The Scottish 100

Duncan A. Bruce

The Scottish 100

Portraits of History's Most Influential Scots

Carroll & Graf Publishers, Inc.
New York

First Carroll & Graf edition 2000

Carroll & Graf Publishers, Inc.
A Division of Avalon Publishing Group
19 West 21st Street
New York, NY 10010-6805

Library of Congress Cataloging-in-Publication Data is available.
ISBN: 0-7867-0770-4

Manufactured in the United States of America

For Tamara

Acknowledgments

MANY PEOPLE ENCOURAGED me in writing this book. Particular thanks to my wife Tamara who read every draft, and offered valuable criticism. My daughters Jennifer and Elizabeth were supportive as were my sister, Christine Astley, and my brother, Roger Bruce. Many friends gave encouragement and advice including Ned Hurley, Alan Bain, Diane and Norman Hunter, Duncan MacDonald, Valerie Cairney and John Reeve, Lynn and Neill Ray, Paul Aronfsky, Fred Bisset, Jan and Dell Bernstein, Karin Henriksen, Bob McLean, Thomas Campbell, Rod Kerr, Maxwell Macleod, Gordon McVie, Ian Ogilvy, Jack Webster, and Jan and Noel Young. Thanks for having confidence in me and in the book are due to publishing pros Hillel Black, Bob Diforio, Claiborne Hancock and Herman Graf who worked to make it happen.

The New York Public Library proved to be, as usual, the Big Apple's greatest cultural asset. My sincere thanks to the many staff members there who helped in innumerable ways, particularly with illustrations. Helen Nicoll was steadfast at the Scottish National Portrait Gallery as were Heather and Elvis at AP/Wide World, Ron at Photofest, and Rebecca at the Metropolitan Museum of Art.

Special thanks go to Bernard Adnet for two original illustrations; to Jim Hutchison for an illustration and explanation of Magnetic Resonance Imaging, and to my good friend Bob Crawford who consulted on various scientific subjects.

Contents

try are Scots. Others think that only people who have *lived* in Scotland are Scots. In the United States there is a general feeling that anyone with even a small amount of Scottish blood is still a Scot. For the most part, I have limited the people in the list to those with significant amounts of Scottish ancestry. I have organized the essays in twenty categories, and listed the subjects chronologically. I have taken away all titles in the headings and used the subjects' names alone. (A man's a man for a' that). I mention people's titles in the essays, however, and in a few places in the Table of Contents to make a few subjects easier to find. In several of the essays, where I thought people's efforts were somehow joined, I have headed essays with more than one person, so that there are, in total, 110 names in the "100." To be specific, 93 of the 110 are made up of 59 men and women born in Scotland; 18 with one or both parents born in Scotland, and 16 more of solidly Scotch-Irish Presbyterian ancestry. The remaining 17 have provable Scottish ancestry in varying degrees, and are on average around half Scottish. The term Scotch-Irish, for those who may not know, does *not* mean someone of Scottish and Irish ancestry. It refers to a mass movement of people from Scotland to northern Ireland in the seventeenth and eighteenth centuries, who stayed there for a generation or several, and then left for North America, or even returned back to Scotland, generally in the eighteenth century. These people were, ethnically, Scots. The Scotch-Irish people in this book have distinctively Scottish names, and are Presbyterians, members of the established Church of Scotland.

I have mentioned Presbyterianism often enough that some readers may think me biased. Let me be clear. I do not recommend one religion over others. But the facts are that Presbyterianism is a good marker of Scottishness, and the Church of Scotland has had an enormous effect on the culture of Scotland, particularly in education. There is no institution of any kind which has had such a profound effect on the Scots, wherever they are, and whatever religion they may now profess.

I note, with no particular motive, that common Scottish surnames predominate in the title names of this book, quite a few more than once. There are two people named Hutcheson/Hutchison; two named Hume; three named Scott; two named Stuart/Stewart; two named Polk/Pollock; two named Bruce; three named Ramsay; two Thomsons; two Murdochs; two Flemings; three Wallaces; two Henrys; two Hunters; two named Livingston/Livingstone; two named Stevenson/Stephenson; and an amaz-

Introduction

THIS BOOK IS a follow-up to my 1996 work, *The Mark of the Scots*, which mentions the achievements of thousands of people with any degree of Scottish ancestry. *The Scottish 100* is an entirely different book. It is a presentation, in one hundred essays, of capsule biographies of the men and women of the Scottish nation who have had the most influence on the world.

There were 287 people considered for the "100," all of whom were distinguished. To cut the list down I removed some men and women who had definite Scottish ancestry, but in rather small amounts, such as the World War II heroes, Churchill, Roosevelt and De Gaulle. Also, I eliminated men such as Jefferson, Newton, and Colbert who claimed Scottish ancestry, but for whom there is only weak or nonexistent evidence. To get from the many to the few has been a difficult task, even after more than thirty years of study, and I am sure that almost every reader will have ideas different from mine as to who should be presented. If one of your favorites is not on the list, I suggest that you consult the index, since I have included, under those honored, quite a few achievers who do not have a separate essay. I have not cast "the first stone," and have ignored the harsh judgments of others on some of the subjects' characters, concentrating rather on the subjects' influence. Regardless of the reader's opinion of my list, I hope all will agree with me that the people discussed are of such quality that it is astonishing to think that they were all born in or have ancestors from such a small country.

There is also the question of who is Scottish? There are many people, particularly in Scotland, who think that only people born in that coun-

List of Abbreviations

ANB	American National Biography
CCB	Cyclopaedia of Canadian Biography
CCE	Concise Columbia Encyclopaedia
CDP	The Cambridge Dictionary of Philosophy
CES	Collins Encyclopaedia of Scotland
CFS	Collins Gem, Famous Scots
CSBD	Chambers Scottish Biographical Dictionary
DAB	Dictionary of American Biography
DNB	Dictionary of National Biography
DSB	Dictionary of Scientific Biography
EB	Encyclopaedia Britannica, 14th ed.
EB 15th	Encyclopaedia Britannica, 15th ed
WA	The World Almanac and Book of Facts 2000

ing three Watsons, one Watson-Watt, and one Watt. I also find a peculiar incidence of cities and towns associated with these titans. We would expect that many would be involved with Edinburgh, Glasgow, Aberdeen, and London. But how can we explain that four of the people were associated with the town of Kirkcaldy? And at least twelve were intimately involved with New York City. Much more unlikely, five of our list had a relationship with Allegheny City, Pennsylvania, which is now the North Side of Pittsburgh. And perhaps the most impressive is that the frontier town of Nashville, Tennessee produced three Scotch-Irish presidents, two of the United States and one of the Republic of Texas, all of whom were living in Nashville at the same time.

I have tried to be accurate and apologize, in advance, for any errors. I have used three principal sources to check facts and learn others: *American National Biography*, the *Dictionary of National Biography* (British) and the *Encyclopaedia Britannica* (the last two founded by Scots). These are marvelous works. I have also consulted dozens of biographies, which are listed in the Bibliography. I have used American spellings except when quoting.

I hope that this book will be an antidote to those who think that Scots equal only Highland games, tartan, haggis, whisky, and bagpipes; or to those who have the view that present day Scotland is entirely the drug scene portrayed by Irvine Welsh and other writers. Of course, these images of the Scots are real, and I like Highland games, tartan, haggis, whisky, and bagpipes as well as the books of Irvine Welsh. But there is another view which I think stands out far above the others: the amazing intellectual achievements of the men and women of a small ethnic group, and how they have influenced the world.

DUNCAN A. BRUCE
New York City
July 25, 2000

Robert Adam

(1728–1792)

ROBERT ADAM, Britain's foremost neoclassic architect, wielded an influence that spread as far to the east as Russia and as far to the west as America.[1] He was born in Kirkcaldy, Fifeshire, the second son of William Adam who was the most prominent Scottish architect of his day. William Adam's work included Hopetoun House and the Royal Infirmary in Edinburgh. Robert Adam attended Edinburgh High School and Edinburgh University. He became friendly with David Hume, Adam Smith and Adam Ferguson.[2]

Between 1755 and 1757 Adam, seeking an improvement in architecture, sought its inspiration in ancient Rome. With the French architect C. L. Clérisseau, he made an intensive study of Roman buildings. He was most interested in the palace of the Emperor Diocletian in Dalmatia. Adam believed that this was the summit of Roman architecture. Although he was arrested as a spy, he was able to take enough measurements to draw the entire palace.[3]

Upon Adam's return to Britain, his neoclassic style caused an immediate sensation, pushing aside the Rococo style popular at the time and gaining him commissions. In 1762 he was appointed architect to the king and queen, a post he held until he was elected to parliament in 1768. He was made a Fellow of the Royal Society, and a Fellow of the Society of Antiquaries. In 1764 Adam published *The Ruins of the Palace of the Emperor Diocletian at Spalatro*. Among his best works are the Adelphi Terrace in London (demolished 1936); Edinburgh University, Culzean Castle, Register House, and Charlotte Square, all in Scotland; and several English country houses, Kenwood Mansion, Luton House and Keddlestone.[4]

Charlotte Square, Edinburgh. COLLECTION OF THE AUTHOR

Robert Adam worked closely with his three brothers, John, James and William, producing furniture and interior fittings in the "Adam style" to match and compliment the buildings they were constructing. But the business grew so fast that they had to farm out work to others, including the great English furniture makers, Thomas Chippendale, and George Hepplewhite.[5] There is no doubt that Chippendale and Hepplewhite were influenced by the Adam brothers.[6] But there is a question as to who designed the furniture, the Adams or their English colleagues. Percy MacQuoid said "that three great houses, Nostell Priory, Harewood and Osterley possessed specimens 'unquestionably designed by Adam and executed by Chippendale.' " This contention is refuted by R. W. Symonds in *Adam and Chippendale*.[7] But the other famous English furniture maker, Thomas Sheraton, "followed upon Chippendale who under the influence of the brothers John and Robert Adam" had refined the work of his predecessors.[8] It would appear that what is acclaimed as an English legacy in furniture is actually rather Scottish.

The Adam brothers can claim, also, to have been "the precursors of the Louis XVI style in France."[9] In the United States, Inverness-born Duncan Phyfe (c. 1768–1854) was the leading exponent of the Adam Style, making a fortune in his New York factory, which employed as many as one hundred artisans.[10]

Other architects with a Scottish background, in addition to Charles Rennie Mackintosh (see p. 4), would include Charles Cameron

(1740–1812) who designed the Great Palace of Pavlosk and the interior of the Summer Palace in Russia for Catherine the Great. In 1981, James Fraser Stirling, born in Glasgow, was awarded a Pritzker Prize. An American Scot, Bruce J. Graham designed the 1,454-foot Sears Tower in Chicago, and another, Ralph T. Walker, called by Frank Lloyd Wright "the only other architect in America," designed number one Wall Street in New York. In 1957 the American Institute of Architects named Walker "Architect of the Century." In Canada, Edward and William Sutherland Maxwell were the architects for the Chateau Frontenac Hotel in Quebec.[11]

Not all of this, of course, derives directly from Robert Adam, but he was probably the most influential Scottish architect ever. When he died an obituary in *Gentlemen's Magazine* said, "Mr. Adam produced a total change in the architecture of this country."[12] Robert Adam was honored with burial in Westminster Abbey. Among the pallbearers were the Duke of Buccleuch, the Earl of Coventry, the Earl of Lauderdale and Lord Frederick Campbell.[13]

Charles Rennie Mackintosh

(1868–1928)

IN THE 1890S and the early years of the twentieth century, a Glaswegian, Charles Rennie Mackintosh, was one of the most influential artists in the world. His posters were a foundation of Art Nouveau. His contributions to architecture were important to the German Bauhaus school of Walter Gropius and Ludwig Mies van der Rohe. His designs were so good that today Mackintosh furniture commands the highest prices of any twentieth-century craftsman.

Charles Rennine Mackintosh was born in Glasgow, the second son of William Mackintosh, a police superintendent, and his wife Margaret Rennie. There were eleven children in this upper-working-class Presbyterian family. Young Mackintosh attended Reid's Public School at age seven, and Alan Glen's School at nine. He was dyslexic, but had an ability to draw, so in 1884 he was apprenticed to an architect, John Hutchison, and attended the Glasgow School of Art at night.[1]

In 1889 Mackintosh joined the architectural firm of Honeyman and Keppie. In 1890 he won an Alexander (Greek) Thomson scholarship to France and Italy. The prize was named after another Glasgow architect who is much better known now than he was in his day. After his return from the Continent, Mackintosh won the competition to design the new Glasgow School of Art, which was built between 1896 and 1909. This outstanding building, still in daily use, was completely innovative, owing nothing to any traditional style. In 1902 Mackintosh became a partner in Honeyman and Keppie, and was awarded the Soane Gold Medal by the Royal Institute of British Architects. He became a Fellow of the Institute in 1906.[2]

Glasgow School of Art.
COLLECTION OF THE AUTHOR.

At the Glasgow School of Art Mackintosh had met and worked with Herbert MacNair. In turn, the two men began to work with the Macdonald sisters, Margaret and Frances. MacNair married Frances in 1899 and Mackintosh married Margaret in 1900. They began to create and exhibit together and became known throughout Europe as "The Glasgow Four" for their Scottish Art Nouveau style. When the MacNairs moved to England, the group lost its cohesion. Despite their excellent reputation in Germany, Vienna, and Holland, the Four did not gain any status in their own country.[3]

In 1897 Mackintosh and George Walton designed and furnished four of Miss Cranston's Tea Rooms, including the 1904 Willow Tea Room on Sauchiehall Street, which still enjoys a booming tourist business. The long-backed chairs and murals are easily recognized and were hailed in Germany as The Glasgow School Style. In 1900 Mackintosh was invited to exhibit at the *Wiener Sezession*, and commissioned to create "A Room for a Music Lover." In 1902 he designed the Scottish Pavillion at the Turin Exhibition, and went on to exhibitions in Venice, Munich, Dresden, Budapest and Moscow. Everything he showed was sold. The *Dictionary of National Biography* says, "Mackintosh's influence on Continental design during the pre-War decade can hardly be exaggerated."[4] Mies van der Rohe, his Bauhaus colleagues in Germany, and the artists of De Stijl in the Netherlands acknowledged their debt to the Glasgow Four and to their style which they called "Mackintoshismus."[5]

In addition to his masterpiece, the Glasgow School of Art, Mackintosh's Scotland Street School in Glasgow and Hill House in Helensburgh are still standing and regularly visited. World War I ended his architectural career. He resigned his partnership in 1913 and moved to London. After the war he and his wife went to the town of Port Vendres in the south of France where the great architect and designer became a full-time painter of watercolors. Mackintosh's *La Rue du Soleil* and *Le Fort Maillet* (1927) put him among the best of British watercolorists.[6]

Charles and Margaret Mackintosh, who had no children, lived a rather ideal life at the Hôtel du Commerce in Port Vendres. M. and Mme. Dejean treated them well with a dining room that looked out over the harbor to the sea. But it all unraveled rather quickly when Margaret left to go to London for medical treatment. Charles wrote to her about the sounds and smells of the harbor and the food of Mme. Dejean, describing it all—soup, sole, asparagus, Roquefort, cherries—all good. Then he found out that he had cancer of the tongue, and joined her in London. He was treated with radium and soon was unable to speak. The couple had a little garden with a small tree where they held hands. He died shortly thereafter.[7]

The Hunterian Museum in Glasgow opened a Mackintosh wing in 1982, which contains several reconstructed rooms and Mackintosh's personal collection of his furniture. The *New York Times* says "For its time, it is astonishing stuff, equaled only perhaps by the work of Frank Lloyd Wright in Chicago and Josef Hoffmann in Vienna."[8] The *Dictionary of National Biography* goes farther, calling Mackintosh a pioneer of Art Nouveau who "was the first anywhere to translate its mannerisms into an architectural idiom, and so to free architecture from the last remnants of historical reminiscence."[9]

Allan Ramsay
(1713–1784)

AND

henry Raeburn
(1756–1823)

LLAN RAMSAY AND Henry Raeburn remain, after two centuries, the best artists born in Scotland. That two such men could come from such a small country at the same time demonstrates the depth of the Scottish Enlightenment of the eighteenth century, and proves that it was not limited to such fields as science, engineering, philosophy and literature, as is sometimes assumed. Their work hangs in the best galleries throughout the world, and continues to influence painting today.

Allan Ramsay was born in Edinburgh, the son of the poet Allan Ramsay (1684–1758) and his wife Christian Ross. The senior Ramsay was an Edinburgh bookseller who in 1825 established what appears to have been the world's first lending library. In 1736 he opened a playhouse which was quickly struck down by the less liberal elements of the clergy. The poetry of the senior Allan Ramsay was a step between the old Scots works and the genius of Robert Burns, who was an admirer.[1] Allan Ramsay, Senior, began a revival of Scottish poetry directed against the use of standard English. His most famous work was *The Gentle Shepherd*, a comedy of rural life.[2]

The poet's son, the younger Allan Ramsay, showed an early talent for art and was encouraged by his father. At the age of twenty he went to London to study with Hogarth. In 1736, having survived a shipwreck, he was studying in Rome. By 1738 he was back in Edinburgh painting and making friends such as David Hume and Adam Smith. In 1756 he returned to London and began to paint the rich and famous, including King George III and Queen Charlotte.[3] In 1767 he was made Principal Painter in Ordinary to the king,[4] and is acknowledged as the best British portrait painter of his time.[5] Ramsay traveled extensively, becoming a friend of Dr. Johnson, Voltaire, and Rousseau. In his last year he became ill and sailed from Italy for Britain, dying at Dover. Ramsay's work preceded and influenced that of the other great British painters of the era—Raeburn, Romney, Gainsborough, and Reynolds, who followed him.

Henry Raeburn was born in Stockbridge, now part of Edinburgh. He was the son of Robert Raeburn, a prosperous manufacturer and mill owner of Border descent, and Ann Elder. He was educated at Heriot's Hospital, leaving at age fifteen to become apprenticed to a goldsmith. He learned portrait painting with David Martin, who was to become his rival. In 1778 he married Ann Edgar Leslie, the prosperous widow of a Frenchman, and it proved to be a most happy union. On their way to Italy in 1785, the Raeburns were introduced to Sir Joshua Reynolds in London, who encouraged the young artist and even offered financial support, which was not needed. Returning to Scotland in 1787, Raeburn quickly established himself as the best portrait painter in the country. Soon David Martin was practically put out of business by Raeburn.[6]

Unlike his predecessor Ramsay, Raeburn made few visits to London. Rather, he stayed in Scotland where he enjoyed a quarter century of success. He painted most of the great Scots of the era such as Adam Smith, James Boswell, Dugald Stewart, Francis Jeffrey and Sir Walter Scott. He worked rapidly with no outline, using the brush from the outset, and keeping businesslike hours. He was knighted in 1822 upon the visit of George IV to Scotland, and died soon after of unknown cause. Many of his paintings are still famous, such as his portrait of the great Highland fiddler, Neil Gow. Sir Henry Raeburn was interested in sports including golf and fishing, and was a builder of ship models. He and his wife had two sons, one of whom showed artistic promise, but who died at nineteen.[7]

In the next century another Scot, Sir David Wilkie (1785–1841) would follow as Painter in Ordinary to King George IV. But among the great portrait painters of Britain in the eighteenth century we find two Scots, Ramsay and Raeburn, to go along with the English triumvirate of Gainsborough, Reynolds, and Romney. Without attempting a ranking of these greats, tiny Scotland should be happy with its two-of-five score.

Sir Henry Raeburn. *Rev. Robert Walker Skating on Duddingston Loch.*
THE SCOTTISH NATIONAL PORTRAIT GALLERY.

Mary Cassatt

(1844–1926)

S HE IS OFTEN called "America's greatest woman painter."[1] In the 1890s she was placed in the second rank of the French Impressionists along with Sisley, Morisot, and Pisarro; behind Degas, Renoir, and Monet but ahead of Caillebot and Guillamin. In 1946 the National Gallery ranked her seventh among American painters after Copley, Stuart, Homer, Eakins, Ryder, and Whistler. But British critics put her second, after only Whistler.[2] However anyone ranks her, Mary Cassatt was, undeniably, a great artist and her success as a recognized colleague of the great male Impressionists has served as a model for women everywhere.

Mary Cassatt. Portrait of the Artist.
THE METROPOLITAN MUSEUM OF ART, BEQUEST OF EDITH H. PROSKAUER, 1975.

Despite her French name, and her nearly lifelong association with France, Mary Stevenson Cassatt was largely of Scotch-Irish ancestry. She was born in Allegheny, Pennsylvania, which is now the North Side of Pittsburgh. Her parents, Robert Simpson Cassat and Katherine Kelso Johnston were of solidly

Scotch-Irish backgrounds. Mary Cassatt was exactly 1/64 French, being descended from Jacques Cossart, a persecuted French Protestant who fled to Holland and then to New Amsterdam.[3] Her family was very prominent. Her father was a successful forwarding merchant, buying in the west and selling in the east, and was also the mayor of Allegheny. Her mother's father, Alexander Johnston, was a director of the Bank of Pittsburgh.[4] Mary Cassatt's brother, Alexander Johnston Cassatt, became president of the Pennsylvania Railroad. It was he who conceived, financed and built "the Eighth Wonder of the World," Pennsylvania Station in New York. This $150 million project (today it would cost billions), patterned after the Baths of Caracalla in Rome, brought trains from the south and west through tunnels under the Hudson River. The tunnels are still filled with trains every day, but the glorious station, with its bronze statue of A. J. Cassatt, was demolished and replaced several decades ago.[5]

When Mary Cassatt was four, the family moved to Lancaster, Pennsylvania, and two years later to Philadelphia. When she was seven, she went to Europe for her basic schooling. During the Civil War she returned to Philadelphia to study at the Pennsylvania Academy of Fine Arts. After the war she returned to France, and with the exception of a few trips home, she lived there the rest of her life. She exhibited at the Paris Salon during 1872–1876, but joined the Impressionists in 1877 along with Monet, Renoir, Pissaro, Morisot, and her close friend Degas. As John Singer Sargent and James Abbott McNeill Whistler (the latter also of Scottish descent) declined to join, she was the only American.[6]

Mary Cassatt's apartment near Place Pigalle was a frequent site of parties drawing important artists. In 1893 she was commissioned to make a mural at the World's Columbian Exposition in Chicago. Her theme was "modern woman." This work brought her to America's attention, and showed, also, that she was becoming a feminist. In 1894 she bought a Château, Mesnil-Beaufresne, some fifty miles northwest of Paris. Here she painted the families of her two brothers when they made annual visits. Many of her paintings were of mother and child. Her best friend during the 1890s was Louisine Elder Havermeyer, a New Yorker who made frequent trips to Paris to purchase art. Mary Cassatt introduced her friend and helped her to buy from Manet and Degas, among others. This team of Cassatt and Havermeyer resulted in the assembly of New York's famed Havermeyer collection.[7]

Mary Cassatt became conservative when the new trend of Fauvism arrived. She didn't like the work of Matisse. With age, her eyes began to fail and she became functionally blind. She did her last work in 1914. During World War I, her house was in a battle zone. She organized aid for suffering local families and invented and patented a hammock for the convalescence of wounded soldiers. She maintained her interest in women's issues, particularly women's suffrage. In 1915 Louisine Havermeyer staged a benefit of her work in New York.[8]

Mary Cassatt maintained her American citizenship. She believed in a woman's right to education and advancement outside the home. She was a strong voice against the many injustices suffered by women. In January of 1926 she recovered from a diabetic coma and was able to return to Beaufresne one last time to visit with her flowers. When she died she was given a state funeral, befitting her rank as Chevalier of the Legion of Honor. She was buried at Mesnil-Théribus.[9] A memorial exhibition followed at Paris, New York, Philadelphia and Chicago.[10]

Alexander Calder

(1898–1976)

A LEXANDER CALDER WAS a genius of the first rank, and in the years before his death was America's most acclaimed artist. As a sculptor, he created two art forms, the mobile and the stabile, which gave him enormous influence in his century, and continues beyond. His front page obituary by John Russell in the *New York Times* is a celebration of a life rather than the cold recitation of facts usually found in such pieces in that staid journal. Calder was not only brilliant, but beloved as well. He was a truly great man.

Sandy Calder (as his friends called him) was born in Lawnton, Pennsylvania, which is now part of Philadelphia. He was predestined from birth to become an artist. His mother, Nanette Lederer, was a painter, and his father and grandfather were distinguished sculptors. Sandy Calder's grandfather, Alexander Milne Calder (1846–1923), the son of a stonecutter, was born in Scotland and studied art at Edinburgh, Paris, and London. In 1868 he immigrated to the United States and continued his education at the Pennsylvania Academy of the Fine Arts under Thomas Eakins.[1] In 1894 he constructed the statue of William Penn atop Philadelphia's famous City Hall. The statue, standing some five hundred feet above the street, is thirty-seven feet high, weighs almost twenty-seven tons, and is the largest sculpture on any building in the world.[2] Alexander Stirling Calder (1870–1945), Sandy Calder's father, also studied under Eakins and at Paris as well. He is responsible for having designed the beautiful Logan Square fountain in Philadelphia.[3] It is possible to stand at this fountain today and see the statue atop City Hall constructed by the first Alexander

Alexander Calder,
AP/WIDE WORLD PHOTOS.

Calder, and also see the Philadelphia Museum of Art, which contains works of the third Alexander Calder.[4]

For health reasons, the second Alexander Calder moved his family to California, and young Sandy graduated from Lowell High School in Berkeley. Deciding to be an engineer, he enrolled at the Stevens Institute of Technology in Hoboken, New Jersey. There he got the highest grade in descriptive geometry ever achieved at the school and graduated in 1919 with a degree in mechanical engineering. For the next several years he wandered, at one point working in the boiler room of a ship which operated between New York and San Francisco through the Panama Canal. In 1923 Calder began studies at the Art Students League in New York, working as a commercial artist to support himself. By 1926 he had his own show of paintings in New York and was off to France as a laborer on a British ship. Living in a small room on the rue Daguerre in Paris, he began to sculpt wire animals, commencing to work on the miniature "Circus" which would make him famous. On a trans-Atlantic trip he met Louisa James, a great-niece of the novelist Henry James. They were married in 1931, beginning an extremely happy marriage which produced two daughters.[5]

In the time he spent in Paris, Calder met and was influenced by other artists including Picasso, Mondrian, Léger and Arp. In 1932 he created the mobile, a sculpture which moved with air currents and balanced parts. Marcel Duchamp coined the word "mobile." Calder's mobiles are hanging in buildings all over the world today. His stabiles (the word coined by Jean Arp), which are stationary sculptures made of heavy metal, also became very popular. His fame and fortune began to grow. He bought houses in Roxbury, Connecticut, and Saché, near Tours in France. His first major exhibition was in New York in 1943, and at his first post-war exhibition in Paris, Jean-Paul Sartre wrote the introduction to the catalogue and Matisse was one of the first visitors. When he won first prize at the Carnegie International at Pittsburgh in 1960, he commented that he finally had the wealth to do "what I want."[6]

Alexander Calder used his talents in many diverse ways. He designed sets for the dancer Martha Graham. He painted the bodies of Braniff airplanes. Louise Nevelson called him "the outstanding creative mind of the twentieth century." Calder received many honors, but perhaps none was so great as the last one. Just weeks before he died, he was given a party at the Whitney Museum in New York in, what John Russell calls, "an atmosphere of universal jubilation." His show at the museum had just opened, to "enormous acclaim." People such as Georgia O'Keeffe and Norman Mailer were there, and some had come from great distances to honor him. John Cage and Merce Cunningham were in attendance. Sandy Calder, an old man now, danced at his own party, not realizing that he was near his end. John Russell calls Calder "one of the people who has best deserved the name of 'American,' " and says of the party, "He loved it, and we loved him, and we shall go on doing it for ever and ever."[7]

Jackson Pollock

(1912–1956)

I T IS OFTEN said that Scots are good at science, but have produced few artists. Such a view presumes that Scottish artists are to be found only in Scotland. If one looks to America, the picture is radically different. We have already discussed Mary Cassatt and Alexander Calder. Gilbert Stuart (1755–1828), a descendant of immigrants from Perth, and famous still for his portrait of George Washington, was America's first important painter. Thomas Eakins (1844–1916), a Philadelphian of Scottish ancestry, is known for his boating scenes. The paintings of James Abbott McNeill Whistler (1834–1903) are in major galleries everywhere, and some critics think that he was the best artist ever produced by the United States. Grandma Moses (Anna Mary Robertson Moses) (1860–1961) was an acclaimed folk artist who painted rural scenes. And Robert Motherwell (Robert Burns Motherwell III) (1915–1991) was a founder of abstract expressionism, and outlived all of his rivals. He was considered to be, at his death, America's foremost painter, and was awarded the Wallace Award of the American-Scottish Foundation.[1]

Jackson Pollock, also an abstract expressionist, was one of a handful of painters who could contend for the title Greatest Painter of the Twentieth Century. His work was revolutionary and has influenced everyone who has followed him. He played a large part in moving the base of the international art scene from Paris to New York after World War II. Pollock was born on a frontier sheep ranch near Cody, Wyoming, to rootless Scotch-Irish Presbyterian parents, Leroy Pollock and Stella Mae McClure. Jackson Pollock's father was a farmer, stonemason, and sometime surveyor, and the family was in constant motion, shifting to new

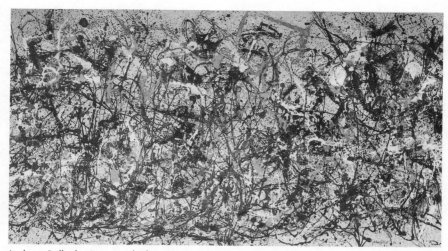

Jackson Pollock. *Autumn Rhythm*. THE METROPOLITAN MUSEUM OF ART, GEORGE A. HEARN FUND, 1957.

places to try to make ends meet. Jackson Pollock was the youngest of five sons. Their mother taught them a pride in workmanship, and four of the brothers became involved in visual arts.[2] The Pollock family moved nine times in sixteen years, shuffling between California and Arizona. In 1928 they settled in Los Angeles where young Jackson attended Manual Arts High School.[3] From the beginning he was depressed, irresponsible, and alcoholic.[4] In 1928, Pollock was expelled from Manual Arts for circulating a pamphlet attacking teachers. He was expelled again in 1929 for coming to blows with a teacher.[5]

In 1930 Jackson Pollock moved to New York where he studied at the Art Students League under Thomas Hart Benton. The next few years he lived in poverty, and in 1938 was hospitalized for alcoholism.[6] In 1940 Pollock met Lee Krasner and his life took on a stable character. Their relationship was volatile, but without her, he wouldn't have been brilliant. They were married in 1945 at Marble Collegiate Church in New York and remained together until 1953. They had no children.[7] In 1943 Pollock had his first one-man show at Peggy Guggenheim's Art of the Century Gallery in New York. But he began drinking again, and he and Krasner escaped to Easthampton, New York on Long Island, almost a hundred miles away from the city.[8]

Pollock stayed sober long enough, between 1947 and 1952, to produce his greatest works, the "poured" paintings, which he made by dribbling paint on the canvas with his hands. In 1949 *Life* Magazine featured him and wrote, "Jackson Pollock: Is he the Greatest Living Painter in the United States?" The publicity got to the very private Pollock. His works were not selling well, and by 1951 he was again drinking heavily.[9]

Pollock's last two years produced almost no important work. Lee Krasner left him and went to Europe. In 1956, drunk at the wheel, he drove his car into a tree and was killed. As Cernuschi, his biographer, says, his work "holds a pivotal place in the art of the postwar era."[10] But Jackson Pollack never got much from his work. The money came far too late. In 1988 a single Pollack entitled *Search*, a 1955 painting spattered with several colors of paint, sold for $4.8 million, a record for any post-war work up to that time.[11]

William Paterson

(1658–1719)

WILLIAM PATERSON STARTED two projects in his lifetime, in completely different fields, and both have had enormous and lasting influence to this day. He is widely acknowledged to have been the founder of the Bank of England, the world's first central bank, a government-sponsored anchor supporting the private banks. This system has been, with various adjustments, copied everywhere. Second, he was a principal and ultimately successful promoter of the political union of Scotland and England. Whatever anyone thinks of that combination today, it must be observed that its immediate effect was greater prosperity in both countries, and an enormous expansion of the British Empire. Paterson campaigned successfully for the union, but the Darién fiasco, of which he was the principal cause, may have had more bearing on its formation.

William Paterson was born in Tinwald, Dumfriesshire, the son of John Paterson and his wife Elizabeth or Bethia. In his youth he traveled to Europe and the West Indies as a merchant, and became so influential that people wanted to settle near him.[1] At some time before 1686 he conceived of a British settlement at Darién on the Isthmus of Panama. Paterson envisioned a colony and transportation center which would cut travel time between the Atlantic and Pacific oceans in half. Returning to England he approached the government of King James II to support the scheme, but this was not forthcoming. He tried on the Continent, but failed there also. As early as 1686 he had become a well-known London merchant.[2] By 1691, Paterson had accumulated a fortune and was proposing the establishment of a central bank, the Bank of England. This was accomplished in 1694, and Paterson was a director. The next year, however, policy differences with the other directors caused him to resign.[3]

In 1695 he was back in Scotland, getting the Scottish parliament to pass an act authorizing the Company for Trading from Scotland to Africa and the West Indies. The Darién scheme, rejected by England and other countries, had become Scottish. It is no wonder that Scotland agreed to what others had refused. This was the era of the Mercantile System, when countries traded, exclusively, with their own colonies. Scotland was shut out of trade with the English colonies in America and elsewhere. The Scots had tried to set up colonies in Nova Scotia (1621), East New Jersey (1683), and South Carolina (1686), but all had failed. Scotland was desperate for a colony, and Paterson was offering what to a desperate people might have seemed like a reasonable venture. It was not. From the beginning, the project smelled of doom. Funds being accumulated went missing, and Paterson was removed from the management. But he would accompany the voyage anyway. Despite this setback, capital for the scheme was subscribed in a patriotic wave of enthusiasm by a broad cross-section of the people of Scotland. Some say that the £400,000 ventured amounted to half of the available money in the country. The disaster was immediate. In 1698 five ships sailed for the Central American jungle. Many died on the way, and those who survived the ocean were further decimated by fever. Predictably, the Spanish attacked, and just as predictably, the English refused to come to the rescue. The Scots fought well, but were overwhelmed.[4]

The Councillors of the pathetic Colony of Caledonia decided to abandon Darién over Paterson's protests. His wife and only child were among the dead, and his own health was so bad that he had to be carried to the ship *Unicorn* which sailed with 250 others bound for home in 1699. By the time the ship reached New York, only half the passengers had survived.[5] In total, 2,000 Scottish lives had been lost, along with an enormous amount of money, and the nation's pride and confidence. It is no wonder that Paterson, and other Scots, now found a merger with England to be more agreeable than they had found it during centuries of fighting. Scotland was bankrupt.

After the catastrophe, Paterson proposed a council of trade, new proposals for Darién, and the union of the parliaments of England and Scotland. He was responsible for the sinking-fund method of paying the English national debt. He advocated free trade and railed at the plan of the French, advocated by fellow Scot John Law (see p. 23).[6]

Paterson published a pamphlet advocating the union of the parliaments of England and Scotland, and went to Scotland in 1706 to help close the deal, which was very unpopular at the time. (It still is in some quarters.) He was prominent in drafting the articles of the treaty which had to do with trade and finance.[7] He was one of the many, it must be said, who received an "indemnity" for supporting the union. The government in London actually gave so much sterling to some of the Darién losers that an English parliamentarian could boast that England had "bought" Scotland. The parliaments of England and Scotland ceased to exist in 1707. The British parliament has existed to the present.

William Paterson died in 1719. He had been married twice, first to Elizabeth Turner, and then to Hannah Kemp, with whom he had a son (both who died at Darién).[8] Paterson was brilliant, but hardly a hero. Yet he leaves two great legacies: the central banking systems of many nations, and the union of Scotland with England.

And how do we evaluate the latter? It must be said that it is *after* the union of 1707 most of the people in this book existed. In 1707 the people of Scotland were in an economic and cultural backwater, much as the Eastern European Jews were two hundred years later. In 1707 the Scots

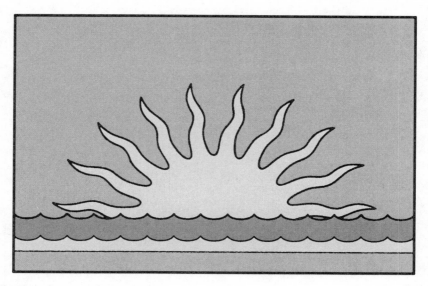

The Flag of Darién. BERNARD ADNET

were bursting with energy and talent, waiting to be allowed into the mainstream of civilization. They were released into the British Empire and flourished, just as the Jews were released from their ghettoes and *shtetls* and flourished in America and elsewhere. Without their participation in the British Empire, the Scots could never have helped to found the United States, Canada, Australia, New Zealand, and many other places. And what would little Scotland have done with the 20 million people of Scottish descent who now live outside Scotland?

Both England and Scotland have benefited by the union. Scotland gained a world-class stage upon which her talented players could perform. England gained the talented players without whom she could never have produced her greatest plays.

Now Scotland has her own parliament and some argue for complete separation. We will now see what the Scottish people will do.

John Law

(1671–1729)

OR A FEW years, John Law was the most talked about man in Europe and the virtual prime minister of France. Starting with the establishment of a bank, Law gradually got financial control of what was then the world's most powerful country. He even took over France's colonies and was in control of Louisiana at the time of the founding of New Orleans. His activities created in France first a wave of prosperity and then a complete collapse. Many call him a scoundrel, while others tend to think that he was deliberately undermined. He was certainly a financial genius.

John Law,

John Law was born in Edinburgh. His father, William Law, a descendant of an Archbishop of Glasgow, was a goldsmith, which in those days meant that he was a banker of sorts. William Law bought the estate of Lauriston near Cramond. He died in 1684. His son, John Law, was educated at

Edinburgh High School, where he excelled in arithmetic and algebra. As a young man, he drifted to London where he had "dissipated habits" and exhibited "foppish" behavior. He was a gambler and at age twenty-one he sold the fee of Lauriston to his mother. In April of 1694 he killed Edward "Beau" Wilson in a duel in London. He was convicted of murder and sentenced to death. On appeal this was reduced to manslaughter and some jail time. But when Law heard that relatives of Wilson would appeal the reduced sentence, he escaped and fled to the Continent. He learned banking in Amsterdam.[1]

In 1700, Law returned to Scotland, just after the disastrous Darién affair had wrecked the country's economy (see pp. 19-21). In the throes of a great depression, Law proposed a far-reaching economic program. He authored *Money and Trade Considered, With a Proposal for Supplying the Nation with Money*.[2] His scheme, which would have produced Scotland's first paper money, abolished monopolies, cut tariffs, and put the unemployed to work, was resoundingly rejected by the Scottish parliament. Undaunted, Law returned to the Continent, gambling and winning. By 1715 it is thought that he was worth about £100,000.[3]

After the death of Louis XIV, the regent, the Duke of Orleans, who was a close friend of Law's, allowed him to open a bank, the first in France. The *Banque Générale* was authorized May 20, 1716. This enterprise was an immediate success. Since French coins were frequently devalued, they were suspect. Law's banknotes were convertible into coin of the same weight and price and rose to a premium. He loaned money at low interest and French industry prospered beyond all expectations. Law, now one of the richest men in France, was hailed as a genius. Had he stopped at this point, he would probably still be a hero. But he had even bigger plans. He hoped to surpass the British colonial companies, and he persuaded Orleans to let him take over Louisiana. The *Compagnie d'Occident* was authorized in August of 1717. The Duke was no doubt pleased when in 1718, the new town of New Orleans was named in his honor. But the French parliament was not amused, and was indignant that this immense concession had been given to a foreign Protestant. The seeds of Law's demise had already been sown.[4]

Louisiana then comprised the entire area drained by the Ohio, Missouri, and Mississippi rivers—about one third of the present United States. Law began to issue bank notes, not only on coin, but upon land. And there was so much land in Louisiana that the amount of notes could be almost unlimited. This was known as the Mississippi Scheme, or simply as "The System." A wave of prosperity, unlike anything which could have been imagined before, swept across France. Law's Western Company acquired the Company of Senegal (1718), the East India and China Companies (1719), and the African Company. Next, he got control of the mint. He then offered to assume the country's entire national debt in exchange for shares in his companies. Speculative fever sent the shares from 500 to 18,000 livres. The regent, Orleans, placated the enemies in parliament by making the *Banque Générale* into the *Banque Royale*, and then he printed money for himself.[5]

It must be said that Law was a good administrator. During his reign, the cost of living in France was reduced by 40 percent, there was free trade between the provinces, and taxes were lowered. The height of The System was reached in 1720 when Law became a Roman Catholic and France's controller-general of finances.[6] Then a royal edict on May 21, 1720 devalued money and the company's shares, bringing about the bursting of the Mississippi Bubble.[7] The panic was on. People demanded gold, which Law could not supply in quantity. Instead he had money printed in enormous quantities. The value of the shares collapsed. It was all over. Law had to be protected from a mob trying to attack him in his house. All of his property was seized and he fled to Holland. There he cried, "Last year I was the richest individual who ever lived. Today I have nothing, not even enough to keep alive."[8]

In Brussels, Law was invited to Russia to run its finances by an envoy of the Tsar. He declined, and traveled to Italy, Germany, and Denmark. The English invited him back and granted him a pardon. He lived in England several years. He ended up in Venice, gambling to the end. He would offer to bet £1,000 against a shilling that his opponent couldn't roll double sixes six times in a row, realizing that there was practically no chance he could lose. He made a living this way.

Law was handsome, with small dark grey eyes and a fair complexion. He had married Katherine Knollys in Scotland in 1708. She died in London in 1774. They had one daughter and one son. The son, William Law of Lauriston, died as a colonel in the Austrian army. A grandnephew James A.B. Law, Comte de Lauriston, was a favorite of Napoleon and was made a marshal of France by Louis XVIII.[9]

The *Dictionary of National Biography* says that French historians agree that despite ruining some people, The System gave a great impetus to the

French economy. The Duke of Saint-Simon said that Law was "innocent of greed and knavery."[10] The best evaluation would probably be that Law was not a criminal running an impossible Ponzi scheme, but rather, an honest genius who went too far too fast. He was on the right track, but he behaved irresponsibly and negligently.

An epitaph was published in 1729 in the *Mercure*:

> Cet Écossais célèbre
>> Ce calculateur sans égal
> Qui par les régles de l'algèbre
>> A mis la France à l'hôpital.

> This celebrated Scot
>> This schemer without equal
> Who by the rules of algebra
>> Has put France in the hospital.

William Jardine
(1784–1843)

AND

James Matheson
(1796–1878)

SCOTTISH TRADERS HAVE been found all over the world in the past eight centuries. At first, they stayed rather close to home setting up bases in the Netherlands, Scandinavia, and Germany. Some became rich and were ennobled. Later they expanded to Poland where they rose from peddlers to court bankers. After Scotland joined England in 1707, Scottish tobacco traders were the main force in the Virginia tobacco trade, the Canadian fur trade and were found as well in Australia, New Zealand, South Africa and many other places. Their influence on all of these countries ranges from significant to dominant in various business-es.[1] But of all of the Scottish traders, it is doubtful if any two had as great an influence on a country, or created an enterprise with such a brilliant and lasting legacy as William Jardine and James Matheson.

William Jardine was born on the farm of his father, Andrew Jardine, near Lochmaben in Dumfriesshire. He was educated in medicine at Edinburgh University and received a diploma from the Royal College of Surgeons in 1802. The same year he accepted a position as ship's surgeon on the East India Company's HCS *Brunswick* and sailed for India. The eastern seas in the early part of the nineteenth century were perilous places where the rule of law was far from established. In his first few years Jardine survived both shipwreck and capture by the French. As a ship's physician he was allowed "privilege tonnage"—cargo space on board to conduct his own trading. By 1817 he was so successful that he gave up medicine and trad-ed regularly between Bombay and Canton on the *Sarah*, which he co-owned. In the 1820s, Jardine lived in Canton, doing business as an agent for opium merchants in Bombay. In 1826 he got control of Magniac & Company.[2]

Nicholas James Sutherland Matheson was born at Lairg, Sutherlandshire, the first of eight children of Captain Donald Matheson and Katherine MacKay, whose father was the parish minister. James Matheson was educated at Edinburgh's Royal High School and at the University of Edinburgh. He spent two years in a London merchant house before leaving for Calcutta in 1815. For a while he was the Danish consul at Canton, and a partner in a firm which traded opium. Somewhere along the way he met his fellow Scot William Jardine, and in 1832 they founded Jardine, Matheson & Company at Canton. It became, quickly, the most influential agency house in the city, flying its emblem, the Scottish St. Andrew's cross flag, with the colors reversed.[3]

Jardine Matheson became a power in banking, shipping, insurance and marketing, usually on commission. There is no doubt about who the Taipan (big boss) of the firm was. It was Jardine, whom the Chinese called "iron-headed rat." There was only one chair in his office, and he sat in it. Everyone else had to stand.[4]

In 1839 Jardine took what he thought was going to be a leisurely trip to London, but when he got to Naples he was informed that the Chinese had confiscated millions of dollars worth of opium. After having hurried to London he advised the great foreign secretary, Lord Palmerston, to seize an island and then negotiate. "You take my opium—I take your islands in return—we are therefore quits—and thenceforth if you please let us live in friendly Communion and good fellowship."[5] During the Opium War (1840–1842) Jardine pursued the firm's interests in banking and insurance from London. And with the Treaty of Nanking, which ended the war in 1842, his strategy was proved correct. Britain got Hong Kong and five "treaty" ports. Palmerston credited Jardine with a "major role" in Britain's successful Chinese policy.[6]

The attitude towards drugs in those days was very different from what it is today. Jardine explained that the opium trade was "the safest and most gentlemanlike speculation I am aware of." According to him, it was the Chinese who were the smugglers, and once the goods had been transferred to them offshore, it was their responsibility as to where the drug went. It is hard to imagine today, but William Jardine was honored and elected to Parliament in 1841.[7]

In 1842 James Matheson went to London, where he found his partner terminally ill. William Jardine died the following year, having never been married. In 1848 Matheson reorganized the London firm into Matheson & Company, which became a powerhouse in the City of London. He was referred to as "Uncle James" and assumed Jardine's seat in Parliament. Eventually he bought the Isle of Lewis and other vast estates in Scotland, and was very generous to the people on his land in bad times. He married Mary Jane Percival, a Canadian. They had no children. He was honored with membership in the Royal Society in 1846, and as Lord Lieutenant and Sheriff Principal in the County of Ross in 1866. He was knighted and died in the south of France.[8] Both he and his partner had contributed heavily to free education and medical treatment for Chinese children.

The Princely Hong, or Noble House, as Jardine Matheson is called, has had by far the biggest influence on China, and in particular Hong Kong, of any business, Chinese or otherwise. In 1834 the company's *Sarah* carried a cargo of tea to London, the first voyage from China on a ship not belonging to the East India Company. This began the rush of British merchants to

Jardine's Noonday Gun, Hong Kong harbor. ROBERT NG/SOUTH CHINA MORNING POST.

China. In 1835 Jardine's bought the first merchant steamship in China. In 1836 the Muckle Hoose (big house), which other Scottish traders called Jardine's, opened the first insurance company in China. (One of those Scots, Thomas Sutherland, founded the Hong Kong and Shanghai Bank, now known as HSBC, which became the most influential bank in Asia and the most profitable in the world.) Jardine Matheson bought the first plots of land offered for sale on Hong Kong for £565 and built the first significant house there. Soon after, offices were opened in Shanghai, Foochow, and Tientsin. William Keswick, a nephew of William Jardine, established the firm in Japan in 1858. Keswicks have been involved in the ownership and operation of the company ever since. In 1941 the Japanese took over the company's interests in Hong Kong, but it was able to continue operating in Chungking, Kuming, and Bombay. When peace came in 1946 the Chinese government, under new laws, issued permissions to conduct business and gave Jardine Matheson certificate number 1.[9]

As the years went by, nine Hong Kong streets were named for various Taipans of Jardine Matheson, which became the world's biggest property owner and employed almost a quarter of a million people. For more than 150 years Jardine's fired a cannon each day in Hong Kong harbor to announce the noonday. And the giant conglomerate never forgot its roots, conducting annual parties on St. Andrew's Day, complete with whisky, Haggis, and pipes.

In 1986 the *New York Times* interviewed the then incumbent Taipan, Simon Keswick, who admitted that he disliked being photographed against the Hong Kong skyline. The *Times* noted that it would be absurd if a businessman in New York or London were thus pictured, surveying his dominions, but concluded that it wouldn't be absurd in Hong Kong.[10]

Andrew Carnegie

(1835–1919)

ANDREW CARNEGIE HAD the distinction of being congratulated by the banker J. P. Morgan on having become "the richest man in the world." The are at least four other men of Scottish ancestry who have claimed this title subsequently. They are Pittsburgh banker Andrew Mellon, oilman J. Paul Getty, John D. Rockefeller of Standard Oil, and Microsoft's Bill Gates. But even in this august company Carnegie stands out, because he was first, and because he gave most of his money away. He is still a controversial figure. Conservatives who view him as a complete hero should realize that he was a brilliant, hardworking, but flawed man. Liberals, who view him as a ruthless tyrant, would do well to reflect upon the simple fact that he gave away more of his money, most likely, than any other extremely rich man before or since. The balance here is in Carnegie's favor. The man who was arguably the greatest businessman in history is also arguably the greatest philanthropist in history.

Carnegie, whose name is correctly pronounced "car-NEG-ie," was born in Dunfermline, Fifeshire, the son of William Carnegie, a prosperous hand-loom weaver who had four looms and three apprentices. The Carnegies' house still stands at the corner of what are now Carnegie and Bruce Streets. The family of Carnegie's mother, Margaret Morrison, included some radicals who wanted to end the monarchy and the House of Lords. But an uncle, George Lauder, passed on to the young Andrew a conservative love of Scottish history and the work of Robert Burns. When the boy went to school at age eight, he was the brightest pupil in his class. But the introduction of steam-powered looms ruined the prosperous Carnegies, who were forced to emigrate. The family left Glasgow on May 17, 1848 aboard the *Wiscasset*. After a journey of ten weeks, they arrived in Pittsburgh, where the young man's Aunt Annie gave them two rooms rent free on a back alley in Allegheny City, a town which has since been incorporated into Pittsburgh. It was probably a worse slum than any extant in Scotland.[1]

It was a grim life for these new Americans. William Carnegie, used to being his own boss, was reduced to menial employment in a textile factory. Twelve-year-old Andrew, with only four years of schooling and no prospects for more, worked in the same factory as a bobbin-boy for $1.20 per week. But Andrew Carnegie never doubted that he would rise above the slum. He was proud to be earning his living, and brimming with confidence. He was encouraged by Allegheny's richest citizen, Colonel James Anderson, who made his library free for all working boys. Andrew Carnegie became his best "customer," and would always remember how books could benefit people's lives.[2]

The career of Andrew Carnegie progressed rapidly. He got a better job as a steam engine tender for $2 a week. Then he became a messenger boy at the Atlantic and Ohio telegraph office at Third and Wood Streets in Pittsburgh. There he met two Scotch-Irish messenger boys, Henry Oliver and David McCargo, and a fellow Scottish immigrant, Robert Pitcairn. All four of these boys, who were supervised by another Scot, James Douglas Reid, would make great marks in Pittsburgh.[3] Carnegie was the best and fastest messenger, able to memorize locations quickly. He then became a telegraph operator, with an unusual ability to read incoming messages by the clicks, ahead of the printed tape. This talent was noticed by Thomas A. Scott, the superintendent of the Western Division of the Pennsylvania Railroad. Scott hired Carnegie as his personal telegraph operator and secretary at $35 per month. When Scott went to Philadelphia in 1859 to become general superintendent of the railroad, he left the twenty-two-year-old Carnegie as his successor. In 1867, with the capital he had saved, Carnegie backed George Pullman, the pioneer of the railroad sleeping car. The venture was extremely successful. By 1868, Carnegie was able to tally his holdings at more than $400,000. He was rich, only twenty years after immigrating.[4]

Carnegie entered the steel business, figuring that it would be the most profitable. But British competition was severe. He decided to build the most modern and largest Bessemer steel plant in the world on the site of Braddock's defeat (see p. 321). He named the plant for Edgar Thomson,

Carnegie Hall, New York City.
COLLECTION OF THE AUTHOR.

the president of the Pennsylvania Railroad who he figured would be his best customer. The mill, nearing its 125th anniversary, was a huge success and is still operating in Braddock, Pennsylvania, today. Gradually Carnegie brought in partners, such as his brother Tom, Henry Phipps, Henry Clay Frick, and Charles M. Schwab. He kept everyone loyal by paying small salaries and giving shares in the company. If anyone left, they would be paid only a nominal value for their shares. The exception was the $25,000 salary he paid to the Welshman Captain William Jones, who was perhaps the best operating steel man in the world. Carnegie merged other companies into his own, including the Illinois Steel Company, which had been founded by another Scottish immigrant, Alexander Leith. He integrated the business vertically, buying a fleet of iron ore boats, a railroad, and Frick's coke ovens. The business was hugely profitable.[5]

The year 1892 brought Carnegie's worst problem. He had acquired the Homestead Works, a little further down the Monongehela River, and it was a union shop, with a contract about to expire. He determined that the plant should be non-union. Whether the fault was Carnegie's, Frick's, or Phipp's is not clear, but Carnegie went to Scotland for a vacation. When the infamous strike arrived, he was not even in the country. The strike was bloody. Three hundred armed Pinkerton agents were brought in. Several men died. Frick had won his non-union shop, but he and Carnegie never fully recovered their reputations after the Homestead strike. The public and the press were incensed.

Carnegie married Louise Whitfield in 1887. He was fifty-one at the time and fathered their only child at sixty-one. He had written his *Gospel of Wealth* in 1889. Its basic message was that it is good to make money, but bad if you don't give it away. He bought Skibo Castle on the Dornoch Firth in the far north of Scotland, and was awakened each day by his piper. He made friends with Gladstone, Theodore Roosevelt, Kipling, Mark Twain, and Booker T. Washington. He was an advocate and diligent supporter of education for blacks and of Tuskeegee Institute.

He moved to New York and built a mansion on Fifth Avenue, which is now the Cooper-Hewitt Museum. He joined the Saint Andrew's Society and became its president. He founded Saint Andrew's Golf Club with fellow Scot John Reid. It continues as the oldest golf club in the United States. In 1901 Schwab asked J. P. Morgan what he would pay for the Carnegie interests. Morgan asked Schwab to name his price. Schwab consulted with Carnegie, who wrote $480 million on an envelope. Morgan, without hesitation, replied, "I accept the price." On March 2, 1901 United States Steel was organized with Schwab as president.[6]

Carnegie's share was over $350 million, a sum that the *New York Times* recently estimated would be worth $112 billion today.[7] In his 1889 essay, *Wealth*, he had said that "the man who dies rich dies disgraced," and he began the task of giving 95 percent of his money away.[8] He built 2,811 libraries, 1946 in the United States, 660 in Great Britain and 156 in Canada, at a cost of about $50 million. He only gave the money if the community would tax itself to support the place. He created pension funds for his former steelworkers. He paid for 7,689 church pipe organs. He created the Carnegie-Dunfermline Trust which gave his hometown baths, parks, and a library. He created the Carnegie Institute of Pittsburgh with a music hall, library, museum, and Carnegie Institute of Technology, today Carnegie-Mellon University. He founded Carnegie Hall in New York.

Andrew Carnegie was sincerely interested in world peace. He thought that if individuals could give up dueling, so could nations. He reasoned that nations could live together just as people did. International courts would be used in place of war. To this end he built the Pan American Building in Washington, D.C. and the Peace Palace at the Hague in the Netherlands.[9]

Carnegie found that giving money away was harder than making it. Despite his best efforts, income kept coming in. Finally, in 1911, he formed the Carnegie Corporation of New York and gave it $125 million. Thus, he had almost completely divested himself of his fortune. Carnegie was showered with honors. He received the freedom of fifty-seven British cities, more even than Churchill.[10] But the greatest honor will be bestowed upon him when people realize that he was the most important founder of private philanthropy, a vital component of today's civilization.

Andrew Carnegie died at his summer home in Lenox, Massachusetts, and is buried in Sleepy Hollow Cemetery, just north of New York City. His grave is marked with a Celtic cross made of stone quarried near Skibo. Five years later, Samuel Gompers, the head of the American Federation of Labor, was buried nearby. They seem to be resting peacefully. There have been no new sightings of ghosts in the cemetery.[11]

Thomas Blake Glover

(1838–1911)

ACENTURY AND A half ago Japan was a feudal nation, deliberately closed off from the rest of the world, without technology, trading with no other country. Today it is one of the most powerful nations on earth, known for its technological prowess, exporting everywhere. The European most responsible for beginning this incredible turnabout is well known in Japan. Two million Japanese tourists visit his mansion every year. But he is almost unknown in his native land.

Thomas Blake Glover was born in Fraserburgh, a fishing port in Aberdeenshire. He was the fifth of the seven sons of Thomas Berry Glover, a lieutenant in the Royal Navy, and Mary Findlay. The Glovers were prosperous enough to move their brood into Braehead House, a large mansion on the river Don. It is now visited annually by thousands of Japanese tourists. Young Thomas Glover attended the excellent gymnasium in the city of Aberdeen. At age eighteen he joined the famous Scottish trading firm of Jardine Matheson (see p. 27) in Shanghai. In 1859 he was transferred to Nagasaki. At that time there was a revolution in Japan with the younger samurai trying to overthrow the Shogun. At first, Glover sold arms to both sides, but gradually, he became interested in and supported the cause of the young samurai. He was able to get several of them into Oxford and Cambridge universities, and some visited his family at Braehead. One of these young samurai was Hirobumi Ito, who became the country's first prime minister in 1885.[1]

In 1861 Glover quit Jardine Matheson and went into business for himself. He made his fortune so rapidly that he was able to build the Glover Mansion and gardens, overlooking Nagasaki Harbor, only two years later.

His achievements came swiftly. In 1865 he imported the first locomotive to Japan and helped to begin the first railway there. In 1869 he operated the first modern coal mine. The Takashima coal mine operated for 117 years, until it was closed in 1986. In 1869 he ordered the first modern dock, the Kosuge Dock, built in Aberdeen and shipped in sections to Japan. In 1853 he ordered the first three ships for the Japanese Navy, also bought in Aberdeen, from the firm of Alexander Hall.[2] He built the first tennis court in Japan and the first paved road. Generally, Glover was the most important European in modernizing Japan. His most lasting and obvious business legacy is as an originator of the Japanese brewing industry. Glover was the actual founder of the still famous Kirin beer, which is named for him. Glover had great facial hair, which was unusual in Japan. The Japanese thought he looked like a kirin, a mythical animal with a flowing mustache. They called him Kirin, and the mythical animal is still pictured on the labels of the beer bottles.[3]

Glover's brother Alfred went out to join the firm in 1870 when he was only eighteen. He founded the Saint Andrew's Society of Nagasaki. Martha, a sister, came later and died in Nagasaki in 1903. Two older brothers, operated the Scottish end of the trade from Aberdeen. Then came the American Civil War, and the Glovers made a great mistake, picking the wrong side to trade with and selling arms to the Confederates. By 1870, the firm was bankrupt. But this didn't stop Thomas Glover. Mitsubishi took over his interests and made him a handsomely paid consultant. In 1908, at age seventy, the Emperor gave him the Order of the Rising Sun.[4]

Another Scot who is much better known in Japan than in Scotland was Henry Dyer (1848–1918), who became the first principal and professor of engineering at the Imperial College of Engineering in Tokyo. Dyer, who was born at Bothwell, Lanarkshire, established a sound program for engineers, beginning the excellence in engineering, which distinguishes Japan today. He sent many Japanese to study in Britain, particularly to Glasgow. When he left what came to be called "Dyer's College" in 1882 to return to Scotland, he, too, was awarded the Order of the Rising Sun.[5]

A Scottish-American woman, Elizabeth Gray Vining (1902–1999) had a profound influence on present day Japan, having served as tutor to the former crown prince and present emperor, Akihito, from 1946 to 1950. Her father, John Gordon Gray, was a native of Aberdeen, and a maker of scientific instruments, including some of those taken to the

North Pole by Peary. As President of the St. Andrew's Society of Philadelphia, John Gordon Gray conceived of that organization's effort to erect the Scottish-American War Memorial in Edinburgh, with its Tait McKenzie sculpture.[6] Elizabeth Gray Vining, whose story parallels *The King and I*, was the first foreigner permitted inside the living quarters of the Imperial Palace, and was closer to Akihito than anyone else outside the imperial household. Akihito's father, Emperor Hirihito, said of her, "If ever anything I did has been a success it was bringing Mrs. Vining here."[7] Elizabeth Gray Vining maintained a lifelong relationship with the emperor and his family. Akihito stayed with her at her house in Philadelphia when he came to the United States. She was the only foreign guest at his wedding to the Empress Michiko in 1959.[8]

But the most significant impression left by Scots in Japan is the Glover Garden at Nagasaki, which houses the Nagasaki Museum of Traditional Performing Arts, the houses of early European traders, and, of course, the centerpiece of the complex, the Glover Mansion, the oldest Western-style building in Japan.[9] Glover led a colorful life, married Japanese women in 1860 and 1867, and had children born to at least three other Japanese women. The child he is most remembered for is Tomisaburo, born to a woman known only as Maki Kaga. When Glover took the boy into his own household, Maki Kaga felt alone and attempted suicide. Tomisaburo was educated at a missionary school at Nagasaki, where the principal was Sarah Correll; she told her brother, John Luther Long, a Philadelphia lawyer, the story of Glover, Tomisaburo, and Maki Kaga. Long wrote the short story *Madam Butterfly*, changing Glover, the Scot, to Pinkerton, an American, and ending the story with the famous suicide. David Belasco produced the play in London, where Puccini saw it and subsequently wrote one of the world's most beloved operas, *Madama Butterfly!*[10]

Glover Garden, overlooking Nagasaki harbor.
SCHAUWECKER'S GUIDE TO JAPAN
WWW.JAPAN-GUIDE.COM

Tomisaburo attended the University of Pennsylvania, which is, perhaps not coincidentally, in Philadelphia, and returned to Japan. When Nagasaki was atom bombed in 1945 he survived, but was so distraught he committed suicide, leaving his fortune for the rebuilding of the city.[11]

Elizabeth Arden

(1878–1966)

U NTIL SEVERAL DECADES ago, conventional wisdom assigned women the roles of housekeeper and mother, with not many other options. Even those who knew that women were valuable workers, teachers, even writers and scientists, were reluctant to believe that a woman could start a business, build it into a major enterprise, and become a multimillionaire on her own. Women weren't thought to be tough enough or interested in such pursuits. A young woman from Canada proved them all wrong, and became, by example, a force for women's liberation.

Florence Nightingale Graham was born in Woodbridge, Ontario, near Toronto, where her parents were farmers. Her mother, Susan Tadd, was of Cornish ancestry. Her father, William "Willie" Graham, was a native of Scotland who passed along his lifelong interest in horses to his daughter.[1] Florence Graham's mother died when she was still a small child. The family didn't have enough money for her to finish high school, so she became a nurse. As she didn't really like that profession, she followed her brother to New York City, in search of a different career. In 1908 she was a cashier in a beauty salon when she decided to master the business. She learned the art of "healing hands." In 1909 Florence Graham went in the salon business at 509 Fifth Avenue with one Elizabeth Hubbard. The partners didn't get along and Florence took over the business. On the salon door was written "Elizabeth Hubbard." Florence ordered the "Hubbard" scratched off and "Arden," a name she liked, in its place. From then on she was Elizabeth Arden.[2]

With $6,000 in capital she made the place look elegant, decorated with antiques and lush carpeting. Elizabeth Arden had a single-minded determination to succeed. Despite World War I, she went to Paris in 1914 to learn the cosmetics business. She discovered the value of mascara, eye shadow, rouge, and lipstick. She brought this knowledge back to New York and began to make huge profits, moving steadily north on Fifth Avenue to the high rent district. She was at 673 Fifth Avenue in 1915, and 691 Fifth Avenue by 1930. She realized that the cosmetics sold because of the *cachet* of her elegant Red Door salons. One of her most successful products was Amoretta, a face cream. In the salons she stressed diet and exercise. She married and divorced Thomas Jenkins Lewis. There were no children.[3]

Elizabeth Arden had a long rivalry with Helena Rubinstein, her competitor who was also quite successful. When Arden was bitten by a horse, Rubinstein remarked, "What happened to the horse?" Elizabeth Arden was, indeed, a successful horse breeder, winning the Kentucky Derby in 1947 with Jet Pilot. Since Rubinstein married nobility, Arden struck back at her rival by marrying Prince Michael Evlanoff, a Russian who was living in New York. They were married in 1942 and divorced in 1944. Again, there were no children.[4]

Elizabeth Arden promoted her business through society functions, particularly charity balls. Her motto was "Hold fast to life and youth." At her death she owned all of the shares of her company which had $60 million in revenue. The business was sold to Eli Lilly & Co. for $37 million.[5] Today the business is owned by Unilever and sells nine Elizabeth Arden fragrances and distributes products from Nino Cerruti, Elizabeth Taylor, and the House of Valentino. There are still eight Red Door salons.[6]

Elizabeth Arden Red Door Salon 5th Avenue, New York City. COLLECTION OF THE AUTHOR.

At her funeral Arden was clothed, for the first time, in a gown made for her by one of her former employees, Oscar de la Renta. She had actually saved it for the occasion! The Frank Campbell Funeral Home, at Eighty-first and Madison, the classiest in the city, was packed with celebrities. The street was choked with limousines and TV crews. Both of her former husbands attended. Estée Lauder could afford to be gracious, what with both Arden and Rubinstein gone: "A great era has passed, leaving us to carry on the fine tradition that Elizabeth leaves us."[7]

Arden was one of the first and is still one of the few women elected to the *Fortune* magazine Business Hall of Fame. Coco Chanel once said, "There is only one Mademoiselle in the world, and that is I; one Madame, and that is Rubinstein; and one Miss, and that is Arden." To which Elizabeth Arden replied, "There's only one Elizabeth like me, and that's the Queen."[8]

Donald Douglas

(1892–1981)

HREE GIANT AMERICAN aircraft manufacturing companies have
Scottish roots. The Lockheed Martin Corporation, currently valued on the New York Stock Exchange at about $10 billion, was founded
in 1926 by the brothers Allan and Malcolm Loughead. The company was
famous for its Constellation aircraft after World War II.

James S. McDonnell, Jr. founded his company in St. Louis in 1939 with
a capital of only $165,000. McDonnell delivered the first carrier-based jet
fighter in 1946, and later built the Mercury spacecraft which carried the
first American into orbit. His company had revenue of many billions of dollars and over 100,000 employees when it was merged into Boeing in 1997.

But no single person had such an influence on commercial aviation,
and few have ever dominated an industry as did Donald Douglas. He was
the man, more than any other, who elevated flying from its adventure
stage and made it routine.

Donald Wills Douglas was born in Brooklyn. His father, William
Edward Douglas, was a banker of Scottish descent. His mother, Dorothy
Locker was of German and Scandinavian origin. At an early age he
became interested in flying. His heroes were the Wright brothers and
Samuel Langley (see pp. 92–93). For his schooling, his parents sent him
across the river to the exclusive Trinity School in Manhattan, where he
graduated in 1909. Young Douglas was accepted at the United States
Naval Academy, where he thought there would be opportunities in fly-
ing. When he couldn't interest the navy in aviation he transferred to the
Massachusetts Institute of Technology. He received a B.S. in 1914.[1]

While at M.I.T. he and Jerome Hunsaker built the first wind tunnel, and, upon graduation Douglas became chief engineer for the Glenn L. Martin Company, a pioneer in the aircraft industry. In 1916 he married Charlotte Marguerite Ogg with whom he had five children.[2]

During World War I Douglas designed a twin-engine bomber for Martin which was a great success. But he longed to be on his own, and in 1920, with a stake of $600, he opened his own office in a Los Angeles barbershop. He was lucky enough to meet a rich man, David R. Davis, who wanted to make the first transcontinental flight. Douglas designed a plane called the Cloudster for this purpose. But Davis pulled out of the partnership, which was dissolved. However, Douglas was able to sell three Cloudsters to the navy and Douglas Aircraft was born.[3]

Douglas raised $1,000 each from fifteen men to finance the sale, which returned $120,000. In 1921 he opened a plant in Santa Monica. In 1922 he built the DT-1 with folding wings. The navy ordered ninety-three of these. In 1923 four DT-1 variants were ordered with the goal of flying around the world and enhancing U.S. prestige. In 1924 two of these planes accomplished the feat.[4] In 1932 TWA airlines asked Douglas for sixty-five all-metal, mono-winged airliners. Douglas designed the DC-1, ("D" for "Douglas," and "C" for "commercial") and filled the order with a modification, the DC-2, at $65,000 each.[5]

On December 17, 1935, Douglas announced a new revolutionary aircraft. It was what proved to be one of the best industrial designs in history, and the most influential in the progress of air transport—the DC-3. It was a beautiful, simple design, and Douglas produced it for a decade, building 10,629 in all. The DC-3 was completely reliable and practically indestructible. In 1985, forty to fifty years after they had been built, 1,500 to 2,000 were still flying; and one plane, still in service after many engine changes, had logged 87,000 flight hours, the equivalent of ten years in the air. The public responded to this, the first commercial airplane in the world to make money carrying only passengers. Airline travel, once considered to be dangerous, boomed. At the end of World War II, the DC-3 was carrying more than 90 percent of all American airline passengers, and large percentages overseas as well.[6]

The "Gooney Bird," as the DC-3 became affectionately called, was reconfigured to become the C-47 military transport in World War II. President Eisenhower called the C-47 one of several American developments that contributed the most to the Allied victory.[7] In 1985 it was said that the C-47 had flown more miles, and carried more freight and passengers, than any

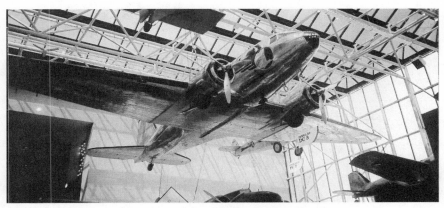

A Douglas DC-3 at the National Air and Space Museum, Washington D.C.
COLLECTION OF THE AUTHOR

other plane ever made. During the war the plane developed a mystique. One story tells of a Japanese Zero which deliberately rammed a C-47, cutting off part of its tail. The Zero crashed into a mountain, while the injured C-47 lumbered safely back to its base.[8] But Douglas built other planes as well. The SBD Dauntless sunk all four Japanese carriers at the critical Battle of Midway in 1942.[9] From 1942 to 1945 Douglas expanded to 160,000 employees, working at plants in El Segundo and Long Beach, California; Tulsa and Oklahoma City, in Oklahoma; and Chicago. During this period the company made 29,385 aircraft, including B-17 and B-24 bombers on license from other aircraft manufacturers.[10]

After the war, the company made the DC-4, DC-6, and the DC-7, all propeller planes which were extremely successful, so successful that the company couldn't see the jet age coming and gave Boeing a one-year advantage. Douglas tried to catch up with the jet DC-8, but couldn't. In 1967 the company merged with McDonnell, becoming McDonnell Douglas Corporation. Eventually, McDonnell Douglas was merged into Boeing.

It was good public relations when Lockheed, acquiring Martin, added aviation pioneer Glenn Martin's name to the company, Lockheed Martin. It was good when Jimmy McDonnell added Don Douglas' name to form McDonnell Douglas. And it is high time for Boeing to recognize two great aircraft-building pioneers in its corporate ancestry and change its name to Boeing McDonnell Douglas.

Donald Douglas spoke proudly of his Scottish ancestry when he received the Wallace Award of the American-Scottish Foundation.

Thomas J. Watson
(1874–1956)

AND

Thomas J. Watson, Jr.
(1914–1993)

THE INTERNATIONAL BUSINESS Machines Corporation, better known as IBM, is the most influential corporation of the twentieth century, having led the world into the computer revolution. The company's story, until recently, is that of the Watsons, father and son who ran and dominated the company for more than half a century.

Three Watson brothers, John, Andrew and David, left the Clyde Valley in southwest Scotland for Ireland, sometime after 1800, to pursue the linen trade. The Watsons, Presbyterians who claimed membership in the clan Buchanan, were disappointed with their lot in Ireland, and around 1840, John Watson emigrated to the United States. In upstate New York he met and married Jane Fulton White whose ancestors, like the Watsons, had migrated from Scotland to Ireland to the United States. The Scotch-Irish Whites had come from Strabane, and Jane Fulton White was related to the Scottish-American steamboat pioneer, Robert Fulton.[1]

The only son of John and Jane Watson was Thomas J. Watson, born in 1874 in Campbell, New York. Young Tom Watson discovered early that he had a talent for selling things that would lead him out of the mean circumstances in which he was raised. He became so good at nailing down sales, in fact, that he was hired by the National Cash Register Company in Dayton, Ohio, which was, at the time, one of the most profitable enterprises in the world. It was founded and run by another Scotch-Irishman, John H. Patterson, who was making the cash register universal in retailing. In a short time, Tom Watson became the company's leading salesman. Gradually, he rose in the company to the point that he became the company's number two man.

THOMAS J. WATSON, JR. AND THOMAS J. WATSON, IBM ARCHIVES

Then he fell in love with Jeannette Kittredge, whose father, Arthur Melville Kittredge, was a leader in the Presbyterian Church and a strict teetotaler. The Kittredges were among the leading families in Dayton. Nevertheless Jeannette accepted the socially inferior but financially successful Watson and the two were married. Patterson was elated and built the couple a house to live in. Their first son was named Thomas J. Watson, Jr. Since Kittredge is an Englishing of the Scottish Mackettrick, all of the ancestors of the Watsons, as far as we know, were of Scottish Presbyterian descent.[2]

Unfortunately, John Patterson was afraid of employees being too good. He didn't want to be upstaged and he had a reputation of getting rid of some of his best people. Tom Watson was an absolute superstar, and Patterson fired him, giving him a very generous $50,000 in severance pay. Thomas and Jeannette were devastated: he because "The Cash" had been his home for sixteen years, and she because they would have to leave Dayton to look for something else. Then things got worse. On February 22, 1912, Patterson, Watson, and several other employees of National Cash Register were indicted on three counts of criminal conspiracy in restraint of trade and maintaining a monopoly. Worse yet, they were convicted and, for the first time in an antitrust case, the defendants were sentenced to prison.[3] Released pending appeal, Tom Watson, protesting that he was innocent, left Dayton in search of employment knowing that his felony conviction would not make things easy.

But the great salesman was able to make another fine sale. There was a company in New York City, the Computing-Tabulating-Recording Company, better known as CTR, which was in desperate need of a manager. The company made time clocks, scales, and tabulating machines and had customers, but was encumbered with $4 million of debt. Some of the directors were talking of liquidation. Watson told them he thought he could turn the situation around, but the directors struggled with his two reputations: his good reputation as a businessman and his bad reputation as a felon. He maintained his position that he was innocent and they agreed to hire him to run the company. He demanded a "gentleman's salary" to support his family, and a percentage of the company's profits after it paid its dividends. Some of the directors must have thought they were giving away nothing on the last part, since the company was in trouble.[4]

Watson went to work immediately. Realizing that the company's products would sell better if improvements were made, he called the firm's banker at Guaranty Trust and asked for another $40,000 loan for research and development. The banker refused immediately, noting the company's unpaid debt of $4 million. But Watson was persuasive and got his money. The products were improved and sales went up. CTR, under Watson, was profitable almost immediately. In a few years, the profit sharing deal he had negotiated for himself would make him the highest paid employee in the United States.

Watson moved his family to Short Hills, New Jersey, an easy commute to New York, and joined the Episcopal Church, the only church in the town. An appeals court set aside his conviction and ordered a new trial. But the government was losing its interest in the case. No new trial developed, and the defendants were asked to sign consent decrees. Watson refused, saying that that would be an implication of guilt, and he was not guilty of anything. Ultimately, the government simply let him go, and the case died. Although he made plenty of money, he spent most of it, living on the edge, buying CTR stock on the generous margins, which were allowed in those days. In 1922 and 1924 he made business trips to open up the European market for the company and borrowed money to take his family along. When the stock market crash of 1929–32 came along, he became financially distressed meeting margin calls, and years later, told his son that if the price of the stock—now called IBM—had dropped only slightly more, he would have been wiped out. But he held on and ended up owning about five percent of the company.[5]

The Great Depression was unkind to most businesses, but not to IBM. The expanding New Deal government needed IBM's punch card technology to process the huge increase in data brought about by programs such as Social Security. The company's revenue doubled in the 1930s. Thomas Watson became a confidant of President Franklin D. Roosevelt, and learned to respect him. When Watson suggested a plan for his industry, Roosevelt quickly said something like, "Tom, forget it. I have to run this entire great country, not just an industry."[6] By the time of the New York World's Fair in 1939, IBM was a well-known international company, but still only medium sized. Yet it attracted an unusual amount of attention, owing to the constant promotion by its leader. At the Fair there was a General Motors Day, a General Electric Day, and an IBM Day. As the younger Watson, then twenty-five, observed, "two elephants and a gnat all getting equal treatment."[7]

During World War II Thomas J. Watson Sr. made an important investment, as much as $5 million, in backing Howard H. Aiken in producing the world's first automatic sequence computer. The Mark I, as it was called, was fifty-three feet long and eight feet high, and was given to Harvard University as a present.

It is useful to discuss the role of various Scots in the development process of the computer. Aiken is, of course, a Scottish name, and one of his most important assistants was Grace Murray Hopper who won the Legion of Honor and over twenty honorary degrees. Hopper retired from the navy in 1986 as a rear admiral, the highest ranking woman and the oldest American naval officer. Amazing Grace, as she was called, was the co-inventor of the early computer language Cobol and also coined the word "bug," meaning a defect in a machine or operating system. She was also of Scottish descent.[8] The role of John Napier in the seventeenth century will be discussed later (see p. 372). In 1843 Ada Byron, the daughter of the half-Scottish poet Lord Byron, wrote a list of instructions for a hypothetical computer theorized by the Englishman Charles Babbage, thus becoming the world's first computer programmer. Some call her the first computer scientist. In 1979 the U.S. Department of Defense named its computer language ADA in her honor In the 1930s Alan Mathison Turing, of Scottish ancestry, built an early computer.

Turing, a mathematical genius, believed that all concrete mathematical calculations could be programmed on his machine, perhaps the most important idea leading to the computer revolution. During the war, Turing built a decoding machine, which was vital to the allied war effort. It has been called the world's first electronic digital computer (see p. 115). Also, the mother of William H. Gates, III, founder of Microsoft, and currently the world's richest individual, was of Maxwell ancestry. Of course, IBM itself was involved in the process of developing the computer. One of its engineers, James Graham Johnston, born in Scotland, developed a tabulating machine—a prototype computer. After the war, Johnston, by then a millionaire, returned to Scotland in triumph to open the IBM facility at Greenock.

Thomas J. Watson, Sr. had spent his life actively. He had taken over a small company in trouble and built it into a profitable international enterprise respected for its technological, and managerial abilities. He had received decorations from more than thirty countries and numerous honorary degrees. His profile in *Who's Who in America* was longer than anyone else's. But he had put a great burden on his wife, first in Short Hills, and later when they had moved to 4 East Seventy-fifth Street in Manhattan. He was continually bringing people home for dinner on a few hours notice, and then was away from home for long periods. His wife, Jeannette, at last asked him for a divorce. Years later she related the story to Thomas Jr. and he was amazed, since he had never heard of the episode. He asked her what had happened, and she answered, "Tom, he looked so shocked, so upset, that I realized how deeply he loved me—and I never brought it up again."

The story of Thomas J. Watson, Jr. is very different from that of his father. Instead of being born poor, he was a child of privilege. Born in Dayton, he was raised in the posh New York City suburb of Short Hills, New Jersey. The tall good-looking Tom Watson, Jr. was a poor student making mostly Ds and Fs. In addition "Terrible Tommy" was a mischief-maker who at age twelve brought skunk juice to school one day, causing its evacuation. When it came time for college his admission test scores were low except in physics, where he scored very high. Princeton refused to admit him but his father used his contacts at Brown to help his son get accepted. Young Watson's academic career was undistinguished, as he admitted: "I spent so much time flying airplanes and fooling around that I barely graduated."[9] In 1939 young Watson joined the Air Force. By 1942 he was stationed in Moscow opening a lend-lease ferry from Alaska to Russia.

He left the service in 1943 as a lieutenant colonel and joined IBM as a salesman, living with his parents on East Seventy-fifth Street. He was gradually promoted through the company's ranks, learning the business, and preparing himself to become the head man. There was an intense loyalty between father and son, but there was also a fierce competition. Many times their disagreements were so severe that they ended in tears. One time, parting at an airport, the younger Watson bid his father goodbye with "Damn you old man!" But this upset him so much that as soon as the flight was over he called his father to apologize.

In 1949 Thomas Watson, Jr. joined Saint Andrew's Society of the State of New York, and, in the same year, was promoted to the position of executive vice president at IBM. From this position he saw clearly that the electronic age was arriving, and that IBM had the possibility of becoming a gigantic enterprise. As Steve Lohr remarked, "Mr. Watson's real business insight was to recognize the profound change that electronics would mean for calculating everything from census data to corporate balance sheets to market research."[10] But he realized that it would take great risks, hiring thousands of engineers and spending tens of millions of dollars to get into the game. His conservative father was against the plan, but by 1950 the son had accumulated enough power in the company to begin the transfer to the new technology on his own. It was by no means certain that IBM would become the leader in this new field. Several other major corporations were in the hunt. But as the technology progressed from vacuum tubes to transistors to silicon chips, Thomas Watson Jr. successfully guided the company's progress to preeminence. By 1953 IBM had produced its 701, the first large-scale computer to be produced in quantity. It was followed by the 702 in 1955.

In 1956, Thomas J. Watson, Jr. was promoted to President of IBM. In his autobiography he said that he was "the most frightened man in America," but in fact he had spent ten years preparing for the responsibility. The two Watsons were photographed shaking hands at the transfer of power. The younger Watson says of the photo, ". . . on my face is a look of great self-assurance . . . but on Dad's face there is a faint, uncertain smile."[11] Only six weeks later, young Watson was all alone; his father dead. The funeral at the Brick Presbyterian Church in Manhattan was more than full, the crowd of the rich and famous extending out onto Park Avenue.

For the next fourteen years, Thomas J. Watson, Jr. ran IBM as the most profitable enterprise in history and led the world into the computer revolution. The logo of "Big Blue" became "a symbol of management excellence and technological prowess."[12] But Watson had a heart attack in 1970 at the age of fifty-six. He resigned as Chief Executive Officer in 1971. During his tenure, the business had grown ten times as big and was turning over $7.5 billion a year. He kept his seat on the Executive Committee, but resigned that position in 1979 to become Ambassador to the Soviet Union. He was an ardent advocate of nuclear arms reduction. He received honorary degrees from Brown University, Columbia, Harvard, Oxford, Yale, and Notre Dame, among others.

In 1987, at the age of seventy-two, he piloted his own Lear 55 around the world on his old Lend Lease route. Crowds of Red Army veterans greeted him at all the stops in Siberia. Thomas J. Watson, Jr. died on New Year's Eve, 1993. Some had called him "the businessman of the twentieth century." *Fortune* magazine referred to him as "the greatest capitalist who ever lived."[13]

Sean Connery

(1930–)

EAN CONNERY IS the best known Scot in the world today, and possibly the best known ever. Millions of Scots, whether in the homeland or in the Diaspora, feel pride at the sight of their handsome kinsman on the wide screen, and to the sound of the glorious remnants of his Edinburgh burr. Although some refer derisively to "007" as the number of times he has visited Scotland in recent years, no one can say that he is not a Scottish patriot nor minimize the effect he has had on Scottish politics. As a highly visible member of the minority Scottish National Party, which seeks an independent Scotland, Connery has had an enormous influence on the country's destiny, and may

Sir Sean Connery, wearing Hunting Maclean tartan, is accompanied by his wife Micheline at the opening of the Scottish Parliament, Edinburgh, July 1, 1999. AP/WIDE WORLD PHOTOS.

have had more to do with bringing about the new Scottish parliament—the first in three centuries—than any politician.

Thomas Connery, the grandfather of Sean Connery, was of Irish ancestry and married a Scottish woman named Jeanie McNab. They were the parents of Sean Connery's father, Joseph Connery, who married Euphamia (Effie) Maclean. Joe and Effie were the parents of Sean Connery who was born in Edinburgh as Thomas Connery. Young Tommy Connery started life in Edinburgh's old Canongate, but the family subsequently moved west to 176 Fountainbridge, and that is where he grew up and where his parents remained for many years.[1] Tommy Connery attended Bruntsfield Primary School and later Darroch where he received a technical education. His maternal grandparents, Helen and Neil Maclean, moved to Fifeshire and Tommy often stayed there, in awe of his grandfather who possessed great strength and drank a bottle of whisky every day.[2]

By the age of eighteen, Tommy Connery had grown to six-foot-two and was known to his friends as Big Tam. He was already working for a living in various jobs which included delivering milk by horse-drawn wagon, polishing coffins, modeling and working as an actor. Big Tam was also defending himself against the tough street gangs of Depression-era Edinburgh. At age twenty-three he went to London with a friend to enter a Mr. Universe contest. He didn't win, but got a chorus part in the traveling company of the musical *South Pacific*, changing his name to the more theatrical Sean. By the time the show reached Edinburgh his talent, good looks and hard work had got him the role of Lieutenant Buzz Adams, which had been played by Larry Hagman, Mary Martin's son, in London.[3]

For the next several years Connery took various roles and in 1957 got his first real recognition in a television program, *Requiem for a Heavyweight*. From then on he worked regularly. In 1962 he married Diane Cliento with whom he had a son, Jason. The next year he became an international star in the first of the James Bond films, *Dr. No*. Such established actors as James Mason and David Niven had been discussed for the role, but Connery got the part, perhaps to some extent because he was cheaper. His accent didn't hurt either as the author, Ian Fleming (also Scottish), had told his readers that James Bond was a Scot. After *Dr. No*, roles and money poured in and Sean Connery became one of the biggest names in the film industry.

Eventually Connery was divorced from his first wife and in 1975 he married Micheline Roquebrune, a French-Moroccan artist who was born in Nice.[4] Sean Connery became a more skillful actor in his later years. He won the BAFTA Best Actor award for his performance in *The Name of the Rose* (1986), and an Academy Award for Best Supporting Actor in *The Untouchables* (1987). He has been generous as well, having given away his entire salary in *Diamonds Are Forever* (1971) to establish the Scottish Education Trust, among many other benefactions. Connery was awarded honorary degrees by Heriot-Watt University of Glasgow in 1981 and by St. Andrews University in 1988. He was a made a Freeman of Edinburgh in 1991, and is a Commander of Arts in France.

There have, of course, been many other Scots and people of Scottish ancestry involved in films. To name a few: Warren Beatty, James Cameron, Montgomery Clift, Ronald Colman, Walt Disney, Faye Dunaway, Clint Eastwood, Ava Gardner, Greer Garson, Mel Gibson, Lillian Gish, Stewart Granger, Hugh Grant, Audrey and Katherine Hepburn, Charlton Heston, John Huston, Deborah Kerr, Alan Ladd, Jeanette MacDonald, Shirley Maclaine, Robert Mitchum, Marilyn Monroe, David Niven, Robert Redford, Cliff Robertson, Mickey Rooney, George C. Scott, Tom Selleck, Alastair Sim, James Stewart, Elizabeth Taylor, and John Wayne.[5]

Sean Connery's membership in the Scottish National Party is, of course, politically incorrect for the majority of Scots. It appears to have kept him from a knighthood for years. But finally the people, even many who don't like his politics, demanded it and, recently, he became Sir Sean. And is there a Scot with soul so dead that didn't swell with pride as Big Tam paraded up the Royal Mile in his kilt, along with all of the other dignitaries including the Queen of Scots, at the opening of the new parliament?

John Muir

(1838–1914)

I T IS ONLY recently that the people of Scotland have discovered a hero—John Muir—previously little known to them. John Muir is recognized everywhere as the founder of both America's grand national parks and the worldwide conservation movement. He is the principal person responsible for establishing Yosemite and for adding 148 million acres to the system. As a result of his pioneering, the world now has more than 3,000 such parks.[1]

John Muir with President Theodore Roosevelt, 1903. COURTESY OF THE BANCROFT LIBRARY, UNIVERSITY OF CALIFORNIA, BERKELEY.

John Muir was born on a farm near Dunbar, a fishing village on the North Sea, about thirty miles East of Edinburgh. His mother, Anne Gilrye, was of the Clan Hay. His father, Daniel Muir, a descendant of Clan Gordon, was an evangelical Presbyterian and religious fanatic who compelled his son to memorize parts of the Bible every day. By the time the family emigrated to Portage, Wisconsin, in 1849, the eleven-year-old John Muir could recite great stretches of both the New and Old Testaments.[2]

On the farm, Daniel Muir worked his son as hard as an adult, and John Muir always felt that this labor had stunted his growth. The young man escaped by reading everything he could find. He even invented a wood-en "alarm clock" so that he would wake early and could read before doing his chores.[3] At the local grammar school, John Muir studied French, English, and Latin. His favorite author[4] was his fellow Scot Alexander Wilson (1766–1813) who was the first American to study the native birds. The Paisley-born Wilson's *American Ornithology* (1808) is still a standard work in the field and inspired Audubon as well as John Muir.[5]

Young John Muir displayed some of his inventions at a Wisconsin State Fair, and that got him into the University of Wisconsin, which he attended from 1859 to 1863. But he was an indifferent student, unwilling to study the prescribed courses, and working instead on geology and botany. He didn't graduate and continued to work on inventions until he injured an eye in 1876 and gave up the profession. He left Wisconsin and walked all the way to the Cedar Key, Florida, keeping a "nature diary" as he went. In 1916, after his death, his *A Thousand Mile Walk to the Gulf* was published. In 1868 he walked from San Francisco to Yosemite, and became enchanted with the place. He stayed there for six years, as Yosemite's unofficial guardian.[6]

In 1880 Muir married Louie Wanda Strentzel, the daughter of a Polish horticulturist who had been one of the founders of the California fruit and wine industries.[7] Muir bought a ranch of his own near Martinez, California, (now a National Historic site) that became very profitable. In 1881 he went to Alaska and discovered the Muir Glacier. By 1891 he had two children, and had made so much money as a rancher he retired and began to travel extensively in Europe, Australia, New Zealand, South America, and Asia.[8]

On one of his trips he visited his old hometown of Dunbar. He writes to his wife, with, perhaps, a bit of pride:

Dunbar, Scotland, July 6, 1893

Dear Louie,

Edinburgh is . . . far the most beautiful town I ever saw."[9]

Back in California, Muir began to write extensively, demanding con-servation of America's priceless wilderness. He promoted the establish-ment of national parks, and blasted developers. In 1890 Yosemite was officially made a National Park, largely due to his efforts, but that was only the beginning of the battle. There were many abuses and not enough resources to maintain and police the parks. He became driven in his pursuit of conservation. In 1892 he organized the world's premier conservation society, the Sierra Club, and served as its first president until his death. In the last years of the century, John Muir wrote articles for magazines that aroused public interest in conservation issues. He is now so well remembered as a conservationist that his very considerable skills as a writer are often overlooked. He hounded the government, which finally established protected forests all over the country. He was an incessant lobbyist and even took the president, Theodore Roosevelt, on a camping trip in 1903. Roosevelt, who had Scottish ancestors, was duly impressed, and bucked the special interests set against the conservation movement. During Roosevelt's administration tens of millions of acres were preserved for future generations. Roosevelt always maintained that his greatest achievement was the additions to the National Parks.[10]

John Muir had much to do with this, and never let up on applying pressure, as excerpts of this letter show:

Martinez, California, April 21, 1908

Dear Mr. President,

I am anxious that Yosemite Park may be saved from all sorts of commercialism . . .

Faithfully and devotedly yours,
John Muir

P.S. Oh for a tranquil camp hour with you like those beneath the Sequoias in memorable 1903![11]

John Muir died in California and is buried at his ranch near Martinez, California.

Rachel Carson

(1907–1964)

I N 1999, THE Modern Library published a ranking of the 100 best nonfiction books written in English in the twentieth century. Fifth on the list was *Silent Spring* by Rachel Carson. The book is important because it was the first to warn and prove to the world the dangers of harsh chemicals in agriculture and other fields. Because of Rachel Carson, birds are singing today which would be otherwise extinct. And millions of humans may have avoided disease and death. Most importantly, we have been warned, and the debate on the subject continues.

Rachel Carson,
PHOTOFEST

Rachel Carson was born in Springdale, Pennsylvania, a town on the Allegheny River near Pittsburgh. The name Carson is a distinctively Scottish name, which originates in Galloway, in southwestern Scotland. Her father, Robert Carson, was born into the working class of Allegheny City, then a Scotch-Irish town which is now incorporated as the North Side of Pittsburgh. His father James Carson, a carpenter, and his wife Ellen, were Presbyterian immigrants from the north of Ireland. Rachel Carson's mother, Maria Frazier McLean, was also Scotch-Irish. Her mother's father, Daniel McLean, was a Presbyterian minister.

Robert Carson sang in the choir in the Fourth United Presbyterian

Church in Allegheny City. In 1893 his quartet participated in a musical evening in Canonsburg, a town about eighteen miles south of Pittsburgh that is best known now as the birthplace of the barber-turned-singer, Perry Como. Also contributing to the evening's entertainment was the Washington Quintette, from nearby Washington, Pennsylvania. This group featured as an alto soloist Maria Frazier McLean. About a year later, and despite their class differences, Robert Carson and Maria McLean were married, and moved to Springdale.[1]

Rachel Louise Carson had a good upbringing in Springdale. There was plenty of accessible nature in the vicinity. It was only a short walk to the river where one could watch the giant paddle-wheelers, belching black smoke, pushing acres of barges ahead, bound for The Point at Pittsburgh, sixteen miles downstream, where the Allegheny meets the Monongehela to form the Ohio. A child could listen to the boats in the night and wonder if they were going to go all the way to New Orleans.

Rachel Carson decided to become a writer while still a child. She wrote stories about animals and won her first literary prize at age ten. In 1925 she received a scholarship to the beautiful campus of Pennsylvania College for Women (now Chatham College) in Pittsburgh. Carson majored in science and graduated *magna cum laude* in 1929. Although jobs for women scientists were scarce, she found employment at Woods Hole in Massachusetts. Soon she was at Johns Hopkins in Baltimore working for an M.A. degree in zoology, which she received in 1932. To support herself she taught part time at Johns Hopkins and at the University of Maryland. Her father died in 1935, and with the country in deep depression, she became the only support for an extended family that included her ailing mother. She was able to get a job at the Bureau of Fisheries, and wrote articles on nature for Baltimore newspapers. In 1941 she published her first book, *Under the Sea-Wind*, just as World War II was starting. It sold poorly, but received excellent reviews.[2]

In 1951 Carson published *The Sea Around Us*. The book was an instant success. Serialized in the *New Yorker*, it was acclaimed by the public and scientists as well for making people aware of the fragility of nature and human life. *The Sea Around Us* won the National Book Award and spent eighty-six weeks on the *New York Times* bestseller list. Carson was established as America's preeminent natural science writer. She had enough money then to retire to a cottage on the Sheepscott River in Maine. In 1955 she published another bestseller, *The Edge of the Sea*.[3]

Sometime, in the next few years, Rachel Carson learned that she was terminally ill with breast cancer. But this did not deter her. In 1962 she published her masterpiece *Silent Spring*. In "clear, often beautiful prose" she indicted the actions and inactions of the chemical industry, the government and agribusiness. The book "demonstrated that chemical pesticides were potential biocides that threatened humankind and nature with extinction."[4] In *Silent Spring* she says, "Incidents like the eastern Illinois spraying raise a question that is not only scientific but moral . . . whether any civilization can wage relentless war on life without destroying itself, and without losing the right to be called civilized. . . ."[5]

Carson was attacked by both the chemical business and by the government, scientifically and personally. Huge sums were spent answering her charges. But her work had been researched so carefully that she was ready to refute the attacks. She proved that DDT had lethal consequences for both fish and birds. She showed that when DDT was used to ward off the Dutch Elm disease, that the worms eating the DDT-sprayed leaves were then eaten by birds whose eggshells were then too weak, causing them to break too early, killing any potential offspring.[6] President Kennedy called for an investigation of the issues Carson had raised, and in 1963 a report of the Presidential Science Advisory Committee supported her. By the end of the year DDT was being regulated by many of the states. The Nixon administration banned all DDT in the United States in 1972.

Rachel Carson was acclaimed by the public and received numerous scientific and literary awards. She was elected into the American Academy of Arts and Letters. But she died in Silver Spring, Maryland, only a year and a half after the publication of *Silent Spring*. She never married, and cared for and lived with her mother until her death in 1958.

Today artificial alterations of nature are met with resistance. American beef, with its additions of hormones, is not welcome in France. And bioengineered crops are shunned by many Americans. This healthy skepticism of modern scientific intrusion into natural life is one of Rachel Carson's legacies. And the last year of the twentieth century was good to her. The peregrine falcon, down to thirty-nine breeding pairs in 1970, has been spared extinction. With 1,650 pairs reported, it was recently removed from the list of endangered species in America. Things are looking up, also, for the bald eagle, the Aleutian Canada goose, and the pelican. The birdcalls of spring have not been silenced.

Robert R. Livingston

(1746–1813)

I T IS INTERESTING to try to imagine what America might be like today if Robert Livingston's ministry to Paris (1801–1803) had not been successful. There could have been a war with France over the Louisiana territory with what results we can only guess. Or he may have negotiated far less well than he did, leaving France in possession of a great deal of land which might not now be part of the United States. This would have made expansion to the West Coast, in all likelihood, impossible. America would be much smaller than it is. It would not be, in all probability, a superpower.

Robert R. Livingston is often referred to as Chancellor Livingston to distinguish him from the many other members of New York's grand Livingston clan, one of the most powerful dynasties in American history. According to one biographer, the New York Livingstons are descended from Lord Livingston who was a guardian of Mary Queen of Scots when she was a child. His daughter was one of "The Four Marys" who accompanied the young queen to France for her wedding to the French dauphin. In 1678 Robert Livingston, born in Roxburghshire, the son of a dissident minister, founded the New York family. In 1686 he put the future of the family on a sound basis by purchasing Livingston Manor, a huge tract, from Indians. Governor Dorgan of the Province of New York recognized this purchase with a patent.[1] Among Robert Livingston's descendants are, in addition to our subject Robert R. Livingston, a governor of New Jersey, a signer of the Declaration of Independence, a mayor of New York City, a justice of the U.S. Supreme Court, a United States secretary of state, a United States senator,[2] and recently, a congressman, Robert Livingston, who almost became Speaker of the House.

Robert R. Livingston, swearing in George Washington as First President of the United States, New York, 1789. MUSEUM OF THE CITY OF NEW YORK.

Robert R. Livingston was born in New York City, and was related to many of the most prominent families including the Schuylers, Van Rensselaers, and Van Cortlandts. He was educated at King's College (now Columbia University), and graduated in 1765. He studied law privately, and within a few years was admitted to the bar. For a short time he practiced law with his college friend and relative, John Jay. But New York was seething with political activity and both Livingston and Jay became involved in the American Revolution.

There were very few people of Scottish birth or ancestry in colonial New York, due partly to the fact that until 1707, when Scotland and England became Great Britain, New York and the other American colonies were *English* colonies, and few Scots were allowed in. But the few Scots became very prominent. Between 1707 and the end of the Revolution, eight different Scottish governors ruled the Province and State of New York. Robert Bruce and Archibald Gracie became rich as merchants. Gracie's summer home, built in 1799, is now Gracie Mansion, in which all of the mayors of New York live. Archibald Kennedy was the largest property owner in New York. He tried to stay neutral in the

Revolution, however, and most of his property was confiscated. His house at 1 Broadway was appropriated by George Washington for his headquarters in 1776. Saint Paul's, New York City's oldest surviving church building, was built between 1764 and 1766 by architect Thomas McBean.[3]

Saint Andrew's Society of the State of New York was founded in 1756 and remains today the oldest charitable institution in New York State. The Society's first President, Philip Livingston, was a kinsman of Robert R. Livingston. Saint Andrew's was so divided between Patriot and Tory that operations were suspended for several years during the American Revolution. Alexander MacDougall, born in Scotland, was the chief founder of the famous Sons of Liberty and became a general in the Revolutionary army.

Robert R. Livingston had accepted the job as Recorder of the City of New York in 1773, but was replaced in 1775 when he signed the Articles of Association at the first Continental Congress in the same year. But the news that year was not all bad. Livingston inherited Clermont, a 500,000-acre Hudson River estate. Then his father-in-law died and he inherited another 250,000 acres in Dutchess County.[4] Livingston was one of the New York delegates to the Continental Congress from 1775 until 1776, and served again from 1779 to 1781. His speaking was of such quality that Benjamin Franklin called him the "American Cicero."[5]

In 1776 he was named as one of five people to draft the Declaration of Independence. The other four were Thomas Jefferson, Benjamin Franklin, John Adams and Roger Sherman.[6] Livingston did not sign the Declaration, however, as he had to be at the New York Provincial Convention on July 8, 1776 when the Province of New York became the State of New York. Robert Livingston was on the committee to draft the State Constitution. His kinsman, Philip Livingston, signed the Declaration of Independence for the family. Two other members of Saint Andrew's Society of the State of New York, Rev. John Witherspoon and Lewis Morris, signed with him.

In 1777, Robert R. Livingston was elected to New York's highest judicial position, becoming the first Chancellor of New York, a post he held until 1801, when his term limit expired. But the war was devastating for him as the British burned Claremont and he had to make ends meet on a low government salary. In the first United States government, operating under the Articles of Confederation, Livingston became America's first secretary of foreign affairs. He carefully monitored the peace negotiations in Paris, and reprimanded his commissioners, Benjamin Franklin, John Jay, John Adams, and Henry Laurens when he thought it was warranted. In 1783, Britain recognized the independence of the United States of America in the Treaty of Paris.

In 1788 Livingston was Chairman of the New York Convention to consider the United States Constitution, and played a very important part in procuring its adoption.[7] A climax in his career came with the inauguration of George Washington as first President of the United States in 1789. New York had been designated as the nation's temporary capital, and President Washington left Virginia for New York in mid-April. Everywhere he went along the way there were crowds of adoring Americans. Church bells rang. Speeches were made. Songs were sung.[8] It should be noted that Washington, of solidly English ancestry, had a Scottish connection in that he was descended from King Malcolm II.

At last, the great hero reached the New Jersey side of the Hudson River where a welcoming committee, headed by Robert R. Livingston, was waiting in a barge ceremonially draped in red. It must have been a majestic sight as the barge was rowed across the harbor to New York among a flotilla of boats, one of which supplied music. The whole party landed at Murray's Wharf where Wall Street met the East River. The President-elect was taken to a house on Cherry Street, which had been newly renovated at private expense as the presidential mansion.[9]

On April 30, 1789 everything was ready for the Inauguration. Cannon were fired in the morning and the streets of New York were soon full of celebrants waving flags. The ceremony took place on a balcony outside Federal Hall at the intersection of Wall and Broad Streets, just a few paces from where the New York Stock Exchange stands today. The atmosphere was festive. The crowd was as large as the space would allow. The military escort for the occasion was commanded by Brigadier General William Malcolm, another member of Saint Andrew's Society, who was attired in a kilt. The tall General Washington walked out on the balcony with the Chancellor of New York, Robert R. Livingston, who administered the oath of office. Livingston was at that time also President of Saint Andrew's Society. As soon as Washington took the oath Livingston shouted, "Long Live George Washington, President of the United States!" That evening there were extravagant fireworks over the little city. The new president of the United States watched from the home of Chancellor Livingston.[10]

Despite his success at the Inauguration, Livingston was soon to be dis-appointed. He sought the positions of secretary of the treasury and chief justice of the Supreme Court, but received neither. He later declined the positions of minister to France and secretary of the navy. But in 1801, President Jefferson gave him a second chance to be America's minister at the court of France during the consulate of Napoleon. Since his term limit as Chancellor of New York was running out, Livingston accepted— a decision which would have great consequences.

When Livingston arrived in Paris there were rumors that Spain had agreed to return Louisiana to France. This was extremely disquieting to America, as tens of thousands of settlers were pouring into the Ohio and Cumberland valleys, and their natural seaport was New Orleans. By the treaty of San Lorenzo in 1795, Spain had given Americans the right to ship American goods from the port of New Orleans duty free, as well as the right to store goods for short periods of time in that port. It was feared that France would be much more difficult to deal with than Spain, and even, that the Mississippi River might be closed to American traffic. Then, in 1802, Spain withdrew the right to deposit goods at New Orleans. The seriousness of the situation was shown when Jefferson, a Francophile and recent enemy of Great Britain, wrote to Livingston, "The day France takes possession of New Orleans, we must marry our-selves to the British fleet and nation." The president further instructed his minister to approach Charles Maurice de Talleyrand and urge him not to complete the deal with Spain, if it had not already taken place; and to try to buy New Orleans, or at least get trading rights there, or at another port, if it had.[11]

But Livingston was not able to talk directly with the great statesman. And when it became known that France owned Louisiana again, he put forward the proposal for trading rights at New Orleans. Not receiving an answer he let rumors be circulated that the United States might attack New Orleans, a threat which most likely was not taken seriously. Then he played his best card. He told the French that he thought, rather than obtain trading rights, it would be better for France to sell all of Louisiana to America, especially since America was considering closer relations with Britain. At this, Napoleon, perhaps for other reasons as well, decid-ed to offer all of Louisiana for sale to the United States. At about this time Jefferson sent James Monroe—another Scottish-American who was retiring as Governor of Virginia—to assist Livingston. This greatly offended Livingston who thought he could do whatever had to be done alone, but he tried to hide his feelings.

Livingston and Monroe did not have the authorization to buy Louisiana but realized immediately that it was the right thing to do, and negotiated the Louisiana Purchase with the Count de Barbé-Marbois. They agreed to purchase 828,000 square miles for a purchase price of $11,250,000 plus the assumption of $3,750,000 in American claims against France, a total of $15 million. For this price—perhaps the greatest real estate deal of all time—Livingston and Monroe had bought what are now the states of Louisiana, Arkansas, Missouri, Iowa, Nebraska, and most of Oklahoma, Kansas, Colorado, Wyoming, Minnesota, the Dakotas, and Montana. They had doubled the size of their country, and provided for its unlimited westward expansion for less than three cents an acre.[12]

After the signing of the agreement, the three ministers, Livingston, Monroe, and the count de Barbé-Marbois rose and Livingston said, "We have lived long, but this work is the noblest work of our whole lives. The treaty which we have just signed has not been obtained by art, or dictated by force; equal advantages to both parties, it will change vast solitudes into flourishing districts. From this day, the United States take their place among the powers of the world. . . ."[13] And Napoleon said to Marbois, "This accession of territory affirms forever the power of the United States, and I have just given England a maritime rival that sooner or later will lay low her pride."[14]

But there were problems with the unauthorized purchase. Jefferson was afraid that a constitutional amendment would be needed. However the Senate, realizing how marvelous the transaction was, approved the purchase twenty-four to seven. Another problem was the treaty's vague borders. In particular, the treaty did not specifically include West Florida, and Livingston was criticized for this. He was also accused of backdating a document to minimize the contributions of Monroe. This may have cost him the Republican nomination for Governor of New York in 1804. To excuse his frustration, it must be said that negotiations were all but finished when Monroe arrived in Paris, only eighteen days before the Louisiana Purchase was completed. It is doubtful that Monroe had had much to do with it. It had been Livingston's show, and he left France as a hero and a personal friend of Napoleon, who gave him a beautiful snuffbox as a token of appreciation.[15]

Monroe went on to become one of the more important presidents. His administration completed a part of the Louisiana Purchase by annexing West Florida in 1819. This was something of a vindication of Livingston's legal theories that the area was part of Louisiana at the time of the Purchase. James Monroe is most famous for the Monroe Doctrine, which has been an important component of American foreign policy ever since. It said, in effect, that there was to be no more European colonization in the Western Hemisphere, that the United States would not intervene in European affairs, and that Europe would not interfere in the affairs of the New World.

Back in New York, Livingston took up an interest he had had before in steam navigation, in part because his estate, Clermont, was more than 100 miles up the Hudson from New York City. As early as 1797, he had joined with his brother-in-law John Stevens and Nicholas Roosevelt trying to develop steam navigation.[16] Governor De Witt Clinton gave them a monopoly, on condition that within one year they would have demonstrated a steam voyage upriver from New York to Albany with a speed of at least four miles an hour. Not being able to buy a Boulton & Watt steam engine, the group built their own, but it was not practical and the project was abandoned.

In Paris, in 1802, Livingston had met Robert Fulton who was constructing torpedoes for the French government. Fulton claimed to have been born in Pennsylvania, but there are those who think he was born in Ayrshire, Scotland and had hid his nationality since torpedo sales by a Briton to France would have been treason. Some say he claimed to be "Irish." Other authorities say that he meant Scotch-Irish. At any rate, Fulton was of Scottish descent and is an inductee of the Scottish-American Hall of Fame. It is alleged, also, that Fulton witnessed the running of the first practical steamboat in the world in Scotland in 1801 or 1802 (see p. 81). With Livingston's financial support, Fulton ran a successful steamboat on the Seine river in Paris in 1803. When Fulton decided to return to New York with Livingston in the same year, they applied for and received another monopoly. By 1807 they had acquired a Boulton & Watt engine and employed a Scottish millwright, Robert McQueen, to build the iron paddle wheel. On August 17 1807 a skeptical crowd watched as Fulton pulled away from the dock at Christopher Street in New York's Greenwich Village. By the next morning the boat, averaging more than four miles per hour, had reached Clermont where Livingston came aboard. They reached Albany the next morning, fulfilling the terms of their monopoly. By September, they were offering regular transportation between New York and Albany. It was the world's first scheduled steamboat service. Their boat was renamed *Clermont*.[17]

Robert Fulton was given a hero's burial. His grave can still be seen clearly, from the Rector Street side of Trinity Churchyard in New York. Fulton Street is named after him.

Livingston received many honors including an honorary LL.D., and was elected Grand Master Mason of New York. He maintained an interest in agriculture and was the principal founder and first president of the American Academy of Fine Arts. He also founded the New York Society for the Promotion of Agriculture, Arts, and Manufactures, which for years was a leading exponent of government support for industrial development.

Robert R. Livingston will be remembered as New York's first Chancellor; as a member of the committees which drafted the Declaration of Independence and the Constitution of New York; as America's first foreign secretary; as the man who swore in George Washington as the first American president; and as a steamboat pioneer. But most of all, he will be remembered as the man who doubled the size of the United States, and made the nation a world power.

James Watt

(1736–1819)

James Watt,

THE FAMOUS STORY of little Jamie Watt, carefully manipulating his mother's teakettle as it changed water into steam, is generally thought to be apocryphal, but it may have a basis in fact. No less a figure than Andrew Carnegie, who was fascinated by Watt, describes this scene in his 1905 biography of his fellow-Scot: "Mrs. Campbell, Watt's cousin, writes in 1798 that Mrs. Muirhead, Watt's aunt, watched him play with a tea kettle for an hour." He goes on to say that the young Watt held a spoon to the steam at various angles to see what the effects would be, and that his aunt chided him for being indolent.[1] Whatever he was, James Watt was not lazy. He went on to produce engineering which became the basis not only of Carnegie's wealth, but of the wealth of the world. Watt became the key inventor of the Industrial Revolution. Before him, progress in manufacturing and transportation had been held back by the lack of an independent engine to drive machinery or power ships and vehicles. Only waterfalls could run factory machines, and ships depended, as they had forever, on the wind. Horses were the principal source of power on land. James Watt's steam engine changed all of that.

Watt was born in the Scottish port town of Greenock on the river Clyde, some twenty miles downstream from Glasgow. His grandfather, Thomas Watt, had been a teacher of mathematics. His father, also named James, was married to Agnes Muirhead and involved in many trades, but is commonly described as a merchant and town councillor. A poor speculation seriously hurt the family finances, and young James' schooling was cut short. He had been a poor scholar anyway, and like so many geniuses, had been taunted by his schoolmates. He was, therefore, sent to London and apprenticed to an instrument maker. Watt learned his trade quickly, and as he disliked his conditions and low pay, returned to Scotland before his term was up.

Watt tried to establish himself in Glasgow as an instrument maker, but the Hammerman's Guild would not accept him as he had not finished his apprenticeship. He was very fortunate that Glasgow University made a position for him in the same field.[2] He soon showed such promise as an engineer at the university that several of its most important figures became his friends; notably the philosopher Adam Smith, the chemist Joseph Black, and the physicist John Robison. It says something about Scotland that these three important and university-educated men accepted the brilliant Watt as an equal, even though he had not even completed an apprenticeship for a trade. It also says something about the raw talent of the young James Watt.

It is, of course, the synergy between Watt and Black which concerns us here, since Black is universally given credit for the discovery of latent heat. (More on this in the section on Black; see p. 377) Although Watt never attended any classes of Black's, the two were intimate friends and often discussed how latent heat related to the steam engine in use in that era—the Newcomen engine—and how it might be improved. This engine, invented in England by Thomas Newcomen about fifty years before Watt's work, had very little utility. For half a century no improvements had been made and it was only marginally useful for its one purpose, pumping water out of mines. The Newcomen engine was so inefficient and required so much fuel that many water-filled mines were being forced to close.

Watt began to study steam scientifically, finding, along Black's line of thought, that water converted into steam heated five times its own weight. Then, in 1764, fortune brought a present. The university acquired a Newcomen engine in need of repair and told Watt to fix it. He was amazed at the great quantity of steam the engine used, and immediately realized that he could build a more efficient engine. Watt saw that the reason for the Newcomen engine's inefficiency was the cold water used to condense the steam being injected into the cylinder itself. This resulted in a cool cylinder that had to be reheated with more steam than would be needed if the cylinder were to remain hot. Over time, Watt found that the optimum engine would require two conditions. The first was that the temperature of the condensed steam should be low, so as to allow for a good vacuum. The second condition he said, was that the cylinder should always be as hot as the steam which entered it. The Newcomen engine was a failure because it could not meet these conditions. Watt would have to build an engine which could. But how was he to do it?

Watt's famous epiphany on Glasgow Green is best described in his own words: "I had gone to take a walk on a fine Sabbath afternoon, early in 1765. I had entered the green by the gate at the foot of Charlotte Street, and had passed the old washing house . . . I had not walked farther than the golf house when the whole thing was arranged in my mind."[3] What he had discovered was something that had escaped everyone trying to improve the almost useless Newcomen engine for half a century. Watt had realized that if he used a separate condenser outside the cylinder, the temperature of condensation could be kept low, leaving the temperature of the cylinder high. His two "conditions" would be met. The only problem was that it was Sunday and, because of his religion, he could do no work. He would have to wait for Monday when he could write down all of his ideas and begin to build his engine.[4]

Watt soon built a new steam engine on these principles. The separate condenser worked perfectly, just as he had surmised it would. Of course, there were many more improvements to be made, and over time, he made them. But progress was slow. Watt had no money to prosecute his invention and investors were slow in coming. In debt, he sold two-thirds of his patent to John Roebuck, the owner of the Carron Iron Works, but this arrangement did not work out. In the meantime, Watt, who had married Margaret Miller in 1763, began to design canals, as his reputation as a civil engineer was growing. In particular, he surveyed the Forth and Clyde Canal, but Parliament didn't act on the project.

But fortune smiled on Watt again. In an incredible string of events, Benjamin Franklin gave a letter of introduction to William Small, the tutor of Jefferson (see p. 279), to Matthew Boulton, an industrialist who owned the Soho engineering works in Birmingham, England. It was Small who told Boulton about Watt's engine.[5] Thus, it came to be that in 1768 Watt and Boulton met, and Boulton agreed to take over Roebuck's share. It was a simple arrangement. Boulton was to run the business and Watt was to do the engineering. Both partners had complete confidence in each other. So at last Watt's engine came to market. The partnership of Boulton & Watt was an immediate success. The partners asked Parliament for an extension of the patent, and this was granted. By 1783 the Newcomen engine was out of business. The energy savings of Watt's engine was so great that Boulton & Watt charged their customers one-third of the reduced cost. The closing of mines ceased.[6]

Watt's first wife, with whom he had had two sons and two daughters, died in childbirth in 1773. In 1775 he married Ann Macgregor and they had two sons and one daughter. The oldest son of this marriage, Gregory, had great ability in both science and literature, but died in 1804, much to the distress of his parents.[7]

Watt made many improvements on his engine including a centrifugal governor that controlled a rotary engine. This is still essential in automation. Of course, he adapted his engine to run machinery, which was to be its greatest use. He also invented the indicator, which diagrams the relationship between the steam's volume and its pressure. The Encyclopaedia Britannica says: "The eminently philosophic notion of an indicator diagram is fundamental in the theory of thermodynamics; the instrument itself is to the steam engineer what the stethoscope is to the physician."[8]

Eventually Watt and Boulton retired, leaving a thriving business in the hands of their two sons, James Watt Jr. and Matthew Robison Boulton. In 1817, James Watt Jr. installed a Boulton & Watt engine on the Caledonia, the first English steamboat to leave port.

Watt withdrew from business, weary from his active life and from the many patent fights he had had to wage and win. He continued to invent, producing a screw propellor. He identified the two components of water and popularized the use of the slide rule. He invented a letter copier using a wet contact process. He invented the term "horsepower" and exaggerated its value considerably, whether by error or with the design of selling more Boulton & Watt steam engines, we do not know. He gave his hometown of Greenock a library.

Imagine the world just before James Watt. Europe and America were beginning to industrialize, but there was no independent source to power factories, which thus had to be located at waterfalls—and the world was running out of waterfalls. After Watt, factories could be built anywhere. Transportation was slow, by sail on the seas, by horse-drawn cart and coach on land. Watt's steam engine would soon power both ships at sea and railroads on land. Andrew Carnegie said, in all sincerity, that Watt was the source of his fortune.[9]

James Watt was elected to the Royal Society in London as well as to the French Academy. Glasgow University gave him an honorary law degree. A statue of him was erected in Westminster Abbey. His name is still used all over the world every day as people discuss units of power in terms of watts, kilowatts, and megawatts. James Watt was the engineer who made the Industrial Revolution possible.[10]

William Murdoch

(1754–1839)

ANYONE WHO HAS walked in darkness down a country road at night knows that it can be a fearful, dangerous experience. Similarly, we know that a city's streets are prone to crime during power failures. And it is hard to imagine, returning to our homes on winter evenings, to find them pitch black and to be groping for candles. But such was the way the world was from time immemorial up to the first part of the nineteenth century. At that time, the Industrial Revolution was in full swing. Great numbers of people were moving from the country to cities and towns where criminals plied their trade under cover of the dark. Factories had to work short hours, especially during the brief winter days.

The solutions to all of these conditions were to be found by a clever engineer from Scotland. William Murdoch was born at Bellow-Mill near Cumnock and Auchinleck in Ayrshire. His father, John Murdoch, as well as his grandfather, had served in the royal artillery. His father was a millwright by trade and worked as a farmer and miller as well. As a boy, William Murdoch was taught his father's trade and became a millwright.[1] He does not appear to have had much, if any, formal schooling. As a boy, he made himself interesting toys. As a young man he constructed a handsome stone bridge over the river Nith. He also invented an oval turning lathe. As Murdoch expressed it he "gar'd (i.e. made) the lathey."[2]

In 1777, having heard of the successes of his famous fellow Scot, James Watt, Murdoch journeyed to Birmingham to the Soho factory of Boulton & Watt in search of employment. It was an unusual thing to do in those times. It was an arduous trip of several days, and Murdoch had no apparent introduction. But throughout his life, he had great confidence in his abilities. Without doubt, he expected to win employment. Perhaps he was hoping, also, that Watt, a fellow countryman, would help him out, but the interview was conducted by someone else, and didn't go well. Then fortune beamed. As he had been unable to afford the customary workman's hat, Mudoch had used his oval lathe to fashion one out of wood. As he was ready to leave the interview unemployed, the hat fell off making a loud sound. The interviewer was favorably impressed with this ingenuity, and Boulton & Watt hired the young Murdoch for fifteen shillings a week if he worked at Soho and seventeen shillings when he was away, except that he was to be increased to twenty shillings if he worked in London.[3]

In 1779, at age twenty-five, Murdoch's progress in the company was such that he was given the responsibility of installing and repairing Boulton & Watt's steam engines in Cornwall, where they were in much demand to pump water out of the mines. He stayed there almost twenty years, often going without sleep, traveling wherever he was needed. The Cornishmen looked upon the young Scot as an intruder, and sometimes his engines were sabotaged by competitors, although one of these tried to hire him away from Boulton & Watt. Occasionally, Murdoch had to fight. Some think that his vast experience with the engines enabled him to make the modifications that made the practical steam engine practical. There is speculation that Murdoch's work was essential to making Boulton & Watt a successful firm.[4]

Murdoch settled in the town of Redruth in Cornwall. Since the English could not say the Scottish guttural at the end of his name, he changed the spelling to Murdock. He married a local lady, Ann Paynter, and they had two sons, William and John. Unfortunately, Ann Paynter Murdock died in 1790, aged only twenty-four.[5]

Between 1781 and 1783 Murdoch made an invention which should have made him rich and famous. He built a model high-pressure, noncondensing locomotive steam engine, nineteen inches long and fourteen high, with a copper boiler with fire-box and flue, a spirit-lamp, and one double-acting cylinder, two drive wheels and a steering wheel. In 1784 he had improved it to the point that it could run in the streets of Redruth. It was the world's first locomotive, and can be seen in the Birmingham Museums and Art Gallery.[6]

The *Dictionary of National Biography* describes the progress of the invention. On August 9, 1786, Thomas Wilson, Boulton & Watt's agent in Cornwall, wrote to Watt: "William Murdock desires me to inform you that he has made a small engine of 3/4 diameter and 1 and 1/2-inch stroke, that he has apply'd to a small carriage, which answers amazingly."[7] It seems incredible, but Boulton and Watt were not interested. It has been suggested that Watt was working in this direction on his own and may not have wanted Murdoch's competition. But in fact, the partners were upset that their star mechanic was not paying enough attention to their fast-growing business. Not wanting to let the opportunity go by, Murdoch left for London to file a patent on the locomotive. But Boulton found out and wrote to Watt, "However, I prevailed upon him to return to Cornwall by the next day's dilligence . . . I am persuaded I can either cure him of the disorder or turn the evil to good." James Watt wrote to Boulton on September 12 1786: "I am extremely sorry that W. M. still busies himself with the steam carriage. I wish W. could . . . mind the business in hand. . . ."[8]

At this point, Murdoch ceased to work on the locomotive. There seems to be little doubt that he had the ability to finish the job, but his bosses had discouraged him and he was a loyal company man, which, in the end served him well. The development and invention of the practical locomotive was therefore credited instead to Richard Trevithick in 1802, eighteen years after 1784, when Murdoch ran his first model on the streets of Redruth. There can be no question that Trevithick was inspired by and profited from Murdoch's work because in 1784, Trevithick was a Cornish boy, all of thirteen years old, living near Redruth. Trevithick was actually a visitor at Murdoch's house, which was situated quite near to that of Trevithick senior, who was one of the mine "captains." Thus, Murdoch was deprived of being the inventor of the practical locomotive, and Boulton and Watt deprived themselves of making another fortune.[9]

It should be noted that subsequent to the invention of the locomotive, Scots had much to do with the development of railroads. Around 1816 or 1817 the Kilmarnock and Troon railway experimented with steam power. And around 1823 Robert Stevenson, the famous Scottish lighthouse engineer and grandfather of author Robert Louis Stevenson, surveyed a railway line running from Stockton to Darlington in England. George Stephenson, an Englishman of Scottish parentage, was the builder of this line, and he persuaded the directors of the company to use steam power. On September 27, 1825, forty-one years after William Murdoch had demonstrated his first model, a steam locomotive pulled the first public passenger steam railway train in the world. Stephenson's triumph has made him universally recognized as the inventor and founder of railways.

In 1792 Murdoch did his first work on a system that would illuminate the world. Experimenting with coal, wood, peat and other substances he generated gasses in a retort in his back yard in Redruth. He then conducted the gas through a pipe into his house and lit it. This was the first gas lighting. In 1795 Murdoch showed his system at the Neath Abbey Iron Works.

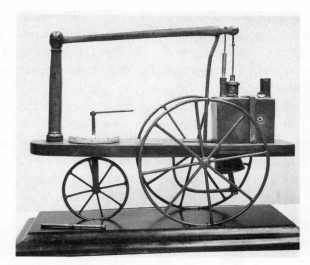

William Murdoch: The Road Engine.
BIRMINGHAM MUSEUMS & ART GALLERY.

A witness noted that the apparatus gave " a strong and beautiful light, which continued burning a considerable time."[10]

Murdoch returned to Birmingham in 1799, and set up his apparatus to show Watt, who was immediately interested. He considered taking out a patent, but delayed due to some pending litigation. A colleague of Murdoch's wrote, "In March 1802 . . . Mr. Murdock first publicly exhibited the gas-light by placing at each end of the Soho manufactory what was termed a Bengal light. The operation was simply effected by fixing a retort in the fireplace of the house below, and then conducting the gas issuing from thence into a copper vase." In 1803 the Soho foundry was regularly illuminated with gas, and a gas-making plant was begun. In 1804 the cotton-spinning firm of Phillips and Lee in Manchester ordered a gas-lighting system for their mill from Boulton & Watt. The gas light was a reality. William Murdoch had brought the world out of the dark.[11]

In 1808 Murdoch read the first paper ever, on the subject of gas lighting, before the Royal Society. He discussed his experiments and the workings of his system. The paper's last words are those of a confident man, the same man who believed the great James Watt would employ him years before. "I believe I may, without presuming too much, claim both the first idea of applying and the first actual application of this gas to economical purposes." The *Dictionary of National Biography* says: "As to the justice of this claim there can be no doubt." Murdoch was awarded the Rumford Medal with the inscription "*ex fumo dare lucem*": from smoke, to give light.[12]

William Murdoch was responsible for many improvements to the steam engine which were assumed to have been Watt's or even more generally those of Boulton and Watt. The famous "sun and planet motion," which was in Watt's original patent of 1781, has been proved to have been the work of Murdoch. In 1785 Murdoch made an oscillating steam engine which was later fitted onto a vessel. In 1810 he took out a patent for making stone pipes, which he sold to the Manchester Stone Pipe Company, the firm supplying that city with water.[13]

In 1798 Murdoch was raised to the annual salary of £1,000 by the firm of Boulton & Watt. After the death of Boulton, he was made a partner. Around 1815 he purchased the estate of Sycamore Hill, on which he built a mansion.[14] It had been a long climb for the young man who wore a wooden hat. William Murdoch died in 1839 and is buried in Handsworth Church beside Matthew Boulton and James Watt.

In 1892, Murdoch was honored on the centenary of his invention of gas lighting, as Lord Kelvin unveiled his bust at the Wallace monument at Stirling.[15] Back in Cornwall, a plaque was affixed to Murdoch's house in Cross Street. It says:[16]

WILLIAM MURDOCK
Lived in this house
1782–1798
MADE THE FIRST LOCOMOTIVE HERE
and tested it in 1784
INVENTED GAS-LIGHTING
and used it in this house in 1792

This was not to be the end of honors for William Murdoch, whose Gaelic surname was similar to that of a Middle Eastern god. In the latter part of the nineteenth century, Nasir ad-Din, the Shah of Persia, proclaimed the light-giving Murdoch a deity and the reincarnation of Merodach, the god of light![17]

William Symington

(1764–1831)

WILLIAM SYMINGTON, A native Scot, was the inventor of the steamboat. There had been engineers in France and America who had made experimental boats, but no one had produced anything that would really work. Even Symington's first tries were in the "experimental" class. But he succeeded, finally, in ushering in the age of steam power on water. Thousands of great passenger liners, freighters and warships were built after he proved that it could be done. Glasgow became one of the most important places in the world for building steamships, and grew to develop into the Second City of the British Empire.

William Symington was born in Leadhills in Lanarkshire. He described his parents as "respectable but not wealthy." His father was "a practical mechanic and superintendent" of the mining company in Leadhills.[1] Young William Symington studied at the universities of Edinburgh and Glasgow, intended by his tutors for the ministry. But he decided, instead, on a career in engineering. He became good at building engines for the mines, and on June 5, 1787, he took out a patent (no. 1610) for an improved steam engine, which he claimed was more efficient than those of James Watt. Watt was well aware of Symington and belittled his efforts. Then in 1788, Patrick Millar (or Miller), who was failing at putting steam power to a boat, heard about Symington and engaged him to make an engine. Millar and Symington operated this boat on Dalswinton Loch in October, 1788. It was a qualified success, but it was still an "experimental" vessel.[2] The poet Robert Burns was either a spectator or a passenger in this trial run. If this seems to be a tall story, it should be known that Burns was then tenant farming at Ellisland, a farm just across the River Nith from Dalswinton, and that Ellisland was owned by Millar. It would be hard to imagine that Millar would *not* have invited his famous tenant to the demonstration.[3]

Symington was disappointed at the way his engine performed, and by 1802 he had designed a better model and received another patent (no. 2544). At this time he was put in touch with Lord Dundas, the governor of the Forth and Clyde Canal. This waterway was of great importance to the early industrialization of Scotland, as it bisected the country at its narrowest point and permited direct travel from the North Sea to the Atlantic Ocean. In March 1802, Symington ran his boat the *Charlotte Dundas* on the Forth and Clyde Canal. The steamboat pushed two barges before it, and made 19½ miles in six hours against a strong headwind. There is no doubt that this was the world's first practical steamboat.[4]

Robert Fulton (see p. 68), who ran the first commercial steamboat service in the world on the Hudson River, had seen the *Charlotte Dundas*. The *Dictionary of National Biography* says that he was on board an earlier version in 1801.[5] Symington also claimed that Fulton was there in July 1801, but it has been alleged that Fulton was in Brest, France at that time.[6] Nevertheless, it was not until 1803 that Fulton ran a seventy-four-foot steamboat on the Seine in Paris before a cheering crowd. It is said that the engine was very much like Symington's.

The Queen Elizabeth 2, built at Clydebank, Scotland. After William Symington's invention of the practical steamboat, Glasgow and its environs became a world capital of shipbuilding, and the Second City of the British Empire. CUNARD LINE LIMITED'S QUEEN ELIZABETH 2.

It is tragic that William Symington, the inventor of the steamboat, did not participate in the revolution which he started. For some reason he was unable to attract capital to his invention. The development of the steamboat proceeded at a leisurely pace. It was not until 1807 that Fulton was able to launch the *Clermont*. And it was not until 1812 that the Scot, Henry Bell, ran the first commercial steamboat service in Europe on the Clyde River in his *Comet*. There was no great hurry to develop steamboats. The sailboat worked, and the "fuel" was free. But it is interesting that all three of these men, Symington, Fulton and Bell, were Scots.

What kept Symington from financial success is unknown. His character was not without blemish. He fathered an illegitimate child, James Symington, with Anne Miller. He was accused in court of drunkenness. He married Elizabeth Benson, and fathered William Symington Jr., a second son and two daughters.[7]

Symington drifted to London, believing that he should be rewarded for his efforts. In 1825 he was given a grant of £100 by the Privy Purse, and later, another £50. But he never got the pension he sought. William Symington died in 1831. He was buried at St. Botolph's in Aldgate, London. The Dalswinton boat still exists in a London museum.[8]

Kirkpatrick Macmillan

(1813–1878)

THERE ARE MILLIONS of pedal-driven bicycles in the world today. The bicycle is the principal means of transportation for uncountable masses of people in countries as different as China and Holland. Acquiring a "bike" is one of the principal rites of passage for many children. Bicycles are used for recreational purposes by people all over the world, and are the focus of one of the world's greatest sports events, *Le Tour de France*. All of this was started by the ingenuity of an obscure Scottish blacksmith.

Kirkpatrick Macmillan was born in the village of Keir near Thornhill in Dumfriesshire. His birth date is not known, but the parish records show that he was baptized September 18, 1812. He was the fifth son of at least eight children born to Robert Macmillan, a smithy at nearby Courthill, and his wife Mary Auld.[1] Kirkpatrick Macmillan, who was called "Pate," had two brothers who were academics, but he chose to stay at home and worked with his father at the forge.[2]

At the age of twenty-two he became the assistant to the blacksmith of one of the richest men in Scotland, the Duke of Buccleugh, at nearby Drumlanrig. One day someone brought in what was called a hobby horse or dandy horse—a bicycle without pedals—for repair at the smithy. Pate was intrigued with it and built himself a copy. Of course, the vehicle had limited use since it had to be propelled by placing a foot on the road every few yards.

Pate realized that it would work much better if he could figure a way to turn the wheels without putting a foot on the street. He returned to Courthill to assist his father and, in his spare time, worked on the problem

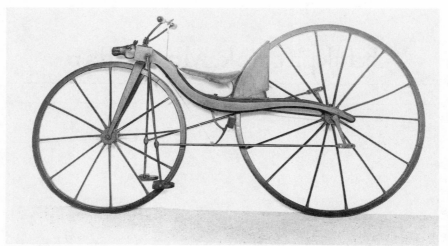

Macmillan's Bicycle, 1839. SCIENCE MUSEUM/SCIENCE & SOCIETY PICTURE LIBRARY, LONDON.

of propelling the hobby horse. His neighbors, not believing in his experiments, now called him "Daft Pate." But four years later he devised a system of pedals and found that he could ride his vehicle for miles, never having to put foot to ground. The *Encyclopaedia Britannica* credits him with having invented "the first ridable bicycle" in 1839.[3] Not only was Macmillan's bicycle the first with pedal power; it also could be steered. It was not at all a crude machine. It had graceful curved lines, anticipating Art Nouveau by half a century.

Macmillan continued to make improvements on the bicycle and rode it often around the local countryside. In the summer of 1842 he decided to ride all the way to Glasgow to see his brother who was Rector of Hutcheson's Grammar School there. His neighbors called him daft again. Only a railroad or a stagecoach could go as far as seventy miles. He would never make it. In the countryside and in the villages along the way people turned out to see the progress of Daft Pate. Word spread from town to town, and by the time he reached the Gorbals section of Glasgow his trip had made him an immediate sensation. People packed the streets to see this deil (devil) on wheels. Unfortunately, with the push of the crowd, a little girl was grazed by the bicycle. She wasn't hurt, but she fell to the ground, crying. Daft Pate was arrested, charged with riding along the pavement "to the obstruction of the passage." The next day, at the Gorbals public bar, he told the magistrate that he had come all the way from Old Cumnock in five hours. This must have seemed to the magistrate an impossible feat. He could have thought Macmillan a liar, but since the girl wasn't seriously hurt, he fined Daft Pate only five shillings. Then the magistrate asked for a demonstration, and Macmillan rode the bicycle in figure eights in the courtyard. The magistrate was so favorably impressed that he returned the fine.[4]

The end of the story should be, perhaps, that Kirkpatrick Macmillan founded a worldwide bicycle empire, but that is not the end. Macmillan was a tall, good-looking, athletically built country boy, widely read and possessed of a good sense of humor. He returned to his forge in Courthill, and resumed his additional duties as free town veterinarian and dentist. He played the fiddle at parties.[5] He never patented his invention, and was quite happy to show it to the many others who came to see and copy it. He couldn't have cared less about making money.

Patrick Macmillan married Elizabeth Gordon Goldie around 1854. They had six children, but only one son and one daughter survived to maturity. Elizabeth died in 1865. After that his sister Ann kept house for her smithy brother, and helped to raise the children.[6]

There is a plaque on his cottage at Courthill.[7]

1939
THE CENTENARY OF
THE BICYCLE
THE NATIONAL COMMITTEE ON CYCLING
HONOURS THE MEMORY OF
KIRKPATRICK MACMILLAN
THE INVENTOR OF THE BICYCLE
He builded better than he knew

Sanford Fleming

(1827–1915)

$\mathcal{S}$ ANFORD FLEMING WASN'T a politician or a business tycoon or a conqueror. He was a rather quiet, reserved man. But he left several monuments which have lasted more than a century and seem likely to last a lot longer—perhaps forever. He was the principal force behind Canada's transcontinental railroad, the Trans Pacific telegraph cable, world Standard Time, and the establishment of the Prime Meridian.

So often it is assumed that someone who served the British Empire so well and has a rather nondescript British name is an Englishman. Sanford

Sir Sanford Fleming,
CANADIAN PACIFIC ARCHIVES,
IMAGE NO. NS 5373.

Fleming was, in fact, thoroughly Scottish. He was born in Kirkcaldy, as was the philosopher Adam Smith. His father was Andrew Greig Fleming and his mother, Elizabeth Arnott. Sanford Fleming studied surveying at the school at Kirkcaldy, only a few years after Thomas Carlyle had taught there.[1]

In 1845, young Sanford Fleming emigrated to Canada. After further training he joined the Ontario, Simcoe and Huron Railway, eventually becoming the line's chief engineer.[2] From 1855 to 1863, Fleming was chief engineer of the Northern Railway. In 1864 he became chief railway engineer of the government of Nova Scotia in charge of building a railway from Truro to Pictou. The government proposed to construct the line in small segments, but this was bringing the costs in too high. Fleming fired the bureaucrats and became the contractor to build the whole line. It was finished in 1867 with a substantial profit to Fleming and a great saving to Nova Scotia.[3]

Fleming was an early advocate of a Canadian transcontinental railway. He realized, as did John A. Macdonald (see p. 364), that the country—with most of its people living near the border with the United States—was strung out over three thousand miles and could not become a cohesive nation without it. At the union of Canada in 1867, Fleming was made chief engineer of the Inter Colonial Railway, completing it in 1876. In 1872 the government decided to proceed with the Canadian Pacific Railway, partly as an inducement to get British Columbia to join the confederation, and Fleming was again named chief engineer. In 1872 he headed the "Ocean to Ocean" expedition to find a route over the Rocky Mountains, and discovered one through Yellow Head Pass. But in 1880, after Fleming had surveyed the entire line, and laid 600 miles of track, the government decided that a private company should finish the road. This was the worst blow in Fleming's life.[4]

In 1876, Fleming took a vacation in Europe visiting Paris, England, Ireland, and of course, Edinburgh and Kircaldy. He also saw the Hebrides and said, "The contrast between Iona and Staffa is striking enough. Iona takes us back to almost prehistoric times; Staffa brings us face to face with the everlasting."[5] In London he met Thomas Carlyle, of whom he was in awe, and was surprised to be welcomed. The two men talked of their days in Kirkcaldy, of the Canadian Pacific Railway, and of Carlyle's *Sartor Resartus*.[6]

In 1883 Fleming became a director of the Canadian Pacific Railway, and was one of those who proposed the present mainline route through Kicking Horse Pass. His party was the first group of white men to cross the Rockies, west and east, by this route. As early as 1876, Fleming had proposed Standard Time. It seems strange, but in those days time was calculated locally. People traveling only a few miles often had to re-set their watches upon arrival at a given place. In 1881, Canada had adopted Standard Time and at Fleming's suggestion, a memo was drawn up and sent to the President of the United States, proposing that he call an international time conference in Washington in 1883. The American Society of Civil Engineers appointed a special committee on Standard Time with Fleming as chairman. Britain, France, Italy, Spain, Germany, Austria, Russia, and Belgium followed. In 1884 the International Prime Meridian Conference met in Washington with twenty-five nations in attendance. And on January 1, 1885, the twenty-four-hour clock was adopted at Greenwich Observatory near London. Due to Sanford Fleming's initiative, the world, however reluctantly, had acquiesced in recognizing that the Prime Meridian was in Britain, and Standard Time began in Britain. From that date, time and distance have been measured from Greenwich.[7]

Soon after, Fleming proposed a Trans Pacific telegraph cable. He said, "It is only necessary . . . to look at a telegraph map of the world to see how dependent on foreign powers Great Britain is at this moment for the security of its telegraphic communication with Asia, Australia, and Africa."[8] Fleming worked to get Australia, Canada, and the Imperial governments to cooperate. He was appointed as an "expert advisor" on the project which was completed between Vancouver and Australia in 1902.[9]

Sanford Fleming was knighted in 1897. He was tall and handsome and spoke gently. He married Ann Jean Hall with whom he had four sons and two daughters. The family lived in Ottawa, and maintained a summer home in Nova Scotia.[10]

Alexander Graham Bell

(1847–1922)

I N THE 1870s there were hundreds of scientists all over the world trying to invent the telephone. The telegraph had been in use for three decades, and telegraph wires were everywhere. It was certain that someone would solve the problem of putting human speech on those wires. Alexander Graham Bell was at a disadvantage—a young man with small resources trying to best huge companies which had scientists on their payrolls. But he also had a great advantage over his many rivals. He was the third generation of Alexander Bells who had studied and worked in the fields of

Alexander Graham Bell,
AP/WIDE WORLD PHOTOS

speech, phonetics, elocution, and aid to the deaf. Bell's own mother, Eliza, was hearing-impaired.

Alexander Melville Bell, born in Edinburgh, and the father of the inventor of the telephone, was a recognized authority on the voice. He was also a teacher of elocution, an author, and the developer of a "visible speech system" which was the basis of subsequent international phonetic alphabets and aids for teaching the deaf. He has his own essay in the *Encylopaedia Britannica*. Alexander Bell, the grandfather of the inventor, started out as a humble cobbler who became an actor and later an author-ity on speech therapy and phonetics.[1]

So when Alexander Graham Bell was inventing one of the most important instruments in all of human progress, he had the benefit of being one of three generations of Bells who had looked with a deep sci-entific interest into the problems of conveying sounds. Bell wasn't just a tinker. He had a profound scientific background in his subject.

Alexander Graham Bell was born in Edinburgh. He was educated at McLauren's Academy and at Edinburgh High School, leaving at age thir-teen. In 1863 he became a pupil-teacher of elocution and music at Weston House Academy at Elgin, Morayshire, in the far north of Scotland. In 1864 he attended Edinburgh University. In 1867 he joined his father, who had taken up *his* father's work in London. At this time Bell studied at London University. But the Bells seemed to have had a genetic predispo-sition to tuberculosis; and, as two of the inventor's brothers had suc-cumbed to the disease and had died at an early age, the family decided to leave the dampness of Britain and emigrated to Canada in 1870.[2]

In 1872 Bell went to Boston where he opened a school for training teachers of the deaf. A year later, he was made professor of vocal physiology and the mechanics of speech at Boston University. As early as 1865, Bell had conceived of the electrical transmission of speech. And in the summer of 1874 he formulated the theory of the telephone at his father's house in Brantford, Ontario. His own words show clearly that he was working against his rivals from a scientific base provided by his family's legacies. "If I could make a current of electricity vary in intensity precisely as the air varies in intensity during the production of sound, I should be able to transmit speech telegraphically."[3] Bell showed his theory to the famous Scottish-American scientist, Joseph Henry, who encouraged the young man.

Bell had no money to pursue his theory, and he tried to raise capital from George Brown, a friend of his father's. Brown owned the powerful newspaper, the *Toronto Daily Globe*, often called "the Scotchman's Bible," as many of its readers were immigrants from Scotland. Brown agreed to put up $600 in installments, but didn't do it. At about this time Bell fell madly in love with one of his students, Mabel Hubbard, who had been entirely deaf since early childhood. Her father, Gardiner Greene Hubbard, did help Bell, but was wary of his trying to invent the tele-phone. Hubbard thought that Bell should concentrate on improving the telegraph, which seemed to him a surer bet. He told Bell, who was standing in front of him wearing a threadbare suit, that he could not marry beautiful Mabel unless he gave up the telephone.[4]

Bell persevered, however, and in June of 1875 he constructed the first rough telephone in Boston with his associate, Thomas A. Watson. With that news, Hubbard, Bell's future father-in-law, relented in his opposition and took the patent application into his own hands. Hubbard filed for the Bell telephone on February 14, 1876. To say that he was just in time would be an understatement. On the same day, two hours later, Elisha Gray filed a "caveat," a provisional patent. Although this makes it clear that Gray was behind Bell, the caveat could have caused Bell a great deal of trouble had Hubbard delayed even a few hours. Of course, Bell's patent was issued on March 7, 1876, just a few days after his twenty-ninth birthday. It is probably the most valuable patent ever issued.[5]

On March 10, 1876 Bell and Watson were trying out a new transmitter, hoping it would work better than the others they had used without success. Watson was in another room, set up, optimistically, to receive a message over the wire. Just then, Bell spilled battery acid on his clothes, and said the world-famous words: "Mr. Watson, come here; I want you."[6] Watson, absolutely stunned, had heard the message over the telephone. Excitedly he ran into Bell's room with the news, and the two men rapidly switched rooms again and again, talking, listening, laughing, and celebrating on the telephone.

During the remainder of 1876 Bell was busy improving and demonstrating his telephone. At the Philadelphia Centennial Exposition he recited Hamlet's soliloquy over the telephone to a highly impressed Emperor of Brazil.[7] Using the wires of the Dominion Telegraph Company, he was able to talk from Brantford to Paris, Ontario—a distance of eight miles. The next year he talked between Boston and New York, and went to Britain and France to promote his invention. The National Bell Telephone Company, which would eventually employ hundreds of thousands of people, was formed in 1877. Bell and his wife owned 1,507 of the 5,000 shares,[8] assuring financial stability for their lifetimes. In 1878 the couple settled in Washington, D.C., where Mrs. Bell's parents had a home. Alexander and Mabel Bell had two daughters.

Thomas Watson, Bell's right-hand man, also received shares in the company which was to become AT&T. Capitalized at $850,000, the stock first traded on June 11, 1897 at $110.25 per share. By December it was trading at $995. Watson said, "I had now nothing more to worry about as far as money was concerned."[9]

There are always people who will question someone's right to call himself the inventor of anything, and so it was with Bell. More than six hundred lawsuits were thrown against him, but every one was decided in his favor, all the way to the U.S. Supreme Court. And, as Forbes Macgregor has observed, even if others had been judged to be first, and they were not so judged (with systems which didn't work) Bell could still be regarded as the inventor of the telephone because of his theory, which laid out the principles of the invention.[10]

Almost everyone can name Bell as the inventor of the telephone, but very few have ever heard of the diverse other works of this remarkable person. For instance, the famous Helen Keller, who became well known as a worker with the handicapped, was his pupil. She came to Bell as a child who could not see, hear, or talk. He meant so much to her that she dedicated her autobiography to him.[11] Bell also invented the photophone, which transmitted sound by light, as well as a phonographic apparatus. In 1903 he was the first to publish the idea of treating deep-seated cancers with radium. He even developed a universal language.

In 1898 Bell became the second president of the National Geographic Society, which was struggling to survive with only a thousand members and over $2,000 in debts. He rescued it, and today it is the largest non-profit scientific and educational institution in the world, with more than ten million members. Bell's great-grandson, Gilbert M. Grosvenor, is the chairman of the Society.

Perhaps the most interesting and least known fact about Bell is that he has a claim to being a co-inventor of the airplane, giving him a share in two of the greatest inventions in history. Bell was a close friend of Samuel Langley in Washington, who became secretary of the Smithsonian Institution in 1887. Langley was trying to invent the airplane at the time, and in 1888 Bell gave him $5,000 for research, although not necessarily for research on heavier-than-air flight. There is no record of what engineering contribution Bell made in Langley's experiments, but it is inconceivable to think that the input of Bell, already a world-famous inventor, would not have been welcome. It is also unlikely that the restless Bell, a hard worker and a keen inventor all of his life, would not have helped in the experiments. At any rate Langley's steam-powered *Aerodrome Five* flew successfully, without a pilot, on May 6, 1896 for about half a mile before settling on the Potomac River. It was then dried off and flown again. The event, the first successful engine-driven, heavier-than-air flight in the world, was recorded on film. The photographer was Alexander Graham Bell. Later Bell said, "No one who was present on this interesting occasion could have failed to recognize that the practicability of mechanical flight had been demonstrated."[12]

In November of the same year, *Aerodrome Six* flew farther, about 4,200 feet. But seven years passed before a manned flight was tried. At last on October 7, and December 8, 1903, a larger aerodrome attempted manned flights from a launcher on the Potomac. Both crashed without flight. On December 17, 1903, Orville Wright flew 120 feet and is credited, with his brother, with having invented the airplane. But that is not yet the end of the story. In 1914, after some design changes, a pilot successfully flew the failed aerodrome of Langley and Bell.[13] It seems possible, maybe even likely, then, that had the aerodrome been properly launched, it would have flown as well as the models had, and that Langley, and perhaps Bell, would have been the inventors of the airplane.

Both Bell and Langley were, of course, very close to the Smithsonian Institution, Bell as a donor and later a regent, and Langley as secretary. So what happened next can be put down at least partly to prejudice in their favor. But for the record, the Smithsonian called the aerodrome the first successful flying machine and displayed the aerodrome and *not* the Wright brothers' plane until 1948.[14]

In 1886 Bell bought a summer home near Baddeck, Nova Scotia which he named *Beinn Bhreagh*, meaning "beautiful mountain" in Scots Gaelic. In his later years he spent more of his time there, and what he did there tends to prove that he was Langley's co-inventor of the aerodrome. In Nova Scotia Bell founded the Aerial Experiment Association, continuing his interest in flight. In 1909 the Scottish-Canadian pilot James Alexander Douglas McCurdy made the Aerial Experiment Association's first flight, which was also the first in the British Empire.[15]

Bell never stopped working. In 1918, only four years before his death, he invented a hydrofoil, powered by an aircraft engine, which set a speed record. He was connected with many organizations and was the founder of the American Association to Promote the Teaching of Speech to the Deaf. Regardless of what else he accomplished in life, his principal motivation was to help bring communication to the handicapped.

Bell was given an honorary degree from Oxford in 1901, and later the freedom of his hometown, the city of Edinburgh. As a special honor for this man who studied sounds, the world calls the standard measure of sound after him: the decibel.

Alexander Graham Bell died at his beloved *Beinn Bhreagh* in 1922. He seldom used the telephone and sometimes stuffed its bell with paper so that he wouldn't be disturbed. "I never use the beast," he said.[16]

Thomas A. Edison

(1847–1931)

T HOMAS EDISON DOES not have a family name commonly found in Scotland. The name Edison belongs to the Netherlands, although his father, Samuel Edison, may have had some Scottish ancestors. His mother, Nancy Elliott Edison, is described by Edison's many biographers as "Scotch" (which was the term used almost universally until the late twentieth century) or as "a Scotchwoman." Edison's Scottishness is confirmed by his induction into the Scottish American Hall of Fame, which is operated by the Illinois Saint Andrews Society.

Thomas A. Edison,
PHOTOFEST.

Thomas Edison was, perhaps, the most prolific inventor of all time. In his lifetime he became an American myth, a genius who could do nothing but miracles. Of course, Edison was not that good. Much of his success had to do with three things other than engineering skills. The first was his ability to get talented people to work for him. The second was his skill at making claims and filing patents. And the third was his unbeliev-able physical and emotional strength, which allowed him to outwork almost everyone.

Edison was born in Milan, Ohio, a town south of Lake Erie which, at the time of his birth, was prospering because of its access to canal trans-portation. Edison's people were Canadians who had fled to the United States due to their support of the abortive rebellion led by William Lyon Mackenzie in 1837. Edison's father was successful in business, so that the inventor's biography is not exactly a rags-to-riches story. Edison's mother, Nancy Elliott Edison, was an attractive, very intelligent, and highly edu-cated woman. Her influence on her son's intellect was profound. As a lit-tle boy Thomas Edison loved to walk about the town shipyard asking incessant questions to the point that he was thought to be dull. His worst day was probably the day that he started a fire in a barn, which was destroyed. For this the boy was publicly whipped in the village square.[1]

When the railroad arrived, the economy of the canal town of Milan collapsed. It was the beginning of a trend. By 1880, of the 4,468 miles of freight canals which had been built in America at a cost of over $200 mil-lion, 1,893 miles had been abandoned. In 1854 the Edisons picked up and moved to Port Huron, Michigan, a town some fifty miles north of Detroit, just across the St. Clair River from Ontario. There, his father became a successful grain dealer. It was in Port Huron that Edison received his only formal education, about three months of study. He didn't do well in school, and his large head made him self-conscious. He was at the bottom of his class and his father was afraid that his son had very low intelligence. But his mother had a different idea. Her opinion of the schools was low, and since she was a former teacher, she decided to educate her son at home. Nancy Elliott Edison instilled in her son a Scottish love of books. With his mother, Edison found learning to be easy. Before he was twelve he had read Gibbon's *Decline and Fall of the Roman Empire*, Hume's *History of England*, and was struggling through Newton's *Principia*.[2]

Edison's boyhood was anything but typical. He didn't play sports with the other boys, preferring to read any book he could get his hands on. By the time he was ten or eleven he built an elaborate chemistry laboratory in the family's basement. He had at least a hundred bottles which he had gathered from all over town. He bought his chemicals at the local drug-store, selling newspapers to finance the operation. At times, there were unpleasant odors in the lab, and, of course, it was dangerous. His mother insisted that he keep the lab locked at all times.[3]

At one point, Edison planted and farmed a market garden in the town, and one summer made the impressive sum of $600, which he gave to his mother. At age twelve he got a job as a railroad newsboy, selling papers on the train from Port Huron to Detroit and back. The train left at 7:00 in the morning and didn't return until 9:30 at night so the days were long and arduous. He used his down time in Detroit to buy vegetables, butter and berries, as well as more periodicals. He opened two stores in Port Huron to sell this merchandise, one for produce and the other for periodicals. The periodical store he closed, as the boy he left in charge could not be trusted. He spent a lot of his days in Detroit at the public library. At one point the railroad decided to run a special immigrant train from Detroit through Port Huron to Minnesota. Every day the train was packed with Norwegian immigrants, and Edison hired a boy to ride that train, selling bread, tobacco and candy.[4]

Young Tom Edison became so popular on the train that he was allowed to use an empty baggage car to transfer his chemistry laboratory from his family's basement to the train! He was making so much in his enterprises that he was able to give his mother a dollar a day. It was 1862 and the Civil War was producing a lot of news. Edison decided to take advantage of this and bought an old printing press, installing it on the train. Here he printed and sold *The Weekly Herald* at 3 cents per copy, or 8 cents a month. The fame of this enterprise reached as far as London where the *Times* claimed that it was the only newspaper in the world printed on a moving train. When the Battle of Pittsburg Landing began, Edison realized that there would be a huge demand for news at each station. So he walked into the offices of the Detroit *Free Press* where he bought a quantity of papers every day. With enough money to buy only 300 papers, he demanded to see the editor to ask to buy 700 more on credit. The credit was extended. But after the train made its first stop on the way back to Port Huron, so many papers were sold that Edison realized he should have bought even more. He decided to raise the price at each station until all were sold, making a tidy, opportunistic profit.[5]

Sometimes Edison would beg to be allowed to ride in the cab of the locomotive, and one night, having done so, the engineer fell asleep. Edison said, "I took charge, reducing the speed about twelve miles per hour," and brought the train of seven cars in to the station safely. But all good things have to end. One night his chemical laboratory caught fire and Edison, his lab, and his printing plant were unceremoniously ejected from the train, banished forever. The railroad man boxed his ears, thus beginning a deafness which affected Edison for the rest of his life.[6]

So, near the end of 1862, fifteen-year-old Tom Edison was out of business. But at this time he saved the life of the son of a telegraph operator from the path of a moving boxcar, and the boy's father, in gratitude, offered to teach him telegraphy.[7] With not much to do, he decided to accept the offer. Soon he had a telegrapher's job on the night shift from 7:00 P.M. to 7:00 A.M. Since he was unsupervised, he was able to read, work with the machinery in the office while on the job, and even go to sleep if there was nothing going on. All unsupervised telegraph operators were required, though, to telegraph "6," every hour to show that they were on the job. Edison rigged a clock mechanism to "six in" when he needed sleep.[8]

For the next five years, Edison wandered around the Midwest. He worked as a telegraph operator in New Orleans; Cincinnati; Memphis; Stratford Junction, Ontario; Adrian, Michigan; Fort Wayne and Indianapolis.[9] He was so good at telegraphy that it was easy to get jobs. But he was fired often for working on unauthorized experiments and careless attention to his duties. He had the ability to read high-speed messages and therefore acquired prestigious press wire positions. In Louisville, he had such a job at Western Union. At one point he considered emigrating to Brazil. In 1867, at the age of twenty, he went home to Port Huron. There he invented a way to send two telegraph messages in opposite directions on the same wire. He published this invention in the journal *Telegraphy* in 1868.[10]

It was also in 1868 that Edison took a job at Western Union in Boston. Here he patented an electrographic vote recorder, and in 1869, the stock ticker. Broke, and looking for work again, he went to New York where he was allowed to sleep in the battery room of Laws's Gold Indicator Company, the owner of which he had befriended with a gift of the ticker. One day, a transmitter broke and the system collapsed with the employees in panic. Edison calmly took charge, and in two hours had fixed the whole complex. Laws made him general manager at $300 a month, which was big pay in those days.[11]

But Edison was restless and started his own electrical engineering firm. It was the beginning of a new professional field. He made telegraphic equipment and fire alarms, and made improvements on the stock ticker. In 1870 he was bought out by the Gold and Stock Telegraph Company which paid him $40,000. With this capital, Edison moved to Newark, New Jersey, to start his own manufacturing business, employing eventually fifty men. It was probably the world's first invention factory, a prototype of such companies as Bell Laboratories.[12]

The next year he married Mary Stilwell. The couple had two sons and a daughter. By 1876 he had moved his operation to Menlo Park, New Jersey and in 1877 patented the "phonograph speaking machine." There is no question of Edison's priority in inventing the phonograph. The U.S. patent office could find no files on anything even similar to it.[13] Later Edison invented wax records and they became popular. He also invented an office dictating machine, the Ediphone. He was becoming famous. Even Lord Kelvin paid him a visit.[14]

In 1878, only two years after Bell's invention, Edison invented the carbon transmitter for the telephone. It was such an improvement over existing technology that the Bell Telephone Company licensed it. Some people think that Edison's work made the telephone practical.[15]

But the biggest day at Menlo Park was October 21, 1879. After spending over $40,000, and long months of mind-numbing work investigating every possible material he could think of, Edison made an incandescent lamp using a carbonized cotton thread filament. It remained lit in a vacuum for more than forty hours. On December 17, 1880, Edison's investors became shareholders of the Edison Electric Company. In 1881 the whole operation was moved to New York City, where Edison cajoled city councilmen to allow him to dig up the streets to lay cables and build a real system. Generators were designed. The lamps were improved. Everything had to be invented. It was an enormous engineering task in a brand new field. At last, on September 4, 1882, in the offices of the financier J.P. Morgan, Edison threw the switch for the famous Pearl Street station near Wall Street. Part of New York's financial district was lit brilliantly. It was a special moment in the history of science.

The Pearl Street station served as a model from which the company could sell dozens of systems. It was an immediate success. In 1884, however, Edison's first wife died. In 1886 he married Mina Miller with whom he had three children. A son, Charles, was Undersecretary of the Navy under President Roosevelt, and later, governor of New Jersey. Also in 1886, the company's principal plant was moved to Schenectady, New York.[16]

In 1877 Edison moved to West Orange, New Jersey, where he turned out countless new products. Throughout his career he was credited with having invented the mimeograph (the first copying machine), the loud-speaker, the microphone, and an efficient electrical generator. Edison made a great business mistake about this time. He sold stock of his com-pany, which would be worth billions today (it is now General Electric) and invested in an iron mine in New Jersey that was to use a process he had developed which would make the mine economical. Although he had made careful calculations, the enterprise failed due to the discovery of the huge Mesabi Range in Minnesota, which could produce iron ore much more efficiently. He lost a lot of money.[17]

In 1892 the Edison Electric Company merged with the Thomson-Houston company to form General Electric, which is now one of the largest industrial companies in the world. It should be noted that Thomson-Houston's founder, Elihu Thomson (1853–1937), had been born in England of Scottish ancestry. He is credited with the inventions of arc welding and electric welding and with developments on the alter-nating current electric motor, among many other accomplishments. His work led to the founding of the giant Thomson S.A. industrial company of France, which today, among many other things, makes more television sets than any organization in the world. Elihu Thomson held more than 700 patents.

In 1888 Edison and his assistant, the French-born Scot[18] William Kennedy-Laurie Dickson (1860–1935), began to achieve the illusion of motion pictures. By October, Edison had drawn pictures of the invention and had filed a caveat with the patent office. Dickson, a skilled photog-rapher and electrician, had joined the firm in 1883. In 1889 Edison, while on a trip to Europe, had been informed that Dickson was working on an exciting "secret." When the boss returned on October 6, 1889, he went straight to the laboratory. Dickson was waiting for him. Edison was brought into a darkened room, which had a projection screen against one wall. In front of the wall was a machine, which looked like a large lantern. Attached to this was a phonograph. Dickson turned a crank, and a crude image of himself flickered on the screen. The film Dickson spoke, "Good morning Mr. Edison, glad to see you back. I hope you are satisfied with the kineto-phonograph." Thus, it is claimed, the first motion picture was also a *talking* motion picture. In an introduction to the book *The Biograph in Battle*, Richard Brown adds: "With Edison's support, Dickson was responsible for designing the world's first fully practical film camera using 35mm celluloid film with a double row of sprocket holes—exactly the same system that is still in use today."[19]

Of course, others, including the Lumière brothers of France, were involved in creating the movies. But Edison's patents, one of his strengths, tied up the industry for twenty years. At last, perhaps, his patents proved to be too strong and antitrust laws forced him to drop the business. Encyclopedias still call *The Jazz Singer* of 1927 the first talking film. But in 1983 the National Broadcasting Company, which is owned by General Electric, discovered a fully talking film which had been made by Edison in 1913.[20]

In addition to his many inventions, Edison made one important purely scientific discovery, which is called "the Edison effect," the movement of electricity from a filament to a piece of metal inside a light bulb. He patented it in 1883, and its principle became the basis of the vacuum tube, which was essential to the development of radio.[21]

In 1927 Thomas Edison was admitted to the National Academy of Science; and in 1928 he was awarded a special Congressional Medal of Honor. In October 1929, the fiftieth anniversary of the testing of the first electric light, he was honored by Henry Ford at the Henry Ford Museum in Dearborn, Michigan. President Hoover attended and Albert Einstein participated by transatlantic telephone. In 1931, Edison filed the last of his 1093 patents, the most ever issued to one person. His epigram, "genius is two percent inspiration and ninety-eight percent perspiration," is best defined by himself. His success came from his almost infinite capacity for work. When he died, it was suggested that the United States be momentarily blacked out in his memory, but this would have been too extreme. Instead the President asked that lights be dimmed for a few minutes at 10:00 P.M. on the day of the funeral.[22] Many Americans paid this last tribute to Edison, and perhaps a larger tribute when the lights came on again.

Guglielmo Marconi

(1874–1937)

I T WAS A beautiful night in 1894 in Pontecchio near Bologna in Italy. The air was cool and sweet in the large house. All was quiet except for the sound of crickets. Sometime past midnight the young man placed a hand on his mother's shoulder, gently awakening her. She put on a dressing gown and went with him across the cool stone floors, following him up several flights of stairs. Near a window in the room upstairs was a telegraph key, which the young man proceeded to tap.

Guglielmo Marconi,

"From the far end of the long double room came a gentle, insistent sound. A bell was ringing. Between the transmitter under his hand and the tiny tinkling lay nothing but air." Thus, Degna Marconi describes the invention of radio in her book, *My Father, Marconi*. This family legend was told to Ms. Marconi by her grandmother, Anne Jameson Marconi,[1] the mother of the inventor.

Anne Jameson was born in Ireland where her father, Andrew Jameson, an immigrant from Scotland, owned a distillery now known throughout the world for its John Jameson Irish whiskey. Anne Jameson was entirely Scottish. Her mother was Margaret Millar and her grandmother Margaret Haig. Annie Jameson had a beautiful voice and as a young woman, decided to go to Bologna to find a career in music. What she found, instead, was Giuseppe Marconi, the scion of a wealthy, propertied Bologna family. Her straight-laced Protestant family, which had tried to dissuade her from a career on the "wicked" operatic stage, was even more shocked when she told them she wanted to marry an Italian Roman Catholic. They forbade the marriage. But this did not stop the blue-eyed young woman from County Wexford. Crossing the Irish Sea, England, and the English Channel, she eloped to Boulogne-sur-Mer in France to be married to Giuseppe Marconi. Their second son, Guglielmo, was born on April 25, 1874 and baptized in the Roman Catholic Church of St. Peter in Bologna.[2]

Young Guglielmo Marconi, like several successful people in this book, had very little formal education. Early on, he studied under tutors. He went to the Instituto Cavallero in Florence at age twelve, but his mother had made him learn English, and the school complained that his Italian, at that time, was poor.[3] He never attended a university. In 1888 he was sent to the technical school at Leghorn (Livorno) where he studied physics, especially the work of Maxwell and Hertz (see p. 390). He became aware that there were predictions that radio waves could be used to communicate without wire, and determined that he would be the one who would discover how to do that. Returning to Bologna, he began to experiment.[4]

From the beginning his Italian father scorned Marconi's work. He would have preferred a career in the navy for his son. But the inventor's Scottish mother believed in her son's work and supported him, even bringing food to his homemade laboratory while he worked. Giuseppe Marconi raged at his wife for allowing their son to "waste years," as he put it. Then came that first successful experiment in the upper floors of the house at Pontecchio. Gradually, Marconi was able to increase the distance he could transmit. When he reached one and a half miles, the limit of the estate, he knew he was on the right track, and approached the Italian government for research money, but the government had no interest in the project of a twenty-year-old school dropout.[5]

At this point he and his mother decided to go to England to try for support. They arrived in 1896, and set up house in the Bayswater neighborhood in London. There Marconi's cousin, Jameson Davis, a practicing engineer, helped file a patent and finance the Wireless Telegraph and Signal Co., which in 1900 became Marconi's Wireless Telegraph Co., Ltd. The patent application, granted July 2, 1897, begins:

I GUGLIELMO MARCONI, of 71 Hereford Road, Bayswater, in the County of Middlesex do hereby declare the nature of this invention to be as follows:—
According to this invention electrical actions or manifestations are transmitted through the air, earth or water by means of electric oscillations of high frequency.

The London County Council placed a plaque on the Bayswater building:

GUGLIELMO MARCONI
1874–1937
THE PIONEER OF
WIRELESS
COMMUNICATION
LIVED HERE
1896–1897[6]

In 1896 Marconi was able to send signals nine miles across the Bristol Channel. In 1897 he was back in Italy at La Spezia where he built a station which could talk to warships as far out as twelve miles. In 1899 a wireless station was built at Foreland, England to communicate with Wimereux, France, a distance of thirty-one miles. By year-end 1900, he had signaled 150 miles. In December 1901, Marconi made the world's first transatlantic transmission by wireless telegraph sending the letter "S" in Morse code from Poldhu, Cornwall to St. John's, Newfoundland, and became world-famous. But there were still skeptics. All of these were gone when complete messages were sent from England to Glace Bay, Nova Scotia in 1902. The effect of these transmissions was sensational. There was scarcely a person in the civilized world who did not know the name Marconi. There were new meanings to the dimensions of distance and time. Marconi's work was, as the *Encylopaedia Britannica* says: ". . . the

starting point of the vast development of radio communications, broadcasting and navigation services that took place in the next fifty years, in
much of which, moreover, Marconi himself continued to play an important part."[7]

After 1902, Marconi was more of a businessman than a scientist,
living and working onboard his yacht *Elettra* as progress continued. In
1910 he transmitted from Ireland to Buenos Aires, a distance of over six
thousand miles. In 1918, it was from England to Australia. In 1916 he
conceived of the potential for transmission by short wave, and in 1923
successfully sent shortwave messages. In 1924 the British Post Office gave
his company a contract to provide service throughout the British
Commonwealth.[8]

Following in Marconi's wake was an American with a Scottish name,
Edwin Howard Armstrong, called by his biographer, Lawrence Lessing,
"the single most important creator of modern radio."[9] His parents were
staunch members of the Old North Presbyterian Church in New York
City, where his father was a trustee. In 1912, as an undergraduate at
Columbia University, Armstrong invented the feedback circuit. In 1918,
as a major in the U.S. Army, he invented the super heterodyne which
greatly amplified signals. For this he was highly decorated. In 1933 he
invented frequency modulation or FM radio, eliminating static. The
Union Internationale des Telecommunications in Geneva, entered
Armstrong's name in its pantheon along with such as Bell, Morse,
Marconi, Ampère, Kelvin, Hertz, Maxwell, and Faraday. Armstrong's wife
was Marion MacInnes, and his funeral was held at New York's Fifth
Avenue Presbyterian Church.[10]

Marconi, of course, was smothered with honors. He was made a knight
of Italy in 1902, a Freeman of Rome in 1903 and was awarded the Nobel
Prize in 1909. He was made a *Marchese* and was nominated to the Italian
Senate in 1929; and was President of the Royal Italian Academy in
1930.[11] He married twice; first to Beatrice O'Brien, an aristocrat; and second to Maria Bezzi-Scali, a woman of Papal nobility. He loved Saville
Row suits and Italian opera, especially, Verdi. He taught himself to play
arias on the piano and befriended Mascagni, Toscanini, and Caruso, the
latter of whom sketched him in 1912.[12] He was a devoted citizen of Italy
and died in Rome, but still spoke the perfect English taught to him by his
Scottish mother.

In Bologna, the Marconi home bears this plaque:[13]

Qui naque
GUGLIELMO MARCONI
che su le onde della elettricita
primo lancio la parola
senza ausilio di cavi e di fili
da un emisfero a l'altro
a beneficio della umanita civile
a gloria della patria
Il Commune decreto
P
MCMVII

Here was born
GUGILELMO MARCONI
Who on the waves of electricity
First threw the human word
Without the aid of cables and wires
From one hemisphere to the other
To the benefit of the civilized world
For the glory of the fatherland
By order of the municipality
1907

John Logie Baird

(1888–1946)

John Logie Baird, By James Kerr-Lawson.
THE SCOTTISH NATIONAL PORTRAIT GALLERY.

N THE SUBJECT of invention, there is always controversy as to identity of the inventor; as to who had the prior claims and demonstrations. In the case of the invention of television, however, the other claimants do not dispute the undeniable string of "firsts" of John Logie Baird. They claim, instead, that since Baird didn't invent the modern electronic system in use today, he cannot be called the inventor of television. That is the equivalent of saying that Edison didn't invent the phonograph because he didn't produce long-playing records or modern compact discs; or that Stephenson didn't invent the railroad because he didn't build a Japanese "bullet" train or a 180-mile-an-hour French *TGV*.

Baird's achievements are all the more remarkable because he was poor and in bad health for his entire life, all the while competing against large companies out to surpass him. As to whether he was the inventor of television, The *Dictionary of National Biography*, one of Britain's most respected sources says, "In spite of his physical and financial handicaps Baird was the first exponent of every development associated with television."[1]

In 1924 Baird, with no capital, made his first TV on a washstand. The *Dictionary of National Biography* describes the device: "The base of his motor was a tea chest, a biscuit tin housed the projection lamp, scanning discs were cut from cardboard, and fourpenny cycle lenses were utilized. Scrap wood, darning needles, string and sealing wax held the apparatus together."[2] On this crude machine Baird was able to transmit a rough image of a Maltese cross. It was the first television in history. In 1925 he became the first to show recognizable human faces. According to Ronald Tiltman, Selfridge's store in London gave Baird space to demonstrate his invention, and invited the public to see for themselves in a flyer. "The picture is flickering and defective, and at present only simple pictures can be sent successfully; but Edison's phonograph announced that 'Mary had a little lamb' in a way that only hearers who were 'in the secret' could understand. Unquestionably the present experimental apparatus can be similarly perfected and refined."[3]

Baird's biggest moment came on January 26, 1926 at 22 Frith Street in the Soho section of London. Here, with an audience of about 50 scientists, including radio engineers, he gave the world's first demonstration of true television. Two journalists, from the London *Times* and the *Daily Chronicle*, attended the event and were able to report to their readers with enthusiasm that television had been achieved. A London County blue plaque marks the site, and Baird's television apparatus is in a London museum.[4] The American journal *Radio News* sent a reporter to London to investigate. In its issue of September 1926 it reported, "Mr. Baird has definitely and undisputedly given a demonstration of real television. It is the first . . . in any part of the world." The *New York Times* in its edition of March 6, 1927 devoted an entire page to Baird with the headline, "How Baird Sees Through Space by Radio: Scotch Inventor Holds the Secret of Television in His Sensitive Photo-Electric Cell." And a year later the *Times* said simply, "Baird was the first to achieve television . . ."[5] Soon after the demonstration in London, Baird started a television station, 2TV; the first in the world.[6] He also demonstrated "noctovision," a method of seeing in the dark by infrared rays.

More "firsts" were to come. In 1927 Baird demonstrated television between London and Glasgow, a distance of 438 miles. In the same year he formed Baird Television and Development, Ltd. In 1928 he achieved the first transatlantic television between London and New York, and also the first from shore to ship, sending vivid images to the *Berengaria* in the mid-Atlantic. In 1929 he began broadcasting over the BBC. In 1930 he began to sell and produce TV sets, the Baird Televisions, and demonstrated big screen television in the London Coliseum. In the same year he demonstrated in Paris, Berlin, and Stockholm. In 1932 the BBC took over the programming which had been provided by Baird up to that point. In the same year a thousand people watched the running of the Derby from Epsom in a theatre near Victoria Station. Baird also demonstrated ultra shortwave television. There were, in Britain, perhaps ten thousand television sets by the mid-1930s. People were watching sports, dance, and plays in their homes.[7]

It would seem that Baird was destined, at last, to leave poverty and become successful. But it was not to be. In a letter to the *New York Times*, dated June 9, 1989, Donald Flamm recounts how, as the owner of station WMCA, he brought Baird to New York in 1931 with the intention of using his system. Flamm says, "But despite Baird's worldwide acclaim, our application was denied . . ." by the Federal Communications Commission. He continues, "By that adverse decision we lost the opportunity of having a second Scottish inventor become a United States citizen, as Alexander Graham Bell did."[8]

Baird was not a businessman. Even though he had invented television, there were soon giant companies competing against him. He was completely alone, trying to do everything himself. He should have attracted capital to his enterprise. He should have developed an all-electronic system. In the mid-1930s the BBC began to use an all-electronic system along with Baird's. It used 405 lines to Baird's 240 lines. In 1937, the Marconi EMI system won out and Baird's system was dropped.[9] Baird had been beaten, but not defeated. He continued to work. In 1939 he demonstrated television in natural colors, and near his death in 1946 he invented stereoscopic television. He admitted that he should have sold his system for shares in a solid company as Bell had done. At one point he turned down an offer of £100,000 for his system, an amount worth millions today, saying that he couldn't sleep at night, being responsible for so much money.[10]

Baird was a son of the manse. His father, Reverend John Baird, was the minister of West Parish church in Helensburgh, Dumbartonshire. His mother, Jessie Morrison Inglis, was of the famous Glasgow shipbuilding family.[11] Baird's life, apart from television, was full of color. Except that his talent raised him to the level of genius, his life was that of the stereotypical bumbling scientist, compounded by his lifelong poor health. He was educated locally, and from an early age showed an astonishing capacity to invent. As a boy Baird made a private telephone system between his family's house and the houses of several of his friends. But the demise of this system came one night when a storm lowered one of the wires, caught a cabman under the chin, and lifted him out of his seat. The telephone company was sued, but it had been Baird's wire that had been at fault.

Baird also constructed an electric power plant for the family home, its dynamo driven by a water wheel worked from the water main. Baird's sister joked, years later, that the Bairds had the only house in Helensburgh with a private electric plant and telephone system.[12]

Baird was educated at the Royal Technical College (now Strathclyde University) in Glasgow. One of his classmates there was J.C.W. Reith, later Baron Reith, who became the most important person in the development of the BBC. It is ironic that Reith was the person most responsible for putting Baird on the air, and also, in the end, for discarding his system. Baird was in his final year at the school when World War I began. He tried to enlist, but was rejected on physical grounds. Instead, he took a job as superintendent engineer at the Clyde Valley Electrical Power Company. With some time on his hands, Baird tried to see if he could turn coal dust into diamonds, reasoning that they were two different forms of carbon. In his experiment, he brought a great deal of power in to bear on the coal dust; fuses were blown; Glasgow was blacked out for eleven minutes, and Baird was fired![13]

Perhaps because of this experience, Baird decided to quit engineering and go into business. His first product was the Baird Undersock, which was to be worn under a regular stocking. The Undersock was medicated, self-absorbent, and prevented dye from passing through to the feet. It was guaranteed to keep the foot cool in summer and warm in winter. The Undersock actually found a limited market, but Baird's frail health made him give up the business.[14]

For health reasons, Baird went to Trinidad. There he found fruit so plentiful, it was often left to rot on the ground, and sugar was extremely cheap. Thus was born Baird's Trinidad Jam. The first attempt at production encountered a slight problem, however, as armies of ants marched into Baird's cauldrons, ruining the jam. When this problem was solved, Baird decided to leave the manufacturing of the jam to an associate while he returned to London to promote the product. His partner, however, failed him and that was the end of Baird's Trinidad Jam.[15]

Back in London in 1920 Baird now went into the soap business. As usual, the product was good and customers bought, but he just didn't have the physical strength to make a go of it. Worse, in trying so hard to succeed, he suffered a complete physical and mental breakdown in 1922. While recuperating in Hastings, Sussex, he decided he must invent television, something he had always hoped to do. As it turned out, despite a life filled with poverty and ill health, he did become the inventor of television.

Baird was married to Margaret Albu, a concert pianist who was the daughter of a South African diamond merchant. They had one son and one daughter. Though his life was filled with repeated failure, Baird could find some happiness in that his real accomplishments did not go unrecognized. In 1937 he was elected an Honorary Fellow of the Royal Society of Edinburgh. Also, he was the first Briton to receive the gold medal of the International Faculty of Science.[16]

John Logie Baird completed the last third of a trilogy of extremely important inventions, all made by natives of the same country: the practical steam engine, the telephone and television. Which powerful country would have been likely to have produced this trilogy: the United States, or England, or France or Germany; all known for their proficiency in science? These inventions did not come from a powerful country. The practical steam engine, the telephone, and television, were invented by Scots.

Robert Watson-Watt

(1892–1973)

Sir Robert Watson-Watt,
AP/Wide World Photos

THE WORLD MIGHT be very different today had it not been for the work of a carpenter's son born in Brechin in the northern Scottish shire of Angus. It was 1940. The German *Wehrmacht* had just crushed the French army and had occupied that country and several others. A German invasion of England, the last Western European country capable of offering significant resistance to Nazism, was being contemplated. If such an invasion had been successful, it would have been catastrophic for all of Europe. Even the United States could have been threatened. The thousand-year *Reich* predicted by Hitler seemed, at the time, to be possible. But before the Germans could launch their invasion, the Royal Air Force of Great Britain would have to be neutralized. So Germany began to attack Britain with the bombing runs of their much greater air force. Things looked black for a while, but the RAF beat back the *Luftwaffe* in the Battle of Britain and the calamitous invasion was prevented.

There were, of course, many British heroes in this conflict. Winston Churchill, who, incidentally, could trace Scottish ancestry from his American mother, said of the brilliant RAF pilots who shot down many more enemy planes than they lost, "Never in the field of human conflict was so much owed by so many to so few." He might have been thinking, also, of that carpenter's son from Scotland, Robert Watson-Watt, the man who developed radar. Because it was radar that gave the RAF an enormous advantage over their German opponents.

Robert Alexander Watson Watt was the descendant of both Watsons and Watts, old families associated with northeast Scotland, and was proud that the genius James Watt was from the same stock as he. Educated in the local schools, he received a bursary to attend Brechin High School, where he received a further bursary to University College, Dundee. In 1912 he received a BSc. degree, after having won many academic prizes. His main interest in college was in radio waves.

In 1915 he volunteered for war duty as a meteorologist at the Royal Aircraft Factory in England. There he located thunderstorms, using radio waves to provide warnings to airmen. He was the first to use cathode ray oscilloscopes, so common in airplanes and air traffic control in later years.[1] He continued his studies of radio waves and the atmosphere in the years between the wars and traveled extensively, as far as the Bay of Bengal.[2] He proposed the word "ionosphere" for the ionized upper levels of the Earth's atmosphere.[3]

In 1933 the Air Ministry became concerned about the growing German air force, and searched for a way to stop bombers. Watson Watt was asked to check out a proposal to heat bombers to untenable levels, by use of radio waves. This idea was immediately rejected, but Watson Watt's assistant, A. F. Wilkins, recalled seeing signals "which fluttered when an aircraft flew nearby." Immediately work was started to develop a practical radar, and on February 12, 1935, Watson Watt was able to present to the government his historic and very precisely detailed proposal to construct the first radar defense system. Two weeks later his five towers performed perfectly in a test. He then organized and coordinated the massive effort of engineers and workmen to construct Britain's radar defense system.[4]

By 1936 Watson Watt's reporters were spotting planes as far away as seventy-five miles. In 1937 he and his wife pretended to be tourists, vacationing in Germany, but could find no development of radar in evidence there.[5] By 1938 Watson Watt had directed the building of a chain of radar stations, had accomplished radar between planes, maritime reconnaissance, radar to control anti-aircraft fire, and the ability to distinguish between friendly and enemy aircraft. By 1940, just when it was needed, Watson Watt had built a reliable air-defense system, which the *Dictionary of National Biography* calls "one of the greatest combined feats of science, engineering, and organization in the annals of human achievement."[6]

The Battle of Britain was won, in large part, because radar told the British how many German aircraft they were up against on a particular day, and where they would be. The *Luftwaffe* never figured out how the Spitfires always knew where to go and how to be at the right place at the right time. The RAF shot down many more planes than it lost. The Nazis were not able to destroy the RAF and, as winter approached, decided not to invade Britain. The tide of World War II had turned against Germany. Britain had held. It could continue to arm itself and could invite America to bring huge amounts of men and materiel to its staging ground.

Sir Robert Watson-Watt hyphenated his name upon receiving his knighthood in 1941. He was thrice married, but had no children. He was short and chubby and very garrulous. He was honored with degrees from St. Andrew's and Toronto, as well as the Medal of Merit, direct from the President of the United States.[7] It was not enough for what he had done. He asked for some compensation from the government, which, in the words of Forbes Macgregor, "made itself contemptuous by an acrimonious resistance" to his request. They gave him, finally, £52,000 for having saved his country.[8] Sir Robert died at Inverness, in the Highlands of Scotland.

But we should not leave the subject of saving civilization with science in the 1940s without discussing briefly a man born in England with a triply Scottish name—Alan Mathison Turing. The Turings, a very small family from Aberdeenshire, possessed a baronetcy. In addition to his paternal descent, Turing's grandmothers bore the Scottish family names of Boyd and Crawford. Alan Turing (1912–1954) was a mathematical genius and was educated at King's College, Cambridge where his great ability was recognized. He was a very odd person, almost childlike, often running ten miles to a meeting, his wild hair streaming behind. He was shy, and awkward, a real eccentric with a total disregard for his personal apperance.[9] In the 1930s he studied under Einstein at Princeton for two years, then returned to Cambridge. In 1937 he wrote a paper for the London Mathematical Society in which he gave a "theoretical description for a 'universal' computing machine." This paper was very advanced in computer theory.

When World War II came, Turing went to the Foreign Office where his work changed the war in an immense way. There, in the top-secret "Ultra" project, he designed a virtual computer to decode the messages sent by the German machine, *Enigma*. The Germans had such confidence that *Enigma's* ciphers could not be decoded that they never changed their procedures. But in fact, with Turing's machine, the Allied High Command was able "to know what the German High Command was planning, almost, at times, from hour to hour."[10]

Turing's work was of incalculable aid to the Allied war effort. In 1951 he was elected a Fellow of the Royal Society, and one of his proposers was Lord Bertrand Russell. But this honor was probably for his work as one of the originators of computers. His work during the war was so secret that he was then still practically unknown. The *Dictionary of National Biography's* essay on him, printed in 1971, says simply, "But his research was interrupted by the war during which he worked for the communications department of the Foreign Office; in 1946 he was appointed O.B.E. for his services." That is all it says. But what were the "services" for which he was honored? The *DNB* at that time, apparently, had never heard of "Ultra" and Turing' immense role in it! He should have been knighted.

Turing died of cyanide poisoning in 1954. It was probably suicide. He received more general public recognition as the subject of the 1987 play, *Breaking the Code*, starring Derek Jacoby.

henry Sinclair

(D. C. 1400)

MORE AND MORE people are coming to accept as fact that Prince Henry Sinclair made a voyage of discovery to America landing in what is now Nova Scotia on June 2, 1398, nearly a century before the first voyage of Columbus. But history changes slowly. All over the world people are still taught that " Columbus discovered America" when we know that Scandanavians were there centuries before him. The excavations at L'Anse aux Meadows in Newfoundland prove this. But Sinclair's voyage is exceptional because it was the first to leave a detailed written record. The Norse sagas, of course, tell of voyages such as that of Bjarne Herjolfsson in 986, but not in detail. Now comes the shocking news that Columbus likely knew about the Sinclair voyage and had access to someone who could tell him all about it.

Prince Henry Sinclair was a member of one of the most distinguished families in the history of Scotland. His ancestor, Henry de Saint Clair, who descended from Normandy, was given lands in Lothian in southern Scotland in the twelfth century. His descendant, Sir William Sinclair, was given the barony of Roslin or Rosslyn just south of Edinburgh in 1280. Another Sinclair was a leader in the Scottish War of Independence who fought with King Robert I, the Bruce. His grandson, sir William Sinclair (d.1330) had set out with Sir James Douglas and others on a trip to the Holy Land carrying the heart of Bruce. The Scottish party was almost entirely killed by Moors in Spain, but the victors were so impressed with the Scots' courage, that they allowed the lone survivor, Sir William Keith, to take back the heart and relics of the dead to Scotland. Sir William's son, also William, (d. c. 1358), married Isabella who was the daughter

Guysborough Harbor, Nova Scotia. The probable spot where a Scottish expedition, which left a written record, landed in the New World, June 2, 1398, almost a century before the first voyage of Columbus. COLLECTION OF THE AUTHOR.

of Malise, the earl of Strathearn, Caithness and Orkney. This marriage gave their son, our subject, Prince Henry Sinclair, a claim to the far northern earldom or jarldom of Orkney, which was then part of Norway.

It should be said that much of the information on Prince Henry and his family is subject to argument and conjecture. Standard sources such as encyclopedias do not agree on basic facts. Early records have been lost; new searches prove to be difficult or impossible. Yet, there is enough information for us to know that in discussing Prince Henry, we are dealing with a subject of great magnitude, who came from a family of almost mystical importance. We find, for instance, a French Sinclair, Catherine de St. Clair, was married to Hugues de Payen, the founder of the Knights Templar.[1] Recent research has shown that the Templars were one of the most powerful organizations existing during the Middle Ages. We know that the Pope, Clement V, gave the French king Philippe le Bel permission to ruin the Templars. We know that on Friday, the 13th, (the reason for the superstition) of October 1307, the king of France gave the order to seize all Templars and their assets. We can guess that many Templars escaped. They could not have fled to most Catholic countries, or they would have been arrested again. But King Robert I, the Bruce had been excommunicated and his loyal subjects were suspect Catholics as well.

There is evidence that some of the fleeing Templars did go to Scotland. There are dozens of Templar graves to be seen in Argyll alone. The Sinclair family's base at Roslin is only a few miles from what was Templar headquarters in Scotland. The formation of the Masons, we have learned recently, occurred in Scotland. The Sinclair family were the hereditary Grand Master Masons of Scotland. Perhaps the Masons began as the Templars gone underground, since when the excommunication of Scotland was lifted, they were vulnerable again to arrest.

All of this is brought together in the building called Rosslyn Chapel, a stone's throw from the Sinclair family's base at what are now the ruins of Rosslyn Castle, a few miles south of Edinburgh. Rosslyn Chapel is not even in the slightest ruined, and is surely one of the most interesting and unique buildings in the world. It was built by the grandson of Prince Henry Sinclair, William Sinclair (d. c. 1480) third Earl of Orkney. It is not possible to leave this building, with only the feeling of having seen another interesting country church. It is used as a church now, but that may not have been its original purpose. The walls and ceiling are covered with pre-Christian Norse and Celtic, as well as Templar and Masonic designs. Rosslyn Chapel is a place where some find the hair standing up on the back of their necks. It is proof that despite how little we know or can surmise, the Sinclair family was in the thick of something strange and important.

Prince Henry Sinclair, by far the most eminent member of an eminent family, was born at Roslin. We do not know the year. His claim to the earldom or jarldom of Orkney was confirmed by King Haakon VI of Norway in 1379.[2] He may have been chosen because he seemed to have the best chance of bringing order to a lawless place, the wild, barren Orkney Islands off the north coast of Scotland. In accepting the earldom, Sinclair was now the vassal of both the King of Norway and the King of Scots. As soon as he arrived in the islands, he must have realized that he could not rule them without a strong fleet, and went about building one. In time Sinclair became a great sea lord, ruling his domain with power approximate to that of a king. He brought the Shetland Islands under his control. He was the premier earl of Norway, second in precedence only to the king. People called him a prince.

As a result of Sinclair's occupation and development of the Orkneys and the Shetlands, more Scots began to settle in the islands, mixing with the Norse. The Norse language, which was still spoken there as late as the early eighteenth century, began to lose ground to Gaelic and English. Gradually, the islands became Scottish in culture, and in 1472 became Scottish in fact, when they were annexed to Scotland. If the Orkneys and Shetlands had not been Scottish, the Hudson's Bay Company would not have had the services of the hundreds of Orkneymen who built trading posts all over Canada. If Prince Henry had never done anything else but control, civilize, and make Scottish the Orkneys and Shetlands, his influence would still have been enough to be recognized in this book.

But two things happened by chance which would give him much greater influence. The story was first uncovered by Frederick J. Pohl in 1974 and augmented by Andrew Sinclair in 1992. There was a shipwreck of a Venetian vessel on one of Sinclair's islands. Incredibly, the captain of this ship was Niccolò Zeno, brother of the famous Venetian naval hero, Carlo Zeno. Niccolò Zeno died, but was survived by his brother Antonio Zeno, who became the admiral of Sinclair's fleet. Then came the second fortuitous event. A fisherman, who had been blown with his companions far to the west, returned home with a tale that was recorded by the Zenos in letters they ultimately carried back to Venice. What is known as the Zeno Narrative speaks:

> The inhabitants are very intelligent people, and possess all the arts like ourselves.
> He says it is a very great country, and like a new world. (*Grandissimo e quasi un nuovo mondo*)[3]

This is, apparently, the first time that the Western Hemisphere was called the "New World." At any rate, Sinclair decided to lead an expedition to this New World, and the party made land at what is now Guysborough, Nova Scotia on June 2, 1398. Later, it is alleged, they went to Westford, Massachusetts, where they proceeded to punch into a rock, still visible, the effigy and arms of a member of the Scottish Clan Gunn.

Standard sources agree that the Zenos traveled at least as far as Greenland with Prince Henry Sinclair. Pohl and Sinclair agree that the explorers got to Nova Scotia. They disagree on the landing site, but the Zeno manuscript describes a smoking hole and a spring of pitch. There are not many locations with these characteristics, but they do occur in Nova Scotia. In addition, legends of the Micmac Indians tell a story of a voyage by Europeans to their land, which parallels the Sinclair voyage.

Independent evidence of Prince Henry's discovery of America can still be seen at Rosslyn Chapel, which was founded in 1446 by Prince Henry's grandson, Sir William Sinclair, third Earl of Orkney. Since we know that construction on the Chapel stopped in 1484, the carvings of Indian corn (maize) and aloe cactus on the Chapel's walls, prove that the Sinclair family knew of these American plants, unknown in Europe at the time, before the first voyage of Columbus in 1492.

The probable reason no one paid any immediate attention to the Sinclair discovery is that there was no practical way of informing the world of it. The Zeno manuscript of the Sinclair expedition had been consigned to a musty Venetian archive some fifty years before Gutenberg's invention of movable type, which was around 1447. However, the new technique of printing was widely available throughout Europe by 1492, in time to give the voyage of Columbus great renown. It seems quite possible that had the Zeno manuscript of the Sinclair expedition been printed and distributed immediately (it lay unpublished for a century and a half), Americans might celebrate Sinclair Day on June 2, instead of Columbus Day on October 12.[4]

So therefore, the Sinclair expedition did *not* have a great influence on the world because few people knew about it. Well, not exactly. Another writer, Ian Brown, has another tale to tell. Prince Henry's daughter, Elizabeth, married one John Drummond. They had a son, also named John, who was born around 1402. In 1419 this John Drummond left Scotland to travel abroad. Since he was never heard from again, he was presumed to have died. But in 1519, another member of the family, Thomas Drummond, journeyed to the island of Madeira, which had been a Portuguese colony from 1420. Here he was astonished to find many Drummonds, including one Manuel Drummond, who proved to be the grandson of the lost John Drummond. The people of Madeira had given John Drummond a sobriquet, *João Escócio*, in Portuguese roughly translating to John the Scot. Presumably, Manuel Drummond would have known something of his ancestry, particularly of the voyage of his great-grandfather, Prince Henry Sinclair. Meanwhile, the Drummonds of Madeira prospered and became one of the island's leading families.[5]

Now come several astonishing facts. In 1478 Christopher Columbus married Filipa Moniz Perestrello. To quote the *Encyclopaedia Britannica*: "He then settled on the island of Porto Santo, Madeira Islands, of which his brother-in-law had inherited the captaincy. From this base he acquired . . . a number of hints[6] . . . as to possible lands beyond the western horizon."[7] This information elegantly provides evidence for Brown's case. But he goes farther, saying that a John Drummond was present with Queen Isabella at the siege of Granada in 1492. He also makes connections, possibly genetic, between the Madeira Drummonds, Columbus' wife, and Queen Isabella![8]

The *Encyclopaedia Britannica* alone corroborates Brown's main case. Perhaps Columbus knew exactly where he was going, informed by one of the Madeira Drummonds of the Sinclair voyage. Perhaps, therefore, Prince Henry Sinclair had a huge influence on the world. The only fact, which needs to be verified, is whether the legend of John the Scot is true. We are fortunate to have a first class witness. It happens that Brazil's greatest poet of the twentieth century was named Carlos Drummond de Andrade. In a letter to the present author he wrote:

Rio de Janeiro, 3 de agosto de 1983

Prezado Sr. Duncan A. Bruce

Em resposta à sua carta de 9 de julho, posso informar-lhe que a família Drummond, do Brasil, é originária da Ilha da Madeira, onde viveu a faleceu, no século XV, John Drummond, chamado João Escócio, que participara de algumas campanhas militares na França e na Espanha. Mantendo-se incógnito naquela ilha, antes de morrer revelou a sua identidade de nobre escocês, fundando o ramo português dos Drummond.

In response to your letter of 9 July, I am pleased to inform you that the Drummond family of Brazil, originated on the island of Madeira, where lived and died, in the fifeenth century, John Drummond, called John the Scot, who had participated in some military campaigns in France and Spain. Keeping himself incognito on that island, before dying he revealed his identity as a Scottish nobleman, founding the Portuguese branch of the Drummonds.

James Cook

(1728–1779)

O F ALL THE people in the world sur-named Cook, most of them Englishmen, it is interesting to know that by far the most eminent represen-tative of this common name is Scottish. Yet despite his continued fame, most people don't even recog-nize James Cook's first name, calling him instead simply Captain Cook. According to the *Encyclopaedia Britannica*, Cook was the first really sci-entific navigator, and did more to enlight-en the literate world about the Southern Hemisphere than had all of the mariners who had gone before him.[1] Further, in ten years of sailing, Cook charted more of the Pacific than had all of his predecessors—Spanish, Portuguese, Dutch, French and English—in the previous 250 years.[2] He had, also, a great influence on the expansion of the British Empire. It is because of the voyages of Captain Cook that Australia and New Zealand speak English.

James Cook,

James Cook was born at Marton-in-Cleveland, Yorkshire, England. His father, also James Cook, was the son of John Cook and Jean Duncan of Ednam, Roxburghshire, Scotland. John Cook and Jean Duncan had been married at Ednam in 1693 by the Reverend Thomas Thomson, who was, incidentally, the father of the poet James Thomson, author of *Rule Britannia*.³ This senior James Cook, the father of Captain Cook, had migrated from Scotland to Yorkshire, looking for work as a common laborer. There he met and married Grace Pace in 1725. Their son, also James, who became known as Captain Cook, was born in 1728. The senior James Cook became a foreman on a farm near Great Ayton and sent his bright son to the village school. By the time he was twenty, young James Cook had shipped out of Whitby on a coal ship. During the winters he studied navigation, and by 1755 he had become a master, commanding colliers along the coast of England.⁴

Cook volunteered as an able seaman in the war with France and by 1758 was master of the *Pembroke*. He crossed the Atlantic, taking part in the siege of Louisbourg and in the assault on Quebec. During this period, he charted the St. Lawrence River. Returning home, he married Elizabeth Batts in 1762, with whom he had six children, all of whom were dead by 1794. In 1763 he made a detailed survey of Newfoundland. In 1766 he observed an eclipse of the sun which was extremely accurate. In 1767 his paper on the eclipse was published by the Royal Society.⁵ This was an unheard of achievement for a noncommissioned naval officer who couldn't spell.⁶

The first of Captain Cook's great voyages of discovery was begun in 1768, with him in command of the HMS *Endeavour*. He sailed from Plymouth on August 25 with the famous botanist, Joseph Banks—later Sir Joseph—on board. The voyage went around Cape Horn, landing at Tahiti on April 13, 1769. Here Banks did his important work, while Cook promoted good relations with the Tahitians. Leaving Tahiti, Cook visited and named the Society Islands, and sailed a figure eight around the two large island of New Zealand, charting them. He was the first European to set foot in New Zealand, and is considered to be its founder. Cook spent a winter establishing good relations with the Maoris, whom he described as intelligent. Before he left, New Zealand's first haggis was served in honor of a Scottish officer's birthday. In 1770, Cook discovered and charted the eastern coast of Australia, which he named New South Wales. An unlucky Scottish crewman, Forbes Sutherland of Aberdeen, became the first Briton to be buried in Australian soil. Cook kept meticulous records, which included his opinion that Australia and New Zealand were ripe for colonization. For the first time, Britain became aware of the potential of the area. By July of 1771 he was home, promoted to commander.⁷

Cook's second voyage left England July 13, 1772 in the ships *Resolution* and *Adventure*. He was determined to prove or disprove the existence of habitable land south of what had already been discovered. By circum-navigating the earth as far south as possible, he demolished the con-tentions of those who thought such land would be found. During this voyage, he crossed the Antarctic Circle twice, reached a record 71° 10' S. and concluded, correctly, that land would be found, but too far south to be habitable. This voyage also discovered, or rediscovered Easter Island, the Marquesas Islands, the Society Islands, Tonga, South Georgia, the South Sandwich Islands, the New Hebrides, and New Caledonia. These last two, for which he chose the names, would seem to pay homage to his Scottish origins. By July 1775 he was home again, and was elected a Fellow of the Royal Society. The Society later awarded him its Copley Award for his paper describing his methods for combating scurvy.[8] As Alan Villiers says, it was "an extraordinary distinction for the farmhand's son, graduate of no school, holder of no degree."[9]

Captain Cook's third and final voyage sailed in 1776 in the ships *Resolution* and *Discovery*. On January 18, 1778 he discovered Hawaii which he named the Sandwich Islands, honoring his sponsor, the Earl of Sandwich. Cook then charted the entire northwestern coast of North America for 3,000 miles, from 45° to 70° 44' N. He sailed the Aleutian Islands and went through the Bering Strait until ice blocked his passage. Returning to Hawaii, he was killed in a skirmish on February 4, 1779.[10]

It was unfortunate for the world to lose such a man at the age of fifty. He could have done much more. As his biographer, J.C. Beaglehole says, ". . . as he grew older he looked still young." Captain Cook was a "tall, large-boned, powerful man, with strongly marked features." His nose, forehead and eyes were all large.[11]

Captain Cook's voyages influenced all subsequent exploration in the seas in which he traveled, and were important to many fields other than geography. In particular his work influenced the progress of the British Empire, which sent the first prisoners to begin the settlement of Australia only a few years after his death.

Alexander Mackenzie

(1764–1820)

ONE OF THE greatest explorers in history is practically unknown in his native Scotland. But Canadian schoolchildren know his name as well as American students know Lewis and Clark. Alexander Mackenzie was the Canadian who extended Britain's claim north all the way to the Arctic Ocean and west to the Pacific. He was the first person to cross the North American Continent north of Mexico.

Alexander Mackenzie[1] was born in Stornoway on the island of Lewis in the Outer Hebrides, the son of Kenneth Mackenzie and Isabella Maciver. In 1775 Alexander and his father immigrated to New York where his father's brother John was a prosperous merchant. This was the time of the American Revolution, and Alexander's father joined the British Army in New York while his young son was sent upstate for the duration. After the war, Alexander made his way to Montreal, where he got some schooling and resolved to become a rich fur trader.[2] To do this he went through a physical-conditioning program, exposing himself to great cold, working out without sleep or food, and learning to fight.[3]

In 1779 he joined in the fur trade in Montreal with Gregory & Company, whose firm was soon absorbed into the North West Company. This latter enterprise, founded by Simon McTavish, was almost entirely Scottish in makeup and was bitterly and sometimes violently opposed to the Hudson's Bay Company, which had previously enjoyed a near monopoly. In 1784 The North West Company sent Alexander Mackenzie to Detroit with some goods and told him to make inroads in the Indian country. But he and his associates encountered other white traders who brought the Indians against them. There was fighting, with one man killed and others wounded, but Mackenzie held his ground, and was grudgingly conceded some of the trade.[4]

In 1788 Mackenzie and his cousin Roderick set up Fort Chipewyan on Lake Athabasca in what is now the far northern reaches of the Province of Alberta. In the howling wilderness they managed to construct not only a trading post, but a library as well. When the other Scottish fur traders heard of the library, which offered classics along with manuals on navigation, they proudly called Fort Chipewyan "The Athens of the North," as if it were a new Edinburgh.[5]

On June 3, 1789, Alexander Mackenzie set out with a party of Canadians and Indians in birch bark canoes on his first great journey. His mind may have been fixed on finding a water route to the Pacific, and the quarter-million-dollar prize to the first man to do so. At any rate, the river he followed kept going north and west, and he must have realized at some point that he was not going to the Pacific. The journey was arduous in the extreme. When the party reached the Great Slave Lake, they found it covered with thin ice and had to walk around it. Along the way the explorers discovered a huge mountain range (named for Mackenzie) and followed Canada's longest river (also named for Mackenzie). Finally, the group reached the Arctic Ocean, where they encountered mild weather. The travelers were entertained by white whales playing in the sea. The Indians had trouble sleeping because of the lack of darkness in the far northern summer. Mackenzie, from the far north of Scotland, was used to it.[6]

Mackenzie marked the northernmost point of the voyage at 69° N. It is now called Mackenzie Bay. Enduring great difficulties, Mackenzie and his party returned to Fort Chipewyan. The entire trip had taken only 120 days. They had covered a distance of 2,990 miles,[7] some 500 miles more than the distance between New York and Los Angeles.

Mackenzie was welcomed as a hero when he returned to Montreal in 1790. He had claimed vast territory for the North West Company and for Britain. Not yet thirty years old, he was made a senior partner of the firm. But he still wanted the prize—to be the first man across the continent. Realizing that he didn't have the scientific training to do it without further education he entered Cambridge University in England studying geography, mathematics, navigation, and astronomy. In London he bought scientific instruments. On the boat back to Canada he practiced shooting the stars. When he arrived in Montreal he found the North West Company awash in money as a result of the territories he had discovered. He advocated merger with the Hudson's Bay Company, but couldn't convince his conservative partners.[8]

In the summer of 1793 Mackenzie set out, but this time with a single canoe which was so light two men could carry it for several miles. By May 17 the party could see the Rocky Mountains. It was a hard trip. There were clouds of mosquitoes and many portages, but at last they could see the rivers flowing to the west. The party was now going downstream, but there were rapids, and at one time the canoe capsized, and much equipment was lost. At last they reached the Dean Channel and could smell the salty water. Mackenzie had reached 52° 21' N., 128° W. No other European had ever even attempted the feat. Mackenzie found a rock and carved into it these words, still visible today:

Alex. Mackenzie
from Canada
by land
22 July 1793

The very next day Mackenzie narrowly avoided being murdered. He was walking alone when two Indians ran at him with knives drawn. He says in his diary, "I could not doubt of their purpose." He assumed a defensive position, but then more Indians arrived. He was surrounded, but saved when a few of his men came to the scene and the Indians ran away. He says, "though I should probably have killed one or two of them, I must have fallen at last."[9]

Rock in British Columbia Inscribed by Sir Alexander Mackenzie. COPYRIGHT KEVIN FLEMING.

Alexander Mackenzie, now a rich man, returned to Britain. In 1801 he published *Voyages on the River St. Lawrence and through the Continent of North America to the Frozen and Pacific Oceans in the Years 1789 and 1793*. The book contains beautiful maps and is dedicated to King George III.[10] Mackenzie was knighted in 1802. He retained his partnership in the North West Company, but started a rival, Alexander Mackenzie & Company, which was merged into the North West Company in 1804. He spent time in Britain and in Canada, becoming even richer and bored. He married a Scottish woman named Geddis Mackenzie from the village of Avoch in Ross-shire and bought an estate there. He was elected to Parliament, and was still bored. Traveling with his family, he died suddenly in 1820 near Pitlochry in Perthshire.

David Livingstone

(1813–1873)

I T IS POSSIBLE to argue that tiny Scotland had more to do with the exploration of Africa than any country, regardless of size. A very brief and by no means complete view of this contention would include James Bruce (1730–1794), a wine merchant, who discovered the source of the Blue Nile. Mungo Park (1771–1806), a surgeon, was the first European to see the upper reaches of the Niger River before being killed by natives. Alexander Gordon Laing (1793–1826), a soldier, was the first European to reach Timbuktu. He was murdered, also. A physician, William Balfour

David Livingstone,
PICTURE COLLECTION, THE BRANCH LIBRARIES,
THE NEW YORK PUBLIC LIBRARY.

Baikie (1825–1864) opened the Niger to commerce and founded the town of Lokoja. Acting as ruler, doctor and educator, he established a market, collected words in a dozen dialects, and translated parts of the Bible into Hausa. In 1823 Hugh Clapperton (1788–1827) and Dixon Denham (1786–1828) were the first to cross the Sahara Desert. Reverend John Campbell (1766–1840) discovered the source of the Limpopo River. James Grant (1827–1892) was one of the British duo which discovered and named Lake Victoria and proved it to be the source of the Nile. Joseph Thomson (1858–1895) discovered Lake Rukwa and Thomson's Falls in what is now Kenya.[1]

But none of these heroes comes near to what was accomplished by Dr. David Livingstone, who is credited with opening the entire southern half of the continent. Having just discussed Captain Cook, whom we can nominate as the greatest of all maritime explorers, we can nominate Livingstone as the foremost explorer on land. In a career which spanned a third of a century, Livingstone traveled an almost incredible thirty thousand miles through hostile country, most of which had never been seen before, let alone lived in, by a European.

David Livingstone was born in Blantyre, Lanarkshire. His father, Neil Livingstone, was a Highlander from the isle of Ulva. The name Livingstone is probably an English rendition of the Gaelic Macleay.[2] David Livingstone's mother Agnes, was of lowland stock. Neil Livingstone was a small dealer in tea at Blantrye. He was very poor but educated, pious, and curious. David Livingstone often compared his father with the cotter in Robert Burn's poem, *The Cotter's Saturday Night*.[3]

Young David was forced by the family's poverty to go to work in a stiflingly hot cotton mill at age ten. It was thought that warmth made the cloth better so the temperature in the mill was kept between eighty and ninety degrees. The workday was fourteen hours, from 6:00 A.M. to 8:00 P.M. But despite these conditions, David went to school from 8:00 P.M. to 10:00 P.M. He perfected, also, a technique whereby he placed a book for study on his jenny and was able to master Virgil and Horace and to study botany, zoology, and geology while he worked. At age nineteen he had been promoted to cotton spinner and made enough money to go to college, without, of course, quitting his job. He studied medicine at Anderson College, and took Greek at Glasgow, studying along with other young men such as the future Lord Kelvin (see p. 385) and James Young (1811–1883), the founder of the petroleum industry. In 1840 he qualified in medicine at Glasgow and went to London where he met Dr. Robert Moffat, a Scottish missionary. He agreed to go to Africa as a missionary and sailed in 1840. On the way, the ship stopped at Rio de Janeiro. It was the only time Livingstone was ever in the Western Hemisphere.[4]

During the early part of his career, Livingstone was mauled by a lion, losing some of the strength in his left arm. He married Moffat's daughter Mary in 1845. Livingstone became obsessed with ending the slave trade, which he called "the running sore of Africa." He practiced what he called "Muscular Christianity" and sometimes freed slaves, at gunpoint. Above all, he tried to find some alternate economy, which would make the slave trade less profitable, and in this he was unsuccessful. Even his discovery of one of the world's greatest natural wonders, Victoria Falls, disappointed him since it meant an obstruction to a possible trade route. Back in London, Livingstone was surprised to find that he was a celebrity. There he wrote his book, *Missionary Travels.*[5]

In 1858 Livingstone discovered Lake Nyasa and a route to the interior. He brought his wife out from Britain, and suffered greatly when she died. He discovered the southern end of Lake Tanganyika as well as Lake Mweru and Lake Bangweulu, all the while, mapping and keeping detailed scientific records.[6]

Then he lost touch with civilization, and perhaps reality as well, forgetting that he was a missionary, and struggling to find the source of the Nile. For several years afterward nothing was heard of him and there were rumors that he had died. Several search parties were sent to find him. One of these, in perhaps the most expensive journalistic venture of all time, was sent by the younger James Gordon Bennett, (see p. 139) publisher of the *New York Herald*. On the morning of November 10, 1871, the *Herald*'s Henry Morton Stanley approached Livingstone's camp at Ujiji. Oliver Ransford describes the scene. "The Stars and Stripes were borne before him; his men were sounding Kudu horns, beating drums and firing off salutes." Stanley then dismounted, walked forward, doffed his helmet, bowed and uttered his famous words, "Dr. Livingstone, I presume." The answer came, "Yes, that is my name."[7]

Livingstone refused to return to civilization with Stanley and continued his work. Two years later, his body worn out, he died in the field after dismissing his servant for the night. His loyal native followers embalmed his body and refusing any suggestion that he should be buried anywhere but Britain, carried his corpse 1,500 miles to the ocean. The return of his body from the depths of Africa was perceived by many as miraculous.[8]

David Livingstone had become a myth in his own time. His life was seen as proof of Britain's "unique mission." On April 18, 1874 huge crowds lined Pall Mall and Whitehall in London. The prime minister and the Prince of Wales were in attendance, as David Livingstone was laid to rest in one of the most conspicuous places in the nave of Westminster Abbey.[9] The large stone reads:

BROUGHT BY FAITHFUL HANDS
OVER LAND AND SEA
HERE RESTS
DAVID LIVINGSTONE
MISSIONARY
TRAVELLER
PHILANTHROPIST
BORN MARCH 19, 1813
AT BLANTYRE, LANARKSHIRE
DIED MAY 1, 1873
AT CHITAMBO'S VILLAGE, ILALA

David Livingstone failed at many things, principally as a missionary. But he was one of the greatest explorers in history. Because of his work, Britain was able to become paramount in southern Africa. He made contributions, also, to linguistics, ". . . tropical medicine, African botany, zoology, anthropology and geology."[10] Perhaps his greatest influence was to change the way Europeans think of Africans. In the *New York Herald* he wrote, "I have no prejudice against their colour; indeed, anyone who lives long among them forgets that they are black and feels that they are just fellow-men . . ."[11] Britain made slavery illegal at Zanzibar in 1873, the year of his death.[12]

Victoria Falls on the Zambesi River is magnificent, a mile wide and 343 feet tall. Overlooking the scene is a huge statue of its discoverer, Dr. David Livingstone. Near the falls is the town of Livingstone. After independence, Zambia exchanged its British place names for African ones, with the exception of Livingstone.[13] Blantyre, named after Livingstone's birthplace, is the largest city in the republic of Malawi, and the Church of Scotland is still very influential there. In 1973, to mark the centenary, a thousand people made a pilgrimage far into the interior to the place of Livingstone's death, led by the Presbyterian President of Zambia, Kenneth Kaunda.[14]

William Stephenson

(1896–1989)

THE GREAT ROLE played by Sir William Stephenson in the defeat of Germany and Japan in World War II began almost accidentally. While doing business in Germany in the 1930s, he noted the massive German buildup of arms, steel, and munitions and immediately informed Britain. As a result Britain, and later the United States, began to re-arm. Without Stephenson's work the allies would have faced World War II relatively unprepared. In 1940 this amateur spy was asked by Prime Minister Churchill to move to New York to set up an agency to coordinate British and American intelligence. Churchill gave Stephenson the code name "Intrepid" and he assumed control of all British intelligence in the Western Hemisphere. Stephenson operated from an office in Rockefeller Center through which hundreds of operatives moved for several years, undetected. His effort was vital to the allies and resulted, directly, in the creation of the OSS, the predecessor to the CIA.

William Samuel Stephenson was born at Point Douglas, near Winnipeg, Manitoba, as the *Dictionary of National Biography* says, "of Scottish ancestry." His father was the owner of a lumber mill, and "Little Bill," so called because of his short stature, attended Argyll High School. In World War I he enlisted in the Royal Canadian Engineers and was gassed. Later, he joined the Royal Flying Corps. As a pilot he became an air ace, shooting down twenty-six German planes, and receiving the Military Cross, the Distinguished Flying Cross and the French *Croix de Guerre*.

After his service in World War I, William Stephenson, an amateur boxer, pursued various business interests, becoming a millionaire by the age of thirty. A component of this success was his invention of the first device to send photographs by radio. His discovery of Hitler's plans for world domination in the Germany of the 1930s, and details of the German build-up for war were relayed through a network, which reported to Churchill, who was soon to become First Sea Lord and later, Prime Minister. From this point on, Stephenson became less interested in business and more in intelligence. As Intrepid, he was sent to New York in 1940 as head of an organization called British Security Coordination, which was to promote British-American cooperation in intelligence. The *Dictionary of National Biography* says that Stephenson was sent by Secret Intelligence Service (MI16), and that he was responsible also for security (MI5) until March 1942, and for the Special Operations Executive (SOE).[1] The *New York Times* says, simply, that Sir William was "Britain's World War II chief of intelligence in the Western Hemisphere."[2] Then the *DNB* makes a mistake, saying "he formed a close relationship with the powerful Herbert Hoover, head of the FBI. . . . " Of course, it was J. Edgar Hoover who was head of the FBI, not the former president.

Because of the secret nature of his work, there is some disagreement as to what Intrepid accomplished in New York. But all sources agree that Stephenson was instrumental in the cooperation between Britain and the United States in trading intelligence before America's entry into the war. It is obvious that any such intelligence was of inestimable value to the government of the United States and that it would have been of utmost importance in rearming the country in readiness for a war that was about to begin. There is agreement, also, that Intrepid was instrumental in forming the OSS, the forerunner of the CIA, with General William J. "Wild Bill" Donovan. Nor is there any doubt that he was knighted and received the Medal for Merit, then America's highest civilian honor, from the President of the United States.

Stephenson's biographers, William Stevenson (no relation) author of *A Man Called Intrepid*; and H. Montgomery Hyde, who wrote *The Quiet Canadian*, with whom Stephenson worked closely, claim that Intrepid was the secret go-between for Churchill and Roosevelt. But John Colville, who was Churchill's private secretary, said that Sir William's assertions that he was in constant touch with the Prime Minister, were completely false. It is obvious that Mr. Colville would be hurt by being told that his boss had been talking often and in secret behind his back. But how would he know what had gone on? If the discussions between Intrepid and

Chruchill were of the utmost secrecy, why would Churchill have told anyone else about them, even his private secretary?

Picking up on Colville's line, the *Dictionary of National Biography* finishes its article on Stephenson in scathing prose, charging him with falsifying information, which he gave his biographers. Sir William was not, they say, a boxing champion. He didn't shoot down twenty-six enemy aircraft; it was only six. He didn't win the *Croix de Guerre*; just the British medals. There was no evidence, says the *DNB*, that he ever even met Churchill. (If their relationship was a secret, why would there be any evidence?)

Fortunately, we do not have to rely on the testimony of the *Times*, the *DNB* or the biographers to settle Sir William's case. We can examine the opinions of three famous men who worked with him in secret at Rockefeller Center in New York for the benefit of all civilized people. Colonel Charles Howard Ellis was one of Stephenson's officers in New York. In his introduction to *A Man Called Intrepid*, he says that the book "clarifies the extraordinary relationship Intrepid maintained in the utmost secrecy between the President of the United States and the Prime Minister of Great Britain."[3] He also says, "Intrepid was the midwife of OSS."[4]

Rockefeller Center, New York City, where "Intrepid" built his powerful intelligence operation.
COLLECTION OF THE AUTHOR.

David K.E. Bruce, a Scottish-American who worked with Stephenson in New York and ran the OSS in London, and was later called by President Eisenhower "the best ambassador the United States ever had" says that Stephenson was "imaginative, resourceful, inventive, practical, persistent, brilliant."[5] Bruce goes on to say that "the finest tribute" to Stephenson was given him by Winston Churchill when he recommended Intrepid for knighthood to King George VI, saying, "This one is dear to my heart." General William J. Donovan said that British Security Co-ordination was built-up by Stephenson "from nothing into the greatest integrated, secret intelligence and operations organization that has ever existed anywhere."[6] "Wild Bill" Donovan said also, "Bill Stephenson taught us all we ever knew about foreign intelligence."[7] And author John le Carre, reviewing *A Man Called Intrepid* noted, ". . . Separatists will not miss the point that in the secret war the job of saving Britain was entrusted to a Scottish Canadian and an Irish American."[8]

James Gordon Bennett
(1795–1872)

AND

James Gordon Bennett
(1841–1918)

THE BENNETTS, FATHER and son, were two of the strangest and least-liked men imaginable. But their newspaper, the New York *Herald*, became the largest circulation paper in the United States in its day, and probably the most influential in the country's journalistic history. The *Herald* revolutionized the news business in many ways. It was the first U.S. newspaper to carry news from Wall Street, the first to employ European correspondents, the first to report a long political speech by telegraph, the first to print news of society, and the first to report a sexual scandal. It was also a pioneer in using illustrations.[1]

The elder James Gordon Bennett was born in Keith, Banffshire, the son of a Roman Catholic farmer. He studied for the priesthood at a seminary in Aberdeen, but left, traveling at his family's expense. In 1819 he emigrated to North America, working his way from Halifax to Boston, where he was employed for three years in a bookstore. He spent some time in Charleston, South Carolina, finally settling in New York in 1823. He became an editor of the *New York Enquirer* and the *Courier and Enquirer*. In 1833 he was chief editor of the *Pennsylvanian*, a Philadelphia paper which supported Andrew Jackson. In 1835 he returned to New York, and with a stake of $500 launched the *Herald* as a penny paper. Its success was immediate, and by 1850 it was the largest in the country with daily circulation of more than fifty thousand.[2]

The *Herald* succeeded because it was much better than any other paper at the time and it was sensational, printing many stories of murder and sex. The paper made its mark in 1836 with the Robinson-Jewett murder story. Ellen Jewett, a beautiful prostitute, had been murdered with an axe;

her last client, Richard P. Robinson, was suspected. Bennett visited the house on Thomas Street and decided that Robinson was innocent. The other papers thought him guilty. Robinson was acquitted and circulation of the *Herald* tripled.[3] Bennett made more innovations. His paper was the first to cover sports. He made himself a story by attacking rival editors. He announced his engagement to Henriette Agnes Crean on the front page, and a week later, their wedding was again front page news. He attacked his own Roman Catholic Church. It was not long before the church, certain members of the business community, and rival papers tried to ruin him. But the *Herald* was too good to be beaten. Bennett had by far the most comprehensive news coverage and he embraced technology ahead of his competitors, buying bigger steam presses to print faster. The fact that he was able to make advertisers pay up front and in cash allowed him to do this. The *Herald* was the first paper to print the peace treaty with Mexico in 1848. It ran a horse express to Washington and to New Orleans during the Mexican War, where it was the only New York paper to have a reporter. Bennett maintained a fleet of boats to meet incoming ships and scoop the other papers.[4]

Bennett made his paper "impudent and intrusive." One of his biographers, Don Carlos Seitz, says, "he became the first real reporter the American press had known."[5] Also, Bennett helped to organize the Associated Press.

As he grew older, he retreated with his wife and daughter, Jeanette, from his palatial home on Fifth Avenue to his estate in Fort Washington, where he puttered with his flowers, and sent specific orders to the *Herald*. A newsman who had worked with him, John Russell Young, described him: "Hair white, prominent nose, long narrow head, keen eye, broad Scottish accent." Another, Junius Henri Browne said, "Bennett is a very honest and strictly moral man." When he died, every one of the most important newspaper editors were pallbearers. James Gordon Bennett realized his ambition, which had been to make the press "the great organ and pivot . . . of all human civilization." Another biographer, Oliver Carlson says, "The power of the Press, as we know it today, is in large measure the product of his genius."[6]

The younger James Gordon Bennett spent most of his youth abroad. He attended the *École Polytechnique* in Paris, and served for a short time in the navy during the Civil War. He worked on the *Herald* for some years, becoming managing editor in 1866 and taking control from his father in 1867. He is remembered, chiefly, as a playboy, and he was that, a handsome daredevil in wild company; a drunk who ruined his engagement by urinating in mixed company and who rode naked in midnight carriage rides. He was probably the only Commodore of the New York Yacht Club to be pressured out of the country by its powerful and influential members. But he was much more than a mere drunken playboy. Running the *Herald* for forty years by remote control from his exile in Europe, he reinvigorated the paper as its circulation reached new heights. Young Bennett outdid even his father in getting the news and would spend almost any amount to get a scoop. He brought in the best journalists, including Walt Whitman and Mark Twain; the latter wrote for the paper for three decades.[7]

The younger Bennett lived lavishly in Europe, maintaining estates and

Monument to the James Gordon Bennetts, Herald Square, New York City.
COLLECTION OF THE AUTHOR.

socializing with royalty. In 1914 he married Maud Potter, the widow of Baron George de Reuter. He died at his villa at Beaulieu in France and is buried in Paris.[8] He is best remembered for sending the reporter Henry Morton Stanley to find the famous Scottish explorer, David Livingstone, who was in Africa and had not been heard of for several years (see p. 131). The meeting between Stanley and Bennett, at the latter's suite in the Grand Hotel in Paris, is reported in Stanley's words: "Entering I found Mr. Bennett in bed. 'Who are you?' he asked. 'My name is Stanley,' I answered. 'Ah yes; sit down. I have important business on hand for you.' And later: 'What!' said I. 'Do you really think I can find Dr. Livingstone?'"[9]

Bennett told Stanley to spend whatever it took to find Livingstone, authorizing him to take down successive tranches of £1,000. Stanley relieved Livingstone at Ujiji in 1871 speaking the timeless words, "Dr. Livingstone, I presume." An enormous amount of attention was paid to the episode, which has secured for Bennett and Stanley the status of all-time media stars.

The two Bennetts ran the *Herald* for a combined 83 years. Yet, as Seitz says, despite the community's disapproval of both the Bennetts and their paper, The *Herald* ruled. "It compelled support by its energy—buying and selling news was its business."[10] After the death of the younger Bennett, the paper was sold, merged with the *Tribune* to become the *Herald Tribune*, and published into the 1960s when it finally expired. But it lives on in the *International Herald Tribune*, which had been founded and nurtured by the younger Bennett in Paris. This journal was the first truly international publication. It introduced the linotype to Europe and was the first paper on the continent to use wireless telegraphy for news dispatches.[11] As of July, 2000 it had a circulation of 234,000, was printed in twenty countries and distributed in 186 others. Now published by the *New York Times* and the *Washington Post*, its masthead says, correctly, that it was founded in 1877. But, continuing the prejudice against the Bennetts, it doesn't say who the founder was.

There is an elaborate monument to the Bennetts in the middle of one of New York City's busiest intersections, Herald Square.

Lila Acheson Wallace
(1889–1984)

AND

DeWitt Wallace
(1889–1981)

eldom have two people come up with such a simple idea and developed it into such an impressive instrument of wealth and power. The idea for the *Reader's Digest* was to create a magazine condensing articles from other published sources so that the reader could obtain the benefit of diverse information in a relatively short period of time. Lila Acheson Wallace and DeWitt Wallace pursued this idea, starting with a few hundred dollars in 1921. By the time their company went public in 1990, it was

Lila Acheson Wallace, DeWitt Walace.

valued at around $2 billion and was producing the most widely read maga-
zine in the world, with over 100 million readers in seventeen languages in
every country on the planet.

William Roy DeWitt Wallace was born in St. Paul, Minnesota, the
son of Reverend Dr. James T. Wallace, president of Macalester College,
which was associated with the Presbyterian Church. Reverend Wallace
was of Scotch-Irish ancestry as was his wife Janet Davis, whose father
was a Presbyterian minister. As a boy DeWitt Wallace was bright enough
to skip two years in grade school, but was better known for athletics and
pranks in high school. He attended Macalester College for two years, but
left after committing some antics.[1] According to his biographer, John
Heidenry, he became a semiprofessional baseball player, barnstorming
throughout the country.[2] Wallace worked for a time at a bank in
Colorado and studied at Berkeley, where he left without a degree. At one
point he visited Tacoma where he met Lila Bell Acheson. He returned
to St. Paul where he worked for a publisher and wrote *Getting the Most
out of Farming* by DeWitt Wallace. This is probably his only byline. The
work sold one hundred thousand copies, mostly because Wallace convinced farm suppliers to buy it and give it away to their customers.
Wallace enlisted in World War I and was wounded. Returning to St.
Paul after the war, Wallace condensed articles from such works as the
Ladies Home Journal, Saturday Evening Post, and *National Geographic,*
then borrowed several hundred dollars from his father and printed a prototype *Reader's Digest.* He tried to sell the concept to publishers, but
there was very little interest.[3]

Meanwhile he again met Lila Bell Acheson who had come to
Minnesota to help form a YWCA. Lila Acheson, born of Scotch-Irish
ancestry in Virden, Manitoba, was the daughter of Reverend Thomas
Acheson, a Presbyterian minister and his wife, Eliza Huston. The
Achesons traced their ancestry to Sir Archibald Acheson whose land-
mark house still stands on Edinburgh's Royal Mile.[4] Lila Acheson had
spent two years at Ward-Belmont, a Presbyterian College in Nashville,
Tennessee, and graduated from the University of Oregon, in 1917, where
she had been active in drama. During World War I she worked in YWCA
"after work" programs aiding women war plant workers.[5]

Lila Acheson went to New York as a social worker, and DeWitt
Wallace went to Pittsburgh to write publicity for the Westinghouse corporation. A recession got him laid off and he followed her to New York.

There, she encouraged him to pursue the *Reader's Digest* idea. Together they mailed out a subscription letter to several thousand people. Then the couple went to Pleasantville, New York where they were married on October 15, 1921 by the Reverend Barclay Acheson. When the Wallaces returned from their wedding trip, they found in the mailbox several thousand dollars worth of subscriptions—enough to publish the first issue from 1 Minetta Lane in Greenwich Village. For the first several years DeWitt Wallace used the periodical room of the New York Public Library as his "office," and did all the condensing himself. The publications from which he compressed his articles charged nothing since to them it was good publicity to be in the magazine.[6] (When the *Digest* got to be big they charged plenty!)

The magazine covered a broad range of interests including nature, art, health, science, sex, and humor. It promoted traditional American values. Even though the first editions were unsophisticated, circulation grew rapidly: to twenty thousand in four years, and to two hundred thousand in seven years. By 1936 the *Reader's Digest* was printing almost two million copies. The Wallaces moved the business to Pleasantville, with DeWitt owning 52 percent and Lila 48 percent.[7]

Lila Wallace designed the couple's house High Winds where they lived, entertained, and sometimes worked. She became a collector of art, especially French Impressionists such as Monet, Matisse, and Renoir. She is quoted in the *American National Biography* as saying, "A painting is like a man. If you can live without it then there isn't much point in having it." The two Wallaces became major philanthropists. DeWitt Wallace gave $50 million to Macalester College while Lila Wallace gave a similar amount to New York's Metropolitan Museum of Art. The impressive continuous floral displays in the main lobby are endowed by her. Lila Wallace also provided funds to restore Monet's home at Giverny. The couple supported dozens of hospitals, churches and made other gifts, including the funds to restore their first "office"—the periodical room at the New York Public Library.[8] As of 1993 the DeWitt Wallace Foundation and the Lila Acheson Wallace Foundation ranked as two of the twenty-one largest charitable foundations in the United States. (Many of the remaining nineteen had Scottish connections as well, such as the foundations started by J. Paul Getty, John D. MacArthur, John D. Rockefeller, Andrew W. Mellon, William L. McKnight and Andrew Carnegie.)

DeWitt Wallace's obituary in the *New York Times* pointed out that his great wealth was not able to break the Scottish habits ingrained from youth. Wallace sent memos on used envelopes, and constantly turned out unneeded lights at the *Reader's Digest*. He proposed for his obituary, "The final condensation."[9]

Rupert Murdoch

(1931–)

THREE DIFFERENT SCOTS have been among the greatest media barons in history. The first was William Maxwell Aitken (1879–1964) who is better remembered as Lord Beaverbrook. He was born in New Brunswick, the son of a Presbyterian minister who had immigrated from Scotland. By age twenty-nine, he was a millionaire stockbroker in Montreal and moved to England where he was elected to parliament. In 1916 he bought control of the *London Daily Express* and two years later founded the *Sunday Express*. He bought the *Evening Standard* in 1923. Beaverbrook greatly increased the circulation of his papers and made another fortune. He held the rank of British cabinet minister in both world wars.[1]

Rupert Murdoch,
News Corporation.

Roy Thomson, who became Lord Thomson of Fleet, was born in Toronto, the son of a Scottish barber, and ended up owning some 150 newspapers, more than anyone else in the world. His son, Kenneth R. Thomson, the second Lord Thomson, now presides over an empire which includes oil properties and the Hudson's Bay Company, and is said by some, to be the richest man in Canada.[2]

But perhaps the most important media mogul of all is Rupert Murdoch, who, starting with one inherited newspaper, now controls influential media properties all over the world. Keith Rupert Murdoch was born in Melbourne, Australia. His mother, Elisabeth Joy Greene is now Dame Elisabeth Murdoch in recognition of her charitable work. Her father, who was in the wool trade, was of Anglo-Scottish ancestry. Rupert Murdoch's father, Keith Arthur Murdoch, was a well-known Australian newsman whose parents were born in Scotland. Keith Arthur Murdoch was knighted in 1933. His father, Rupert Murdoch's grandfather, Reverend Patrick John Murdoch, was moderator of the Presbyterian church in Australia.[3]

The Murdochs were and are a very distinguished family. Rupert Murdoch's father made his mark as a reporter covering the British fighting at Gallipoli in Turkey during World War I. He observed that Australian and New Zealand troops were being slaughtered in a hopeless operation against overwhelming forces. Murdoch took a boat to Marseilles and wrote a story about what he considered to be the incompetent British leadership in Turkey. His essay was confiscated when he reached France. But in London he obtained an audience with Lord Northcliffe, who got him a meeting with the Prime Minister, David Lloyd George. In part because of Keith Murdoch's efforts, the British military leaders were changed, and, ultimately, Gallipoli was evacuated. He returned to Australia as a national hero.[4]

Rupert Murdoch was educated at the Geelong School in Australia, and at Worcester College at Oxford. He was something of a left-wing radical at Oxford, and wasn't much interested in his studies. He barely graduated with a third class. While he was finishing his father died and the family prevailed upon him to take over the family paper, the Adelaide *News and Sunday Mail*. When he assumed control, Murdoch found the paper to be in difficulty, and, despite the family's prominence, there wasn't much money.[5] From that day to this, Rupert Murdoch has dedicated himself to making sure that there would be profits and an ever-expanding business.

But he is not a one-dimensional man. He is interested in skiing and sailing. He has been married thrice; first to Patricia Booker; then to Anna Maria Torv; and most recently to Wendy Deng, who was born in China. The first two marriages ended in divorce, but produced his heirs— Elisabeth, thirty-two, Lachlan, twenty-nine, and James, twenty-eight.[6] In May 2000, Elisabeth Murdoch announced that she was leaving the family business to go out on her own. Now that Rupert Murdoch has made it known that he has a low-grade prostate cancer, there is speculation that either Lachlan or James will succeed him as the head of News Corporation, which controls all of the Murdoch properties.

Rupert Murdoch is a controversial figure who claims not to understand why some people are so negative about him. It probably has to do with his conservative politics and the sensational style of some of his publications. But there are many who see him differently. He has, for instance, no problem socializing with the royal family.

But there is no doubt of his credentials as a businessman. He has built one of the first truly global media companies. He owns Britain's largest daily newspaper, the *Sun*; its largest weekly, *News of the World*; its most prestigious daily, the *Times*; and its most prestigious weekly, the *Sunday Times*. Among his other papers are the *New York Post* (America's oldest continuously printed paper, founded by Alexander Hamilton in 1801); and the *Australian*.

He controls the national magazine *TV Guide* in the United States and the *Times Literary Supplement* in Britain. He owns the Los Angeles Dodgers baseball team and the giant international publishing company HarperCollins. He owns Twentieth-Century Fox films.

Perhaps it is in television where he has left his biggest imprint. Since the beginning of radio in the 1920s up until recently there were three radio-television (ABC, CBS, NBC) networks in the United States. No one thought there would ever be another. But Murdoch's Fox network broke that barrier to provide competition for the three other networks. In addition to the Fox network in the United States, News Corporation controls British Sky Broadcasting (BSkyB) in Europe and Star TV in Asia. Murdoch now has the potential of reaching more than two-thirds of the world's people with his global network.

Someone once tried to compare Rupert Murdoch with the American newspaper baron William Randolph Hearst. But Murdoch would have none of it. He said, "Hearst had great gifts . . . but he was a spoiled boy, self-indulgent. I'm more Presbyterian, Calvinistic, more Scottish."[7]

James Wilson

(1742–1798)

T HE UNITED STATES of America is one of the oldest countries in the world, not of course, in the ordinary sense that China is old or that France is old; but one of the oldest in a political sense. China is thousands of years old, but politically; constitutionally, it is only, perhaps, half a century old. France, one of the oldest states in Europe, with kings recorded back to the fifth century, is, constitutionally, only a few decades old. But the Constitution of the United States of America has stood like a rock for more than two centuries and has even survived a civil war, which tested it, as Lincoln said.[1] Each state still gets two senators

James Wilson,
SMITHSONIAN AMERICAN ART MUSEUM,
MUSEUM PURCHASE THROUGH THE CATHERINE
WALDEN MYER FUND.

and representatives based on population. The president and vice president are still elected by an archaic electoral college. The separate powers of the legislative, executive and judicial branches still exist, unchanged. There have been amendments, but the Constitution of the United States continues to stand, a model of political stability. At the convention which wrote this unusually strong document, there was a collection of great men which has seldom, if ever, been matched. But even in this

august company, there was one man who stood out, universally acknowledged as one of the document's principal creators. Some think he was *the*
principal creator, yet most people in the United States, and in his
Scottish homeland, have never heard of him.

James Wilson was born in the village of Carskerdy in Fifeshire. Very
little is known of his early life. He studied at nearby St. Andrews
University from 1757 to 1759. He was, perhaps, at Glasgow from 1759 to
1763, and at Edinburgh from 1763 to 1765. He received no degree from
any of these universities. He began to study accounting, but didn't finish
that either. Soon, he left Scotland for America, arriving in Philadelphia
at the time of the Stamp Act disturbances. In February, 1766, Wilson was
hired as a tutor at the College of Philadelphia (now the University of
Pennsylvania). In May of the same year he was granted an MA degree,
and subsequently went to work in the law office of John Dickinson. He
was admitted to the bar in 1767.[2]

In 1768 Wilson went west to the Pennsylvania frontier, first to
Reading, where he practiced law among the Pennsylvania Dutch. Then
he moved to the Scotch-Irish region near Carlisle. Here he became a
legal phenomenon. By 1774 he was a lawyer in half the cases in
Cumberland County and was practicing in seven other counties as well.
In 1771 he married Rachel Bird, bought a house, livestock, and a slave.
By 1773 he began to borrow money to speculate in land. He was an
imprudent speculator for the rest of his life, and this weakness caused his
downfall.

From 1768 to 1774 he lectured in English Literature at the College of
Philadelphia. But in that year he was elected to the first provincial conference, and later as a delegate to the first Continental Congress. Then
he made an audacious move. While few were prepared, at that time, to go
on record for American independence, Wilson published *Considerations
on the Nature and Extent of the Legislative Authority of the British
Government*. This paper was distributed to members of the congress and
drew the conclusion that the British Parliament "had no authority over
the colonies in any instance."[3]

In 1775 Wilson was elected to the second Continental Congress, and
was assigned to a committee to gain the alliance of the western Indians. He
went to Pittsburgh to do this, but was unsuccessful. On July 2, 1776 Wilson
was one of three of the seven delegates from Pennsylvania to vote for independence, and one of the first delegates to advocate a strong central

government. Then, in 1778, perhaps because he needed money to sustain his land speculations, the frontier lawyer became politically conservative, switched from the Presbyterian to the Episcopal Church (as so very many Scottish-Americans have done), and became a lawyer for Loyalists! These activities brought on the Fort Wilson Affair in 1779. A mob attacked Wilson's home, where some of his loyalist friends and their sympathizers had gathered. Wilson defended his home, and several were killed. Finally the house was rescued by Philadelphia's famous First City Troop.[4]

In June, 1779, Wilson became *avocat général* for the French government in legal cases involving commercial and maritime law. He held this position until 1783. In 1780 he advised Robert Morris in the formation of the Bank of Pennsylvania. Then he was elected to Congress in 1782, and again in 1785.

James Wilson's great moment on the world's stage came at the Constitutional Convention of 1787, which was held in Philadelphia. His principal idea, gradually adopted by his colleagues, was that sovereignty rested with the people, that the people had the final authority, and that the government should be elected by popular vote. Men such as Hamilton and Jefferson didn't really trust the people. That America has a constitution which gives the ultimate power to the people is more due to Wilson than to any other person.[5]

The Constitutional Convention was packed with political talent: Washington, Madison, Hamilton, Franklin, Mason and many others. Jefferson, who was in France at the time, referred to the Convention as "an assembly of demi-Gods."[6] Yet even in this star-studded cast, James Wilson stands out. Lord Bryce describes him as "one of the deepest thinkers and most exact reasoners."[7] William Pierce, a fellow delegate, said that Wilson "draws the attention not by the charm of his eloquence, but by the force of his reasoning."[8] And Wilson spoke more often at the convention than any delegate but one,[9] more often even, than Madison who is sometimes described as the most important of the delegates. Wilson's biggest moment came when the delegates were discussing how many persons would comprise the executive branch. Wilson stunned them all by moving that the executive department should consist of "a single person." Charles C. Pinckney seconded the motion, and a great debate raged for days. Some delegates were afraid that a single executive would lead to a king. Edmund Randolph called the single person executive "the foetus of monarchy." But Wilson countered, "All know that a single Magistrate is not a King." And further, "That Unity in the Executive, instead of being the foetus of Monarchy would be the best safeguard against tyranny." Eventually, Wilson's motion won. He had created the American Presidency.[10]

Wilson was a member of the committee which drafted the Constitution. His draft copy is held by the Historical Society of Pennsylvania. He signed the document and fought hard for its adoption. In 1789 he became the first law professor in America at the College of Philadelphia. President Washington attended the first lecture on December 15. Wilson taught against Blackstone who defined law as the rule of a sovereign superior. Wilson, whom we know argued for the people at the Constitutional Convention, taught that the law needed "the consent of those whose obedience the law requires."[11] This argument was, of course, advanced in the Arbroath Declaration in Wilson's native Scotland, 469 years before (see p. 217).

In 1789 James Wilson was named by President Washington as a justice of the first Supreme Court of the United States. In 1790 he was the dominating force at the Pennsylvania constitutional convention and was its chief drafter. His opponents heckled him as "James de Caledonia," and he was burned in effigy at Carlisle. In 1792 he was deep in land speculation again, and owned—with lots of debt—several hundred thousand acres in Pennsylvania and New York. His wife, with whom he had had six children, had died. In 1793 he married Hannah Gray, who was only nineteen years old. They had a son who died in infancy. In 1797 when the speculative bubble burst, Wilson, a sitting justice of the United States Supreme Court, fled justice to avoid arrest for a debt. He was sheltered at the home of Judge Iredell at Edenton, North Carolina. There was talk of his impeachment from the Supreme Court. "I have been hunted like a wild beast," was Wilson's lament. His health was ruined, and this great, flawed Founding Father died "of a violent nervous fever" at Edenton in 1798.[12]

But James Wilson is the unknown Founding Father, and should be well known. He is one of only six people to have signed both the Declaration of Independence and the United States Constitution. Francis Hopkinson confided to Jefferson, who had missed the Constitutional Convention, that "Wilson exerted himself to the astonishment of all hearers. The powers of Demosthenes and Cicero seemed to be united in this able orator." R.G. McCloskey, a Wilson scholar, says, "It is not too much to say that the ideas of James Wilson more nearly foreshadowed the national future than those of any of his well-remembered contemporaries. No one of them—not Hamilton, or Jefferson, or Madison, or Adams or Marshall—came so close to representing in his views what the United States was to become."[13]

John Marshall

(1755–1835)

FOR THE FIRST decade of its existence, the government of the new United States of America moved around like a traveling show, sitting in eight different temporary capital cities. This proved to be a very difficult burden in trying to build the national government, and by 1800 much remained to be done. But in that year, the federal government settled into its new capital, the town of Washington, and this act gave the Congress and the president a sense of permanence. It was time then to move forward. But no one was really sure what the government's power was, or what its obligations or its limitations were. Was the United States a federation or a nation? The Constitution was a grand experiment, but there was no framework of law which could be agreed upon. The country needed for the Supreme Court to create what the *Encyclopaedia Britannica* calls "a body of coherent, authoritative and disinterested doctrine around which opinion could mass and become effective." Someone had to define the American government. This task fell to one of the greatest jurists in all history, the

John Marshall,

greatest the United States has ever produced.[1]

John Marshall, the fourth chief justice, was born, the eldest of fifteen children, in what is now Midland, Virginia. His father, Thomas Marshall, was a man of some property and a personal friend of George Washington. Thomas Marshall was not, however, a gentleman farmer, but operated on the frontier. His ancestry is quite cloudy. There were plenty of Scots in the area, but whether or not Thomas Marshall had any Scottish ancestry we cannot say. It is different, though, with the maternal side of John Marshall's ancestry, which is quite clear. His mother, Mary Randolph Keith, was the daughter of an immigrant Episcopal minister from Scotland, James Keith. James Keith was very intelligent and had been well educated at Aberdeen. He was, apparently, descended from the historic family who were hereditary Earl Marischals of Scotland. One of the family had been a field marshall in the army of Frederick the Great[2] (see p. 230). James Keith, although a man of the cloth, was a warrior as well. He had been "out" in the rebellion of 1745 fighting for Prince Charles on the losing side. After the catastrophic Battle of Culloden Moor in 1746, James Keith fled to Virginia.[3] His grandson, John Marshall, took a great pride in his Scottish heritage. Throughout his life John Marshall wore an amethyst ring bearing the motto of the Keiths, *Veritas Vincit*.[4]

Thomas Marshall, who married Mary Randolph Keith, and was the father of John Marshall, had been an assistant to George Washington, in surveying the huge estate of Lord Fairfax. He had probably only a few months of formal schooling, but was elected to the Virginia House of Burgesses, then Sheriff of Fauquier County, then Clerk of Dunmore County. When the American Revolution began in 1755 young John Marshall joined his father as a lieutenant in a Virginia regiment. Later he joined the Continental Army, serving under Washington. John Marshall was one of the heroes who stood by the General in the awful winter of 1777–1778 at Valley Forge, Pennsylvania.[5]

After the war, John Marshall took a brief course in law at William and Mary, and was licensed the same year. He returned to Fauquier County and was elected to the Virginia House of Delegates in 1782 and 1784. He established a law practice in Richmond, and in 1783 married Mary (Polly) Ambler. This was the beginning of a long and extremely happy marriage. For the next fifteen years, Marshall gained stature in his state. He was a member of the Virginia convention to ratify or reject the United States Constitution. It was closely contested, and because

Virginia was then the largest and most populous state, a vote in favor was vital. The "pros" included James Madison and Edmund Randolph. The "cons" were led by Patrick Henry and George Mason. Marshall was pro-Constitution, and partly because of his arguments, it was ratified in Virginia.[6]

By then John Marshall had become a power in Virginia, and in 1795 President George Washington offered him the post of attorney general, but Marshall declined it. The next president, John Adams, made Marshall a member of a commission to France to improve relations between the two counties. But the Americans were told that they would get nowhere unless they paid bribes. The commission refused and returned home to one of the earliest American political slogans, "Millions for defense, but not one cent for tribute." As a result of his mission to France, Marshall had become a well-liked public figure throughout the United States. He was offered a seat on the Supreme Court, but declined it. In 1799 he was elected to Congress, and in 1800 President Adams offered him the cabinet post of Secretary of War. Again, he refused. Marshall was then offered the position of secretary of state, then carrying the stature, almost, of assistant president. No sooner had Marshall accepted than Adams went home to Massachusetts, leaving his new secretary of state virtually in charge of the country. Adams lost his bid for re-election and Chief Justice Ellsworth resigned. As one of his last presidential acts, Adams appointed Marshall as Chief Justice of the Supreme Court. He was confirmed by the Senate on January 27, 1801.[7]

John Marshall came to the Court prepared for his role in determining the shape of the government of the United States. Over a thirty-five-year term he and his court developed a consistent block of constitutional law. And, unlike the precedent of England, where each justice rendered an opinion, the Chief Justice, Marshall, pronounced all of the decisions of the United States Supreme Court. This gave the impression of finality, even unanimity to the law. Marshall's language was always elegant and clear, and the Court gained in status as the years went by. The main issue was always the same: whether laws passed by Congress or the state legislatures were constitutional. Nothing explicit in the Constitution gives the Supreme Court the powers to determine these issues. Marshall's court just assumed them.[8]

Marshall's first great case was *Marbury vs. Madison* in 1803. William Marbury had been appointed as a justice of the peace in Washington, and when he wasn't confirmed, he sued the new Secretary of State, James Madison. The court found that the law created by Congress allowing such a suit was unconstitutional, and that the suit must proceed in a lower court. Thus, the Court assumed the capacity of judicial review. Marshall said that no judge could uphold a law which was in conflict with the Constitution.[9]

The next significant case was decided in 1819. In *McCulloch vs. Maryland*, the Court upheld the authority of Congress to create the Bank of the United States. Although the Constitution said nothing about such a bank, the Court decided that, since it had given Congress the power to tax, to borrow and to regulate commerce, that its action was appropriate. Marshall said that if the end was legitimate, and not prohibited by the Constitution, then all laws which "consist with the letter and spirit of the constitution, are constitutional." This decision allowed the government to expand. It was also a positive decision of judicial review, as opposed to the negative decision in *Marbury*.[10]

The next case was *Gibbon vs. Ogden*, which came in 1824. In this case it was decided that a steamboat from New Jersey could navigate in New York waters, despite the fact that New York had given a monopoly for steam navigation to Robert R. Livingston and Robert Fulton (see p. 68). The court held that since the New Jersey steamboat had a federal license it had the right to sail anywhere in the United States, overriding the New York monopoly. This decision was important for making federal law superior to state law, and for an unrestricted interstate commerce.[11] John Marshall was, simply, a genius. During his term the majority was almost always with him. His court made the United States work, and laid the groundwork for its stability, which continues today. Thus we have in the previous essay, James Wilson, a native Scot who had a great deal to do with what the Constitution says, and in this essay we have the grandson of a Scottish minister John Marshall, who had a great deal to say about what the Constitution means, and how the new government would work.

In 1831, at the age of seventy-six, John Marshall had a kidney removed. He survived this, but his beloved wife of almost half a century, Mary, or Polly as she was sometimes called, died in the same year, at Christmas. Marshall never recovered from this loss and his health declined. He died in July 1835 in Philadelphia, where the Constitution had been created half a century before. Hundreds of people went to the wharf, where his body was put on a ship for Richmond. On July 9 the boat, containing many important people including General Winfield Scott landed at Richmond in the late afternoon. Bells were tolling, stores were closed, a three-gun salute was fired and a great procession followed the body.[12] The *Encyclopaedia Britannica* says that "... it is his lasting memorial that when the phrase 'the great chief justice' is used, the reference is unmistakably to John Marshall."[13]

Marshall was also very human, the best kind of person. At Christmastime, on the first anniversary of his wife's death, he broke away from the celebrations and wrote a moving letter. It begins, "This day of joy & festivity ... is to my sad heart the keenest affliction which humanity can sustain."[14] Through tears he writes, movingly, about his lost wife, and how he never, during their entire marriage stopped thanking Heaven for her. He closes with a short poem that he says he has recited to himself a thousand times, that was written by another bereaved husband about his wife. Marshall changes the name to his wife's name, Mary. The poem ends:

> My Mary's worth, my Mary's charms
>   Can never more return.
> What now shall fill these widowed arms?
>   Ah, me! My Mary's urn!!
> Ah, me! Ah, me! My Mary's urn!!![15]

James Macpherson

(1736–1796)

James Macpherson, Unknown artist, after Sir Joshua Reynolds. THE SCOTTISH NATIONAL PORTRAIT GALLERY.

THE POEMS PUBLISHED by James Macpherson, which he claimed were translations from the Gaelic of the third-century poet Ossian, were the most popular in the English language in the eighteenth century, and, with the exception of Byron, in the nineteenth century as well.[1] These poems were important in bringing about the Romantic movement in European literature and in stimulating new interest in Gaelic studies. One poem, *Fingal*, enchanted some of the great minds of Europe for half a century. Goethe admired it and Napoleon carried an illustrated Italian copy with him on all of his campaigns.[2] Among others influenced were Schiller, Coleridge, Scott, Byron, Diderot, Massenet, Schubert, and Mendlesohn.[3] Thomas Jefferson was so moved by the poem that he attempted to study Gaelic and said, "I am not ashamed to own that I think this rude bard of the North the greatest Poet that has ever existed."[4] As to its quality, let the poetry speak for itself. Here is the beginning of Fingal, describing a Norwegian invasion:

Cuchullin sat by Tura's wall; by the tree of the rustling leaf. His spear leaned against the mossy rock. His shield lay by him on the grass. As he thought of mighty Carbar, a hero whom he slew in war; the scout of the ocean came, Moran the son of Fithil! "Rise," said the youth, "Cuchullin rise; I see the ships of Swaran. Cuchullin, many are the foe: many the heroes of the dark-rolling sea."[5]

Later there are these romantic lines:

Bards sing the battle of heroes; or the heaving breast of love. Ullin, Fingal's bard was there; the sweet voice of the hill of Cona. He praised the daughter of snow; and Morven's high-descended chief. The daughter of snow overheard, and left the hall of her secret sigh. She came in all her beauty, like the moon from the cloud of the east. Loveliness was around her as light. Her steps were like the music of songs. She saw the youth and loved him. He was the stolen sigh of her soul. Her blue eye rolled on him in secret: and she blest the chief of Morven.[6]

But a controversy raged for over a century as to whether Macpherson had really found and translated these poems or simply augmented traditional Gaelic poems which he had found with his own work. The argument continues even today.

James Macpherson was born at Ruthven in the far northern parish of Kingussie in Invernessshire. His father, Andrew Macpherson, was a farmer closely related to the chief of the Macphersons, and his mother, Ellen, also belonged to the clan. James Macpherson was educated at the district school in Badenoch. In 1752 to 1755 he studied at Aberdeen University. Later he was a divinity student in Edinburgh. He never received a degree. By 1759 he was a wandering tutor and met the author John Home. Macpherson recited some Gaelic poetry, and Home urged publication. In 1760 Macpherson published *Fragments of Ancient Poetry Collected in the Highlands.* Many people, including the philosopher Adam Ferguson, were enchanted by the poems, and helped to finance two more expeditions by Macpherson to the Gaelic-speaking areas. Macpherson visited Skye, Uist, Benbecula and Mull.[7]

In December, 1761, Macpherson issued *Fingal*, telling his supporters that he had been lucky in finding it. But the controversy was almost as immediate as the acclaim. Most of the people on the island of Britain had a great dislike for Highlanders in general, and Gaelic in specific.[8] From England Samuel Johnson, a noted Scot-hater, led the attack. In Macpherson's defense it should be pointed out that most of his enemies knew not one word of Gaelic. Adam Ferguson, a native Gaelic speaker, supported Macpherson.[9]

Throughout the controversy, Macpherson refused to produce what he said were his Gaelic originals. At one point he did deposit them with his publisher and advertised for subscribers. Since there were none, he withdrew his offer and never again made any attempt to defend himself. Instead, he went into business and made a fortune. Along the way he fathered four illegitimate children,[10] was elected to Parliament and was, for a time, Surveyor-General of the Floridas. When he died he was allowed burial in Westminster Abbey, although it was at his own expense.[11] He left £1000 to publish what he always claimed were his Gaelic originals, which appeared in 1807. Some people became convinced by these, but others have said that they are translations from Macpherson's English to Gaelic.[12]

There is a growing movement to review Macpherson and, perhaps, evaluate him in a different way. Howard Gaskill, in *Ossian Revisited*, says that there is now "the common conviction that his work should be taken seriously. Whatever its status as 'translation,' whatever its intrinsic merits—and I would insist that one may still reasonably argue about both—there can be no doubt that it is historically, extremely important."[13] And Gaskill goes on to point out that the poems were published just after the Highland clans were broken and decimated after the Battle of Culloden in 1746. For a while afterward, even speaking Gaelic was illegal. If he did nothing else, James Macpherson helped to save something beautiful and significant from destruction.

Robert Burns

(1759–1796)

IN HIS SHORT, chaotic life, Robert Burns became one of the most famous and influential poets in the world, and by far the most influential in the history of Scotland. And, it is not too much to say that he was also the most important person responsible for saving the uniqueness of Scottish culture and of the Scottish people. He was born at Alloway in Ayrshire, the son of William Burnes and the former Agnes Broun. His father was a tenant farmer who eventually worked himself to death trying to coax a living from the weak Scottish soil and the country's harsh climate.

Statue of Robert Burns, Central Park, New York City. COLLECTION OF THE AUTHOR.

William Burnes (the poet changed the spelling to Burns upon his first publication) came from a long line of farmers in Kincardineshire in the northeast of the country who had moved south in hope of finding a better life. In this they were disappointed. But William Burnes saw to it that his eldest son received the elements of an education. It was not at all unusual for even the poorest people in Scotland to be literate. In fact, the country probably had the highest literacy rate of any in Europe at that time.

Robert Burns was taught at several schools, but most of his instruction came from his father. He borrowed such books as *Salmon's Geographical Grammar* and a life of the Scottish patriot, William Wallace. Burns read Locke, *The Spectator*, and the Scottish poets Robert Fergusson and Allan Ramsay. He studied French and Latin. The neighbors noted his unusual talent and his father predicted great things for his son, who began to write poetry at an early age. But poverty weighed heavily on the family, which grew to seven children, and by the age of thirteen, Robert Burns was in the fields.[1] And it was as a ploughman that Burns's lifelong interests in women and poetry began to develop. He even saw them as a sort of unity. "There is certainly some connection between Love and Music and Poetry . . . I never had the least thought or inclination of turning Poet till I once got heartily in love, and then rhyme and song were, in a manner, the spontaneous language of my heart."[2]

Burns knew much about love. He fathered more than a dozen children, most of them born out of wedlock. His behavior, while not common in its excess, was part of the immense dichotomy of eighteenth-century Scotland, which had one of the world's most severe and puritanical national churches presiding over one of the world's most libertine populations. Scotland has a long tradition of lewdness. Few people realize that many of Burns's songs and poems are sanitized versions of earlier bawdy songs. An example is the famous *Comin' Thro' the Rye:*[3]

> Gin a body meet a body,   (if)
>   Comin' thro' the rye;
> Gin a body f—k a body,
>   Need a body cry.

Burns also wrote a short piece, which gave his own attitude:[4]

> Say, Puritan, can it be wrong
> To dress plain Truth in witty song:
> What honest Nature says we should do,
> What every Lady does, or would do?

Even among the most prudish of Scots, Burns is revered, and his behavior somehow justified to a sort of respectibility.

As he passed into manhood, his life became more complicated with women, children, his poverty as a farmer and ill health caused by the residue of rheumatic fever. Everything changed in the pivotal year of 1786. He wanted to marry Jean Armour who was pregnant with his twins, but her father forbade it and made her break her promise to him. Angrily, Burns resolved to emigrate to Jamaica, but decided that as a last hope to stay in Scotland, he would try to publish some poetry with a publisher in nearby Kilmarnock. To say that the famous Kilmarnock edition was a success is not nearly enough. The book absolutely stunned the people of Scotland, rich and poor, and Burns became famous, immediately.

It is easy, looking back, to see why, in addition to possessing great talent, Burns was so successful. Scotland had lost its independence in 1707 when it merged its Parliament with that of England. This was still depressing to a proud people, and everyone knew that it was brought about by the Darien fiasco, which bankrupted an already poor country (see pp. 19-21). Scotland's technological success in the Industrial Revolution was making a few people rich, but not enough wealth had yet been created to elevate the ordinary man. The country was very poor. Even worse, Scotland was losing its identity. The Scots language was dying out. The country's authors wrote in standard English. The country's rich history was being negated. Scotland was in danger of losing its heritage to become a shire of England.

But into this darkness came a very good-looking, strongly-built, charismatic, self-educated peasant genius whose poetry awakened something very basic in the Scots. Burns didn't invent Scottish philosophy; it was part of him. "An honest man's the noblest work o' God." "A Man's a man for a' that." These are ideas entrenched deeply in the Scottish psyche. The people saw and heard words that belonged to Scotland alone. Burns didn't write in the old Scots language: he did better. He created a new dialect, easy to understand, combining Scots and English. Burns went from totally unknown to famous in a matter of weeks. It was as if the Scottish people were like a crystal glass, humming with the sympathetic vibrations of his words. He had returned the country's identity to its people. Here are some excerpts:

SCOTCH DRINK

> O thou my muse! Guid auld Scotch drink!
> Whether thro' wimplin worms thou jink,   (winding; frisk)
> Or, richly brown, ream owre the brink,   (cream)
>   In glorious fame,   (foam)
> Inspire me, till I lisp an' wink,
>   To sing thy name!

THE COTTER'S SATURDAY NIGHT

> O Scotia! My dear, my native soil!
> For whom my warmest wish to Heaven is sent!
> Long may thy hardy sons of rustic toil
> Be blest with health, and peace and sweet content!

TO A MOUSE

> Wee, sleekit, cowrin, tim'rous beastie,   (sleek)
> O, what a panic's in thy breastie!
> Thou need na start awa sae hasty
>   Wi' bickering brattle!   (hurrying scamper)
> I wad be laith to rin an' chase thee,   (loth)
>   Wi' murdering pattle!   (plough-staff)

ADDRESS TO A HAGGIS

> Ye Pow'rs, wha mak mankind your care,
> And dish them out their bill o' fare,
> Auld Scotland wants nae skinking ware,   (watery)
>   That jaups in luggies;   (splashes in bowls)
> But, if ye wish her gratefu' prayer,
>   Gie her a Haggis!

But this was not all that Burns did. Scotland had one of the richest traditions of folk music in the world, and that too, was being corrupted, lost and in danger of dying out. Burns began to collect hundreds of tunes from all parts of the country, and wrote lyrics to those which had none, and improved other lyrics. He contributed to the Scots Musical Museum and refused pay for this work, although he remained poor. The old tunes with their new, brilliant lyrics became popular again, and many are still sung today. On New Year's eve, millions of people all over the world sing the Scots words of "Auld Lang Syne," without even knowing that they mean "old long ago." The song ranks with "Happy Birthday" and "For He's a Jolly Good Fellow" as one of the three most often sung songs in the English language.[5] In this role, Robert Burns became one of Britain's greatest songwriters, and one of the best in the world. Burns is Scotland's national poet. He is revered by Scots as is no other person. Throughout the Cold War Burns was even celebrated as a champion of the common man in communist countries such as China and the Soviet Union. But this does not mean he would have been a communist. He would have hated its totalitarian dictators. He is still revered in those countries, and in China, at least, is probably better known than is any other western poet. Burns was for freedom, and sympathized with both the American and French revolutions.

Eventually Burns was given a job in Dumfries collecting taxes and was able to leave hardscrabble farming. But his health had been broken and he died, not even close to completing forty years.

On his birthday each year, Robert Burns is celebrated at thousands of Burns Suppers and Burns Nichts in practically every country of the world. Whisky is poured, the "immortal memory" toasted, haggis served, and Burns's poetry read, even in areas where there are not even any Scots or Scots-descended people in attendance. Hundreds attend at locations as remote from Scotland as Shanghai. As the *Encyclopaedia Britannica* puts it, Burns' birthday is ". . . celebrated annually with rites associated with no other man of letters anywhere in the world . . ."[6]

His poetry is universal, his message straightforward and understood by all. He preaches sympathy, tolerance, honesty, reason, freedom, humility, fairness, and perhaps most of all, brotherhood.

> Then let us pray that come it may
>   (As come it will for a' that)
> That Sense and Worth o'er a' the earth
>   Shall bear the gree an' a' that!   (have the first place)
> For a' that, an' a' that,
>   It's comin' yet for a' that,
> That man to man the world o'er
>   Shall brithers be for a' that.

Walter Scott

(1771–1832)

IN EDINBURGH, SCOTLAND'S capital city, the most prominent monument is not dedicated to a king or a great soldier, but rather to a writer. This demonstrates the power of the Celtic tradition, which Scotland shares with Ireland and Wales, where words and language are of the highest importance. The monument to Sir Walter Scott rises two hundred feet above Princes Street and contains statues of Scott and some of the characters he created. It is a tribute paid by a grateful people to the man who put them on the map. Before Scott, the world knew very little of Scotland. His work, drawing on his immense knowledge of the country's unique history, and embellished by his art, created the very positive image of the country, current to this day throughout the world. Scott had an enormous influence on the literature of the world, because he created the historical novel, so common today. In doing so, he was the first novelist in the English language to become famous, breaking the ground for such as Charles Dickens, Mark Twain and Ernest Hemingway.

Walter Scott, compared with Robert Burns, was born at the opposite, privileged end of Scotland's social spectrum. He was the son of Sir Walter Scott, a solicitor, and his wife Anne Rutherford, the daughter of a professor of medicine at Edinburgh University. Scott was raised in Edinburgh, where he was given a proper Calvinist upbringing. But he spent much of his youth with relatives in the Scottish Borders where his father's family had originated. Between his first and second years he contracted polio, which weakened his constitution and gave him a lifelong limp. It was to try to restore his health that he was sent to the Borders, the wild area near England where smuggling, cattle reiving, and feuding between families such as the Johnstons, Kerrs, and Armstrongs, was a way of life. At Sandyknowe, his grandfather's farm near Kelso, the young Scott became fascinated with the local people and their old tales. Here, also, he heard the old Border ballads.[1]

Scott was a prodigy. Before he was seven years old he had studied history and could quote poetry extensively. In 1778 he went to the high school at Edinburgh, and by age ten had become fluent in reading Latin. In 1783 he was sent to the Old College of Edinburgh. In 1786 he was apprenticed to his father to become a solicitor, and in 1792 he qualified as an advocate. Despite this legal education he spent very little time practicing law. Perhaps that was because, in the winter of 1786–1787 he had met Robert Burns.[2]

At about this time Scott had a passionate love affair which ended with his beloved marrying someone else. It was a tragedy from which he never fully recovered, but he fought on with hard work. In 1797 he married a French woman, Charlotte Charpentier, who was really more of a friend than a woman for whom he had a grand passion. Eventually, they had two girls and two boys.

In 1802 Scott began his formal literary career upon the publication of *The Mistrelsy of the Scottish Border*, a collection of poems which he had edited, and restored as he thought fit. He says, "By such efforts, feeble as they are, I may contribute somewhat to the history of my native country; the peculiar features of whose manners and character are daily melting and dissolving into those of her sister and ally."[3] *Minstrelsy* was enough of a success that Scott began to write in earnest. In 1805 he published *The Lay of the Last Minstrel*, which established him as a poet in his own right. *Marmion* was published in 1808 and *The Lady of the Lake*, his most successful poem, in 1810. Scott was by then Britain's most famous poet, and in 1806 he was appointed clerk of session, a position which paid him £1,300 annually after 1811.[4] He had fame, respect and money. But trouble was ahead.

Scott Monument, Edinburgh. COLLECTION OF THE AUTHOR.

In 1812 the half Scot, Lord Byron, burst on the poetic scene with *Childe Harold's Pilgrimage* and, in an instant, became the most famous British poet, indeed the most famous Briton of the day. Scott chose, seeing Byron's popularity, to switch to prose and became a novelist, publishing one or two novels a year for the next several years. Again, he was extremely successful. *Waverley* (1814) and *Guy Mannering* (1815) were immediate successes as were *Rob Roy* (1818) and *Ivanhoe* (1820). Things were back on track.

But Scott had made two fatal decisions which were to encumber him financially for the rest of his life. The first was to purchase a great deal of land near Melrose, in the Borders, to construct his country mansion, Abbotsford. This beautiful estate, today a major tourist attraction, consumed a great deal of money over many years, which he couldn't afford. Scott was prosperous, not rich. Also, he became involved, financially, in the actual publishing of his works. This was in an era before limited-liability corporations and liberal bankruptcy laws. When the publishers failed, Scott was personally liable for their debts. For the rest of his life, he was forced to write more and more to support Abbotsford, his high living style and the debts of his publishers. These were almost impossible tasks.

In 1822 King George IV made his famous visit to Scotland, and Scott became involved as a sort of ringmaster, orchestrating the events. It was at this time that the image of Scotland—of tartans, kilts and bagpipes—developed. It is ironic that the Hanoverian kings had banned these things after the Battle of Culloden in 1746. But this Hanoverian king participated eagerly, resplendent in a kilt. It makes no difference whether Walter Scott was the creator of these Highland images by which the world knows Scotland today. Most of the people of Scotland had some Highland and Gaelic background, and some sort of tartans, kilts, and bagpipes had existed for a very long time. At any rate, many took up the enthusiasm of Scott and the king, family tartans were created and ordered and the pipes skirled. These images, of course, continue today, honoring an earlier Scotland, and serving to distinguish the Scots from two other nations, which inhabit the southern part of the island of Britain. As the Collins Encylopaedia of Scotland says, Sir Walter ". . . created a consciousness of Scotland which has sustained a sense of nationhood in a country without statehood."[5] The climactic scene of *The Lady of the Lake* illustrates this. It could not belong to any other country. The Lowland noble Fitz-James is touring through a rugged Highland glen, looking for the outlawed Highland chief of Clan Alpine, Roderick Dhu, not realizing that his "guide" is that chief.

Fitz-James: Twice have I sought Clan-Alpine's glen
               In peace; but when I come agen,
               I come with banner, brand and bow,
               As leader seeks his mortal foe.
               For love-lorn swain, in lady's bower,
               Ne'er panted for the appointed hour,
               As I, until before me stand
               This rebel Chieftan and his band!

Roderick: "Have then thy wish!"—he whistled shrill,
               And he was answered from the hill;
               Wild as the scream of the curlew,
               From crag to crag the signal flew.
               Instant, through copse and heath arose
               Bonnets and spears and bended bows;
               On right, on left, above, below,
               Sprung up at once the lurking foe;

               And every tuft of broom gives life
               To plaided warrior armed for strife.
               That whistle garrisoned the glen
               At once with full five hundred men,

               Then fixed his eyes and sable brow
               Full on Fitz-James—"How say'st thou now?
               These are Clan-Alpine's warriors true;
               And, Saxon,—I am Roderick Dhu!"

The hectic pace of his life, with its great financial pressures, finally got to Scott in 1831 when he suffered a paralytic stroke. In order to give him a chance to recover, the government put a frigate at his disposal and Scott cruised the Mediterranean in the winter of 1831–1832. But there were more strokes and he was taken home to his beloved Abbotsford to face his end. The creator of the historical novel and of the popular image of Scotland died there September 21, 1832.

Washington Irving

(1783–1859)

WASHINGTON IRVING WAS not America's greatest author, but it is easy to argue that he was the most influential, simply because he was the country's first great man of letters. Before him others such as Jefferson and Thomas Paine had written, but had not made it a career. Irving's career was writing. It was his vocation. The rest of the things he did were avocations. He showed Americans that it was possible to become very prosperous, just by writing, and taking advantage of the marketplace. This paved the way for all of the others to follow him, many of them Scottish-Americans. To

Washington Irving,

name an even dozen of these: James MacGregor Burns, Erskine Caldwell, Michael Crichton, William Faulkner, John Kenneth Galbraith, David McCullough, John D. MacDonald, Ross Macdonald, Helen MacInnes, Catherine A. MacKinnon, Herman Melville, and Margaret Mitchell. But Irving is much more than just a forerunner. He is credited with the invention of the short story, with the first important American comedy, and with the re-creation and popularization of Santa Claus. More than any of these, he eased the tension between Britons and Americans who had fought an angry war only a few years prior to the publication of his first widely read work. He made everyone laugh, and showed Britain that there was talent and elegance in the new country.

Washington Irving was born in New York City, in the year the British Army left the occupied town. He was named for America's hero warrior, and a few years later, when Washington came to New York to be inaugurated as the first president, Irving's Scottish nanny approached the great man in the street saying, "Please your honor, here's a bairn was named for you." The president placed his hand on the little boy's head and gave him his blessing.[1] Washington Irving's father, William Irving, was born on the island of Shapinsay in the far northern Orkney Islands of Scotland. William Irving was a successful merchant in New York and a Presbyterian deacon and elder. He had emigrated to New York in 1763 with his wife, Sarah Sanders, an English woman. The couple had five sons and three daughters. Washington Irving was the youngest child, and his mother and three sisters lavished affection on him.[2]

Washington Irving displayed an interest in writing at an early age, but at that time writing was considered to be, at best, an avocation, and his Calvinistic father made him study law. Irving never really took this profession seriously. His brother, Peter, a physician, had started a small, short-lived newspaper, *The Morning Chronicle*, and Washington Irving was one of the contributors. Irving was never in robust health—he had signs of tuberculosis—so in the hope that a change would do him good, his family sent him on a grand tour of Europe. In two years he covered France, Italy, Switzerland, the Low Countries, and Great Britain. Back in New York he was admitted to the bar in 1806. He began to practice with his brother John, but didn't much care for it. He represented the Irving family's interests, and because of his contacts and easygoing personality, the Irvings moved up socially in the city.[3]

In 1807, under various pseudonyms, he and his brother William printed *Salmagundi*, which parodied upper-class New Yorkers and politicians. Later, Irving began his first important work with his brother Peter, who dropped out early in the project. Then Irving fell in love with Matilda Hoffman, whom he very much wanted to marry. Her father would not consent since Irving could not support her and insisted that he become a partner in Hoffman's law firm. Reluctantly, Irving agreed and went to work in the firm. Then Matilda died. Irving was overcome with grief, resigned from the partnership, and went to work as an author. He never married. In 1809 he finished and published *History of New York from the Beginning of the World to the End of the Dutch Dynasty*. The work is an exaggerated and humorous history of New York. It is America's first great comic literature.

The "author" of the *History* is one Diedrich Knickerbocker, an old man who, according to personal advertisements placed by Irving in various newspapers prior to the book's publication, disappeared from his room at the Independent Columbian Hotel on Mulberry Street leaving behind this work. This may have been the first public relations "hype" for a book in history. At any rate, it worked. Irving made a lot of money, and in a few weeks, everyone knew who the real author was. But some of the old New York families were not so amused. Listen to "Diedrich Knickerbocker" on some of New York's early governors:

> "The renowned Wouter (or Walter) Van Twiller was descended from a long line of Dutch burgomasters who had successively dozed away their lives and grown fat . . . in Rotterdam. He was exactly five feet six inches in height, and six feet five inches in circumference."
> "Wilhelmus Kleft, who, in 1634, ascended to the gubernatorial chair, was of lofty descent, his father being inspector of windmills in the ancient town of Saardam . . ."

Sir Walter Scott got a copy of the *History*, and filed this report: "I have been employed these few evenings in reading it aloud to Mrs. Scott, and two other ladies who are guests, and our sides have been absolutely sore with laughing."[4] This sentence, alone, demonstrates how Washington Irving had gained status for American letters, and how he had managed to transcend the ill will, which existed between Britain and the United States.

The *History* also changed Christmas in America. December 6 had been celebrated for centuries as the day of Saint Nicholas, the patron saint of the Netherlands. But the dour Dutch Protestants of New York played down the day of *Sinter Claes* (Saint Nicholas in Dutch). In the *History*, Irving portrayed a jolly old Dutch Saint Nicholas who brought "bounteous gifts for the sleeping children of the city on his feast day." This took root immediately, and was boosted a dozen years later when another New

Yorker, Clement Clarke Moore, wrote the poem, *A Visit From St. Nicholas*, better known as *The Night Before Christmas*.[5]

By 1811, Washington Irving was lobbying for the Irving family's hardware importing business with the federal government in Washington, D.C. He served as a noncombatant in the War of 1812. By 1815 he was off on another tour to Europe, but stopped at Liverpool, where he found his brother Peter in financial trouble. He worked for two years trying to help save Peter's business, but it failed. During this period he made many excellent contacts including the great London publisher John Murray (also Scottish). He visited Sir Walter Scott at his home in Scotland, and was charmed by Edinburgh. At this time he published his *Sketch Book*, which included the first three modern short stories ever published. Two of these stories are still read, *Rip Van Winkle* and *The Legend of Sleepy Hollow*. His treatment of Christmas touched off a revival of that holiday in England and influenced Dickens. The *Sketch Book* was published simultaneously (with the help of his brothers) in Britain and the United States, to ward off copyright "pirates."[6]

Irving spent the years 1822–1823 in Germany where he wrote a German "Sketch Book." This was published in 1824 as *Tales of a Traveler*, but was a failure. In 1826 he was in Madrid where he wrote a biography of Columbus. With the prodding of Irving's family, President Van Buren (a New Yorker) named him secretary to the American legation in London. Apparently, he was a good diplomat. In 1832, after seventeen years abroad, he returned to New York as a national hero. He bought a pretty old Dutch-style house, north of the city, overlooking the Hudson River. Sunnyside is visited by thousands of tourists every year. Five of his nieces lived with him there. He was happily in semiretirement. But he was called again to serve, from 1842 to 1846, as minister to Spain.[7]

His final project, completed at Sunnyside just before his death, was a biography of his personal hero. The title is *Life of George Washington*. On November 28, 1859, a frail Washington Irving was watching the sunset from his dining room overlooking the Hudson. He called in his "womankind" to admire the colorful sight. He died that same night. Flags were lowered to half-mast throughout New York City. His funeral was held on a beautiful Indian summer day in the Hudson River Valley. The ghosts of Rip Van Winkle and Ichabod Crane must have watched, as a parade of carriages bearing dignitaries and neighbors buried America's first great man of letters in Sleepy Hollow Cemetery.[8]

George Gordon Byron

(1788–1824)

THE MOST INFLUENTIAL poet of the nineteenth century, and to his supporters the best poet of any century, was Lord Byron. His scandalous lifestyle has been apologized for by many, forgiven by others and even applauded by some. His poetry and his sins made him, in his day, the most famous and infamous Briton in the world. Byron's popularity was so great that the famous Sir Walter Scott switched from writing poetry to writing prose.

George Gordon Byron was the only child of John "Mad Jack" Byron, a dissolute scion of one of England's oldest families, and his second wife, the Scottish heiress Catherine Gordon of Gight. Catherine Gordon gave her son royal genes and descent from the Scottish King James I. To her husband she brought a fortune of £23,000. With diligent squandering, pursuing the high life in France, Mad Jack managed to reduce most of this wealth in a very short time to about £3,000. If it hadn't been for the iron hand of a trustee, that remnant probably would have been lost also. The straitened couple returned to England where the poet was born with a clubfoot which left him with a permanent limp. Byron later compensated by becoming an expert boxer, fencer, horseman, and swimmer. Soon Catherine Gordon Byron took her son to Aberdeen, where she was able to live on the £150 per year afforded by her reduced estate. Mad Jack skipped out to France and died a few years later, possibly a suicide.[1]

In Aberdeen, his mother treated young George Gordon Byron, alternately, with tenderness and violence. So did their Calvinist serving girl who taught him the Bible and initiated him in sex at age nine. He attended grammar school in Aberdeen from 1794 to 1798. In the latter year, at age ten, the boy inherited the title of Lord Byron from his uncle, and moved with his mother to England. The title produced enough money to send the young Lord Byron to Harrow where, despite his handicap, he acquitted himself well in the Eton-Harrow cricket match, making eleven and seven runs. He went on to Trinity College, Cambridge where a glimpse of his later lifestyle appeared when he brought a bear to the college. Byron boxed at Cambridge and lived a riotous life on £500 a year. He also exhibited bisexual tendencies. He received an M.A. in 1808.[2]

In 1806 Byron published his first book of poems, but they were so erotic that the book was recalled. A newer edition was published in 1807. But this early promise was soon struck down by scathing criticism in the most influential magazine of that era, Francis Jeffrey's *Edinburgh Review*. Byron was so upset at the review he is said to have drunk three bottles of claret. In 1809 he began a tour of Europe, reaching Lisbon, Seville, Cadiz, Gibraltar, Malta, Patras, Athens, Smyrna and Constantinople. He fell in love with Greece and spent eighteen months there, before returning to England in July 1811. He took his seat in the House of Lords and made his maiden speech February 27, 1812. But politics was not to be his *metier*. A month later he published *Childe Harold* and became instantly

Sir Walter Scott talking with Lord Byron at the window of John Murray, publishers, London, 1815. JOHN MURRAY.

famous. The Scottish-founded London publishing firm of John Murray paid £600 for the copyright.[3]

From then on Lord Byron pursued his dual careers of poetry and sex, both with great success. Byron was very good looking, of medium height with a fair complexion. He had numerous affairs with women such as Lady Catherine Lamb, Lady Oxford and with his half sister, Augusta Leigh. There were numerous affairs with actresses and prostitutes. In 1815 he contracted what proved to be a disastrous marriage to Annabella Milbanke. Their daughter, Augusta Ada (see p. 49) was born in December 1815. Soon after, Ada was taken by her mother to visit the child's grandparents. In a short time Byron was informed that his family would not return to him. In the wake of the Leigh affair, he signed the separation papers from Annabella and left Britain forever. He traveled to Waterloo and then to Geneva where he enjoyed the company of Shelley. He also renewed his acquaintance with Claire Clairmont, with whom he had an illegitimate daughter, Allegra. In the fall of 1817 he lived in Rome and Venice, having affairs with—by his count—over two hundred women. In 1818 he published Canto IV of *Childe Harold*. His literary reputation was still on the rise and he began his masterpiece, *Don Juan*. In 1819 he met Teresa, Countess of Guiccioli, who had been married for a year and was only twenty years old. She became the most important woman for the rest of his life. But tragedy struck when his daughter Allegra died and then he witnessed the death, by drowning, of his friend Shelley near Livorno. A grisly cremation on the beach followed.[4]

In 1823 Byron, now the most famous Briton in the world, was asked by a committee in London to help Greece in its struggle for independence from Turkey. Byron, of course, loved Greece. "If I am a poet," he had said, "the air of Greece made me one." He had written in *Don Juan*:

> "The Isles of Greece, the Isles of Greece!
>   Where burning Sappho loved and sung,
> Where grew the arts of love and peace,
>   Where Delos rose, and Phoebus sprung!
> Eternal summer gilds them yet,
> But all, except their sun, is set.[5]

The poet accepted the invitation, eagerly. He left Italy for Greece in 1823 with an "army" consisting of nine servants, five horses, two cannon, two helmets with the family crest, medical supplies, money and colorful military uniforms. It was comic opera, of course, but his fame made his "invasion" watched all over the world. Important people began to support the cause. Byron actually made plans to attack the Turkish-held stronghold of Lepanto. But suddenly, he became ill and died. Immediately he became a mythological figure, not only in Greece, but around the world. The death of the handsome young martyr who had fought for the liberty of Greece inspired a great enthusiasm for the country. Within a few years, Greece was independent. A Director General of Cultural Affairs of Greece, George Kournotos, said that Byron's death "inflamed the imagination of European public opinion" and that it "was a very great factor for the progress of Greek liberation." Children in Greece are still named Byron and his name has been used on everything from cigarettes to hotels. Greek students still memorize an ode to him by the Greek poet, Dionysius Solomos.[6]

Byron is probably near his best when writing of love:

> She walks in beauty, like the night
>   Of cloudless climes and starry skies,
> And all that's best of dark and bright
>   Meet in her aspect and her eyes,
> Thus mellowed to that tender light
>   Which heaven to gaudy day denies.[7]

Or of his upper class life:

> The gentlemen got up to shoot,
>   Or hunt: the young, because they liked the sport—
> The first thing boys like after play and fruit;
>   The middle-aged, to make the day more short;
> For *ennui* is a growth of English root
>   Though nameless in our language:—we retort
> The fact for words, and let the French translate
> That awful yawn which sleep can not abate.
>
> The elderly walked through the library,
>   And tumbled books, or criticized the pictures,
> O sauntered through the gardens piteously,

And made upon the hot-house several strictures,
Or rode a nag which trotted not too high,
    Or in the morning papers read their lectures,
Or on the watch their longing eyes would fix,
Longing at sixty for the hour of six.[8]

Lord Byron's body was brought back to Britain, and was refused burial in Westminster Abbey. But a century and a half after his death, a statue of him was placed there.

Thomas Carlyle

(1795–1881)

Thomas Carlyle,
PICTURE COLLECTION, THE BRANCH LIBRARIES,
THE NEW YORK PUBLIC LIBRARY.

ECCLEFECHAN IS A quiet village in Dumfriesshire. Two centuries ago it boasted a weekly swine market, a monthly cattle market and an annual fair. To accommodate the visitors to these events it offered four hotels and twenty-two pubs.[1] The town is famous now as the birthplace of one of the most important British writers of the Victorian age, Thomas Carlyle. The output of the Sage of Ecclefechan was huge and included essays, histories, biographies, translations from French and German and several major works. He wrote on morals, the negative aspects of the machine age, ethics, and religion. Since his time was without radio or television, his works were read eagerly by the public and widely discussed. Carlyle set the tone for the era, which was the height of the British Empire and the Industrial Revolution.

Thomas Carlyle was born in the house built by his master-mason father, James Carlyle. It still stands, now owned by the National Trust for Scotland and maintained as a Mecca for literary pilgrims. Carlyle's mother, Janet Aitken, taught him reading and his father taught him arithmetic.

At age five he went to the village school. In 1805 he was sent to the grammar school at Annan where he learned French, Latin, Greek, Geometry and Algebra. In 1809 he walked the one hundred-odd miles from Ecclefechan to Edinburgh University.[2] His Calvinist father expected him to study for the ministry, but Carlyle wasn't interested. In 1814 he became a teacher at Annan, and in 1816 accepted another position at Kirkcaldy. But teaching didn't suit him, and he returned to Edinburgh to study law for three years. He didn't like the law either, and began an intensive study of German. In 1824 he published a translation of Goethe's *Wilhelm Meister's Apprenticeship*. In 1826 he married the attractive, intelligent Jane Baillie Welsh, who was descended from both John Knox and William Wallace.[3] The couple lived in Edinburgh where Carlyle wrote articles for Francis Jeffrey's *Edinburgh Review*.[4] In 1826 they moved to a farmhouse Jane had inherited at Craigenputtock, near Dumfries. In 1833–1834 Carlyle published in installments *Sartor Resartus* in *Fraser's Magazine*. It was a hodge-podge of fictionalized autobiography, religious experience and German philosophy, and contained an introduction by Ralph Waldo Emerson.[5]

In 1834 Thomas and Jane Carlyle moved to 5 Cheyne Row in London, which quickly became ground zero for the literary establishment there. Everyone wanted to talk with Thomas, and Jane entertained with wit and style. Carlyle wrote a manuscript for his famous *The French Revolution* which John Stuart Mill agreed to read. Unfortunately, Mill's servant used it to light a fire, and Mill was obliged to pay some compensation to Carlyle, as the latter was out of money and needed time to do it all over again. The book was published in 1837 and was both a popular and critical success.[6]

In the 1860s and 1870s Carlyle was "the acknowledged head of English literature." His biography *Frederick the Great* was published in 1858–1865. By that time he had plenty of money and was very generous with it. In 1865 he was elected Rector of Edinburgh University, and made a famous speech at his installation in 1866. But just after that triumphant moment, Jane Carlyle died, and the author never recovered from the loss. In 1874 he was awarded the Prussian Order of Merit. The same year Disraeli offered him the Grand Cross of the Order of the Bath and a pension, but he declined both. On his eightieth birthday he received a letter from Prince Bismarck. He walked daily until he no longer could. When he died the government proposed burial at Westminster Abbey, but Carlyle had requested that he be buried next to his parents at Ecclefechan.[7]

Walt Whitman said: "As a representative author, a literary figure, no man else will bequeath to the future more significant hints of our stormy era, its fierce paradoxes, its din and its struggling parturition periods, than Carlyle."[8] The *Encyclopaedia Britannica* states, "He stirred the conscience of his century; he helped thousands to . . . find new meaning in a monotonous and drab existence; and in an age of prolonged and burdensome physical toil, he inspired thousands with belief in the dignity of their work."[9]

Edgar Allan Poe

(1809–1849)

DGAR ALLAN POE was a unique genius. His writing is like that of no other person. The quantity of literature he produced was limited, but the quality was of the highest class. No one has ever written better short stories, and some of his poems are among the most famous existing. He is recognized as the inventor of the detective story.

Poe suffered through a difficult life made worse by his addiction to alcohol. He was born in Boston, the son of actors. His mother, Elizabeth Arnold, was English. His father, David Poe Jr.

Edgar Allan Poe,
PICTURE COLLECTION, THE BRANCH LIBRARIES,
THE NEW YORK PUBLIC LIBRARY.

was of Scotch-Irish descent. The family's earliest known Scottish ancestor was also David Poe, a Covenanter who left Irvine, in Ayrshire, for Ireland in 1666. It is thought that the name Poe is a corruption of the Scottish Pollock, which has been written and pronounced, variously, as Polk, Pollo, and Pook. David Poe Jr. was the son of David Poe, born in Ireland, and Elizabeth Cairnes, who was also Scotch-Irish. David Poe was, in turn, the son of John Poe and Jane McBride, the daughter of Reverend Robert McBride, a Presbyterian minister. Edgar Allan Poe's father, David Poe Jr. was baptized at the First Presbyterian Church in Baltimore.[1]

Edgar Allan Poe's father deserted his family and is thought to have died in 1810. His mother died in Richmond in 1811, only twenty-four years old. The orphaned boy was taken in, but never adopted, by John Allan, a Scottish merchant in Richmond, whose wife had no children. John Allan gave Poe his middle name but no love. The boy was sent first to a school run by an old Scottish woman and later to another operated by Master William Ewing. In 1815, John Allan took his family to Britain to promote his business. Edgar Allan Poe was sent to his ancestral town of Irvine to study, but when the business purpose of the trip failed, the family returned to Richmond.[2]

In 1826 Poe was sent to the University of Virginia where he excelled in Greek, French, Latin, Spanish, and Italian. He swam six miles against the tide on the James River, a feat about which he maintained a lifetime pride. Allan didn't send him enough money and Poe tried to gamble his way through college. He became $2,000 in debt and was threatened with jail, so he fled to Boston where he published his first professional work, *Tamerlane and Other Poems*. He joined the army, but Allan bought his release. Poe then applied to West Point in 1830. He was accepted, but Allan, who had remarried when his kind wife died, wrote Poe that he was not supporting him any longer. Poe, who had no means of paying for the academy, deliberately missed all his classes and drills until he was dismissed. He then went to New York City where he published a volume of poems in 1831.[3]

By 1835 Poe was in Richmond as editor of the *Southern Literary Messenger*. He became known as an excellent literary critic, and married his cousin, Virginia Clemm, who was only thirteen. His young wife (Sissy) and his mother-in-law (Muddy), who was also his aunt, began traveling with Poe throughout the seaboard. Poe would be hired as a critic, then be fired for drinking, then hired again because of his ability. He and Sissy and Muddy lived, at various times, in Baltimore, Richmond, Philadelphia, New York and Providence. In between, Poe began to develop a literary reputation. In 1839 he published *The Fall of the House of Usher*, which is one of the best tales of horror ever written. In 1841 he authored *The Murders in the Rue Morgue*, which established the detective story. In 1843 he produced one of the most clever of stories, *The Gold Bug*.[4]

In 1845 Poe wrote one of the world's most famous poems, *The Raven*. It is an eerie work which ends:

And the Raven, never flitting, still is sitting, still is sitting
On the pallid bust of Pallas just above my chamber door;

And his eyes have all the seeming of a demon's that is dreaming,
And the lamp-light o'er him streaming throws his shadow on the floor;
And my soul from out that shadow that lies floating on the floor
    Shall be lifted—nevermore!

Two years later Sissy died of tuberculosis, and the despondent Poe wrote, in *Ulalume*:

But Psyche, upliftng her finger,
    Said—"Sadly this star I mistrust—
    Her pallor I strangely mistrust:—
Oh Hasten!—oh, let us not linger!
Oh fly!—let us fly!—for we must."
In terror she spoke, letting sink her
    Wings until they trailed in the dust—
In agony sobbed, letting sink her
    Plumes till they trailed in the dust—
    Till they sorrowfully trailed in the dust.

Poe fell into a rapid decline, and his life became chaotic. In 1848 he was drinking heavily and involved with three different women in three different cities. He tried suicide but didn't take enough poison and recovered. He determined, without conviction, to marry the widowed Elmira Royster, his love of many years previous, in Richmond. On September 27, 1849, he left Richmond for New York. Nothing is known of his movements until he was found on October 3rd in a Baltimore bar, semi-conscious, in rumpled clothes, and delirious. He died four days later of a fatal dose of alcohol.[5]

Edgar Allan Poe was buried in the churchyard of the Westminster Presbyterian Church in Baltimore. A monument was erected there in 1875.[6] But the author of *The Pit and the Pendulum*, *The Tell-tale Heart*, and *The Cask of Amontillado*; and of the poems *Annabel Lee*, *To Helen* and *The Bells*; will never really die. Beaudelaire, translated his works into French and called him America's first great poet. He has been translated into many other languages since then. One of his biographers, Arthur Hobson Quinn, calls him "... the one writer in the English language, who was at once foremost in criticism, supreme in fiction, and in poetry destined to be immortal."[7]

Robert Louis Stevenson

(1850–1894)

ROBERT LOUIS STEVENSON was one of the foremost writers born in Scotland. In addition to having written several novels, still popular a century after his death, he was well known as a poet. Of his masterpiece for children, the Encyclopaedia Britannica says, the poems in A Child's Garden of Verses "represent with extraordinary fidelity an adult's recapturing of the emotions and sensations of childhood: there is nothing quite like them in English literature."[1] Stevenson's health was frail from birth, but his refusal to give in to his handicap, and his determination to enjoy the world to its fullest, makes his life inspirational as a triumph of work and will over adversity.

Robert Lewis Balfour Stevenson (he later changed to the French Louis and dropped the Balfour) was born in Edinburgh, the son of Thomas Stevenson, scion of the family that were Britain's leading lighthouse engineers. His mother, Margaret Isabella Balfour, was the daughter of a minister. Poor health kept the young Stevenson from regular schooling, but he was able to travel with his father to various lighthouse projects.[2] Stevenson's nanny frightened him as a child with wild horror stories, but this may have given him a start on a literary career. At age sixteen, he published *The Pentland Rising* about the Covanenters of Scotland.[3]

In 1867 Stevenson entered Edinburgh University. His poor health made his attendance irregular, but he read a lot in English and French, and devoured Scottish history. During this period he rebelled against his religious parents, living a Bohemian high life in Edinburgh's Old Town, but then returning to the gentility of his parents' home in the New Town. He studied engineering in preparation for entering the family firm and won a silver medal from the Edinburgh Society of Arts for a paper rec-ommending an improved lighthouse apparatus. He spent two years work-ing on lighthouses in the wild north and west of the country, but he was too frail for this career and instead took up the study of law. He was admitted to the bar in 1875 but never practiced. In 1873 friends had con-vinced him to take up writing as a profession.[4]

Soon Stevenson was in London, dressed as a Bohemian. Then he was off to France. In 1876 he met Mrs. Fanny Vandegrift Osbourne, an American woman separated from her husband, living in Paris with her children. Stevenson and Mrs. Osbourne became romantically involved, and she returned to California, where she was divorced. In 1879 Stevenson published *Travels With a Donkey in the Cevennes*, and then fol-lowed Fanny to California, much to the consternation of his parents. Without much money he had to travel by immigrant ship and train, and when he arrived in California, he was gravely ill.[5] He stayed at San Francisco and Monterey for eight months, recovering from pleurisy, malaria and exhaustion. Fanny nursed him back to passable health and they were married in San Francisco by a Presbyterian minister.[6]

In 1880 the couple returned to Edinburgh where Fanny charmed Stevenson's parents. It was easy to see that they were perfect companions. All of Stevenson's best work was done after his marriage. The Stevensons moved to the town of Hyères in France in 1883. There they had a chalet with a garden. Stevenson's health was better, and he realized his first suc-cess with *Treasure Island*. In 1885 he published *A Child's Garden of Verses*, which contains poems such as:

> In winter I get up at night
> And dress by yellow candlelight.
> In summer, quite the other way,
> I have to go to bed by day.

and

> Of speckled eggs the birdie sings
> And nests among the trees;
> The sailor sings of ropes and things
> In ships upon the seas.

Robert Louis and Fanny Stevenson. With their friends, Nan Tok and Nei Takauti, Butaritari, 1889. THE WRITERS' MUSEUM, EDINBURGH.

One night Fanny had to wake Stevenson from a nightmare. He immediately got up and began to write *The Strange Case of Dr. Jekyll and Mr. Hyde*.[7] It was published in 1886 along with *Kidnapped*, and Stevenson was established in the first rank of young writers in English.[8] But his health began to fail again, and he took his mother, wife, and stepson to New York to winter at Lake Saranac in 1887. In 1888 it was on to Hawaii for six months, and in 1889 to Samoa and Sydney. At last the extended family established a permanent home in Samoa on four hundred acres, which they called Vailima, meaning five rivers. The natives called Stevenson *Tusitala*, the teller of tales. His health improved. He was almost six feet tall, and had dark, wide-spaced eyes, and possessed a good voice.[9]

He was enjoying his life, his family and his work, and took an active part in the affairs of the island. In 1894 he began to dictate *Weir of Hermiston* to his stepdaughter, and it was published in 1896. Although he never finished it, it is considered by some to be his masterpiece. Carol P. Shaw says of the work "every sentence summons vivid pictures and strong emotions," and calls the book "the finest work ever produced by a Scottish writer."[10]

Stevenson was stricken with a brain hemorrhage, and died almost immediately. Throughout the night the Samoans labored to hack a path up the mountain where he had asked to be buried. The next day his coffin was covered by a Union Jack procured from a British ship. The Samoans, following their custom of placing woven mats on the grave of a loved one, filed past, laying the mats on the grave, and chanting, *Tofa, Tusitala*, meaning "sleep, teller of tales."[11] The grave contains Stevenson's brave, heartbreaking epitaph which he had prepared:

> Under the wide and starry sky,
> Dig the grave and let me lie.
> Glad did I live and gladly die,
> And I lay me down with a will.
> This be the verse you grave for me:
> "Here lies he where he longed to be;
> Home is the sailor home from the sea,
> And the hunter home from the hill."

Fanny was buried, eventually, next to Stevenson under a large block of concrete, adorned with the carvings of a thistle for Scotland and a hibiscus for Samoa. On each November 13, Stevenson's birthday, the natives would decorate the tomb with flowers and sing a dirge, which went in part:

> Let her majesty, Queen Victoria, be told
> That *Tusitala*, the loving one, has been taken home.
> Refrain, groan and weep, oh my heart in its sorrow!
> Alas! For *Tusitala* who rests in the forest.[12]

William hunter
(1718–1783)

AND

John hunter
(1728–1793)

John Hunter. PICTURE COLLECTION, THE BRANCH LIBRARIES, THE NEW YORK PUBLIC LIBRARY.

URING THE SCOTTISH Enlightenment of the eighteenth century, the arts and sciences flourished, and none more so than medicine. Between 1751 and 1800, 87 percent of all British physicians, as well as many Americans, had been trained in Edinburgh.[1] The country produced a wealth of medical practitioners. Robert Whytt (1714–1766) discovered the sympathetic nervous system. Charles Bell (1774–1842) discovered motor, sensory and motor-sensory nerves. William Cruickshank (1745–1800) discovered the ovum in mammals. William Cullen (1710–1790), the foremost medical teacher of his day, wrote *The Edinburgh Pharmacopoeia* (1776), the most modern at the time. James Lind (1716–1794) conducted what is believed to have been the world's first controlled clinical experiment when he prescribed lime juice to prevent the scourge of scurvy on ships. Gilbert Blane (1749–1834) convinced the navy to use Lind's technique, causing all Englishmen to be called "limeys." James Currie (1756–1805) was the first physician to use the thermometer in clinical medicine.[2]

More influential than any of the above, however, were the Hunter brothers, William and John, who made momentous scientific progress in each of their specialties. In effect, they created two disciplines, and did so on the big stage of London where their work had, probably, a greater effect than it would have had in their native Scotland.

William Hunter was born at Long Calderwood, Lanarkshire, the seventh of ten children born to John Hunter, descended from the Hunters of Hunterston, and Agnes Paul, whose father was the treasurer of the city of Glasgow. William was intended for the church, but when he arrived at Glasgow University at the age of fourteen, the great William Cullen persuaded him to study medicine. In 1741 he went to England where he learned surgery, and in 1748 he was at Leyden and Paris. In 1750 he received his MD at Glasgow, and by 1756 was a licentiate of the Royal College of Physicians in London. William Hunter was a brilliant anatomist, but it is as an obstetrician that he gained fame. He was the man who made obstetrics a science, raising midwifery to a branch of medicine. In 1762 he was appointed Physician Extraordinary to Queen Charlotte, and attended her during three pregnancies. William Hunter taught many students, including his brother John. He spent twenty-five years gathering information for his greatest work, the *Anatomy of the Human Gravid Uterus* (1774) in which he credits John for assistance in dissecting work. In 1767 he was made a Fellow of the Royal Society, and in 1782 was honored by the Academy of Sciences in Paris.[3]

William Hunter was slightly built but strong, possessing a refined face and intelligent eyes. He lived frugally, devoting almost all of his time to work. He was a great collector of ancient coins and medals, rare Greek and Latin books, and anatomical and pathological specimens. He had some 35,000 coins and many weapons brought back by Captain Cook.[4] William Hunter started his own museum in London, and when he died, it became the property of Glasgow University, and is now known as the Hunterian Museum. He left £8,000 for its maintenance.

John Hunter was the last of the ten Hunter children. Unlike his studious brother William, he had little interest in books, preferring sports. In 1748, his twentieth year, he went to London to see William who taught him dissecting. Although he never received a degree, John Hunter became a huge presence on the medical scene of London. He made many significant anatomical discoveries. After serving with the army in Portugal, he returned to London to begin practice as a surgeon in 1763.

His rise was swift and his teachings were significant. (One of his students was Edward Jenner, who conquered smallpox.) His surgery was impressive. He was, for instance, the first to tie an artery "above the seat of a disease in aneurysm."[5] John Hunter was the man who took surgery from the barber's grasp and made it into a science based on sound biological principles. He is still known as the founder of scientific surgery.

John Hunter was of medium height, with light blue eyes and reddish hair, which gradually turned white. He is described as being "patient, blunt, rude and overbearing." He married Anne Home with whom he had four children. Hunter was made a Fellow of the Royal Society in 1767. In 1787 he received the society's Copley Medal. His most important work, published after his death, was *Treatise on the Blood, Inflammation, and Gunshot Wounds*, which helped surgery to progress for decades. After 1788 he was "undisputed head of the surgical profession." As did his brother William, John Hunter founded a museum, which cost him more than £40,000. It is now to be seen at the Royal College of Surgeons. John Hunter died of heart disease and is buried in Westminster Abbey.[6]

The two Hunter brothers became estranged after about 1780, apparently due to arguments as to which brother should be credited for various discoveries. William was more the scholar, while John was more the doer. William taught John, yet it is John who is honored by the Hunterian Orations and the Hunterian Society.[7] Both brothers were great in their own ways, each one the founder of a modern science, and both exemplify the overwhelming dominance of Scotland in the medicine of the eighteenth century. As William Hunter said, "May no English noblemen venture out of the world without a Scottish physician, as I am sure there is none who ventures in."[8]

Ronald Ross

(1857–1932)

Surgeon-Major Ronald Ross (later Sir Ronald)
With his wife and laboratory assistants,
Calcutta, 1898. COURTESY LONDON SCHOOL OF
HYGIENE AND TROPICAL MEDICINE.

MALARIA IS THE world's most deadly disease. Tens of millions have died of it, but uncounted millions have been saved as well, largely because of the work of Sir Ronald Ross, who found the exact cause of the disease. The work of Ross has perhaps prevented more human suffering than that of anyone, save Alexander Fleming (see p. 199).

Sir Ronald Ross was born three days after the start of the Indian Mutiny, in Almora, a hill station of British India very near to Nepal. His father, Captain Campbell Claye Grant Ross, was a soldier of Scottish extraction in the Indian service, who would retire as a brigadier general. His mother, Matilda Elderton, was English.[1] As a boy he spoke English with his parents and Hindustani with the servants.[2]

Ronald Ross was sent to Springhill near Southampton in England for his schooling. He was very happy as a student with particular interest in zoology. His ambition was to be an artist, but he deferred to his father's wishes and studied medicine at St. Bartholomew's Hospital in London.

Upon becoming a physician, young Ross went on several voyages as a ship's surgeon. In his free time he wrote a novel and a play. From 1881 to 1888 he was in the Indian Medical Service, serving at Madras and Moulmein and at Port Blair in the Andaman Islands. This career left him plenty of leisure time, which he used to study French, Italian, and German. He also wrote poems, plays and novels. In 1888 he visited England where he met and married Rosa Bessie Bloxham. In 1894 he was introduced to the Scottish physician Patrick (later Sir Patrick) Manson, and this meeting changed the course of his life. Manson, who had found-ed a medical school that became the University and Medical School of Hong Kong,[3] was convinced that malaria was caused by biting insects. By 1895, Ross was back in India, pursuing malaria with a passion. In 1895 Ross proved that malaria was transmitted to man by mosquitoes. The *Dictionary of National Biography* says that he "was the actual discoverer of the quite unsuspected mechanism of transmission, which once and for all exploded the view, so far universally held, that malaria was contracted from air or water." For the next several years, Ross studied all of the con-ditions of malaria including the life cycle of the malaria parasite. On July 28, 1898, Manson read Ross's results at the Edinburgh meeting of the British Medical Association.[4]

In 1899, Ross retired from the Indian service and became professor of tropical medicine at the University of Liverpool. He was made a fellow of the Royal Society and received its royal medal. In 1902 he received the Nobel Prize, and many wonder why Patrick Manson was not included (he was knighted in 1903). For the next few years, Ross studied methods of killing mosquitoes. In 1910 he published his most important work, *The Prevention of Malaria*. In 1911 he was made a Knight Commander of the Bath. During World War I, Ross was a consultant to the War Office on malaria.[5]

In 1926 Sir Ronald Ross became the first director of the Ross Institute for Tropical Medicine at Putney. He and his wife, with whom he had two daughters, are buried beside each other at Putney Vale Cemetery.[6]

Scots have made many other important contributions to the conquest of disease, as we shall see later in this section. We must mention, also, Alexander Patrick Stewart (1813–1883) who distinguished typhus from typhoid, and Sir William Leishman (1865–1926) who perfected the typhoid vaccine in 1913. David Bruce (1855–1931), an Australian of Scottish descent, discovered the cause of sleeping sickness and Malta fever. When he isolated the bacteria of Malta fever it was renamed brucellosis after him, and the genus of bacteria causing it, Brucella.[7]

Perhaps the most interesting in the group is Carlos Juan Finlay (1833–1915), born in Cuba to a Scottish father and a French mother. Finlay was the first to report that yellow fever might be transmitted by mosquitoes. He expounded this idea in public as early as 1881, even before Manson and Ross were theorizing about the mosquito and malaria. Finlay was, of course, proved right. There is a statue of him in Finlay Square, Havana.[8] In 1908 the French government made Finlay an officer in the *Legion d'Honneur*, its highest honor for a foreigner. In Paris, there is a street named rue du Docteur Finlay.[9]

The motivation for the intense quests of these Scottish scientists was elegantly expressed by Sir Ronald Ross, several years before his discoveries:

> The painful faces ask, can we not cure?
> We answer, No not yet; we seek the laws.
> O God reveal thro' all this thing obscure
> The unseen, small, but million-murdering cause.[10]

John J.R. Macleod
(1876–1935)

AND

Frederick Grant Banting
(1891–1941)

A S A RESULT OF the dis-
covery of insulin treatment
in 1921, millions of people
throughout the world have been
spared the suffering caused by diabetes. Untreated diabetics may
experience boils and other skin
maladies as well as gangrene.
They are more likely to get tuberculosis, heart problems, and ultimately, the dreaded diabetic
coma and death. That the discovery of the use of insulin to treat
diabetes occurred at a laboratory
at the University of Toronto has
never been in question. But for

Sir Frederick Grant Banting, co-discoverer of
Insulin. PICTURE COLLECTION, THE BRANCH
LIBRARIES, THE NEW YORK PUBLIC LIBRARY

more than three-quarters of a century a controversy has raged as to exactly who should be credited with the discovery, usually focusing on which
two men should be credited. The situation was finally sorted out by
Professor Michael Bliss of the University of Toronto.[1] There were actually four men involved, and articles in the *Dictionary of National Biography*
bear this out.

To begin with, the 1923 Nobel Prize for the discovery was awarded to
John J.R. Macleod, a native of Scotland, and Frederick Grant Banting, a

Scottish-Canadian. Since a Nobel award can be shared by no more than three people, the selection of these two men, after reviewing all of the evidence, seems to have been well justified. Macleod was the captain of the team. Banting did the most crucial research.

John James Rickard Macleod was born at Clunie, near Dunkeld, the ancient cathedral town in Perthshire. His father, Robert Macleod, was a minister of the Free Church. His mother was Jane Guthrie McWalter. Young Macleod was educated at Aberdeen grammar school, and at Marischal College, Aberdeen. He received an M.B. and a Ch.B. with honors in 1898. He was granted a "travelling fellowship" and worked for a year at Berlin and Leipzig. In 1901 he won the Mackinnon research studentship of the Royal Society. In 1902 he became lecturer in biochemistry at the London Hospital. In 1903, at age twenty-seven, he married Mary Watson, also Scottish, and accepted an appointment as professor of physiology at Western Reserve University in Cleveland. He stayed there fifteen years, until his appointment as professor of physiology at Toronto in 1918.[2]

Frederick Grant Banting was born on a farm near Alliston, Ontario. His father, William Thompson Banting, was of Northern Irish extraction. His mother, Margaret Grant, was the daughter of Alexander Grant, a millwright, and Sarah Ann Squire, both of whom were of Scottish descent.[3] Young Banting entered the University of Toronto in 1910. In 1912 he began studies at the medical school, receiving his degree in 1916. He was then given a commission and served overseas in World War I. At the Battle of Cambrai in 1918, he was awarded an M.C. for "exceptional bravery."[4] He was wounded and almost lost an arm. In 1920 he was back in Canada, practicing medicine in London, Ontario.

Macleod had been interested in diabetes as early as 1905, and by 1921 had published thirty-seven papers on problems connected with the metabolism of carbohydrates.[5] Then Banting came to see Macleod at Toronto. Macleod was then already a distinguished researcher, whereas Banting was a war hero, having only just begun his career in medicine. Banting told Macleod of his hypothesis for a diabetes treatment, and the older man was interested. He offered Banting the use of a laboratory, animals, and an assistant. As summer approached in 1921, Macleod proposed that another young man, Charles H. Best, join Banting in the project. Then, according to Professor Bliss, Macleod went over procedures and technical problems with his young team, and after having left "fairly explicit instructions," sailed away for a vacation in Scotland. Over the summer, Macleod kept in touch with the laboratory. By the time he returned, on September 21, 1921, Banting and Best had found that injections of their "pancreatic extract into the veins of diabetic dogs sometimes worked spectacularly."[6] Macleod was delighted, but insisted on more work to refine the process and make certain that it worked. He turned the entire laboratory over to the project, and added another young biochemist, J.B. Collip, to the team, over the objections of Banting and Best. At times, the jealous researchers came near to fighting. It was Collip who purified the extract, and early in 1922 one Leonard Thompson was injected with an extract made by Banting and Best, which failed. But a second, using an extract prepared by Collip, succeeded.[7] Thompson, who had been near death, was restored to health. Then, incredibly, Collip forgot how to make the extract! By May, the team had re-learned the process, but the demand for it far exceeded their ability to supply the substance. Accordingly, the University of Toronto made a deal with the American pharmaceutical firm of Eli Lilly, and insulin, the name adopted by Macleod, has been available ever since.

Then the wars over the honors began. Banting and Macleod received the Nobel Prize in 1923, and this seems reasonable, inasmuch as they were the most important participants. Macleod gave half of his reward money to Collip, and Banting gave half of his award money to Best. These bequests seem quite fair, and in the circumstances, very proper.

In 1924 Banting married Marion Robertson, and after having one son they divorced. In 1934, Banting was made KBE, an award which Macleod did not receive. In 1939 Banting married Henrietta Ball. In the same year he became head of the central research committee of the National Research Council of Canada. He was killed during World War II as a bomber taking him to England crashed in Newfoundland. Sir Frederick Grant Banting had also been one of Canada's best amateur painters. He is memorialized by the Banting Institute, The Banting Research Foundation, and the Banting Memorial Lectureship, all at the University of Toronto.[8]

In 1928 Macleod returned to Scotland to his old campus as Regius Professor of Physiology at Aberdeen, a position he held until his death in 1935. He was a cheery man, a gardener and a golfer, well read and interested in the arts. He received honorary degrees from many institutions including Aberdeen, Pennsylvania, Toronto, Western Reserve and Jefferson Medical College. He was made a Fellow of three Royal Societies; of Canada in 1919, of London in 1923 and of Edinburgh in 1932.[9]

Alexander Fleming

(1881–1955)

T HE FRENCH GENIUS Louis Pasteur said that chance favors the prepared mind. But he could not have guessed that a Scottish farm boy would someday become the best-known exponent of his axiom. Sir Alexander Fleming was born at Lochfield, Ayrshire, the son of Hugh and Grace Morton Fleming. His father died young and consequently the financial pressure on the family made the boy's early schooling sketchy. He was sent off to London to live with several brothers, and spent some years there as a clerk.

In 1901 he was enrolled at St.

Professor Alexander Fleming, By Wolf Suschitsky. THE SCOTTISH NATIONAL PORTRAIT GALLERY.

Mary's Hospital Medical School in London. From the very beginning he showed a talent for research, and won many prizes and scholarships. Academics were easy for Fleming, and he had plenty of time for the school's golf, swimming, shooting and theatrical clubs. He received his degree from London University in 1908, with honors in five subjects, and the university's gold medal. After graduation he was accepted at the laboratory of Sir Almroth Wright at St. Mary's in Paddington. Wright had been impressed by Fleming's research skills, and also by his marksmanship on the university rifle team. His career took off immediately and brilliantly. He wrote a paper on acne and devised a simple method of diagnosing syphilis.[1]

Fleming joined the Royal Army Medical Corps in World War I, and was struck by the fact that contemporary antiseptics were not very effective in preventing or combating disease in wounds. But he made significant contributions in the field, including his demonstration that most streptococcal infections occurred *after* the patient was admitted to the hospital. Fleming held the rank of captain and was mentioned in dispatches.[2]

By 1920 he was back at St. Mary's, where he was to remain for the rest of his career, and was appointed as lecturer in bacteriology. He was the first to use antityphoid vaccine on humans and was a pioneer in the use of salvarsan to combat syphilis. He continued to search for antibacterial substances which would not harm humans. In 1921–1922 he found such a substance, lysozyme, which is found in body fluids such as tears, mucous, and saliva. Fleming called it the body's natural antibiotic.[3]

Then, on a summer day in 1928, Pasteur's axiom came into play. Fleming noticed that an airborne mold had landed on a plate containing staphylococcus, that the mold had created a circle around itself, and around the circle the bacteria was being destroyed. The mold was identified as *penicillium notatum* and Fleming named the substance discharged by the mold penicillin. Years before, Fleming had had a similar experience when he discovered lysozyme. He said, "But for that previous experience, it is likely that I would have thrown the plate away as many bacteriologists must have done before . . . then I made dilutions of the fluid to see how strong the inhibiting substance was and found that dilutions of something close to one in one thousand still inhibited the staphylococcus."[4]

Since innumerable types of fungi are in the air, odds of this chance discovery must be calculated at something like one in ten thousand or even higher. But chance favored Alexander Fleming's prepared mind. As he investigated further he was able to say: "The action is very marked on the pyogenic cocci (i.e. staphylococcus, streptococcus, gonococcus, pneumococcus and meningococcus) and the diphtheria group of bacilli. Penicillin is nontoxic to animals in enormous doses."[5] He predicted the use of penicillin against venereal diseases.

But penicillin proved to be difficult to produce in any quantity. And Fleming was not a chemist; he was a bacteriologist. He has been criticized for not making more of an effort to bring his discovery to market. But he had other priorities. In the same year that he made his discovery, 1928, he was made professor of bacteriology at London University. He seemed to have thought it enough to have given the world his discovery. He was willing to wait for the chemists to finish the job. There wasn't much interest until World War II, when Britain was looking for something to save lives on the battlefield. Finally, at Oxford University, two chemists, Howard Florey and Ernst Chain used penicillin, supplied by Fleming, on mice. They were immediately impressed at what the substance could do against certain infections and set about perfecting a manufacturing process which soon gave the world the first "wonder drug."[6]

Sir Alexander Fleming was a brilliant man who shared the Nobel Prize with Florey and Chain in 1945. He might have been deserving of a prize even if he hadn't discovered penicillin. He was showered with honors including: Fellow of the Royal Society (1943), knighted (1944), Fellow of the Royal College of Physicians of London (1944), Fellow of the Royal College of Physicians of Edinburgh (1946), Honorary Fellow of the Royal Society of Edinburgh (1947), and the French Legion of Honor.[7]

But for all this, he was a simple man. He said that the most powerful influences on his life were "tramping the upland moors and learning the Shorter (i.e. Presbyterian) Catechism." He was married twice, the father of one son. He was also a biologist, with a great knowledge of birds, plants and trees. He was short and strongly built, an indefatigable worker, loyal to friends, unaffected by honors, and commanding respect.[8] He had a sense of balance, too, and could say, "If penicillin cures illnesses, sherry resuscitates the dead."[9] Always in modest financial circumstances, he turned away offers of money to keep doing what he wanted to do.

Sir Alexander Fleming died in 1955, and his cremated remains were buried in St. Paul's Cathedral. At his funeral it was said, "by his work he has saved more lives and relieved more suffering than any other living man, perhaps than any man who has ever lived."[10] And he did not make a single penny out of it.

Ian Donald
(1910–1987),

AND

Allan MacLeod Cormack
(1924–1998),

AND

James M.S. hutchison
(1940–)

I N THE LAST several decades of the twentieth century, three revolutionary noninvasive technological developments occurred which
have made it possible to see with great clarity inside the human body.
Significant advances in medicine have resulted from the use of these
machines. Tens of thousands of surgeries and misdiagnoses have been
avoided. Millions of lives have been improved or saved by these inventions, and all three of them have significant Scottish engineering components.

The first of these is ultrasound, the prenatal scanner in use all over the
world, which was developed in Glasgow largely from the work of Dr. Ian
Donald. Donald, the son of John Donald, a Paisley doctor,[1] and Helen
Barrow Wilson, was born in Cornwall, the eldest of two sons and two daugh-
ters. Ian Donald was educated at the Warriston School in Moffat, Scotland
and at Fettes College in Edinburgh. He received his B.A. degree from
Capetown University, and his medical training at St. Thomas Hospital
Medical School in England. During World War II he served in the Royal Air
Force medical branch, was mentioned in dispatches and awarded the MBE
for gallantry. He received his medical degree from St. Thomas in 1947.[2]

In 1952 Donald developed a respirator for the newborn at

Hammersmith Hospital. In 1954 he was appointed to the Regius Chair of Midwifery at Glasgow, a position he held for more than two decades. He became interested in ultrasound as a diagnostic technique when he heard that Americans were experimenting with it. Unfortunately, their patients had to be immersed in water to get any kind of result. Donald knew that ultrasound with oily probes was being used to detect flaws in metal, and in 1955 took some specimens to the nearby Clydeside plant of Babcock and Wilcox, which made metal products. As he had supposed, it was possible to tell the differences between the substances using the company's metal scanner.[3]

Donald went to work to make a usable scanner with T. G. Brown, an engineer with the firm of Kelvin Hughes. At first only a crude prototype could be built, using, as one of its parts, a contraceptive sheath. But by 1958 Donald had made a practical ultrasound scanner and he and Dr. John MacVicar reported the results in the June 1958 issue of *Lancet*. The medical community laughed at the new machine until Donald began to prove that it worked, and Glasgow became a center for manufacturing ultrasound scanners, with demand from all over the world.[4]

Ian Donald was tall and red-haired and had a certain personal magnetism. He was married for fifty years to his wife, Alix ,with whom he had four daughters. He painted watercolor landscapes, and played the piano, with Chopin being his favorite. He had a deep knowledge of the Bible and of English literature, and didn't like abortion. At his death he was trying to invent a device that would warn a woman of the approach of ovulation, and thus make abortion unnecessary. He was the author in 1955 of *Practical Obstetric Problems*, which was a best seller. His motto was, "the art of teaching is the art of sharing enthusiasm." Donald received many honors, including the CBE in 1973.[5]

The CAT scan (sometimes called the CT scan) stands for Computerized Axial Tomography. It is an advanced X-ray technique which permits parts of the body to be scanned and viewed in detailed slices. The machines are very expensive, but work better in certain situations than anything else. The 1979 Nobel Prize in physiology and medicine was awarded to two men for having created the CAT scan. The first, Godfrey Newbold Hounsfield, an Englishman, actually built the first CAT scan. The second, Allan MacLeod Cormack, was the first to theorize the CAT scan and wrote the formulas with which it could be built.

Allan MacLeod Cormack was born in Johannesburg, his parents having left Caithness in the far north of Scotland for South Africa just before World War I.[6] He received a B.Sc. degree in 1944 and a master's degree in 1945 from the University of Capetown. He studied another two years at Cambridge, but never received a doctoral degree. In 1957 he moved to the United States, joining the physics faculty at Tufts University. In 1963 he published the first paper containing the theory and formulas with which a CAT scan could be built. Cormack married the former Barbara Jane Seavey and fathered three children. He became a citizen of the United States in 1966.[7]

The newest of the three viewing technologies is Magnetic Resonance Imaging, or MRI. The patient's entire body can be placed in the machine while a powerful magnetic field is generated, producing extremely clear images. MRI has an advantage over the CAT scan, inasmuch as it does not use X-rays and is completely safe. However, it is extremely expensive, often costing more than $1,000 for a single MRI session. Nevertheless, it is being used more and more. The development of MRI took place, largely, at Aberdeen University in Scotland, and during the long process one man, Dr. James M. S. Hutchison, was in a leading role from start to finish.

In the 1960s, Professor John Mallard brought some equipment to the school, and Dr. Hutchison supervised a student, Roy Gordon, in early experiments in 1970. Gordon left the school, but Hutchison continued working with other students. In 1974 a crude 2–D image was produced— the now famous "mouse" picture. Mallard began to inform the world about what was going on in Aberdeen, and this publicity brought a large research grant from the British Medical Research Council. With the funds, the Aberdeen team and Oxford Instruments designed the first ever whole-body magnet, and a new system was finished in 1978, but the images were not nearly good enough.[8]

By now Hutchison's team included Glyn Johnson and Bill Edelstein, who is now a key man at General Electric in the United States. A paper by Richard Ernst suggested a slightly different technique and the Aberdeen team applied this to their project in 1979 calling it the "Spin Warp" method, and the machine suddenly worked. Originally Hutchison called it "Spin Twist," but his wife, a *Star Trek* fan, insisted on Spin Warp. (Once at a conference, the name Spin Warp was introduced as: "by Jim Hutchison, with apologies to Jim Kirk!")[9]

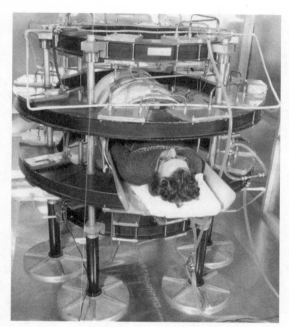

MRI scanner at Aberdeen University, 1978.
DEPARTMENT OF BIO-MEDICAL PHYSICS AND BIO-ENGINEERING, UNIVERSITY OF ABERDEEN.

In August 1980 Hutchison's team scanned their first patient, one who was dying of liver cancer. Their machine clearly showed the difference between the patient's liver and a normal liver, and also showed another cancer tumor on the spine which had not been previously found. This was the world's first clinical whole-body MRI scan. The Aberdeen group had over 1,000 patient referrals in its first two years.[10]

James M.S. Hutchison was born in the village Alyth near Dundee. His father, also James Hutchison, was an insurance agent. His mother, Isabella Strachan, was the daughter of a Presbyterian minister. Hutchison was educated at local schools at Alyth and nearby Blairgowrie. He received a B.Sc. Hons. (1st) Physics in 1962, and a Ph.D. in 1968, both from the University of St. Andrews. He is married to Dr. Margaret Ann Foster Hutchison who is a biologist/physiologist by training but also served on the MRI team. In its early years she was president of the European MRI Society. Dr. James Hutchison currently holds the title Reader, University of Aberdeen, and has won numerous scientific awards. He is the co-inventor on seven patents currently held by the British Technology Group. He says, "The royalties from these patents have attracted substantial funds to the University of Aberdeen, as well as the inventors."[11]

William Wallace

(C. 1270–1305)

PERHAPS ONLY ONCE in the history of a nation will someone seize the stage and with a single act change the course of that nation irrevocably. Such a man was William Wallace, the son of Malcolm Wallace, a small landholder at Elderslie, near Paisley; vassal of James, fifth Steward of Scotland.[1] The name Wallace or Waleys or Walensis means, usefully, "Welshman" and is probably an indication of descent from the Stathclyde Britons of southwest Scotland. His father's name, Malcolm and his mother's maiden name, Crawford, however, indicate likely descent from Gaelic and Anglian ancestors as well. This would be typical at that time when the diverse peoples of the north were blending into what would become the Scottish nation.

There is almost nothing known of William Wallace until the fateful year of 1297. In that year the English King Edward I, who styled himself The Hammer of the Scots, was occupying Scotland using as an excuse the country's unsettled royal succession. The King of Scots, John de Balliol, was held prisoner in the Tower of London. Most of the Scottish nobility, many of who were of largely Norman descent, deferred to Edward's rule. Many held lands on both sides of the border and had given homage to the foreign king. But the ordinary people of the country hated their English rulers and were beginning to rebel. They found their leader and champion in May when William Wallace and a small band burned the town of Lanark and killed the English sheriff, William Hazelrig.

This single act shocked the people of both Scotland and England. To the English, Wallace was simply a savage to be hunted down with vengeance. To the Scots, he was a great, noble hero. What his motive was is not certain, although tradition says that the sheriff had killed Wallace's love, Marion Bradfute.[2] But it is certain that in one stroke, Wallace had galvanized the people of Scotland, and he had also created a force which still exists today for good and evil—nationalism. According to Winston Churchill, Wallace and his Scots were the first—a cen-

The letter of 1297 to Lübeck.
COLLECTION OF THE AUTHOR.

tury before Joan of Arc—to say to a conqueror, "We are not the same people as you are and we will not live under your rule."

The Scottish War of Independence had now begun. Robert Bruce, later King Robert I, raised an army but surrendered at Irvine to Sir Henry de Percy and Sir Robert de Clifford.[3] But recruits were drawn to Wallace and he fought and won often in the name of the imprisoned King John. In the north, Andrew de Moray raised a Gaelic army and joined with Wallace. Together they came to control most of the north. Then came the news that the enraged King Edward was sending an army north to re-conquer Scotland.

Wallace and Moray prepared for battle below Stirling Castle. On the morning of September 11, 1297 the English, under John de Warenne, Earl of Surrey, offered the outnumbered Scots a surrender, but Wallace answered, "We have come not for peace, but ready to fight them to their beards."[4] Then the English began to cross the narrow wooden bridge across the Forth. This was a terrible mistake and the Scots made use of it. Wallace told his men not to move until he gave the order. Cleverly, he allowed about half of the English force, which he thought he could handle, to cross the bridge. When this was completed the Scots fell upon their enemy in a wild frenzy, which stunned the English who could not send any more troops across the bridge, clogged, as it was, with English bodies. Almost all of the English who had advanced were killed or drowned in the river, about 5,000 in all. The remainder of the English army fled, pursued by the Scots, back to England.

Wallace had basically freed the country. He and Andrew de Moray felt so confidant that they wrote the famous letter of October 11, 1297 to the north German towns of Hamburg and Lübeck. This document, which asked for the resumption of courtesies for Scottish merchants in Germany, advised that German ships were now, once again, safe in Scottish ports "because the Kingdom of Scotland has, thanks be to God, by war been recovered from the power of the English."[5] Soon after, de Moray died of wounds he had sustained at Stirling Bridge.

To consolidate his victory, Wallace punished the north of England with several weeks of brutal violence. When he returned to Scotland in December, he was elected or had himself elected Guardian of Scotland and was somehow knighted. He seems to have ruled well at the head of an army which was disciplined by the threat of the death penalty. But many of the Scottish nobles, especially those holding lands in England, were still not committed to his cause.

In the spring of 1298, Surrey returned, relieving the castles of Roxburgh and Berwick which were still in English hands. In July, the Hammer himself crossed the Tweed and with a massive army moved towards Stirling. Wallace chose to situate himself near Falkirk. The Scots, outnumbered about three to one, fought valiantly but succumbed in the end to the deadly English archers. At least 10,000 Scots were killed and Wallace's reputation as a military leader was tarnished. He retreated to the north with his survivors and resigned the guardianship in favor of Robert Bruce and John Comyn, who had the best claims to the throne.

For the next several years there is not much information concerning Wallace. It appears that he was on the continent at the French court of Philip the Fair asking for help against the English in 1299. He may have gone to Rome on a similar mission.

But the war continued and the English were winning back what they had lost. Bruce submitted to Edward in 1302 and in 1304 Stirling fell. Wallace was pursued by the English and their Scottish noble allies. With the country largely in English hands again, it was inevitable that he would be caught. Tradition tells us that he was betrayed by Sir John de Menteith, who gave a signal to the English by turning over a bannock on a table when the patriot entered an inn. Whatever the accuracy of that, Wallace was arrested August 5, 1305.[6]

The Scottish loyalist was immediately taken to London where his case became one of the most famous in English criminal history. To the English, Wallace was the most barbarous, the most wicked man on the entire island—an animal to be dealt with as if he were the devil himself.

The importance of the trial is shown in part, by the fact that it was held in Westminster Hall, one of the most beautiful buildings in the world. It is a space that has been reserved for ultra-important events such as the trials of Sir Thomas More, Charles I, and Guy Fawkes. In an ironic twist, it was two Scots, Walter Elliot and C.P. MacDuell who, by their quick fire-fighting actions, saved the Hall from destruction by German incendiary bombs on the night of May 11, 1941.[7]

Wallace's trial was conducted on August 23, 1305. The charges of treason were vague, except for the killing of Hazelrig. Wallace argued that he could not be guilty of treason since he had never sworn allegiance to Edward. But, of course, the verdict of guilty was a certainty. "You shall be . . . hanged and drawn, and as an outlaw beheaded."[8] Wallace was taken the same day to receive this gory punishment to Smithfield, which is, of course, the London meat market.[9] There his innards were drawn from his body and burned before his eyes. He was then beheaded and quartered with the parts sent to four different cities, usually given as Newcastle, Berwick, Stirling and Perth, as a warning to others not to trifle with King Edward I.[10]

But Edward's punishment had the opposite effect on the Scots who now became united against the tyranny of England. Only months after the torment of Wallace, Robert Bruce was crowned at Scone as King Robert I. Bruce resurrected the Scottish cause in its darkest hour. The War of Independence was on again just when Edward thought it to be over, with him the victor. The ailing English king raged against the Scots again, determined to subjugate them. He mounted another campaign, but on the way to invade Scotland he died on May 7, 1307. The Hammer of the Scots had succumbed, farther than ever from subduing Scotland only two years after he thought he had won it.

Robert Bruce was the most influential of Scots because he rallied the country in what seemed to be an impossibly uphill battle, and established its independence. Without The Bruce, there would be no Scotland and no Scottish people, and the world, deprived of the achievements of the Scots, would be the poorer.

But without the first nationalist, William Wallace, who started the War of Independence, there would have been no war for Bruce to win.

Robert Bruce

(1274–1329)

K ING ROBERT I, known as The Bruce, was without a doubt, the most influential person in the history of Scotland. Without him, there would be, almost certainly, no Scotland and no Scottish people. His leadership defended Scotland as an independent country, and he encouraged his disparate and multiethnic subjects to become the Scottish nation. Without The Bruce, it is likely that there would be today, where Scotland now is, a northern county of England called something like Scotshire, and the people living there would think of themselves as English—a little different, perhaps from their fellow Englishmen farther south, but still English. Without King Robert, there would have been no Scottish culture to produce the extraordinary men and women we are discussing here. Without the Bruce, the world would not have benefited from the unusual and significant contributions of the Scots.

Robert de Bruce, as he was called in Norman French, was a member of one of the world's oldest and most distinguished families. His ancestor, also Robert, was said to have been a supporter of *Guillaume le Conquerant,* William the Conqueror, who invaded England in 1066 to claim what he believed was his right to the crown of that kingdom. The Bruces of Normandy lived at the time in a town presently called Brix between Valognes and Cherbourg on the Cotentin peninsula, which juts out into the English Channel. The ruins of the eleventh-century castle of Adam de Bruce, called Chateau d'Adam, are still visible. Whether the Bruces named Brix after themselves or took the name from the town is not clear or certain. Whether they are descended from Brussi, a Scandinavian king of Orkney, who came with other Northmen to found Normandy cannot be proved. Others say that the Bruces originated in Flanders with the name of de Bruges.

At any rate, this first Robert Bruce was given lands at Cleveland in Northern England by the Conqueror. His son, also Robert, was given lands by his friend, the Scottish King David I, at Annandale in southern Scotland. Thus was created a dual loyalty which was not at all uncommon in the Norman world. Most of one's peers were speaking French; most of one's peers were Norman; being Scottish or English didn't really matter that much. But it began to matter a lot after William Wallace—the subject of the previous essay—created Nationalism, deciding that he was a Scot, that Scots were not Englishmen, and that English soldiers should not be occupying his country. It mattered to the Bruces especially because they had married into the old Celtic aristocracy of Scotland, could prove their necessary descent from the Scottish royalty all the way back to Ireland, and, due to a series of royal deaths, had a very good claim to the throne.

The Bruces vacillated between loyalty to the English and Scottish kings as did many Normans when Wallace and his patriots began the Scottish War of Independence. The eighth Robert Bruce, who was to become king, was no exception. He appears, at first to have fought with Wallace, but later went over to the English King Edward I, who styled himself The Hammer of the Scots. But all this confusion of loyalty resolved itself in 1306 in a stunning fashion. Bruce invited his chief rival to the throne, John Comyn or Cumming, to a meeting at Greyfriars Church in the town of Dumfries. It may be that Bruce had knowledge that Comyn was plotting against him. At any rate, the two powerful nobles met at the high altar, words were exchanged, knives were drawn, and Bruce stabbed Comyn. Tradition says that he told one of his supporters, Roger Kirkpatrick, "I doubt that I have slain the Red Comyn." Whereupon Kirpatrick answered, "then I'll mak sikker" (I'll make sure) and went back to the church to finish the job.

In this decisive moment the history of Scotland was changed forever. Bruce had risked everything on this act. He knew that he must now become King of Scots or die. (There would be no more vacillation. What follows here, makes the last scene of the film *Braveheart* ludicrous.) Immediately he and his small band captured Dumfries castle which had been occupied by the English. Scots, hearing of this success, began to join his cause. He had a strong ally in the Scottish church, which like

Scotland, was resisting rule from England. Bruce, knowing this, next went to see the Bishop Wishart of Glasgow who forgave him his violent and sacrilegious act and promised him the support of the clergy.[1]

On March 25, 1306, Bruce was crowned King of Scots at Scone, the traditional seat of authority, with all of the pomp which could be mustered at the time. The golden circlet which was put on his head is probably the base of the Scottish crown on view in Edinburgh today. Bruce was not, however, crowned on the Stone of Destiny. The coronation stone had been stolen by King Edward in 1296. All of the Kings of England, and later Great Britain, have been crowned upon the stone in Westminster Abbey since that date. It was not returned to Scotland until the last decade.

This, however, was only a beginning. Bruce still faced formidable odds, not the least of which was an outraged and powerful King Edward who, upon hearing the bad news from the north, vowed retribution and began mobilizing troops. Also, many of the Scottish nobles, including supporters of the Comyns, were hostile to Bruce. The Pope, at Edward's request, excommunicated the new king. Nonetheless, Robert kept the support of the Scottish church. He was able to raise a small army and proceeded to move against the English garrison at Perth. But he was badly beaten near Methven, a few miles away from Perth in June 1306, and soon after at Dalry near Tyndrum. Nigel Bruce, the King's brother, was captured, dragged through the streets of Berwick, hanged and beheaded. Bruce's wife, Queen Elizabeth, was held hostage for the next eight years. His sister Mary was put in a cage hanging from the walls of Roxburgh castle. She was to stay there in humiliation for four years. The King's daughter, Marjorie, was taken to the Tower of London.[2]

Bruce had no choice but to retreat in order to regroup, and may have made his way to Rathlin, a tiny island off the northern coast of Ireland. King Edward sent a party after him but by the time they arrived, Bruce was already back on the mainland. But he had few supporters save for his brother Edward Bruce. At one point he became desperate, hiding by himself in a cave, grieving over the injuries to his family and at the overwhelming forces arrayed against him. The traditional story is that he saw a spider trying to establish the first thread of a new web. The spider had tried six times and had failed six times. But on the seventh try it succeeded, and Bruce reasoned that if a little insect could overcome failure, he could too.

Thus Bruce began to fight again. Now he became the genius, perhaps the inventor of guerrilla warfare—hiding in the hills with only a few men; moving his base of operations to a new place daily; taking castles by surprise and at night; thrusting and quickly retreating; harrying the enemy and avoiding the pitched battles which were so common in the Middle Ages; and all the time gathering supporters. It would be hard to believe that Fidel Castro had not studied the tactics of The Bruce when he took over Cuba in 1959.

In the next several years Robert won many battles and added much support. One of his best men was Sir James Douglas (The Black Douglas) who captured his own Castle Douglas in 1307, killing most of its English occupants. He then burned the castle with their bodies still inside. This great roast is known, cheerfully, as the Douglas Larder. Another crucial fighter was King Robert's blood nephew, Thomas Randolph, whom he made Earl of Moray and who is claimed to be an ancestor of Thomas Jefferson. Randolph captured Edinburgh Castle, thought to have been an impossible task. Edward Bruce subdued the southwest and the King himself took Perth. Other prominent nobles supporting The Bruce included Gilbert de la Haye, Angus Macdonald of the Isles, and Robert Boyd.

As the war progressed to the year 1312, Bruce found himself in control of the greater part of the country. Heroic as his efforts and those of his associates had been, it must be said that they had been helped by the death of their arch enemy, the English King Edward the I. His son, Edward II was, compared to his father, relatively inept. In July, Bruce and his Parliament decided on an invasion of England. The Scottish army ravaged the north of England pillaging and burning as it drove. When it reached Durham the terrified populace offered £2,000 for a ten-month truce, which was accepted by Bruce. Similar tribute was received in other English towns and counties. The following year, 1313, the Scots were so feared, they merely had to send messengers to collect the tribute.[3]

It was also in the summer of 1313 that Edward Bruce made the great mistake, which led, paradoxically, to the Scots' decisive victory over England. Almost all of Scotland was under Scottish control. But the most important stronghold, Stirling Castle, was still held by the English. Stirling is on high ground at the narrow waist of the country, only a few miles from the Firth of Clyde on the west and the Firth of Forth on the east. With easy access to both the Atlantic Ocean and the North Sea, Stirling is the strategic heart of Scotland. Edward Bruce besieged the castle, impatiently waiting for its supplies to run out. The English commander, Sir Philip Mowbray, realized that he could not possibly hold out much longer and would have to surrender the castle. So, with nothing to lose, he made a chivalrous offer to Edward: he would surrender Stirling if it could not be relieved by Midsummer Day 1314. In the words of Barbour:

> That gif, at midsummer tyme ane yeir
> To cum, it war nocht with batall
> Reskewit, than withouten faill,
> He suld the castell yeld quytly,[4]

When news of the impetuous Edward's acceptance of this bargain reached King Robert, he realized that by the customs of chivalry he would have to honor his brother's pledge, and that all that he had gained, he now stood to lose. The English would, almost certainly, mount a great attack upon Stirling. And when they did, the highly successful Scottish guerrilla army would have to fight a pitched battle against a greatly superior English force, something which Robert had avoided for years. All of Scotland knew that a climactic battle would be fought at long odds against a powerful enemy. The Scots now rallied to their king and volunteers poured into central Scotland from all parts of the country. By June 1314, word was received that the army of King Edward II was in Scotland taking on provisions. By June 21 it had reached Edinburgh.

The last act of the drama began to play on June 23, 1314 as the largest English army ever to take the field up to that time advanced on Stirling along the old Roman road from Falkirk. Imagine what a sight it was! A mile or more of men, animals and wagons; perhaps 20,000 men in arms; the sunlight dancing on the armor; the colorful coats-of-arms of the great families of England; horses' heads bobbing above the cloud of dust which rose high in the summer sky. Even the bravest of Scots ready to defend their position must have had a thought or two of failure and death. But the Scots, outnumbered probably about three or four to one, had some advantages, not least the motivating advantage of people defending their homeland. Also, their king had used his military genius to augment his forces with that of the land. The Scots were arrayed on high ground, and to get at them the English would have to cross the Bannock Burn. Also, the Scots had dug camouflaged pits with spikes on the field in front of them. To the north was a marsh.

On the afternoon of June 23, there was a skirmish between the armies.

In full view of the Scots, the English knight Henry de Bohun raced across the burn on his horse in search of glory. What he found, instead, was the Scottish king, astride a pony holding a battleaxe, ready to meet him. Bohun charged King Robert who waited until the last second to move his pony out of the way, then raised his battleaxe and clove the head of de Bohun in two. Then a detachment of English cavalry under Sir Henry de Beaumont and Sir Robert de Clifford moved towards the position of Thomas Randolph, Earl of Moray, whose spearmen formed a schiltron. Spears pointed ahead, they advanced on the English knights, winning after a harsh fight. These two small battles boosted the morale of the Scots and discouraged the English.

On the next day, June 24, 1314, one of the pivotal battles in world history was fought, although few realize it. If the Scots had lost, there would have been, almost certainly, no Scotland and the world would not have had the benefit of all of the vast achievements of the Scottish people. It was Midsummer Day and the sun rose early, a little before four o'clock in the morning. The Scottish forces were drawn up under commanders whose names resonate throughout the history of Scotland: Sir Gilbert Hay, Lord High Constable; Sir Walter Stewart, Lord High Steward; the king's brother Sir Edward Bruce; the king's nephew Thomas Randolph, Earl of Moray; Sir Robert Keith, Earl Marshall; and Sir James Douglas.[5] The battle began as the English, under the Earl of Gloucester, attacked the position of Edward Bruce who was able to hold as Gloucester was killed. Then Douglas and Randolph moved in line with Edward Bruce and all three Scottish divisions advanced against the English cavalry with great effect. The English king then called upon his archers but they were routed and fled before the light cavalry of Robert Keith. At this, King Robert, seeing the victory in sight, called up his reserves and added their pressure against the English who began to be driven back. What happened next is not clear, but another group of Scots emerged on the field running down from the high ground. They are generally said to have been camp followers, but some think they may have been a remnant of the Knights Templar who had fled France seven years before. Whoever they were, they apparently frightened the English who retreated in disarray. When King Edward II left the field with the English royal standard, demoralizing the English further, the battle became a rout, and although it would still be years before the independence of Scotland was recognized, there was never another credible attempt by England to prove otherwise.

King Robert would reign another fifteen years after the Battle of Bannockburn. The warrior king turned himself to consolidating his kingdom. One of his first acts was to tell his nobles who held lands in England to renounce them or leave Scotland, surrendering their lands in the north. Hoping to be recognized as an independent king by the defeated Edward, he made a gesture towards reconciliation, returning the Great Seal of England, which had been taken on the battlefield. King Edward ignored the gesture. Robert then decided to apply more pressure and began raids against England under the familiar commanders Randolph and Douglas.[6] He sent his brother to Ireland to fight for Irish independence, and the Irish, realizing that the Bruces were of royal Irish descent and might be able to free them from the English yoke, crowned Edward Bruce High King of Ireland, on May 2, 1316. This expedition ended badly, with Edward Bruce being killed at a battle near Dundalk in 1318. But his career as King of Ireland had lasting consequences for the English, who never again regained control of all of Ireland, as well as for the Irish who never afterward lost their independent identity.

Perhaps King Robert's most important work was in uniting the diverse elements of the people of Scotland, who during his reign were speaking several languages including French, English (Scots), Flemish, Norse, Gaelic, and Welsh (or something like it, in the Southwest). Even though the mixing of these disparate peoples had begun long before (the King himself was of mixed ancestry) there was a tendency for parts of the population to think of themselves as distinct from the rest. As late as 1199 a charter had been addressed to "Francis et Englis et Flamingis et Scotis." But continued intermarriage and the united effort to win the war had begun to make these distinctions disappear. King Robert's intelligent rule made them fade more, and as the people mixed, the Scottish nation was created. By 1320 all of the men who signed the Arbroath Declaration were claiming to be (and most probably were) of a common ancestry, descended from the ancient aristocracies of Ireland and Scotland.

The Arbroath Declaration of Independence was the crown jewel of King Robert's reign, and appears to have had a marked effect on the American Revolution, four and a half centuries later. Six years after their victory at Bannockburn, the Scots were no closer to being recognized as separate from England. The forces of Bruce were ravaging northern England and Edward II was besieging Berwick. In desperation, the Scots turned to what was then the international court of appeals—the Vatican.

On April 6, 1320, they sent to the Pope what is one of the most advanced political documents of the Middle Ages. The Declaration, written in Latin by the Abbot of Arbroath Abbey, Bernard de Linton, Chancellor of Scotland, was signed by thirty-nine nobles representing all of Scotland. Their names show the diverse origins of the Scots—Norman, Gaelic, English and Norse, yet all are claiming a common Scottish ancestry, different from that of the English people.

This is the first declaration of one country's independence from another, and it is eloquent in several respects. It asks the Pope to tell the English to leave Scotland to its people, that the English have been harassing them and that the Scots want nothing more than the remote land which they possess. It warns the Pope that "For so long as a hundred remain alive, we never will in any degree be subject to the domination of the English." Four and a half centuries later the Scottish-American radical, Patrick Henry, would spark the American Revolution with the words, "I know not what course others may take, but as for me, give me liberty or give me death!" The Declaration tells the Pope that King Robert is ruling "with the due consent of us all" and insists that "if he were to desist from what he has begun . . . we would immediately expel him as our enemy and the subverter of his own rights and ours, and make another our king." In the medieval world of authoritarian governments, this is highly advanced political philosophy. The year 1320 is 456 years before 1776. Yet Jefferson wrote in the American Declaration of Independence these words: "Governments are instituted among Men, deriving their just powers from the consent of the governed—That when any Form of Government becomes destructive of these ends, it is the Right of the People to alter or to abolish it, and to institute new Government."

There are many other similarities between the Arbroath Declaration and the American Declaration of Independence:[7]

DECLARATION OF INDEPENDENCE Philadelphia July 4, 1776	ARBROATH DECLARATION Arbroath, Scotland April 6, 1320
All men are created equal	nor distinction of Jew or Greek, Scots or English

We mutually pledge our lives	we will maintain even to the death
The history of the present king of Great Britain is a history of repeated injuries death Desolations	The mighty king of the English . . . perpetrated . . . injuries slaughters deeds of violence
He has . . . sent hither swarms of officers to harass our people	. . . in most unfreindlywise harassed our kingdom
A prince whose character is marked by every act which may define a tyrant	. . . this prince perpetrated . . . these evils innumerable
Merciless Indian savages	the most savage tribes
In the most barbarous Ages	people however barbarous
He has plundered our Seas . . . burnt our towns	plunderings, burnings
an undistinguished Destruction of all ages, sexes and conditions	sparing no age or sex
appealing to the Supreme Judge of the World for the Rectitude of our Intentions	to Him, as the Supreme King and Judge we commit the defence of our cause
With a firm reliance on the Protection of Divine Providence	Divine Providence firmly trusting that He will bring our enemies to nought

At the convention in Philadelphia in 1776, which met to write and adopt the Declaration of Independence, there were two native Scots and numerous Americans of Scottish and Scotch-Irish descent who might have been familiar with the Arbroath Declaration. In addition, many of the delegates had been educated in Scotland or in America by Scottish tutors. It appears that the older Scottish document served as an inspiration for the newer American one. Curiously, each Declaration has a signatory named Ross. And Thomas Randolph, who signed at Arbroath, is the alleged ancestor of Thomas Jefferson.[8]

Unfortunately, Scotland's petition to the Pope was not immediately effective. Edward II invaded Scotland and Bruce continued to expel him and to ravish the northern shires of England. At last, in 1324 the Pope told King Edward II that he would address Robert as "King," almost recognizing the independence of Scotland, but still, the English would not give

The Declaration of Arbroath, 1320. The National Archives of Scotland, SP13/7. REPRODUCED WITH THE PERMISSION OF THE KEEPER OF THE RECORDS OF SCOTLAND.

in. In 1327 Edward III replaced his father and moved an army northward trying to capture a Scottish army in the English borders. But the Scots were too nimble and escaped, and the English Parliament would spend no more money for war against the Scots. King Robert demanded a treaty with full independence. As he had exhausted England, he got it. In the early part of 1328, Edward III signed the treaty promising that the Kingdom of Scotland "shall remain for ever separate in all respects from the kingdom of England . . . "; and calls The Bruce "the magnificent prince, the lord Robert, by God's grace illustrious king of Scots, our ally and very dear friend . . . "[9] A long way had been traveled.

Of course, Edward III eventually repudiated the treaty and war between the two countries continued for several centuries, but the Scots never lost their nationhood after Robert—not even when they agreed to join in a united kingdom in 1707. In the merger of its Parliament with that of England, Scotland kept its separate law, church and system of education.

King Robert I, The Bruce, died June 7, 1329 and was buried in Dunfermline Abbey where he rests still. His legacy is, simply put, Scotland and the Scottish people. The king's heart was taken from his body and given to Sir James Douglas to take on a crusade. Douglas died in a battle against the Moors in Spain still carrying the heart. Somehow it was conveyed back to Scotland where it was buried at Melrose Abbey. In the 1990s it was exhumed, examined, and re-buried. It was, indeed, a brave heart.

John Hepburn

(c. 1589–1636)

EUROPE'S BLOODY THIRTY Years War (1618–1648) decided among many other things, that large parts of Germany, and all of Scandinavia, would remain Protestant against the Roman Catholic tide of Counter Reformation. The intervention of Sweden under King Gustavus II Adolphus on the Protestant side was decisive. But a 1991 book review in the *New York Times* implies that the success of the Swedish army in the war was due to the fact that it was the first national, one language, one religion army, not dependent on mercenaries.[1]

This view is impossibly incorrect. In fact, the army of Gustavus contained somewhere between 10,000 and 40,000 Scottish mercenary troops, including at least four field marshalls, five generals, nine major generals and forty-one colonels. More than sixty Scottish officers served as governors of conquered German castles and towns. The Scots, of course, were usually Presbyterians and Roman Catholics, not Lutherans as were their Swedish comrades. And for the most part they spoke Scots and Gaelic, not Swedish. The Scottish presence in the Swedish army was so great that one could postulate that Scots were the decisive force in Sweden's decisive army. Field Marshall Alexander Leslie, for instance, secured Russian cooperation and relieved the besieged town of Stralsund (1628), without which further Swedish progress would have been blocked. Robert Douglas, whose descendant General Archibald Douglas commanded the Swedish army during World War II, made a dashing strike at the important Battle of Jankovitch, near Prague, in 1645. The Swedish Minister of War was Alexander Erskine, who represented Sweden at the conference which led to the Treaty of Westphalia (1648) which ended the war.[2]

But the Scot who may have made the most difference in the Swedish army was Sir John Hepburn, a colorful soldier of fortune who was born in Athelstaneford near Haddington. Very little of his early life is known but he studied at St. Andrew's in 1615, and visited Paris and Poitiers in the company of his schoolfellow Robert Monro, with whom he later shared distinction in the Swedish army. In 1620 Hepburn, a Roman Catholic, joined the Scottish troops under Sir Andrew Gray who were fighting on the Protestant side. Later Gustavus made him a colonel of one of his Scottish regiments. Incidentally, this regiment was the direct ancestor of the Royal Scots, which is claimed as Britain's oldest, and Hepburn was, therefore, its de facto founder.[3]

In 1626 Hepburn fought at Danzig under Sir Alexander Leslie. In 1627 he was in Prussia and Hungary, and in 1628 in Poland. In 1630 he relieved his old friend Monro at Rügenwalde, and became governor of the town. In 1631 Gustavus joined four Scottish regiments into the Scots Brigade, also called the Green Brigade, and gave its command to Hepburn. He blew up the town gates of Frankfurt-on-the-Oder, and was shot in the leg while leading his men inside.[4] Hepburn's greatest moment (it was for Gustavus also) came at the Battle of Breitenfeld near Leipzig on September 7, 1631. This was one of the pivotal battles in European history. *The Encyclopaedia Britannica* says that Breitenfeld "ensured the survival of German Protestantism, and it made Gustavus for a time the arbiter of Germany."[5] The *Dictonary of National Biography* says of Hepburn's participation, that the battle "was decided by the charge of his brigade."[6] James Grant describes the scene: "In full armour, with laurel in his helmet, sword in hand, and conspicuous on his richly caparisoned horse, Sir John Hepburn, who outshone all the army in the splendor of his military trappings, led his Scots brigade . . . ," while his drummers beat "The Scots March" the "old national air, which was the terror of the Spanish in Holland and of the Austrians in Germany." Once inside Leipzig, Gustavus publicly thanked the Green Brigade in front of the whole army.[7]

In 1632 Hepburn marched to Frankfurt-on-the-Main, where he was publicly thanked by Gustavus again. Hepburn was the first to enter Munich, where Gustavus made him governor of the city. Also the Scots Brigade was made bodyguard to the king, an honor which caused the seething resentment of the Swedish soldiers. Perhaps this was the beginning of the end for both Hepburn and the King of Sweden. In Nürnberg, Gustavus teased Hepburn about his colorful uniforms, and complained that his best soldier remained a Roman Catholic. The king realized, immediately, that he had made a mistake, and tried to contain the damage, but Hepburn replied, "Sire, I will never more unsheath this sword in the quarrels of Sweden."[8] Gustavus was killed at Lützen later that year.

Hepburn made his way to France, where the army of Louis XIII eagerly admitted him. He went to Scotland to recruit 2,000 men, arriving at Boulogne in March, 1633. In August they were merged with the remnant of the Scots Archery Guard, the famous *Garde Écossaise*, which claimed to be the oldest French regiment. The Scots took part in the conquest of Lorraine, and Hepburn was made *maréchal-de-camp*, or brigadier general. In 1634 he took Heidelberg and fought in many more battles. He was captured, but spoke German so well that the Germans let him go. His regiment, now known as the *régiment d'Hebron*, became 8,300 strong, and Hepburn asked that it be given precedence, "intimating that otherwise his dignity would not allow him to remain in the French army."[9]

In 1636, while walking the fortifications at Saverne in Alsace, Sir John Hepburn was shot in the neck and died. Cardinal Richelieu said of Hepburn's death, "I am, indeed, quite inconsolable. . . . He was just the man needed. . . . I have ordered that all honour should be shown to his memory. . . ." Hepburn was buried, with sword and helmet, in Toul Cathedral in Lorraine, with the leading nobles and chevaliers of France in attendance. A monument was erected by Louis XIV which was destroyed during the French Revolution. But the Latin inscription can still be read. It says, eloquently, "To the best soldier in Christendom."[10]

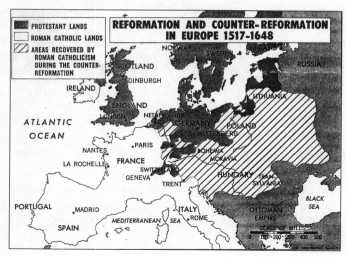

COPYRIGHT: HAMMOND WORLD ATLAS CORP.

John Paul Jones

(1747–1792)

John Paul Jones,

JOHN PAUL JONES is the mythical hero of the United States Navy. All American naval officers know of his feats during the American Revolution and have been inspired by them. The tiny American Navy was not a great factor in the Revolution. But the many sensational victories of Jones and his courage and seamanship during the war gave the Americans a much-needed psychological boost. Jones gave the Revolution a credibility which was important in getting foreign help. His exploits undercut the British people's determination to win the unpopular war and strengthened the British anti-war parties. Jones put doubt into the minds of all Britons, as to whether they could prevail against the United States. His legend has spread around the world.[1] People find Jones fascinating. Many people have written about him, including Carlyle, Churchill, Disraeli, Dumas, Kipling, Melville, and Thackeray.[2]

Jones was born near Kirkbean in Kircudbrightshire on the Solway Firth in southwestern Scotland. His entire name at baptism was John Paul. Paul as a family name is probably an English rendition of MacPhail (son of Paul in Gaelic). Some think the Pauls descend from Clan Mackay; others think that this disctictively Scottish family name is of Flemish origin. John Paul's father, also John Paul, was a landscape gardener. His mother was Jean Duff, or MacDuff.

Young John Paul was educated in the local Presbyterian school, but not for long. At age thirteen he was apprenticed on a Kirkcudbright merchant ship as a cabin boy. By this method he got a chance to visit his brother William Paul, a successful tailor in Fredericksburg, Virginia. When the ship owner went bankrupt, John Paul signed on a Jamaica slaver as chief mate. He quit this after two years, calling the slave trade "abominable." He took passage from Jamaica on a brigantine bound for Scotland. When both the master and the chief mate died, John Paul brought her safely in and was made a master.[3]

Young John Paul "was a man of distinguished talent and originality, a thorough seaman, and of the most determined and tenacious courage."[4] He was small, but strongly built. He could be charming, but he was more often tough, impatient, and aggressive.[5] At Tobago in 1770, John Paul flogged a ship's carpenter for laziness. The man deserted to another ship and died soon after. When John Paul once again reached Scotland he was arrested, charged with murder, and released on bail. He then returned to the West Indies looking for evidence for his defense. By 1772 he had bought a ship and made several voyages. Then he made what he called "the great misfortune" of his life when he killed "the ringleader of a mutinous crew." Although the killing may have been justified, his friends advised him to leave rather than rot in a courthouse. He fled Tobago and changed his name to John Paul Jones.[6]

For the next two years his movements are hazy, no doubt because he was travelling undercover. He did get to Fredericksburg in 1774 when his brother died, and shared in his estate. Through his contacts as a Freemason Jones met several government leaders, so that when the completely improvised U.S. Navy was formed in 1775, he was made a senior lieutenant. On December 3, 1775, he was given the honor of raising the Grand Union flag on the ship *Alfred*. The tiny American fleet sailed for the Bahamas in March of 1776. Largely because of Jones's knowledge of the islands, the Americans were able to capture New Providence bloodlessly, taking away a large quantity of stores. On the return trip the British ship *Glasgow* got away from the American fleet, but during the chase Jones distinguished himself on the *Alfred*, while the captain of the *Providence*, by contrast, was later court-martialed for cowardice. Jones was then given command of the *Providence*. He sailed her on a six-week tour from Bermuda to Nova Scotia. On this voyage he took eight prizes and sank or burned eight more. In October 1776, he brought the prizes safely into Rhode Island. Then it was back to Nova Scotia aboard the *Alfred*. Jones burned an oil warehouse and brought more prizes to Boston in December. Probably because of his cloudy reputation, the Navy made him only 18th on the seniority list. It was discrimination, and some in Congress tried to change it, but in the end, nothing was done.[7]

But Jones had made a great impression. He was obviously the best sailor/fighter in the navy. Most of the other masters were inept, so Jones was picked for a bigger assignment in Europe.[8] On November 1, 1777, he sailed from Portsmouth, New Hampshire on the new ship *Ranger*, bound for France. He was disappointed to find plans changed when he arrived, but persuaded the U.S. Commissioner at Paris to allow him a cruise. Before sailing he had the honor of receiving the first salute of the new Stars and Stripes flag by the French fleet in Quiberon Bay.[9] The voyage was delayed, however, by the fact that Jones had spent time seducing Madame de Chaumont, the wife of the French minister who was in charge of handling clandestine aid to the Americans. Jones never married and was such a Don Juan that the English, in disparagement, named a dance after him, the Paul Jones, in which people change partners in rapid sequence.[10]

With the first of two cruises that would make him famous forever finally underway, Jones headed for the Irish Sea, capturing prizes as he went. In the early morning of April 23, 1778, he went ashore with thirty-one volunteers at Whitehaven, England on the Solway Firth. He spiked the cannon at two forts but wasn't able to take or destroy any ships. At noon on the same day he invaded St. Mary's Isle, his boyhood home on the Scottish side of the firth. Jones's intention was to take Lord Selkirk hostage. But the great Earl wasn't home, and Jones returned to his ship. Unfortunately his men had made off with the household silver. Embarrassed, Jones wrote an apologetic letter to Lady Selkirk saying that he would buy back the silver and return it.[11] But he was very candid also. "It was perhaps fortunate for you Madam that he [Lord Selkirk] was from home; for it was my intention to have taken him on aboard the *Ranger*..."[12] The next day, off

Carrickfergus, Ireland, Jones captured the *Drake* in a battle lasting an hour.

By the time he returned to France in May with his prizes, Jones had become an international celebrity and had changed the psychological balance of the war. The British press went wild with lurid stories. One of the country's premier noblemen had almost been kidnapped! The homeland was threatened! The morale of the British people was turning against the war, and the anti-war parties were strengthened. Although he hadn't done much damage, the stunning fact was that John Paul Jones had invaded Great Britain and he was still out there and might come back. The coastal towns were fearful. But as it turned out Jones's visit to Lady Selkirk would be the last invasion of Britain by any foreign country.

In France Jones was hailed as a hero and the government wanted him in its service. But his friend Benjamin Franklin, who was then an American commissioner to France, was able to get him a fleet of eight ships to put him back in action. Jones named his forty-two-gun flagship *Bon Homme Richard* out of respect for Franklin, the author of *Poor Richard's Almanack*. Jones sailed on August 14, 1779 heading around Ireland and Scotland, taking prizes as he went along. He planned to attack Edinburgh's port town of Leith, putting the residents into panic. But he could only make a feint as contrary winds kept him offshore. Continuing southward he reached the Yorkshire coast. There, off Flamborough Head, just south of Scarborough, Jones came to the scene that would make him immortal. On September 23, 1779, he engaged the bigger, better-gunned British ship *Serapis* in a battle that is still one of the most famous in naval history. For more than three hours the *Bon Homme Richard* and *Serapis* pounded each other in close quarters with everything available. *Serapis* was on fire and *Bon Homme Richard* was sinking when the British captain yelled for Jones to surrender. Jones's famous reply was, "I have not yet begun to fight!" Eventually Jones was able to board *Serapis* and take her as a prize. The victory was expensive. The *Bon Homme Richard* was lost along with 302 sailors. The British never released their staggering number of dead. As Jones said, "No action before was ever, in all respects, so bloody, so severe and so lasting."[13]

When Jones brought in his prizes, Louis XVI gave him a gold-hilted sword and made him a Chevalier of France. Back home Congress hailed him on April 14, 1781, and in 1787 gave him a gold medal. In 1783 Jones was sent back to France to settle the prizes, working with Franklin and his replacement, Thomas Jefferson. While in France he was also able to pursue his vigorous sex life.[14] In 1788 Jones was sent to Denmark to seek restitution for two prizes which had been transferred to England. Then, on the advice of Jefferson, he accepted the post of Rear Admiral of the Russian Navy. The Empress Catherine the Great promised him supreme command in the Black Sea against the Turks.[15] But the Russian Navy had little tolerance for outspoken Scots. Jones was succeeding Samuel Carlovitch Greig (see p. 230). Ethnic prejudice caused Russian sailors to infringe his authority and some even took credit for Jones' victories. To end it all he was accused, probably on trumped up charges, of raping a ten-year-old girl. It was Catherine's way of getting rid of him and Jones was permitted to return to France without a trial. Jones, old beyond his years, suffered from nephritis and jaundice. He contracted pneumonia and died, dejected and depressed, at 19 rue de Tournon on the Left Bank of Paris.[16]

The government of the puritanical United States ignored this hero's death, but the French would not. An elaborate funeral was arranged by the French Assembly. The procession to the Protestant cemetery wound through several miles of the streets of Paris. The cortège included "a detachment of grenadiers in uniform with loaded muskets, and drums that beat a mournful cadence." There were carriages full of members of the Assembly and following behind, ordinary Parisians. Thousands of people turned out along the route "to see the last of the 'Le célèbre Capitaine Paul-Jones'."[17]

More than a century later the United States woke up. President Theodore Roosevelt dispatched four cruisers of the Navy to France to conduct the remains of John Paul Jones to the United States Naval Academy at Annapolis, Maryland. His coffin was found in an unmarked grave in the Protestant cemetery in Paris. The body was well-preserved and easy to identify. On July 6, 1905, Jones's 158th birthday, his body was escorted to a train station by French cavalry and infantry, various French dignitaries, and 500 American sailors. A special train was run to the port of Cherbourg. When the flotilla reached Nantucket, seven battleships were sent to join the escort.[18]

The body of John Paul Jones is buried in a special marble crypt below the beautiful chapel of the Naval Academy. The tomb, an ornate sarcophagus resting on dolphins, resembles Napoleon's tomb in Paris. It is one of the most extravagant tombs in the United States and is a national shrine.

Mikhail Andreas Bogdanovich Barclay de Tolly

(1761–1818)

ALTHOUGH WE NATIVE English speakers are proud of our roles in having defeated first Napoleon and later Hitler, we tend to forget that neither of these things could have been accomplished without the help of the colossal country of the east, Mother Russia. Just as France was weakened beyond repair by its hapless excursion into Russia in 1812, so was Germany's prowess fatally diluted as World War II climaxed at Stalingrad. In both cases the aggressor, having used up enormous quantities of men and materiel, was stopped by the might and fierce pride

Barclay de Tolly,
PICTURE COLLECTION, THE BRANCH LIBRARIES, THE NEW YORK PUBLIC LIBRARY.

of the Russians. What is not so well known is that one of the world's greatest soldiers, a Russian general of Scottish descent, Barclay de Tolly, was the originator of the successful strategy used in both events.

It should be pointed out that Barclay was by no means the only Russian warrior of note to be connected with Scotland. The special services of General Patrick Gordon and later John Paul Jones are discussed separately in this book. Field Marshall James Bruce (1670–1735), known in Russia as Yakov Vilemovitch Bruce, negotiated the cession of the Baltic provinces to Russia at the Peace of Nystadt in 1721. By that time he had become the right-hand man to Peter the Great, directing the tsar's schools of navigation, artillery and military engineering, and had become a count and senator. James's brother, Lt. Gen. Roman Vilemovitch Bruce, was commandant at St. Petersburg and one of the builders of the city. Around 1700 he drove the Swedes away three times and is considered to have been the city's savior. From 1781 to 1786, Count James Alexandrovitch Bruce was governor of Moscow. There is a Bruce family museum near Moscow. Samuel Carlovitch Greig (1735–1788), born in Scotland, is known as the father of the Russian navy. Greig destroyed the Turkish fleet in 1770 and when he died was given a state funeral by Catherine the Great. But it would be hard to match the incredible story of Scottish-born General James F. E. Keith (1696–1758) who commanded the Russian army against the Swedes. Keith might actually have become tsar. It appears that the Empress Elizabeth wanted to marry this dashing hero. But the canny Keith realized that the powerful friends of a noblewoman named Catherine wanted *her* to succeed Elizabeth as Catherine the Great. Fearing the wrath of Russia if he accepted the marriage, and that of Elizabeth if he refused, Keith, no doubt with thoughts of Siberia in mind, fled to Prussia where he was immediately made a field marshal and governor of Berlin by Frederick the Great.[1] Despite these exploits none would have the influence of Barclay de Tolly, whose strategy influenced world history in the outcomes of the Napoleonic Wars and World War II.

Barclay was born at Ludha-Grosshof in Livonia, which now comprises parts of Latvia and Estonia. All standard sources say that he was of Scottish descent. There were many thousands of Scottish traders, teachers, and soldiers in the Baltic for centuries before his birth. The usual pattern was for the Scots to import their wives from Scotland, to have their own charitable societies, and after the Scottish Reformation of 1560, to build Presbyterian churches wherever they went. Generally, this insular stance would last for several generations and then they would gradually "marry in" to the general population, change their names and religions, and disappear. But this branch of the Barclays of Towie (hence Tolly, a Slavic rendering of Towie), however "married in" they may have been, kept their name, and the knowledge of their Scottish descent. And these Barclays kept in touch with each other throughout their eastern European Diaspora. It is likely therefore, that General Barclay de Tolly possessed a relatively small proportion of Scottish blood. On the other hand, as we shall see later on, he was interested in and proud of his Scottish descent.

The parents of the boy, who would become Field Marshal and later Prince Mikhail Barclay de Tolly, died when he was very young and he was sent to Russia to be raised by foster parents. But throughout his life he kept in touch with all branches of the Barclays "in a glowing sentiment of kinship."[2] Barclay entered the Russian army in 1786 and rose rapidly. He served against Turkey 1788–1789, against Sweden in 1790, and against Poland in 1792–1794. He commanded the advance guard at Pułtusk and was wounded in 1807 at Eylau, losing an arm. He was then promoted to lieutenant general. He served with distinction in forcing a surrender of the Swedes by leading an army across the frozen Gulf of Bothnia in 1808. In 1810 he was made Minister of War by Tsar Alexander I.

When the assault came from Napoleon in 1812 the defense of Russia was given to Barclay. As commander he pursued a strategy of calculated retreat, which caused the French to move farther into Russia and farther from their supply base. This policy, of course, cost Russia huge areas of land and great misery to millions of Russians. The policy became unpopular in the extreme, and there were suggestions of treason being perpetrated by the "foreign" commander with the Scottish name. After Barclay's defeat at the battle of Smolensk in 1812, he was replaced by General Kutuzov, who used the exact same strategy. When the French eventually ran low on materiel and began their catastrophic retreat, Kutuzov was able to destroy their armies. Kutuzov became Russia's hero, in effect, because he had a solid Russian name.

But Barclay's talent was still needed and he was commander-in-chief again in 1813. He served at Dresden and Leipzig in that year and in 1814 took part in the capture of Paris, where he was made field marshal. In 1815 he was commander-in-chief of the Russian army which again invaded France, and with Napoleon defeated, this time for good, he was made a prince.

After Waterloo Barclay went to London and is said to have called on Colonel Sir Robert Barclay. "The Field Marshall told the Colonel that 'he was perfectly acquainted with his descent from the Barclays of Towie in Scotland . . .'" He also added that he had heard that Towie Castle was for sale and had briefly considered buying it, then decided that he belonged in Russia and would return there.[3]

The great Russian poet, Alexander Pushkin, wrote a poem to Barclay called *The Commander*. Here are some excerpts, translated by W.W. Arndt:

> Luckless commander! Ah your fate was bitter gall:
> To alien soil in sacrifice you brought your all.
>
> But, fastening on your name's outlandish sound for bait,
> And letting loose on you its hue-and-cry of hate,
> While being rescued by your stratagem, the nation
> Reviled your venerable head with execration.[4]

Barclay's career and strategy have been vindicated now. The Encyclopaedia Britannica says that in World War II Stalin's strategy "... following the traditional Russian pattern of 1812, [i.e. Barclay's pattern] was to withdraw, to conserve strength ... and to force the attacker to spend his impetus and extend his lines ..."[5] The truth always comes out. Barclay's strategy of calculated retreat was crucial in beating Napoleon and Hitler and changing world history. He was, probably, Russia's greatest and most influential soldier.

Winfield Scott

(1786–1866)

WINFIELD SCOTT WAS one of America's greatest soldiers, but is not as well known as many others. During his half-century career he was a general in three wars: the War of 1812, The Mexican War, and the Civil War. Scott was the soldier who brought California, Utah, Arizona, and parts of New Mexico and Colorado into the United States. He wrote the first good regulations for the army. He fought Indian tribes, but was also a success at making peace on the Anglo-American border. He was the army's commanding general for twenty years and ran unsuccessfully for President. Behind his back he was called "Old Fuss and Feathers," for his fancy uniforms and insistence on protocol. But everyone knew he could fight.

Gen. Winfield Scott, Scott Circle, Washington.
COLLECTION OF THE AUTHOR.

Winfield Scott's grandfather, James Scott, the son of a Lowland "small landed proprietor," had fought on the losing Stuart side at Culloden, and fled to Virginia in 1746. His son William Scott, General Scott's father, fought in the American Revolution and General Winfield Scott fought in the War of 1812, making three consecutive generations of their family to have borne arms against the Hanoverian government.[1] Winfield Scott was born at Laurel Branch, his father's farm near Petersburg, Virginia. His mother was Ann Mason. By the time he reached the age of seventeen, both parents had died. Scott had only about two years of schooling. He entered the College of William and Mary but stayed only a year. After another year of studying law he was admitted to the bar in 1806. But the law didn't suit him and he joined a cavalry outfit. He then asked President Jefferson for a commission, which he received in 1808. He was assigned to duty in New Orleans.[2]

Almost immediately Scott showed a rowdy temperament that was to get him in trouble many times. He called a superior "a liar and a scoundrel" and was court-martialed, losing his rank and pay for a year. He was reactivated and posted to Lake Erie in 1812 where he was captured by the British, but later exchanged. He was restored as a full colonel, and became adjutant to General Henry Dearborn. Scott began to put the troops on a professional basis using a French manual for guidance. He led an invasion of Fort George in May of 1813, and broke his collarbone when a magazine exploded. He was promoted to brigadier general. He was next sent to Buffalo, where he became very good at drilling his soldiers. He brought the young American army to a new level of professionalism. Scott beat the British at Chippewa in July of 1814, and was wounded twice while winning at Lundy's Lane. These victories were a great boost to American morale (and a reverse for the British) as it was the first time in the war that British regulars had been beaten. Congress gave Scott a gold medal and he was promoted to brevet major general.[3]

In 1817 Scott married Maria Mayo, whose father John Mayo was one of the richest men in Richmond. They had seven children, but the marriage wasn't ideal. Maria liked to travel and frequently went to Europe without her husband. In 1832 Scott was ordered to the Black Hawk War. He had prepared himself for a cholera epidemic which fell upon his troops, and received great acclaim for his success against the disease, often treating his soldiers with his own hands. In the belief that cholera was made worse by the use of alcohol he ordered drunken men to dig their own graves, so as to spare others from having to toil for their folly. In 1836 Scott was in Florida fighting against the Seminole Indians, and then moved on to Georgia to deal with the Creeks. President Jackson, who didn't like Scott, accused him of delaying, but Scott was acquitted in court. President Van Buren sent Scott to the Canadian border to prevent

Americans from helping to arm Canadian rebels. Scott quickly took control of the situation, blocked shipments of arms, and pacified the countryside. He went south again, this time to relocate the Cherokees. Then it was back to the Canadian border to solve a boundary dispute between New Brunswick and Maine. He got the opposing armies to withdraw until negotiations could be completed. All of this got Scott the attention of the country and he was talked of as a presidential candidate.[4]

Scott's greatest days were still ahead. In 1841 he became commander in chief of the U.S. Army, and President Polk sent him to the Mexican War in 1846. Polk fumed as Scott stayed in Washington carefully planning his moves. At last, Scott landed at the port of Vera Cruz on March 9, 1847. He spent two weeks making preparations to besiege the city. Vera Cruz surrendered on March 29. Scott then battled through Mexico against the army of General López de Santa Anna, winning a great victory at Cerro Gordo on April 18. Scott reached Puebla on May 15, where he picked up men and supplies. He was now so far from Vera Cruz that he decided to cut off communications with the rear and march forward to Mexico City. The Duke of Wellington predicted, "Scott is lost. He has been carried away by success. He can't take the city and he can't fall back on his bases."[5] But Scott won again at Contreras, and at Molino del Rey on September 8. He won again at Chapultepec, forcing the Mexican Army to leave the capital. Scott entered the main plaza of the city on September 14, 1847, while a stunned crowd watched from behind windows. His dirty, tired men stood at attention as the band played "Yankee Doodle."[6] He had marched 10,000 men from Vera Cruz to Mexico City, more than 250 miles. Now Wellington called him "the greatest living soldier."[7]

Scott helped in negotiating the Treaty of Guadalupe Hidalgo, in which the United States gave Mexico $15 million in exchange for the American Southwest. Incredibly, Polk recalled Scott for an inquiry of his conduct of the campaign! But he was such a hero that the inquiry was dropped, and Scott was appointed as brevet lieutenant general.

Scott ran for President as a Whig in 1852, but lost to Franklin Pierce. Then Pierce appointed Jefferson Davis as Secretary of War and he and Scott quarreled. In the later 1850s Scott built a soldiers home and increased officers' pay. In 1859 he was called upon again to settle a border dispute with Britain involving San Juan Island in the Pacific Northwest. When the Civil War loomed he assured Lincoln that although a Southerner he was loyal to the Union. Scott also tried unsuccessfully to retain the loyalty of General Robert E. Lee. At the outbreak, Scott predicted a three-year war with the North winning, and a need after that for federal troops to control the defeated states. This forecast proved to be quite accurate. Scott proposed a blockade of the southern ports and a drive down the Mississippi River. These plans were initially rejected but as the war progressed they were eventually adopted. As commander of the army Scott appointed General Irvin McDowell, who was thoroughly defeated by the Confederates at Manassas (Bull Run). General George McClellan replaced McDowell and treated Scott with contempt. Many thought that Scott was too old to be running a war, and he resigned November 1, 1861, and took a boat to Europe.[8]

Old Fuss and Feathers was proud, vain, and not well liked by many. He spent most of his last years at West Point writing his memoirs. He was well-read and a sincere Episcopalian, a Southerner who remained loyal to the Union and who advocated the ending of slavery by all means "not incompatible with the safety of both colors."[9] His greatest achievement was his leadership in the Mexican War. Above all, Winfield Scott was the brilliant soldier who added California and the southwest to the United States.

Thomas Cochrane

(1775–1860)

T HOMAS COCHRANE, TENTH Earl of Dundonald, was the only person to command the navies of four different countries, and is credited with helping all four of them to gain their independence. Some of his exploits on the sea have never been matched. He survived disgrace and ended his life with honors. He is one of the most interesting personalities ever produced by Scotland, and one of the greatest sailors ever.

Thomas Cochrane, born in Annsfield, Lanarkshire, was the son of Archibald Cochrane, the ninth Earl of Dundonald and Anne, daughter of Captain James Gilchrist. Archibald Cochrane was an excellent inventor and a poor businessman

Thomas Cochrane, 10th Earl of Dundonald, By Patric Park. THE SCOTTISH NATIONAL PORTRAIT GALLERY.

who developed products out of coal such as tar, varnish, lampblack, coke, and coal gas. He also invented the smoke screen. But none of these products, all of which became very useful, ever made him any money and the family became poor.[1] Young Thomas, therefore, was sent out to sea at age seventeen in a ship commanded by his uncle, Alexander Forrester Inglis Cochrane. Captain Cochrane had entered the young man on the books of various ships for several years so that he would have to wait less time to qualify as an officer. Thomas progressed well as a sailor, but his temper got him in trouble and hurt his reputation. He criticized the admiralty and demanded reforms. At one point he was court-martialed for disrespect.

In 1800 his career began in earnest as he was given command of the *Speedy*, a brig of 158 tons, armed with fourteen four-pounders, and "crowded with, rather than manned with, ninety officers and men."[2] Cochrane was ordered to cruise the Spanish coast and did very well, capturing merchant ships and privateers. Annoyed, the Spanish government sent ships to find him but Cochrane painted *Speedy* to look like a well-known Danish ship, and dressed a Danish quartermaster to stand on board in a Danish uniform. All went well until a Spanish ship insisted on boarding *Speedy*, at which point Cochrane ran up a quarantine flag, and the Spaniard went away.

In 1801, at the height of the Napoleonic wars, Cochrane put in at Valletta and went to a French costume party dressed as a British seaman. Someone suspected that he really *was* a British seaman and things got ugly. Cochrane decked a Frenchman and was put in jail. A duel followed in which the Frenchman was shot in the leg. Cochrane was grazed, his side bruised. But this tawdry incident was the prelude to a high point in his career. In December, 1801, the Spanish sent the 600-ton *El Gamo* to confront Cochrane and the *Speedy*. *El Gamo*'s thirty-two heavy guns outclassed *Speedy*'s fourteen lighter guns. Further, *El Gamo* carried a crew of 319 men, while *Speedy* was down to 54. What followed is absolutely unparalleled in naval history. *Speedy* attacked and soon boarded *El Gamo*. It was all over very quickly. Cochrane defeated his outsized foe with a loss of only four men killed and seventeen wounded. The Spaniards suffered fourteen killed and forty-one wounded. To control the huge number of prisoners and convey the prize to port Cochrane ordered all Spaniards belowdecks and trained their own guns, pointed down the hatches, at his prisoners. Stationed by each gun was a British sailor standing by, where all could see, holding lighted matches.[3]

Cochrane expected a promotion for this victory but his reputation had cost him. He was already so unpopular that the admiralty's Lord St. Vincent, who used the excuse that only a few had been killed in taking *El Gamo*, denied the advancement. Cochrane had the audacity to point out that there were more killed on the *Speedy* than on the ship for which his lordship had been made an Earl!

Finally, the *Speedy* was trapped among three French ships. Cochrane fought hard and well, but finally submitted. The French captain refused to accept Cochrane's sword because he had put up such a gallant fight in a hopeless cause. In the thirteen months of Cochrane's command, the undermanned, ill-armed *Speedy* had captured more than 50 vessels, 122 guns, and 534 prisoners.[4]

In the next few years Cochrane commanded other ships, winning huge amounts of prize money. He studied at Edinburgh University for a while and was elected to Parliament. Then in 1809, what should have been his greatest victory turned out to be the beginning of his worst days. With the bulk of the French fleet holed up in Aix Roads, Cochrane submitted a plan to cripple the French Navy. At great personal risk he would attack the fleet with fireships, each loaded with 1,500 barrels of powder, hoping to cause terror in the French. Then in the confusion the British fleet would come in and finish the job. The plan worked exactly as he expected. The French panicked, trying to escape, and many of their ships ran aground. Cochrane signaled by semaphore for the British to attack but Lord Gambier, the British commander, refused to do so. A major naval victory was canceled by his inaction. Several French ships were destroyed, but many more could have been. At least Cochrane was given the Order of the Bath.

When a resolution was offered in Parliament to congratulate Lord Gambier on the victory, Cochrane could not hold his tongue. According to the *Dictionary of National Biography*, he told parliament that the resolution should be denied, "on the ground that the commander-in-chief had not only done nothing to merit a vote of thanks, but had neglected to destroy the French fleet in Aix Roads when it was clearly in his power to do so."[5] The resulting court martial cleared Lord Gambier, and found Cochrane guilty of libel.

Then things got worse. In 1814 some friends of Cochrane bought British funds and then spread a rumor that Napoleon had been killed. The funds rose, they took their profits, and the funds fell. Most sources say that Cochrane was innocent, but he was found guilty of fraud along with the others. He was struck from the Navy list, deprived of his Order of the Bath, jailed, fined, and expelled from Parliament. But his constituents didn't believe he was guilty and re-elected him a few days later! He escaped from prison but was returned and fined again, refusing to pay on the grounds that he should never have been imprisoned in the first place. Amazingly, Cochrane was so popular with the people that pennies were collected and the fine was paid.

In 1817 Cochrane accepted an offer from Chile to organize and command its navy in the country's quest for independence from Spain. When he arrived he found seven pitiful ships. But in 1819 he captured the entire town of Valdivia, taking huge quantities of stores back to Valparaiso. General O'Higgins, another hero of Chile, welcomed him, but the other officers were jealous to the point that Cochrane tendered his resignation. It was refused and he was promised a better deal. In 1820 he sailed with the incompetent General San Martín to attack the Spaniards in Peru. Cochrane was so disgusted with the inaction of his commander that he broke away and without any orders captured the Spanish flagship *Esmeralda*. Cochrane was severely wounded, but this was a key victory in the battle for the independence of both Chile and Peru. He demanded and got 600 soldiers from San Martín and harassed the coast from Callao to Arica, compelling Lima to surrender on July 6, 1821. San Martín got all of the credit and was loaded with honors.[6] Cochrane denounced him as a traitor and resigned.

In 1823 Cochrane became "first admiral of the national and imperial navy" of Brazil. Within a few months, he had established the superiority of the Brazilian navy that led to the country's independence from Portugal. The *Encyclopaedia Britannica* says, "With the cooperation of Lord Dundonald (Thomas Cochrane), an able British naval officer who had entered Brazilian service, the strong Portuguese garrisons were forced to return to Europe."[7] Brazil had become the third country to become independent with the help of Cochrane.

But corruption and intrigue once again got the best of the sea king, who resigned and sailed for Europe. In 1827 Greece sought his services in the war of independence against the Turks. Cochrane agreed to have "sole, independent, uncontrolled command of the entire Greek fleet."[8] He also demanded steamships, made in the United States and Britain, that he would have been the first to use in warfare. These were ordered but by the time he arrived at Hydra there were no ships, no money to pay the men, and worst of all, not much patriotic spirit shown by the Greek sailors. In Greece, Cochrane accomplished very little. In 1828 he resigned his command and went home. Still, he had participated in the liberation of a fourth country. In 1832, Turkey recognized the independence of Greece.

Back home Cochrane demanded reinstatement in the Navy, and was restored in 1832. He was back at sea in 1848 commanding in the

Caribbean until 1851. He had succeeded his father as Earl of Dundonald in 1831. In 1841 he was restored to the Order of the Bath. In 1851 he was promoted to admiral. That made five countries in which he held the top naval rank. He continued to advocate reform, proposing to the admiralty the use of steam, and devised a secret war plan that has never been used, but those who have seen it say would massacre an enemy. It is probably too horrible to use.

Cochrane followed his father as an inventor, proposing the use of screw propellers and devising a rotary steam engine. His personal life was as hectic as his life at sea. In 1812 he eloped to Scotland with sixteen-year-old Katherine Corbett Barnes. After the rushed marriage ceremony the bridegroom left the bride alone in her room to attend to other pressing business! The couple were later married again in an Anglican church, and years later by the Church of Scotland in Edinburgh.[9] They had four sons, including Admiral Arthur Auckland Leopold Pedro Cochrane. Kate, Lady Dundonald, died in 1865. It was by all accounts an excellent marriage. Writing from jail Cochrane asked his wife not to visit him. "This is not a place favourable to morality . . . Oh my dear soul, you do not know how much I love you. . . ."[10]

Thomas Cochrane, tenth Earl of Dundonald, was honored with burial in Westminster Abbey. The four corners of the memorial stone depict the four countries he helped to become free. Although largely forgotten in his own country, in South America Cock-RAH-nay, as his name is pronounced there, is still a hero.

Ulysses Simpson Grant

(1822–1885)

ENERAL GRANT WAS the most influential American soldier of the nineteenth century. His bold strategy and brilliant tactics won important battles in the American Civil War. His leadership defeated the Confederates and preserved the United States. His charisma energized the North and demoralized the South. At his death America treated him as the greatest hero of his time. He has been elected to the Scottish American Hall of Fame.

Grant's Tomb, New York City. COLLECTION OF THE AUTHOR.

Hiram Ulysses Grant was born on a farm near Point Pleasant, Ohio. His father Jesse Grant was of New England stock and ultimately descended from Matthew Grant, an immigrant described by the *Encylopaedia Britannica* as "a Scotsman."[1] General Grant's mother was Hannah Simpson, part of the large Scotch-Irish population of Pennsylvania. She was the daughter of John Simpson and Rebecca Weir and granddaughter of John Simpson, a Scotch-Irish immigrant from Dergenagh, near Dungannon in County Tyrone, Northern Ireland.[2]

As a boy, the future General Grant attended the local log schoolhouse, and later the Maysville Seminary in Kentucky and the Presbyterian Academy at Ripley, Ohio.[3] At age seventeen Grant won an appointment to the U.S. Military Academy at West Point, New York. An error by a clerk at West Point changed his name to Ulysses S. Grant. Sometime later Grant made the S. stand for Simpson, for his mother's family. His record at the Academy was not distinguished and he finished in the middle of his class of thirty-nine. He did establish a record in the high jump, however, which stood for a quarter of a century. Also, he was the best horseman in his class.

When he graduated in 1843, he visited the St. Louis home of Frederick Dent Jr., a classmate. There he fell in love with Dent's sister Julia, who was an excellent horsewoman. Before they could marry Grant was ordered to join Zachary Taylor's army, which was stationed on the Texas-Mexican border. Although Grant was a quartermaster working behind the lines, he couldn't resist fighting. In Monterey, in 1846, he led a successful charge. At one point he brought up ammunition by riding back through sniper-infested streets, galloping Indian-style on the "off-side" of his gray mare Nellie. Neither Grant nor Nellie suffered a scratch.[4]

In March 1847, Grant transferred to the army of General Winfield Scott (see p. 235), serving at Vera Cruz. At Molino del Rey he was breveted as first lieutenant for his gallantry, and as captain at Chapultepec. On September 16, 1847, he was commissioned as a first lieutenant. As the army approached Mexico City none other than Robert E. Lee took notice of young Grant. Lee wrote in a dispatch that when the battalion was within musket range, "lieutenant Grant came up handsomely, pushed forward with our men and drove the enemy flank. . . . Grant behaved with distinguished gallantry."[5]

After the Mexican War, Grant returned to St. Louis in triumph to marry Julia Dent. The best man, James Longstreet, another of Grant's contemporaries at West Point, would become a Confederate general in little more than a decade. In the awful times to come, the friends would have to fight each other and Longstreet would deal a severe setback to Grant at the Battle of the Wilderness, while sustaining a severe wound from Union fire. But when Grant became president he appointed Longstreet as U.S. minister to Turkey![6]

Grant was made a captain and sent to Oregon. There he got in trouble and in 1854 resigned his commission. It is not known whether his resignation was voluntary, but the incident was caused by rumors of his drinking. Back in St. Louis he had a hard time making a living as a farmer. In 1860 he moved to Galena, Illinois where he found employment in his father's leather-goods store. At this point no one could have predicted that this poor, depressed, perhaps alcoholic man would become the hero of millions.

But the Civil War started and Grant, a born soldier, took his opportunity. He drilled the militia so well he was made colonel of the Twenty-first Illinois infantry regiment, and soon was made a brigadier general by President Lincoln. Without any orders, on September 6, 1861, Grant seized Paducah, Kentucky, an important town at the confluence of the Ohio and Tennessee Rivers. In early 1862 he took Fort Henry and Fort Donelson. Grant was almost beaten at Fort Donelson, but with great calm redeployed his forces and attacked the Confederates, cutting them off from any possible reinforcements. The southern general, Simon Bolivar Buckner, another friend of Grant's from West Point, asked Grant for terms of surrender. Grant replied, "No terms except an unconditional surrender can be accepted." Fifteen thousand Rebel soldiers were taken prisoner and from this time forward U. S. Grant became Unconditional Surrender Grant; the hero was born.[7]

In 1862 Grant won an important victory at Shiloh, and Union victories at Iuka and Corinth in Mississippi gave him the opportunity to try to take Vicksburg, the most important Confederate fortification in the west. Vicksburg gave the South control of the Mississippi River, and Grant realized that he could not only open up the river for the North, but also cut the South off from the West by capturing the town. After months of brilliant maneuvering, Grant forced the Confederates into Vicksburg and besieged it. The city surrendered on July 4, 1863—the day after the Battle of Gettysburg ended on the other side of the country. Grant took 30,000 prisoners in his crucial victory.

Despite these heroics many seized on Grant's mistakes and denounced him as incompetent and a drunk. But Lincoln stood by him—asking the critics to find out what brand he drank so that he could supply it to his other, less successful generals. "Grant is my man," said the president, and promoted his soldier to major general. After the Union defeat at Chickamauga, Grant was promoted to lieutenant general, a rank not held by anyone since the days of George Washington. A major Union force was trapped in Chattanooga. With Grant in charge, the Union won at nearby Lookout Mountain and Missionary Ridge, and the Southerners retreated into Georgia. For this great victory Grant was made general in chief of all Union armies.

It was then left to Grant to finish the South. He forced the abandonment of Richmond, the Confederate capital. Then he pursued the Southern army in its final retreat. When the dignified General Robert E. Lee surrendered to Grant at Appomattox in April 1865, ending the war, Grant was not elated. He said instead that he felt "sad and depressed at the downfall of a foe who had fought so long and valiantly and had suffered so much for a cause, though the cause was, I believe, one of the worst for which a people ever fought."[8] Later, he forbade any prosecution of Lee for treason.

Grant was only one of the Scottish-American leaders in the Civil War. Among the other generals of Scottish descent were Joseph E. Johnston, George B. McClellan, Irvin McDowell, T. J. "Stonewall" Jackson, and J. E. B. "Jeb" Stuart. Franklin Buchanan was the only full admiral of the Confederate Navy. Union Admiral David Glasgow Farragut became famous by yelling, "Damn the torpedoes!"

Ulysses S. Grant was elected President in 1869 and again in 1873, but is generally ranked very low on a list of American Presidents. His administration was full of corruption and scandal, although he was never any part of this. His mistake was trusting friends and relatives. Still, his administration promoted civil rights, the national parks, and a sound dollar, and he should be given some credit for the economic boom which followed his presidency.

After leaving office in 1877, Grant went on a two-year triumphal world tour with his wife and one son. In Britain, he met with the Earl of Seafield, the chief of Clan Grant. The Grants also visited India, China, and Japan. In 1881 the Grants moved to New York City, and Grant lost everything he had to a fraud on Wall Street. Then things got even worse when a physician advised Grant that he was dying of throat cancer. At this news Grant retreated to the country to write his memoirs, hoping to leave his family with something. His publisher was none other than the famous author, Mark Twain.

Grant labored on the work day after day in great pain, the disease closing in on him. The public was informed of this activity, at least as heroic as anything he had done in war, and gained a new respect for their old hero. Grant regained his legendary status. The work was completed just a few days before the old soldier died and produced for his heirs a phenomenal $450,000 in royalties.

General Grant's adopted city, New York, "did better for him in death than it had in life. Grant's body lay in state at City Hall for three days, then embarked on a six-mile-long funeral procession through the city's streets, past an estimated million and a half spectators . . ."[9] Several presidents were in attendance, and Civil War generals from both North and South rode together.

Ulysses S. Grant and his wife Julia rest in what is known as Grant's Tomb on Riverside Drive in New York. It is the largest mausoleum in the United States.

Douglas MacArthur

(1880–1964)

ENERAL OF THE Army Douglas MacArthur was, arguably, the greatest soldier that America has produced. As commander of the South West Pacific Area Theater in World War II, supreme Allied commander in occupied Japan, and as commander of the forces of the United States and the United Nations in Korea, he put together ten years of brilliant service that would be hard to match for influence. And there is much more to his story.

It begins in Glasgow where Arthur McArthur, Douglas MacArthur's grandfather, was born in 1817, the son of Arthur McArthur and Sara MacArthur. He always joked that he was a "double distilled" MacArthur. (For those not familiar with the Gaelic patronymic, "Mac" can be translated as "son of," and so the name means "son of Arthur" and is used to mean "descendant of Arthur."

Sara McArthur, a native of Dumbarton, was a young widow when she brought her son Arthur to America. But from this inauspicious start her son Arthur (Douglas MacArthur's grandfather) grew up to be a judge in Milwaukee. He was also on hand on January 25, 1859, Robert Burns's birthday, as a founding member of the Saint Andrew's Society of Milwaukee. The city then was largely German and the tiny Scottish community must have felt relatively isolated. The first president of the society was another Scottish immigrant, Alexander Mitchell, who entered the banking business and became "the Rothschild of Milwaukee."[1] Judge Arthur McArthur was elected first vice president.

Judge Arthur McArthur married an American woman and they produced a son, Arthur MacArthur Jr. (1845–1912), who was Douglas

MacArthur's father. Arthur MacArthur Jr. became a genuine war hero fighting on the side of the North in the Twenty-fourth Wisconsin regiment in the American Civil War. After the battle of Missionary Ridge in 1863, his commanding officer wrote, "I would most respectfully mention Adjutant Arthur MacArthur Jr. for his bravery. When the color sergeant was exhausted he carried the flag in front of the regiment, cheering his men to follow him up the ridge." For this feat Arthur MacArthur Jr., still a teenager, was given America's highest honor, the Medal of Honor, and promoted to major.[2] Captain E. B. Parsons wrote home to the judge, "Arthur was magnificent. He seems to be afraid of nothing. . . . He seems the hero of the regiment."[3] Rising rapidly, Arthur MacArthur Jr., now in command of the Twenty-fourth, was seriously wounded in the chest and leg at the battle of Franklin. Major General David S. Stanley wrote, "In this feat the regiment was gallantly and well led by your boy colonel, Arthur MacArthur."[4]

After the war MacArthur rose steadily, being promoted to major general in 1898, while in command of the First Brigade, First Division, Eighth Army Corps at the battle of Manila. He was military governor of the Philippines in 1900–1901. In 1906 he became a lieutenant general, the highest-ranking officer in active service in the United States Army. He retired in 1909 after almost a half century of service. General Arthur MacArthur died suddenly while making a speech and was given a Presbyterian funeral.[5]

General Arthur MacArthur married Mary Pinkney Hardy who bore him three sons, all given distinctively Scottish names: Arthur III, Malcolm, and Douglas, the youngest, who was born in the military barracks in Little Rock, Arkansas. Young Douglas MacArthur idolized his father and was raised in various army posts in Texas and the American southwest. He never thought of being anything but a soldier and won appointment to the United States Military Academy at West Point, New York, scoring ninety-three on the entrance examination. He was graduated in 1903 with highest honors, first in his class, and senior officer of the corps of cadets. He served in the Philippines and Korea in 1905 and at Veracruz, Mexico in 1914.

In World War I he was with the Forty-second (Rainbow) Division and became one of the most, perhaps *the* most decorated American foot soldier in the war. He fought in Champagne-Marne, St. Mihiel, and Meuse-Argonne. He was nominated for the Medal of Honor but didn't receive it. He seemed to be fearless, and showed unusual leadership abilities. At one point when he had ordered a soldier to do something extremely dangerous, he is said to have given one of his own medals to the soldier saying, "I see that you are going to do it!" MacArthur rose to the command of the Forty-second and was promoted to brigadier general.

After the war he commanded the U.S. sector of occupation on the Rhine. From 1919 through 1922, he was superintendent at West Point. In 1925 he was one of the judges at the military court martial of his boyhood friend, General William "Billy" Mitchell, whose grandfather had founded the Milwaukee St. Andrew's Society with MacArthur's grandfather. Mitchell, who commanded the Army Air Force, which scarcely existed between the world wars, had been a strident and consistent advocate of the Air Force, but had overstepped his authority in criticizing the Army for its lack of interest in air power. He had gone so far as to predict (very correctly) the debacle at Pearl Harbor seventeen years before its event. The public and the American Legion supported him, but he was found guilty. It is said—although it can never be known—that Douglas MacArthur cast the only dissenting vote.[6] The people of Milwaukee were not favorably impressed with this verdict and named the city's airport Mitchell Field.

During the 1920s MacArthur saw some service in the Philippines and in 1922 he married Louise Cromwell Brooks. Their marriage ended in divorce seven years later. From 1930 to 1935 MacArthur was U.S. Army chief-of-staff. 1932 was the low point in America's economic history and also the bottom of Douglas MacArthur's career. Thousands of unemployed veterans marched on Washington demanding payments which were not due to them until 1945. President Hoover ordered MacArthur to control the encampment of these "bonus marchers," but his actions were clumsy in the extreme, involving tanks and tear gas. Throughout the Depression, MacArthur dealt with the new president, Franklin D. Roosevelt, helping to implement the New Deal, particularly in the Civilian Conservation Corps. Neither man liked the other, and Roosevelt even called MacArthur "dangerous" but approved his promotions anyway.

From 1935 through 1937 MacArthur was in the Philippines (then controlled by the U.S.) developing the Philippine army. He retired in 1937 and in the same year married Jean Faircloth. He was then made a Field Marshal of the Philippine Army. On July 26, 1941, in response to the developing threat from Japan, MacArthur was recalled to active duty as a lieutenant general in command of U.S. forces in the Far East. When the Japanese attacked Pearl Harbor on December 7, 1941, America was unprepared and suffered a great loss of warships and men. The Japanese bombarded the Philippines the same day, destroying many American aircraft. MacArthur was criticized for being unprepared, as were his counterparts in Hawaii.

As World War II was the pivotal event of the twentieth century, it is appropriate to mention two other generals of Scottish ancestry who were among the most prominent men at arms in this supreme conflict. General George S. Patton, "Old Blood and Guts" to his troops, was one of the most successful and colorful American soldiers ever. Patton was a great tank commander—with Scots on both sides of his ancestry—who swept through the Germans in France with a relentlessness that will be remembered forever. British Field Marshall Bernard Law Montgomery was the most famous British soldier of modern times. His 1942 victory over Rommel at El Alemein was one of the decisive battles of all history. Up to that time the Germans hadn't lost a major battle. After El Alamein, they never won one. "Monty" was born in London of Scotch-Irish ancestry.

As for Douglas MacArthur, he defended the Philippines as best he could but the odds against him were overwhelming. The *Encyclopaedia Britannica* calls his actions "gallant," but he simply hadn't the troops to withstand the Japanese assault. On March 17, 1942, President Roosevelt ordered MacArthur to depart for Australia from the last American fortress at Corregidor. He and his family left by PT boat, a 3,000-mile dash past the Japanese. As he left he uttered his famous words, "I shall return." He was awarded the Medal of Honor that he might have been more deserving of in World War I. Roosevelt said later that "public opinion" got MacArthur the medal. General George Marshall called it "propaganda." Others said he deserved it.[7]

When MacArthur arrived in Australia he found the country in a siege mentality. Everyone was convinced that it was necessary to get ready to defend the all-but-certain Japanese invasion. MacArthur, however, told everyone that an invasion could be prevented by offensive strategy. He began his "island hopping" tactics in the fall of 1942 with the capture of New Guinea and proceeded to move toward Japan, one island at a time, skipping over others. Not only had an invasion of Australia been prevented, MacArthur's forces made steady progress toward the Japanese homeland. When the Philippines were approached MacArthur had to convince Roosevelt that it was right to take the islands instead of bypass them. He made good on his promise to return; soon the Philippines were under American control.

Perhaps MacArthur's biggest moment came on September 2, 1945 when he was in charge of the proceedings that ended World War II. The ceremony took place on an overcast day on Tokyo bay on the decks of the U.S.S. *Missouri*. Signing the papers for Britain was another Scot, Admiral Sir Bruce Fraser. MacArthur signed as supreme commander of the Allied powers. As if on cue the sun broke through the clouds. MacArthur ended the greatest war in all history by saying, simply, "These proceedings are now closed."

MacArthur was given the rank of general of the army and became the supreme Allied commander in occupied Japan. Here he made an enormous impact, demobilizing millions of Japanese servicemen. He purged militarists and promoted unions. He decreed great land reforms, some said greater than Mao had done in China. He promoted women's rights and strengthened the police and the educational system. He imposed a written constitution on the country in 1947. He revived a devastated economy. Practically everyone agrees that he did a superb job as dictator of Japan.

But a new challenge came in 1950 when North Korean troops crossed the Thirty-eighth parallel. MacArthur was put in charge of all United Nations forces. The situation he was presented with was grim. The northern forces had almost completely overrun the country and the United Nations forces were penned into a very small beachhead in the southeast of the country near Pusan. There was a real danger that they would be pushed into the sea. MacArthur's response was immediate. Korea is a narrow peninsula, only about 500 miles long and 100 or so across. MacArthur's idea was to make an amphibious landing at Inchon, far to the north. He noted that Inchon was near Seoul, the capital, and that most of the enemy's troops were near Pusan in the southeast waiting to deal the death blow. At first the Joint Chiefs of Staff rejected the plan, saying that the thirty-foot tides at Inchon would make a landing suicidal, and that there was not sufficient time to prepare. In the end MacArthur convinced everyone on the soundness of his plan and the famous Inchon landing took place on September 15, 1950. The strategy worked exactly

as MacArthur had planned. By September 26, Seoul was under his control and the North Korean Army was "completely shattered." One hundred twenty-five thousand prisoners were taken, and all of the lost territory was retaken. The *Encyclopaedia Britannica* says, "In its conception, its
execution, and its results, the Inchon landing takes its place beside the
great battles of history."[8]

But this brilliant stroke was the beginning of the end for Douglas
MacArthur. In November, a "new war" came as Chinese troops invaded.
MacArthur stabilized the situation, but he proposed a bombing of
Manchuria, a blockade of China and the use of Nationalist Chinese
troops. These were all against the policies of the United States government, but MacArthur kept on talking about them. This conflict of views
caused President Truman to relieve him of his duties on April 1, 1951.

MacArthur came home to an unprecedented welcome. The ticker-tape
parade was, according to the New York City police, the largest in the
city's history. He was invited to address both houses of Congress, explaining his views to the public. He ended his speech dramatically by quoting
an old song, "old soldiers never die; they just fade away." And except for
a few political forays he did just that.

Gen. Douglas MacArthur making good on his promise "I shall return" at Leyte, Philippines,
1944. AP/Wide World Photos.

What was MacArthur really like? According to Brigadier General Le Grande Diller, who spent much time with him, "He had an ability to take a large problem apart, study the segments, and then put it back together again; come up with a solution that was so simple and so direct that one always said, "Why didn't I think of that myself?"[9] Biographer William Manchester calls him many things including, flamboyant, imperious, inspiring, outrageous, arrogant, and shy. He also says, "Yet he was also endowed with great personal charm, a will of iron, and a soaring intellect." Manchester goes on, "Unquestionably he was the most gifted man-at-arms this nation has produced. He was extraordinarily brave. His twenty-two medals—thirteen of them for heroism—probably exceeded those of any other figure in American history." MacArthur even exposed himself, deliberately, to enemy snipers, yet he was not able always to convey this bravery to his men, some of whom called him "Dugout Doug."[10]

Truman called MacArthur "a counterfeit." But Churchill said he was "the glorious commander," and Montgomery said he was the "best soldier" of the United States in World War II. Lord Alanbrooke called MacArthur "the greatest general and the best strategist that the war produced." George Marshall disliked him, but admitted that he was "our most brilliant general."[11]

It is interesting that three of the key players who saved civilization in the 1940s were actually related. Through his great-great grandmother, Sarah Barney Belcher, Douglas MacArthur was an eighth cousin of Churchill and a sixth cousin once removed of Franklin D. Roosevelt.[12]

Stephen Foster

(1826–1864)

Stephen Foster, FOSTER HALL COLLECTION, CENTER FOR AMERICAN MUSIC, UNIVERSITY OF PITTSBURGH.

STEPHEN FOSTER CAN be considered as the founder of popular commercial music. He is the spiritual ancestor of George Gershwin, Frank Sinatra, Elvis Presley, The Beatles, Sting, and Sheryl Crow, whether they know it or not. There were songwriters before Foster, but none of them sold copies of their works by the tens of thousands. No one before him was able to captivate a public with hit after hit. Most importantly, perhaps, Foster was the first songwriter to be able to make a living by his music alone. He was, therefore, the first professional songwriter, and led the way for those who followed him. Two who must be mentioned were Scottish-Americans: Hoagy Carmichael and Johnny Mercer.[1]

Stephen Collins Foster was born on July 4, 1826 in Lawrenceville, Pennsylvania, which is now The Strip section of Pittsburgh. His father, William Barclay Foster, was of entirely Scotch-Irish Presbyterian ancestry. William Barclay Foster's grandfather, Alexander Foster, had emigrated from Londonderry in 1725. Alexander Foster's son, James Foster, whose brother was a Presbyterian minister, married Ann Barclay and settled in Washington County, Pennsylvania, southwest of Pittsburgh. There they were in the company of a great many Scotch-Irish Presbyterians whose interest in education was almost an obsession. They started one of the dozens of Presbyterian Log Colleges on the frontier; this one in Canonsburg, Pennsylvania with Dr. James McMillan as the first President. This is now Washington and Jefferson College, and the original log schoolhouse is preserved.[2] (Princeton University is the most famous institution descended from a Presbyterian Log College.) James Foster's Son, William Barclay Foster, became a successful merchant and moved to Pittsburgh. He owned, named, and subdivided Lawrenceville, which is situated on the Allegheny River. William Barclay Foster contributed money to help equip Andrew Jackson's army for the Battle of New Orleans, but eventually suffered the loss of most of his fortune. Yet he was prominent enough to become a Pennsylvania state legislator and mayor of Allegheny City, which is now Pittsburgh's North Side.[3]

William Barclay Foster married Eliza Clayland Tomlinson, a woman of mostly English descent, whom he met on a business trip. Stephen Foster was the tenth of their eleven children, and the youngest of the seven who survived to adulthood. As is so often the case in Scottish-English marriages, the Anglicans won out over the Presbyterians and Stephen Foster was baptized in an Episcopal Church. From a very young age his sister, Charlotte Susanna, played the piano and the guitar for him. He could pick out tunes on the guitar before he was three. But his sister died at an early age and some say that Stephen Foster never got over this loss. He received a private school education and was good with languages. His music tutor, Henry Kleber, was a native of Germany and the most prominent musician in Pittsburgh at that time. Stephen Foster wrote songs as a boy, and at age seventeen wrote his first published song "Open Thy Lattice Love Listen to Me."[4] It is obvious to anyone who knows Foster's music that this song is a continuation of an older tradition. It is not the kind of song which is now associated with him. He had not yet developed his own style.

Stephen Foster's brothers were successful in engineering and trade. Dunning McNair Foster was a steamboat agent down the Ohio in Cincinnati, in partnership with another Scotch-Irishman (this one still a Presbyterian), Archibald Irwin Jr.[5] The firm of Irwin and Foster was quite successful in selling passage on all the boats operating between Pittsburgh and New Orleans. In those days the traffic on the Ohio and Mississippi

Rivers was huge, boosting prosperity and growth in places like Memphis, St. Louis, and Louisville. Stephen Foster joined his brother's firm as a bookkeeper and wrote songs on the side. There was even a period when Dunning went off to the Mexican War that the Foster in Irwin and Foster meant Stephen Foster.[6] But professional singers started to sing Foster's songs. In 1848 he published "Oh! Susanna," and this changed his life. The song gained immediate, almost universal popularity. In 1849 it became the marching song of the wagon trains moving west over the vast continent to the California Gold Rush. All races, ethnic groups, and classes sang "Oh! Susanna."[7]

Stephen Foster left the steamboat agency business and returned to Pittsburgh, where he married Jane Denny McDowell, the daughter of a physician. Her father, Dr. Andrew McDowell, had had the honor of attending Charles Dickens when he visited Pittsburgh in 1842.[8] (After observing the night sky ablaze with the fire and smoke of the steel mills, Dickens pronounced the city, "Hell with the lid lifted.") Stephen and Jane Foster were forever poor and never even had their own home, usually staying with relatives in Allegheny City, and in or near New York City. They separated several times, in 1861 for good. Jane Foster supported herself as a telegraph operator in Greensburg, Pennsylvania. The Fosters had one daughter, Marion.[9]

From 1850 until his death in 1864, Stephen Foster supported himself entirely by writing music. He sometimes spent weeks on one song, starting with the words, then adding the melody, and last the accompaniment. His songs were usually about the South, for two reasons. One is that he paid a visit while he was based in Cincinnati to his father's cousins, the Rowan family, in Bardstown, Kentucky. Judge Rowan had been a United States Senator and a justice of the Kentucky Supreme Court. According to Stephen Foster's brother, Morrison Foster, the judge was their father's first cousin.[10] Kentucky made a great impression on Stephen Foster with its beautiful farms and relaxed ways. He was especially impressed with the black people, and with their music. The second reason was that it was the era of the minstrel show, which the Encyclopaedia Britannica calls "the only indigenous American theatrical form."[11] These shows featured white actors and musicians in blackface, and pseudo-Southern culture with "Ethiopian" music. The largest of the minstrel companies was Christy's Minstrels, which was so popular that it played in one New York theater for a decade. Stephen Foster wrote most of his songs, including the 1851

"Old Folks at Home" ("Swanee River"), for Christy's. E. P. Christy paid Foster for first performance rights.[12] "Swanee River" has since sold over 20 million sheet music copies, possibly the most for any song ever written.[13]

While many minstrel shows depicted blacks in a vulgar way, Foster portrayed sympathetic and compassionate black characters. He used the minstrel "dialect" but not in a demeaning way. His "Nelly Was a Lady," was the first song by a white composer to depict a faithful black couple, and the first to call a black woman "lady" without sarcasm. In a letter to Christy in 1852, he said that he intended "to build up a taste for Ethiopian songs among refined people" by using good words, "instead of the trashy and really offensive words which belong to some songs of that order."[14]

In 1854 one of Foster's closest friends, the abolitionist poet Charles Shiras, died, and soon after Foster lost both of his parents. Foster became depressed and stopped writing as the debts mounted. Finally in 1860 he began again, moving to New York City to be near the theaters and his publishers, Firth, Pond & Co. In these last few years, he turned out over 100 songs, but with the exception of "Beautiful Dreamer", none were as good as those he had done before.[15] There were no more such as "Camptown Races," "My Old Kentucky Home," which is played before every Kentucky Derby, "Jeannie With the Light Brown Hair," and "Ring, Ring de Banjo."

Stephen Foster wrote 286 songs and lived in poverty on an average of about $1,400 per year. Since he was the first in the business, there was no means of enforcing copyrights or collecting royalties. Twenty-eight publishers put out "Swanee River," but only one paid Foster any royalties. In the next century Irving Berlin and others founded ASCAP, taking the example of Foster's exploitation to make sure that other successful songwriters would get the benefits of their work. In his last years Foster declined into alcoholism and despair.[16]

The beautiful Stephen Foster Memorial on the campus of the University of Pittsburgh includes a library, museum and a theater. It is visited by thousands of people every year. The quality of Stephen Foster's songs have been recognized by many including Jenny Lind, Paul Robeson, Marilyn Horne, Fritz Kreisler, and Antonín Dvořák. At times, his work is seen to be politically incorrect, and in some cases, banned from use. This has happened despite Foster's insistence on a good portrayal of black people. On the other hand, Foster's songs remain among the best-known

American music throughout the world. They have been recorded in remote areas of China, have been taught to black South Africans, and have been used in Japanese schools for more than a century. Stephen Foster's songs have become a vision of the United States to many people.[17]

On the morning of January 10, 1864, in a room at the New England Hotel at the corner of Bayard Street and the Bowery in what is now New York's Chinatown, Stephen Foster fell, putting a nasty gash in his head. The chambermaid found him in a pool of blood. A neighbor, George Cooper, lifted him up and Foster told him, "I'm done for." He was taken to Bellvue Hospital where he died a few days later. His brother Morrison came to get him, but found the body already in the city morgue. The custodians gave Morrison Foster the composer's clothes. In a coat pocket was a small purse. Its contents were 38 cents and a fragment of paper with the words, "Dear friends and gentle hearts." A few days later a funeral was held at Pittsburgh's Trinity Episcopal Church, where Foster had been baptized. The Pennsylvania Railroad gave free fares to the funeral party on the way to Allegheny Cemetery. Kleber, Foster's music tutor, was in charge of the band. It must have been a truly tragic sound when they played "Swanee River."[18]

Edvard Grieg

(1843–1907)

Edvard Grieg,
PHOTOFEST

O N A LIST of approximately fifty or so universally recognized composers of serious music in the past three centuries, three have Scottish surnames. The first was Edward Alexander MacDowell (1861–1908), a New Yorker of Scottish ancestry who was known for his piano works but whose compositions are not much played now. He has been called by some, "America's greatest composer." The second was another American, Virgil Thomson, (1896–1989) who is best known for his opera *Four Saints in Three Acts*, written to the libretto of Gertrude Stein. The third, and most important, was Edvard Grieg, whose Scottish surname is disguised by its Norwegian spelling. Grieg is the romantic composer who founded the Norwegian national school, and is, according to Bernard Holland, writing in the *New York Times*, probably that nation's greatest cultural hero. Holland calls his Concerto in A minor "perhaps Norway's most successful export."[1]

Edvard Hagerup Grieg was born at Bergen, the son of Alexander Grieg, the British Consul there. The Scottish name Greig, pronounced

Gregg, and sometimes spelled that way, is often thought to be a substitute, along with Greer, for MacGregor, having been used during the time that clan was outlawed. The composer's grandfather came to Norway in the aftermath of the Battle of Culloden Moor.[2] The name was changed from Greig to Grieg in order to help Norwegians pronounce it. Edvard Grieg's mother, Gesine Hagerup, also had Scottish ancestry, being descended from one Andrew Christie and his wife Anne Guthrie.[3] Although the Scots merged into the Norwegian population, it is reported that Norwegian Christies and Wallaces went back to Scotland for study.[4]

Edvard Grieg received piano instruction from his mother and at age fifteen was encouraged by the musician Ole Bull, to whom he was distantly related,[5] to study on the continent. Grieg went to the Leipzig Conservatory and when he returned to Norway four years later, he was a well-trained musician and composer. Grieg began composing and continuing to learn, particularly more about Norway's folk music. In the winter of 1864–1865 he helped to found the Copenhagen Concert Society. In 1867 he married his cousin, Nina Hagerup. He spent time in Rome where he met the Norwegian playwright Henrik Ibsen (also a descendent of Scottish ancestors)[6] and the Hungarian composer Franz Liszt.[7]

In 1870 Grieg put forth his "Piano Concerto in A Minor." It is his masterwork and, somehow evokes Norway. In a televised interview the pianist Artur Rubinstein said that the great composer of concertos, Rachmaninoff, had told him that Grieg's "Concerto" was the best ever written "without exception."[8] It is played all over the world, along with his other major compositions such as "In Holberg's Time" and the "Peer Gynt Suite," both of which rely on Norwegian folk tradition.

Grieg knew all about his Scottish connections. He even had a Scottish godmother, a Mrs. Stirling. The Rev. W. A. Gray, a Scot visiting Norway, met Grieg and reported his saying in fluent English: "I have various ties to Scotland. I know something of your Scottish writers, too, especially Carlyle. And I admire Edinburgh—Princes Street, the gardens, the old town, the castle—ah, they are beautiful, beautiful!"[9]

In his last years Edvard Grieg and his wife were supported by a stipend from the Norwegian government, and lived peacefully at their home near Bergen, Troldhaugen. Despite poor health, the composer and pianist went on several tours of Scandinavia, Britain, and the continent. His music became extremely popular.

Grieg was much more than a composer to Norway. He was its cultural icon. When he began composing, Norway didn't have a great deal of musical tradition. Grieg retrieved and used what there was, and invented the rest. Bernard Holland says, "A small society had a ready-made tradition dropped in its lap, even though it was less the voice of a nation than that of one citizen."[10]

Martha Graham

(1894–1991)

MARTHA GRAHAM RANKS as one of the great artistic innovators of the twentieth century, and is often mentioned as such along with Joyce, Picasso, and Stravinsky. Although she danced until she reached the age of seventy-five, it is as a choreographer that she is most remembered. The "Graham technique," which is used by dance companies throughout the world, was the first style to succeed classical ballet. The technique trains the inner, visceral muscles' to motivate movement from the center of the body to its extremeties,

Martha Graham,
PHOTOFEST

adding a dramatic third dimension to Graham dance."[1] The name Martha Graham is synonymous with modern dance.[2]

Martha Graham was born in Allegheny, Pennsylvania, which is now the North Side of Pittsburgh. Both her father, Dr. George Graham, and her mother, Jane Beers, were of Scotch-Irish heritage and were strict Presbyterians, and saw to it that their children attended church and Sunday school.[3] Her mother also claimed descent from the Pilgrim Miles Standish.

Dr. Graham was a stern father, and Martha Graham found relief from the family's Irish-Catholic maid who gave the child a sense of fantasy. In

1909 the family moved to Santa Barbara, California. In 1914 Dr. Graham died, leaving his family poor. Martha Graham graduated from Santa Barbara High School in 1913, and from Cumnock College in 1916. She enrolled at the Denishawn School in Los Angeles, a dancing school run by Ruth St. Denis and Ted Shawn. By 1920 she had starred in Shawn's *Xochitl* in New York and appeared in the Greenwich Village Follies between 1923 and 1925.[4]

But Martha Graham decided that she must do her own dances. In 1926 she made her debut at New York's Forty-eighth Street Theater, performing eighteen pieces. Initially, the critics were harsh, but she attracted talented dancers to her troupe. By 1929 the Martha Graham Dance Company had been established. In 1937 she became the first American dancer to perform at the White House. The next year she had her first big success with *American Document*. This dance, which turned the minstrel show toward injustice and suffering, toured the country in sold-out houses. The star of *Document* was Erick Hawkins, who married Martha Graham in 1948. They were divorced in 1954.[5]

Martha Graham's masterpiece was *Appalachian Spring* (1944). Its strong American themes were seen as patriotic during World War II. The piece portrays a wedding and is supported by an Aaron Copeland score. After this success however, Martha Graham went into a period of unproductive depression, drinking heavily. Yet she emerged several years later in her Greek and Hebrew period, exploiting the ancient myths and culminating in *Clytemnestra* (1958), a full-length dance which had a great impact. In 1961 she produced *Samson Agonistes*. As age began to overtake her, she wrote less demanding roles for herself and finally gave the roles to younger dancers and became solely a choreographer.

In her later years Martha Graham became an institution, clothed in beautiful gowns, surrounded by celebrities, and receiving many honors. In 1975 Dame Margot Fonteyn and Rudolf Nureyev appeared with her company, signifying the end of the divide between ballet and modern dance. Mikhail Baryshnikov danced with her group from 1987 to 1989. The little girl who had danced up the aisle of a Presbyterian church[6] had come to the top of her profession.

Several other people of Scottish ancestry should be mentioned as connected with dance. Isadora Duncan (1878–1927) was the principal originator of modern dance. Gelsey Kirkland (1953–) had a spectacular partnership with Baryshnikov. Sir Kenneth MacMillan (1929–1992), born in Dunfermline, was one of the great choreographers and was a director of the Royal Ballet and an associate of the American Ballet Theater.[7]

But the legacy of Martha Graham will last beyond any of these. She collaborated with Isamu Noguchi, Gian-Carlo Menotti, Norman Dello Joio, Paul Hindemith, Leopold Stokowski, Katherine Cornell, and Archibald MacLeish, among others. She taught Gregory Peck, Woody Allen, Bette Davis, Eli Wallach, and Joanne Woodward. She started other companies in London and Israel, and some of her dancers, such as Merce Cunningham, have started their own. Her two hundred-odd pieces and the Martha Graham technique have changed modern dance and ballet forever. She received many honors, including honorary degrees from Harvard and Yale and the Presidential Medal of Freedom, America's highest civilian honor, from President Ford in 1976. In 1984 she received the Legion of Honor at the Paris Opera. Her last piece, *Maple Leaf Rag* (1990), was composed when she was well over ninety years old. As she said, "No artist is ahead of his time. He *is* the time; it is just that others are behind the time."[8]

Joan Sutherland

(1926–)

I N THE UNITED STATES she was called "The Voice of the Century." In Italy she was *La Stupenda*. She helped to revive the difficult and flowery singing known as coloratura, and brought it to a new height. Many critics think she was the best ever at this style. She was without question the best of her time. She renewed interest in the Italian operas of the early nineteenth century of Rossini, Donizetti, and Bellini, among others and brought them to new prominence.

Joan Sutherland,
Photo courtesy of Patrick Jones

Joan Sutherland was born in Sydney, Australia, the daughter of William McDonald Sutherland, who was born at Portskerra in the far north of Scotland, the son of a fisherman. William Sutherland went to Glasgow to learn English and tailoring and at age twenty-two left Scotland for Australia, never to see his parents again. He became a successful tailor and eventually president of the Highland Society in Sydney. He was also an elder in the Presbyterian Church. Joan Sutherland's mother, Muriel Alston, was also of Scottish Presbyterian ancestry. Muriel Sutherland was an excellent singer and taught her daughter until she was about nineteen.[1]

Young Joan Sutherland won a singing competition in Sydney, and was accepted to study at the Royal College of Music in London. One voice coach, Ivor Griffiths, told her that she had the strongest vocal cords he had ever heard, including those of her fellow-Scottish-Australian,[2] Madame Melba.[3] In 1952 Joan Sutherland made her debut at Covent Garden in Mozart's *Die Zauberflöte*. In 1954 she was married to Richard Bonynge, a vocal coach from Sydney who was convinced that she could become a coloratura. Together they trained her voice and she sang in various roles. Then in 1959 she became a sensation in her first performance in Donizetti's *Lucia di Lammermoor*, which Covent Garden had revived especially for her. This became the first of her signature operas, and was followed by her debut as Elvira in Bellini's *I Puritani* in 1960, and as Norma in *Norma* in 1963. She made her debuts at both La Scala and the Metropolitan Opera in 1961 singing *Lucia*.

Joan Sutherland sang all over the world until her retirement in 1990. In particular she liked to sing light roles such as Rosalinde in Strauss' *Die Fledermaus* and Anna Glavari in Lehár's *The Merry Widow*. But it was always the *Bel Canto* roles to which she returned. On her sixtieth birthday, which was the twenty-fifth anniversary of her New York debut, she sang *I Puritani* at the Met. There was so much applause on her first appearance that she had to retreat and start over. The music critic, Fritz Spiegel called her "an institution almost beyond praise or criticism," and ". . . the voice of the century . . ."[4]

Joan Sutherland has a son, Adam Bonynge. She was made a Dame of the British Empire in 1978. Twenty years later, Rudolph Giuliani, the opera-loving mayor, declared a Dame Joan Sutherland day in New York City.

Francis hutcheson

(1694–1746)

Francis Hutcheson,
PICTURE COLLECTION, THE BRANCH
LIBRARIES, THE NEW YORK PUBLIC LIBRARY.

T HE FOUNDER OF the Scottish Enlightenment was the philosopher Francis Hutcheson, who was born at Drumalig, County Down, Ireland. If he had emigrated to the American colonies instead of to Scotland he would have been called Scotch-Irish, that is, someone living in Ireland—usually northern Ireland, who was ethnically Scottish. Hutcheson's family roots were in Ayrshire and he was the son and grandson of Presbyterian ministers.

In 1710 he began his studies at Glasgow University in theology, classics, and philosophy. He left Scotland in 1716 to open a Presbyterian school in Dublin, but in 1729 he was back in Glasgow as professor of moral philosophy. Here he began a modern era by being the first to teach in English instead of Latin, which was then the universal custom.[1] In 1738 he ran into trouble with the Glasgow presbytery for his philosophical views that the standard of good morals was making others happy and that people could know good and evil without knowing God.

During his teaching years, Hutcheson was writing many works which became his Moral Sense philosophy. He rejected the ideas of others that morality was merely in one's self-interest. Instead, he says that, like beauty, virtue is something which is perceived not by reason but by an 'internal' sense. We can prove that we have a moral sense because we take actions which are not related to or are even contrary to our own interests. This shows that not all actions are based on reason.[2] He also argued that the action which is best is that which gives the greatest happiness to the greatest number of people. The was circulated in France as "*assurer the plus grand bonheur possible à la plus grande population possible.*"[3]

In the growing dispute between the American colonies and Britain, Hutcheson took the American side. His writings were read throughout the colonies. He says: "Large numbers of men cannot be bound to sacrifice their own posterity's liberty and happiness, to the ambitious views of the mother country . . . There is something so unnatural in supposing a large society, sufficient for all good purposes of an independent political union, remaining subject to the direction of a distant body of men who know not sufficiently the circumstances and exigencies of this society."[4] To see Hutcheson's influence read Thomas Paine, the greatly influential and revolutionary American pamphleteer, who paraphrased this by saying, "As to government matters, it is not in the power of Britain to do this continent justice: the business of it will soon be too weighty and intricate to be managed with any tolerable degree of convenience by a power so distant from us, and so very ignorant of us. . . ." He added that the colonies would always be "running three or four thousand miles for an answer."[5]

Three decades before the American Revolution Hutcheson said that human rights include the right of a people to oppose tyranny by their governors, and the right to turn independent when the mother country uses "severe and absolute" policies.[6] This of course was not new in Scotland. It was merely a paraphrase of part of the Arbroath Declaration of 1320 which said: "But if he [King Robert I, the Bruce] were to desist from what he has begun . . . we would immediately endeavour to expel him as our enemy and the subverter of his own rights and ours, and make another our king." What was new was to send this message to America and England.

Hutcheson said also, "unalienable rights are essential limitations in all governments."[7] These are words familiar to all Americans. Thomas Jefferson, James Madison, and John Adams all read Hutcheson. His philosophy was carried by thousands of Scotch-Irish Presbyterian pioneers, pushing across the Allegheny Mountains like a giant stream, bringing civilization to the valleys beyond. Hutcheson's work marks the beginning of the ascendance of Scottish thought and the beginning of the decline of English thought (Berkeley, Locke, Hobbes, etc.) on the world.

One of Francis Hutcheson's early allies was Henry Home, Lord Kames (1696–1782) who was born at Kames, in Berwickshire. He became a lawyer and later a judge in the Court of Session and a lord of justiciary in 1763. As a philosopher Kames believed that beauty was what was pleasant to sight and hearing. He was an influence on David Hume and Adam Smith, and numbered among his friends, Benjamin Franklin and Thomas Reid. Kames was in turn influenced by Hutcheson, agreeing that morality was part of the human constitution and that action was the object of philosophy. He thought, also, that sympathy was the "cement of society." As a judge, he believed that the purpose of law and government was the well-being of the people.[8]

Francis Hutcheson had a great influence as the predecessor to the philosophers of the Scottish School of Common Sense, which we will discuss later in this section. He was not part of the school but he was in effect its godfather. His influence on America as the pioneering Briton to take up the colonials' cause, was enormous. Hutcheson was taught in the American Colonies at the College of New Jersey (now Princeton), the College of Philadelphia (now the University of Pennsylvania), and at King's College in New York (now Columbia).

Adam Smith's *Wealth of Nations* was filled with Hutcheson's ideas. Smith, of course, had been his student, and often referred to "the never to be forgotten Hutcheson."[9]

David hume

(1711–1776)

I T IS NOT overreaching to say
that the Scottish Enlightenment
of the last half of the eighteenth century had an enormous effect on the
entire world. It is also possible to say
of Scotland at this time that not since
the days of ancient Greece had so
much creativity come from such a
small place in such a short time.
Indeed, people in this era referred to
Edinburgh as the "Athens of the
North." All of the arts and sciences
were flourishing. Scotland's four universities were packed with students

David Hume,
PICTURE COLLECTION, THE BRANCH LIBRARIES,
THE NEW YORK PUBLIC LIBRARY.

from as far away as the American colonies, while England's two universities were in decline. Thomas Jefferson thought Edinburgh University to
be the best in the world. Benjamin Franklin, who became Dr. Franklin
with an honorary degree from St. Andrews, thought that Scotland in that
era possessed "a set of as truly great men . . . as have ever appeared in one
Age or Country."[1]

In an era without the distractions of television and spectator sports,
philosophy was a subject widely discussed throughout the civilized world
in private and public houses. And philosophy is what propelled things
along in tiny, remote Scotland which at that time was leading the world
as an intellectual center. It is not a coincidence, as we shall see later, that

the American and French revolutions took place in the same half century as Scotland's prominence.

Francis Hutcheson, as we have said, was the philosopher who sparked the Scottish Enlightenment, but he was not its beacon nor its center. Those positions belong to one of the greatest men of all time, David Hume, who is almost universally recognized as the greatest philosopher ever produced by Great Britain. Hume was the son of Joseph Hume and Catherine Falconer. He was born on his father's small estate, Ninehills, near Berwick-upon-Tweed in 1711. He entered Edinburgh University at age 12. Later he studied law but didn't show much interest in it. In 1734 he went to France to pursue his interest in philosophy, living most of the time at La Flèche near the great *chateaux* of the Loire Valley. It was during his three years in France that Hume composed his masterpiece, *A Treatise of Human Nature*, which was published in 1739. He thought he had produced a great work and historical assessment agrees, but at the time there was little interest.[2]

The *Treatise* is an attempt by Hume to introduce the experimental, scientific approach into philosophy. In the book's introduction he claims to be changing philosophy completely. His idea was to put philosophy on a scientific basis using observation and experience for his input. Hume's philosophy is skeptical and questions everything including religious beliefs, saying that what has been shown to be true may not be true. According to some Hume proved that there could not be a rational belief and that experience and reason have no connection with each other.[3] He says that neither the senses nor reason can show that an object (a cause) is related to another object (an effect). For instance it is not possible to prove that a ball dropped from a tree will fall to the ground, just because that has been observed to have happened before. Yet although we cannot prove this causality, we believe in it and should believe in it. He thinks it would be ridiculous to say that the sun will probably rise tomorrow, even though we cannot prove that it will. He asks us to imagine the first man's first day. Adam at his first sunset would have had no idea when or whether the sun would rise again. The difference between Adam and ourselves is experience.[4]

In 1741, Hume published *Essays, Moral and Political*, which met with some success. In 1744 he made application for the chair of moral philosophy at Edinburgh, but because of his heretical image, it was denied. He wandered for several years, and worked for a time as secretary to General

James Sinclair in such places as Vienna and Turin. He returned to Edinburgh from 1751 to 1763, and tried to succeed Adam Smith in the chair of logic at Glasgow, but again charges of atheism denied him a post. In 1752 he was made custodian of the Advocate's library in Edinburgh, and here, fortified with 30,000 books, began to write his *History of England*, which, for its time was far better than anything written previously. The book was written in an easy style and was published in dozens of editions. Upon its publication, David Hume became famous.[5]

In 1763 he became secretary to the British embassy in Paris, and despite his portly build and unsophisticated manners, he became a celebrity. The French welcomed and honored him in the *salons* and referred to him as *le bon David*. In 1766 Hume went to London with Jean Jacques Rousseau, who was escaping persecution. Rousseau was given a country place to live in, but suspected a plot and hurried back to France. He accused Hume in the plot, so there soon appeared *A Concise and Genuine Account of the Dispute Between Mr. Hume and M. Rousseau.*[6]

In 1769 Hume returned to his beloved Edinburgh and wrote many other works including an autobiography. In his political writings he says, "Divide the people into many separate bodies; and then they may debate with safety, and every inconvenience seems to be prevented."[7] His *Essay on Miracles* is one of the most famous, as it states that the supporting evidence for any given miracle is suspect. Hume says that violations of the laws of nature may have occurred, but that beliefs in these miracles are not justified by evidence.[8] Hume believed that man was more of a creature of sentiment than of reason. He thought also that the Creator may have made too many competing species who constantly attacked each other.[9] This view of course, preceded the ideas of Darwin.

The skeptical Hume provoked a reaction to his ideas, which became the Common Sense school of Scottish philosophers. Their relatively uncomplicated ideas put him at odds with them. But when Thomas Reid, whom we discuss in the next essay, had an intermediary show Hume the manuscript of his Common Sense ideas, which were harshly opposed to Hume's, Hume's reply was considerate and cordial. In fact Hume put aside his skepticism on one subject, morality, because of Hutcheson's idea (see p. 267) that morality was self-evident.[10] Thus, Hume, the great doubter, became a Common Sense moralist. Hume thought that the moral sense of man came from sympathy for his fellow man, and noted that from the earliest times people have been social, as he himself certainly was.

Everyone liked him and he had many friends, even ministers, in the intellectual clubhouse that was Edinburgh during the Golden Age. He died in his Edinburgh house in 1776 and is buried on Calton Hill.

Adam Smith, whose own work had been influenced by the writings of Hume, was Hume's literary executor. Smith wrote in the autobiography *The Life of David Hume, by Himself,* that his friend was "approaching as nearly to the idea of a perfectly wise and virtuous man as perhaps the nature of human frailty will permit."[11]

The influence of David Hume is immense. Germans think that his work pushed Kant into creating the "critical" philosophy. He led Auguste Comte toward "positivism," and had influence on the work and ideas of Jeremy Bentham and John Stuart Mill. He received tributes from Voltaire, Diderot, Montesquieu, Gibbon, and Kant;[12] and James Boswell called him "the greatest writer in Britain."[13] In the latter part of the eighteenth century and the beginning of the nineteenth, Hume's influence was pushed aside by the Scottish Common Sense school, which made a stunning and immediate impact on the world, particularly in America and France, as we will see in the next essay. But as the centuries have progressed Common Sense has become relatively unimportant and the work of Hume is exalted.

But the greatest influence of David Hume was on his own country. He was the giant force in eighteenth-century Scotland, during the magical half-century which made that country the envy of the world. In Hume's time, Scotland produced a torrent of scientific discoveries and inventions, brilliant literature, wondrous art, and deep scholarship in quantities and in quality, which would have been enough for a major nation. Yet even today many educated Scots will respond to the question, "Who was the most influential Scot?" with the answer, "David Hume."

Thomas Reid

(1710–1796)

Professor Thomas Reid after James Tassie. THE SCOTTISH NATIONAL PORTRAIT GALLERY.

A S WE HAVE said, David Hume was in his time recognized as the foremost British philosopher. But before he could get really comfortable with all of the adulation, he was knocked off his feet by an upstart from the northeast of his own country who was shocked at his skepticism, and tried to prove him wrong. Thomas Reid, the founder of the Scottish School of Common Sense, was born at Strachan in Kincardineshire, the son of Lewis Reid, a minister and his wife, Margaret Gregory, of the notable family of mathematicians. The famous James Gregory (1638–1675) who had invented the reflecting telescope and anticipated the discovery of differential calculus was Thomas Reid's great uncle. Reid studied at Aberdeen's Marischal College and was licensed for the ministry in 1731. From 1733 through 1736 he was the librarian at the school. In 1740 he was married to his cousin Elizabeth who eventually bore him nine children.[1]

In 1737 he was appointed to minister at New Machar, near Aberdeen, and here he became aware of Hume's *Treatise on Human Nature*, and began his life's work of refuting its ideas. In this he was influenced by the work of Francis Hutcheson. In 1751 he was given the chair of philosophy at King's College, Aberdeen; and in 1764, succeeded Adam Smith in the chair of moral philosophy at Glasgow.[2] In the same year he published *An Inquiry into the Human Mind on the Principles of Common Sense*.[3]

Reid's idea is that the philosopher's duty is not to challenge facts, which we all know to be true. Rather it is his job to take these facts and find out what it is that we know about them; to analyze them. Reid berates other philosophers' reliance on ideas. He says sarcastically that it has been found out by the means of ideas that "fire is not hot, nor snow cold, nor honey sweet; and in a word, that heat and cold, sound, colour, taste, and smell, are nothing but ideas or impressions."[4] Reid says that our natural faculties are trustworthy and are the footing of all of our behavior and that without them we will fall into the abyss of skepticism. "The basic beliefs in our faculties must be assumed to be trustworthy without argumentation, because all argumentation assumes the trustworthiness of our faculties."[5] He adds, directly aiming at Hume, "But the triumph of ideas was completed by the *Treatise on Human Nature* . . . which leaves ideas and impressions as the sole existences in the universe."[6]

Reid argued that there are many instinctively known moral principles, some of which are displayed in the Ten Commandments, which all people can comprehend. He held that certain moral "truths" were "self-evident." He even said that if a philosophical argument goes against common sense, then the philosophy must be in error.[7] He continues, saying that in an ordinary man's life, situations and sensations are not just ideas or impressions, but are believed to be real. Such beliefs Reid says, "belong to the common sense of mankind." And in matters of common sense, "the learned and the unlearned, the philosopher and the day-labourer, are upon a level."[8]

David Hume was presented with the manuscript of Reid's *Inquiry* and his magnanimous answer does not suggest that he thought he was treated unfairly. There was no real personal animosity between the two men, although they clashed like medieval jousters in the philosophical arena. Reid even called Hume "the greatest metaphysician of the age."[9]

From Germany, Immanuel Kant blasted Common Sense and said it was a way that the "emptiest talker" could best "the profoundest thinker."[10] But Reid was not claiming that Common Sense was a revelation of truth (as Kant thought he meant) but that there is in everyone common-sense knowledge.[11]

Adam Ferguson (1723–1816) was another member of the Scottish Common Sense school. He was born at Logierait in Perthshire and attended St. Andrews, eventually becoming a minister. In 1745, Ferguson, a native Gaelic speaker, became chaplain of the Black Watch regiment and at the battle of Fontenoy actually led an attack, sword in hand. In 1759 he succeeded Hume at the Advocate's Library, and in 1764 he became professor of moral philosophy at Edinburgh. His greatest work was his *A History of Civil Society*, published in 1767. His main argument is that human well-being is the result of pursuing social goals, rather than private goals. Ferguson thought that there was a danger in the unbridled self-interest of commercial society. For this he is sometimes called the "father" of Sociology. His work is said to have influenced German philosophers, notably Schiller and Hegel.[12]

Reid's student, Dugald Stewart (1753–1828) greatly enhanced his tutor's reputation and also linked Reid with Hutcheson, giving the idea of a "Scottish school" credibility. Stewart was born in Edinburgh, the son of a mathematics professor. He was educated at Edinburgh and Glasgow, and in 1775 joined his father, Matthew, as co-professor of mathematics at Edinburgh. In 1785 he succeeded Adam Ferguson as professor of moral philosophy. Stewart's work, *Elements of the Philosophy of the Human Mind*, clarified Reid's philosophy. He was praised also for his *Life and Writings of Adam Smith*. Stewart numbered among his students Sir Walter Scott, and James Mill, the father of John Stuart Mill. His stature is attested to by the elaborate monument to him on Calton Hill in Edinburgh.[13]

The effect of Common Sense was immediate and far-reaching. The esoteric skepticism of Hume was shunted aside for a century as the new philosophy began to dominate Scottish thought. Common Sense made religion reasonable and Scotland was a very religious country. Faith and reason were made compatible. A scientist saw no reason why he should not be a Christian. A devout Christian saw no reason why he shouldn't be a scientist or a businessman. As Adam Smith gave moral justification to self-interested money-making; now Common Sense justified Christianity as the moral status quo. Productive work, religion, and education were seen to be complimentary to each other. And elevating the views of the common man promoted democracy. After all, if the observations and reasoning of ordinary people put "the philosopher and the day-labourer" "on a level," as Reid had said; then there was no reason why the day-laborer could not aspire to become a philosopher or any other position.

There was also no reason why the vote of the common man would not be valued. If Common Sense was anything it was egalitarian, and it swept through Scotland in the sermons of Presbyterian ministers. Scotland had always been more egalitarian than other countries and now the country's clergy was proclaiming a divine basis for the equality of man. Robert Burns echoed the Scottish sentiment when he said:

> What though on hamely fare we dine,
>   Wear hoddin grey, an' a' that?
> Gie fools their silks, and knaves their wine—
>   A man's a man for a' that.
>
> Ye see yon birkie ca'd a 'lord,'
>   Wha struts, an' stares, an' a' that?
> Tho' hundreds worship at his word,
>   He's but a cuif for a' that.
> For a' that, an' a' that,
>   His ribband, star, an' a' that,
> The man o' independent mind,
>   He looks an' laughs at a' that.

Soon these ideas swept the north of Ireland just as tens of thousands of disaffected Scottish-descended Presbyterians were embarking by the boatloads for the American colonies. Many preached Common Sense in the Presbyterian churches of Philadelphia where most of them landed, and took it with them to the Presbyterian churches of western Pennsylvania in towns they founded such as Tyrone, Derry, and Donegal. They took it to the new, heavily Scotch-Irish city of Pittsburgh, and further west throughout the frontier.

It was not long until Common Sense reached the College of New Jersey at Princeton where a new president, an immigrant minister from Scotland, arrived in 1768. John Witherspoon (c. 1723–1794) took over what was then a small, struggling school for the Presbyterian ministry and began to turn it into one of the most respected universities in North America, adding courses, raising money, and enticing students. Witherspoon, whose mother claimed descent from John Knox, had declined to minister to the Scottish kirk at Rotterdam.[14] But an American visitor, Benjamin Rush, who had studied at Princeton, convinced him to come to America.

Witherspoon became an enthusiastic American early on, almost immediately siding with the colonists in their dispute with the mother country. Only eight years after he arrived in America, he was in Philadelphia helping to write the Declaration of Independence. At one point he objected to a racial slur against the Scots in an early draft which complained that King George III had used "Scotch and foreign merce-naries" against the colonists. The offensive words were removed and Witherspoon became the only clergyman to sign the Declaration.[15]

In Scotland Witherspoon had studied with Adam Smith, David Hume, and Thomas Reid, and became convinced of the validity of Reid's philosophy. He preached Common Sense at Princeton, and so effective was he that it became the dominant philosophy in America. The histori-an Garry Wills thinks that Witherspoon may have been the most influ-ential teacher in the history of American education. Included in the 478 Princeton graduates during his term were:[16]

1 president of the United States (James Madison)
1 vice president of the United States (Aaron Burr)
3 Supreme Court Justices
5 cabinet members
12 delegates to the Continental Congress
12 state governors
21 United States senators
29 United States representatives
33 Judges
56 state legislators
6 signers of the Declaration of Independence
9 delegates to the Constitutional Convention
31 Revolutionary army officers, and more than
100 ministers

The effect of these men on revolutionary America was magnified even more by the fact that Princetonians, unlike the graduates of Harvard, Yale, Columbia, Penn, and William and Mary, did not come primarily from their college's locality. Princeton men came from all over the colonies and when they graduated, returned to their various homes, spreading the sober Scottish philosophy throughout America. There were nine Princeton graduates at the Constitutional Convention. Harvard and Yale together had only seven.[17]

Common Sense also was taught at the College of Philadelphia (now the University of Pennsylvania) by the immigrant Scottish professor William Smith. Thomas Carlyle thought that Hume's influence on America was mainly as a historian and that it was Reid, along with Smith, Ferguson, and Stewart who had the philosophical power. As an example he pointed out that as a student, Emerson was required to study Reid and to write a paper on Dugald Stewart.[18]

Americans were thoroughly exposed to the Scottish philosophy when traveling to Scotland. They preferred the Scottish universities to those of England to the extent that there was even a Virginian club at Edinburgh. Benjamin Franklin visited Scotland twice, in 1759 and 1771. He said that the country had far exceeded his expectations and that the weeks he spent there were the best of any in his life. He even said that if he did not have reasons to return to America he would choose to live out the rest of his life in Scotland.[19] He knew most of the Scottish philosophers, and spent his last night in the country in the company of Adam Ferguson.

Many of the better tutors in the colonies were Scots. Jefferson had three Scottish teachers, Samuel Finley, William Douglas, and most importantly William Small, who Jefferson said, "probably fixed the destinies of my life."[20] James Madison studied with Archibald Campbell and boarded for five years with Donald Robertson who taught him to speak French with a Scottish accent.[21] Many other Americans who were to become influential studied with Scots, including George Mason, Alexander Hamilton, and Richard Henry Lee.

The radical Thomas Paine attended lectures by Adam Ferguson in London just prior to emigrating to America.[22] When Paine later wrote one of the most influential pamphlets ever published calling for the people of America to take action for independence—selling tens of thousands of copies in the six months preceding the revolution—he actually called it *Common Sense*. Was this just a coincidence? Or did Paine and Benjamin Rush, who suggested the title, realize that the Scottish philosophy fit with the budding revolution around them and that by then was so well-known in the colonies that it had become American rather than Scottish? The Americans wanted reason *and* faith. They wanted democracy, free trade and low taxes. They wanted a harmonious society. They wanted uncomplicated ideas which would help them to conquer a continent. They wanted egalitarianism and they wanted freedom from Great Britain. All of these had been promised by Adam Smith, Francis

Hutcheson, and most directly by Thomas Reid. The English Parliamentarian Horace Walpole said it best: "There is no use crying about it. Cousin America has run off with the Presbyterian parson, and that is the end of it."[23]

The simple Scottish philosophy founded by Thomas Reid reached out to Europe as well, particularly to France, which was looking at America with a view toward its own revolution. When the Marquis de Lafayette wrote the first draft of the Declaration of the Rights of Man and the Citizen, at the very beginning of the French Revolution in 1789, he was assisted by Thomas Jefferson. The ideas expressed were those of the Declaration of Independence, which relied heavily on Scottish philosophy. In fact, from 1816 to 1870, the Scottish Common Sense philosophy was adopted as the official philosophy of France.[24]

It is absolutely unprecedented in all of history that in one century, a small country like Scotland could produce philosophers of the caliber of Adam Smith, David Hume, Francis Hutcheson, Lord Kames, Thomas Reid, Adam Ferguson, and Dugald Stewart. There is no question that Scottish philosophy was dominant in the same half century which brought both the American and French revolutions, or that these movements were heavily influenced by the Scottish School. It happened. It was Scotland's Golden Age.

After its preamble, the American Declaration of Independence begins: "We hold these Truths to be self-evident, that all Men are created equal, that they are endowed by their Creator with certain unalienable Rights . . ." It is straight from the pen of Thomas Reid.

Adam Smith

(1723–1790)

*T*HE *WEALTH OF Nations*, published over two centuries ago in remote Scotland, has had the most influence on economics and politics of any book ever written. It remains the Bible of free trade. Its author, Adam Smith, observed many things which few others could see at the time. One was that the then current economic system—the mercantile system, whereby countries established colonies and exclusive trading policies with those colonies—was doomed to failure. Inherent in the system was the idea that the main benefits of the colonial trade would belong to the mother country and Smith saw clearly that this could not prevail. He also thought that the mother countries would profit more by letting their colonies go free. These revolutionary and perhaps even seditious ideas would soon be widely embraced. Within a short period of time mercantilism began to be abandoned in favor of free trade.

Adam Smith was born in the Scottish town of Kirkcaldy in Fifeshire several months after the death of his father, the local customs official. He was kidnapped by gypsies at age three, but a relative was able to find and return him to his mother.[1] He was a good student and was able to enroll at Glasgow University at the age of fourteen. There he studied under the great philosopher, Francis Hutcheson. In 1740 he won admission to Balliol College at Oxford, but didn't take to the place. He left in 1746, returning to Scotland where he became a noted lecturer. Here he became a close friend of philosopher David Hume and many other Scottish luminaries. In 1751 he was appointed professor of logic at Glasgow and in 1752 professor of moral philosophy.[2]

In 1759 Smith published his *Theory of Moral Sentiments*, which brought him to the top of the robust intellectual society of Scotland during the country's golden age. In this broad philosophical work Smith suggested that sympathy is a key to human behavior. He also says that the commonly held values of a society restrain the people of that society. In 1763 he was appointed tutor to third Duke of Buccleuch and his brother, a position which paid him handsomely. From 1764 to 1766 he traveled with his pupils to France where he broadened his contacts further, then returned to Kirkcaldy to live with his mother and to write his masterpiece.[3]

An Inquiry Into the Nature and Causes of The Wealth of Nations was finally published ten years later in the earth-shaking year of 1776. Among the words it contains are these: "Under the present system of management, therefore, Great Britain derives nothing but loss from the dominion she assumes over her colonies." He suggests that Britain should let the colonies go, but admits that this idea is "to propose such a measure as never was, and never will be adopted, by any nation in the world." Then he says, "If it was adopted, however, Great Britain would not only be immediately freed from the whole annual expence of the peace establishment of the colonies, but might settle with them such a treaty of commerce as would effectually secure to her a free trade, more advantageous to the great body of the people, though less so to the merchants, than the monopoly which she at present enjoys. By thus parting good friends, the natural affection of the colonies to the mother country, which perhaps, our late dissensions have well nigh extinguished, would quickly revive." He adds that the newly freed colonies might actually "favour us in war as well as in trade, and, instead of turbulent and factious subjects, to become our most faithful, affectionate, and generous allies . . . ."[4] Of course as Smith foresaw, Great Britain did not let the colonies go. War was necessary to accomplish American freedom. And all the benefits of separation, which he predicted, came true. The United States of America and Great Britain have enjoyed a vigorous trade since the Revolution. Despite periods of tension, the two countries have retained a mutual affection and have fought as allies throughout the twentieth century in what some presidents and prime ministers have referred to as a "special relationship."

When The Wealth of Nations was published it must have acted as a philosophical beacon for the besieged Americans. Here was Smith, a Briton who was risking charges of treason, agreeing with them and giving their struggle a moral basis. In his section, Prosperity of the New Colonies, he says, referring to the oppressive British trade laws in America, "To prohibit a great people, however, from making all that they can of every part of their own produce, or from employing their stock and industry in the way that they judge most advantageous to themselves, is a manifest violation of the most sacred rights of mankind."[5] In other words, property rights are the equivalent of human rights.

In his section *"America and East Indies"* he blames the mercantile system for the rebellion of the colonies and says, "The monopoly of the colony trade, therefore, like all the other mean and malignant expedients of the mercantile system, depresses the industry of all other countries, but chiefly that of the colonies, without in the least increasing, but on the contrary diminishing, that of the country in whose favour it is established."[6]

Smith goes on to suggest that the Americans would win the war. ". . . it is not very probable that they will ever voluntarily submit to us; and we ought to consider that the blood which must be shed in forcing them to do so, is, every drop of it, the blood either of those who are, or of those whom we wish to have as our fellow citizens. They are very weak who flatter themselves that, in the state to which things have come, our colonies will be easily conquered by force alone."[7] He also proposes what the colonists insisted upon, American representation in Parliament, and says ". . . there is not the least probability that the British constitution would be hurt by the union of Great Britain with her colonies."[8] Undoubtedly George III and his parliamentarians were aware of *The Wealth of Nations*, but despite its reasoned approach to the conflict, they pursued the war to its inevitable end.

The largest idea in Smith's treatise is however, that individuals competing against each other without a great deal of government regulation can produce more wealth than they can with oppressive regulations. And further, that as people pursue their own gains they may very well increase the wealth of others. As he put it every individual "intends only his own security; and by directing that industry in such a manner as its produce may be of greatest value, he intends only his own gain, and he is in this, as in many other cases, led by an invisible hand to promote an end which was no part of his intention. By pursuing his own interest he frequently promotes that of the society more effectually than when he really intends to promote it."[9] These words gave a philosophical basis to the Industrial Revolution, then just getting underway.

For the next century Smith was the world's dominant economic philosopher, but towards the end of the nineteenth century he was challenged and then overtaken by a voice, completely contrary to his own, that of Karl Marx. Until the twentieth century neared its end, most of the world's intellectuals sided with or at least leaned toward Marx. But when the Berlin Wall fell, the ideas of communism which had produced despotic governments but not a single prosperous country were exposed as failures. Today all over the world, even in Russia and China, communist economic systems are being dismantled and free trade and individual enterprise encouraged. Marxism is in disrepute, and the ideas of Adam Smith are embraced almost everywhere.

In addition to its central messages, *The Wealth of Nations* is full of interesting, liberal ideas, and despite what some say Smith was not an exponent of unbridled *laissez faire*. Throughout the book Smith's sympathy for the common man comes through and he advocates things like good conditions for workers. Although he is generally against tariffs on imported goods, he admits that there are situations in which they are justified, such as when an industry is necessary to the defense of the country. On the other hand he says "The natural advantages which one country has over another in producing particular commodities are sometimes so great, that it is acknowledged by all the world to be in vain to struggle with them. By means of glasses, hotbeds, and hotwalls, very good grapes can be raised in Scotland, and very good wine too can be made of them at about thirty times the expence for which at least equally good can be brought from foreign countries. Would it be reasonable to prohibit the importation of all foreign wines, merely to encourage the making of claret and burgundy in Scotland?"[10] On the same subject he says ". . . if we consult experience, the cheapness of wine seems to be the cause, not of drunkeness, but of sobriety. The inhabitants of the wine countries are in general the soberest people in Europe; witness the Spaniards, the Italians, and the inhabitants of the southern provinces of France. On the contrary, in the countries which, either from excessive heat or cold, produce no grapes, and where wine consequently is dear and a rarity, drunkenness is a common vice. . . "[11] Years later, Thomas Jefferson appropriated a paraphrase of these words as his own.

One can open *The Wealth of Nations* to almost any page and find a fascinating discussion on diverse subjects. On slavery Smith says "But if great improvements are seldom to be expected from great proprietors, they are least of all to be expected when they employ slaves for their workmen. The experience of all ages and nations, I believe, demonstrates that the work done by slaves, though it appears to cost only their maintenance, is in the end the dearest of any. A person who can acquire no property, can have no other interest but to eat as much, and to labour as little as possible."[12] This pragmatic argument against slavery might have been a better argument against the practice than a moral one.

On the American Indians Smith talks about ". . . the injustice of coveting the possession of a country whose harmless natives, far from having ever injured the people of Europe, had received the first adventurers with every mark of kindness and hospitality."[13]

So broad is the reach of *The Wealth of Nations* that it is difficult to comprehend that it was only a part of what Smith intended to write about. He had conceived to discuss all aspects of human experience and already had planned two major works, one on law and the other on science and art. A few days before his death he had his notes on these subjects burned. In 1788 his renown had brought him the post of Commissioner of Customs for the city of Edinburgh. He died there in 1790 and remains buried in Canongate Churchyard.

Adam Smith was one of the geniuses of history. His masterwork founded, essentially, the science of political economy and gave the world an

explanation of, and justification for free trade which it continues to do to this day. The book promoted and propelled the Industrial Revolution just at the time that it was beginning to gain speed, and serves and will continue to serve as an eloquent argument in favor of freedom and against despotism among the developing countries of the twenty-first century. Smith's largest message was his belief in free trade. Were he to come back to

The grave of Adam Smith.
Canongate Churchyard, Edinburgh.
COLLECTION OF THE AUTHOR.

life he would be delighted to find things like the EEC, GATT, and rampant globalization. He believed that any country however backward, would achieve economic success if it were at peace, had low taxes, allowed relatively free trade, and had just courts. *The Wealth of Nations* is still studied throughout the world.

His work brought Smith the respect, admiration, and friendship of many great men including the scientist Joseph Black, and the architect Robert Adam. As celebrated as he is today, he was even more so in his own day. At a formal dinner in London William Pitt insisted that Smith be seated before anyone else on the grounds that the rest of the company were all his "scholars."[14]

Immanuel Kant

(1724–1804)

IMMANUEL KANT WAS Germany's most important philosopher and one of the most important in world history. All of the brilliant writing produced by Germans since 1781, when Kant produced his *Kritik der reinen Vernunft* (*Critique of Pure Reason*), was influenced by him.

Immanuel Kant was born in Königsberg, a city in what was then East Prussia. Since 1946 it has been known as Kaliningrad and is in Russia. There is very little known about Kant's life. The lack of detail is unusual for someone whose influence has been so profound. This is probably attributable to the fact that he never in his life traveled beyond this provincial town's environs. His

Immanuel Kant,

father was a saddlemaker "of very small means" and his mother uneducated, but "remarkable for her character and for her natural intelligence." The *Encyclopedia Britannica* does not even give us his parents' names. Kant was educated at the Collegium Fridericianum in Königsberg, and attended the University of Königsberg in 1740. He became a tutor and in 1755 was given the position of *Privatdozent* at Königsberg. For the next fifteen years he taught science, mathematics, and philosophy. In 1770 he was promoted to professor of logic and metaphysics, a position he held almost to his death.[1]

Kant's philosophy was an attempt to reject all previous metaphysics and start over. He disagreed with Gottfried Wilhelm Leibniz (1646–1716) the founder of German philosophy who assumed that human intelligence had powers which a careful examination shows is nonexistent. Kant drew on the philosophy of the Enlightenment, which occurred for the most part in three countries. England had produced Hobbes, Locke, Berkeley, Shaftsbury, and Burke. Scotland had Hume, Reid, Hutcheson, and Smith. France had given Condorcet, Diderot, Rousseau, and Voltaire. Kant's preeminence in Germany rests upon the fact that his great mind was able to draw from The Enlightenment and begin a new era.[2] He said that David Hume "woke him from his dogmatic slumber."[3]

Kant wanted to vindicate the authority of reason. He argued that reason is the means by which experiences are made understandable.[4] He said that the existence of God could not be proved by science. But Kant believed in God and in a future life and "was certain nothing could shake these beliefs." This belief was not logical, but "a moral certainty." A man should say "I am morally certain," not "it is a moral certainty." Nevertheless the authorities warned him that writings such as these were "too rationalistic."[5]

It may be difficult for some to understand that this insular German genius was in any way Scottish, but in fact most books about Kant offer some reference to his grandfather's having come from Scotland. Many authorities think that this can not be demonstrated but they have not read a little-known book written a century ago by Th. A. Fischer, the only expert on the Scots in Germany. According to Fischer, this is what the philosopher said: "It is very well known to me, that my grandfather, who was a citizen of the Prusso-Lithuanian town of Tilsit, came originally from Scotland."[6] Fischer has much more to say, but there are two things that the reader should know before taking this farther. The first is that Cant, according to the best authority, George Fraser Black, is an obscure but very old and very definitely Scottish name.[7] It would have been all but certain that the spelling of the name in Germany would change to Kant, because that is the way that sound is spelled in Germany. Coffee is kaffee, and corn becomes korn. The second thing is that at the time of Kant's birth, the Prussian coast of the Baltic was teeming with Scottish traders and had been for several centuries. And most of these traders were not integrated into the German nation. They imported wives from Scotland. They maintained their own, usually Presbyterian, churches, their own schools, charities, and hospitals.[8] It is possible therefore to postulate that Immanuel Kant came from a Scottish-Presbyterian exile community on the Baltic seacoast.

Fischer has evidence of this. He found a contract which he labels in an appendix: *Agreement between Hans Kant, the Grandfather of the Philosopher, and Hans Karr, his Brother-in-Law.* It is dated June 4, 1670. To quote part of the agreement: ". . . the contracting parties for the sake of peace and brotherly love have agreed, that Hans Karr should pay to Hans Kant 150 Thaler in all, together with ten yards of linen, at five shillings a yard, in return for which Kant resigns all and every claim to the public house at Werdden . . ."[9] Notice that the contract is written in English! Since Hans Karr is related to Hans Kant it would seem possible, perhaps even likely, that he might be Scottish also. Consulting Black again we find that Karr is a variant spelling of the ancient Border surname, Kerr.[10] Now come the knockout blows. Fischer notes that a fine of ten thaler is fixed in case of a breach of the contract payable at the Presbyterian Church at Memel! And further, that two of the four witnesses were Scots, Thomas Sckrumsor (Scrimgeour) and Wilhelm Murray![11]

It appears that we have a picture here of men from a Scottish community settling a dispute without recourse to German law. Perhaps they were not even entitled to or were suspicious of German justice. And what of Kant's intelligent mother? Immanuel Kant did not like women, and never married. Could that be why he doesn't discuss his maternal ancestry? In a tight knit community as this may have been, perhaps his mother was Scottish, also. It may be that Immanuel Kant was entirely Scottish.

Immanuel Kant was very short, just over five feet tall, and small chested. But he was able to live a full life, healthy almost to the end. It is amazing that German philosophy and letters bloomed as never before or since, for forty years after he wrote his major work in 1781. The strength of the movement which Kant started is especially impressive inasmuch as the country was under French occupation for much of the time. Germany was at its lowest ebb, politically, but at its highest intellectually. Fichte, Hegel, Schopenhauer, Schleiermacher, Herbart, Schiller, and Goethe were all born between five and thirty-two years before or after the publication of the *Kritik* in 1781. All of these geniuses were influenced by Kant and his work. This was the era when people all over the world spoke of the German *Weltanschauung*. In this movement, the work of Kant was of "incomparably high historical importance."[12] And his influence continues today.

John Stuart Mill

(1806–1873)

John Stuart Mill,

J OHN STUART MILL is thought
of as one of Britain's greatest
philosophers, but he was much more
than that. He was an observer of
everything from capitalism to religion to women's rights, and a prolific
writer whose ideas had a great influence on the British Empire at its
height. His ideas are still being
debated today.

Mill was born in London, the
son of the famous Scottish intellectual James Mill. James Mill was in
turn the son of James Milne, a shoe-
maker in the village Logie Pert in
Forfarshire. (Milne is the Scottish form of Mill, just as Millar is the
Scottish form of Miller.) James Milne married Isobel Fenton who had
been a servant in Edinburgh. The Fentons had once been of much higher social standing, but were ruined after having backed the Stuart side in
the rebellion of 1745–1746. Isobel Fenton Milne was determined that her
son would redeem her family and was not disappointed. After changing
the family name to Mill, which she thought had more class to it, her son
James Mill was given the best education which could be afforded, and he
proceeded to make the most of it. The good-looking young man became
a tutor at age seventeen, and this got him to Edinburgh University where

he studied under Dugald Stewart, alongside Jeffrey, who was to become famous with his *Edinburgh Review*, and Brougham, who was to become Lord Chancellor, the head of the judiciary of Great Britain. Then James Mill's life suddenly changed when his patron, Sir John Stuart, bought him a ticket to London.[1]

In London James Mill became a companion and ally of the philosopher and economist, Jeremy Bentham, and became a well-known intellectual in Britain. His best work was *The History of British India*, written in 1817.[2] He married Harriet Burrow who brought him a dowry of £400 and a house at £50 annual rent. James Mill named their son John Stuart Mill after his sponsor. Young Mill was educated entirely by his father who was a stern taskmaster. He learned Greek words at age three. By age eight he had read Aesop, Herodotus, and Plato, as well as works by Hume and Gibbon. At eight he began Latin, Euclid, and algebra. By age ten he was teaching other children and could read the Greek classics with ease. At twelve he had read much of Virgil, Horace, Livy, Ovid, and Cicero in Latin, as well as Homer, Thucydides, and Aristotle in Greek. By age thirteen he was reading Adam Smith and David Ricardo.[3] A study of genius in 1926 estimated the I.Q. of John Stuart Mill in the range of 190–200, the highest for anyone ever.[4]

But all of this had a price. John Stuart Mill had been under stress for a long time and hadn't had a normal boyhood. In 1820 he went to France and stayed until 1821 near Toulouse. At least this was some change, but his work habits continued and he studied nine hours a day, learning French and becoming a Francophile. Although he wasn't an athlete he loved walking in the countryside. Back in London the tall, slightly built Mill began to be noticed. He was fair-haired and always wore black. He began to write articles for several papers on various subjects and studied German. He found employment as an examiner at India House, the headquarters of the East India Company. In 1830 he began a long, apparently platonic romance with Mrs. Harriet Taylor who was an invalid. His parents were outraged at the scandal which ensued. When Mr. Taylor died in 1851, Mill and Mrs. Taylor were married. They were a devoted couple. On a vacation to Avignon in 1858 Harriet died. Mill's response was to buy a house near to her grave so that he could visit. Ever afterward he spent significant time in Avignon.[5]

Over the years Mill published many works, including *System of Logic* (1843), *Political Economy* (1848), and *Three Essays on Religion* (1874). His most important work was probably *On Liberty* (1859), which is the classical liberal statement on the importance of individual freedom. Mill defended "absolute freedom of opinion, nearly absolute freedom of expression, (the qualification turning on circumstances where expression constitutes 'a positive instigation to some mischievous act') and freedom of action so long as it does not harm others."[6] He was elected to Parliament in 1865 and generally followed Gladstone and his liberal ideas. In particular, Mill advocated permanent tenancy for tenants in Ireland. In 1866 he was elected Rector of St. Andrew's University, an honorary position bestowed on someone of substance and popularity. But he lost his seat in Parliament in 1868.[7]

John Stuart Mill was one of the early and leading exponents of women's rights. He believed in the equality of the sexes, women's suffrage, and equal access to education and employment. He thought women's suffrage "an essential step toward the moral improvement of humankind."[8]

Mill spent his last years often at Avignon in the company of his stepdaughter, Helen Taylor. On Saturday, 3 May 1873 he took a train to Orange to pursue a botanical interest with a friend. Although he was sixty-seven, he walked about fifteen miles that day, and took a train back to Avignon. By Monday he had a fever, perhaps a symptom of erysipelas, which was common in that area then. He died May 7, with Helen Taylor by his side. He was buried at Avignon beside his wife. A few awkward sounds were made about reburial at Westminster Abbey, but this did not happen. Instead, there is a bronze statue of John Stuart Mill on the Thames Embankment in London.

Michael Scot
(C.1175-1235?)

AND

John Duns Scotus
(C.1265-1308)

I N THE ERA when Europe was beginning to move toward the Renaissance two scholars from remote Scotland, a country which in their day possessed not even one university, were among the most influential thinkers.

Michael Scot was not the first important Scottish scholar. Richard Scot (*c.* 1123–1173) preceded him. Ricardus de Sancto Victore Scotus was prior at the abbey of St. Victor in Paris and placed love first in his theological system.[1] Michael Scot (or Scott) was born at Balwearie in Fifeshire. He went to Oxford as a young man and later to Paris where he acquired the title "mathematician." Next he studied at Bologna, and from there went to Palermo in Sicily at the court of Frederick II. It is probable that Scot taught the young king. Scot appears next at Toledo in 1217. There he came in contact with Jewish and Arab scholars who taught him Arabic. His most important work was in translating works of Aristotle the Greek and Averroes the Arab into Latin and therefore making available in the West, such works as Aristotle's *Historia Animalium* and *De Caelo.* He also translated Avicenna from the Persian and wrote *Abbreviatio Avicennae* which the Vatican colophon dates as "*explicit anno domini* MCCX. "[2]

At some point Michael Scot became the court astrologer to Frederick II in Sicily. His own writings were on alchemy, astrology, and occult sciences. Thus the legend of Michael Scot "The Wizard" was born and soon outgrew Michael Scot the scholar. Throughout Europe, all the way back to Scotland, people believed he could see the future and part mountains. Scot took holy orders, and Pope Honorious III became his patron. He received several posts in Italy and was offered the Bishopric of Cashel in Ireland, but rejected it as he could not speak Irish. In 1230 Scot showed up at Oxford with works of Aristotle in Latin which he had translated *ex Arabico* (from Arabic). Some say he died and is buried at Melrose, Scotland. Italians claim him also.[3]

The legend of Michael Scot was observed in Dante's *Inferno*, c. XX., which says, "That other there, whose ribs fill scanty space, was Michael Scott, who truly full well knew of magical deceits the illusive grace." Boccaccio wrote, "Not long ago there was in Florence a great master of necromancy who was called Michele Scotto, because he was from Scotland."[4] People said that Michael Scot rode through the air on a "demon horse," and that he possessed a magic wand. In Scotland people still blame unusual happenings on Auld Michael.[5]

We know nothing of what Michael Scot looked like except for Dante's brief reference. Michael Scot said that four things made a man wise: intelligence of reason, diligence of doing, experience of knowledge, and a living memory. He is one of the important people who recovered the works of Aristotle to the West, providing the fuel for the Renaissance. His biographer, Lynn Thorndike, says that Michael Scot "may be regarded as the leading intellectual in western Europe during the first third of the thirteenth century."[6]

John Duns Scotus, also known as Doctor Subtilis is called by the *Encyclopaedia Britannica* "the greatest medieval British philosopher and theologian." He was was born in Duns, Berwickshire, about 1265 and entered the

John Duns Scotus's, *Quodlibetum*.

Franciscan Order in 1280. He studied in Scotland, Oxford, and Paris, and was ordained in the church of St. Andrew at Northampton, England, by the Bishop of Lincoln. He returned to Paris (1291–1296) and studied under "the master" Gonsalvus of Spain. He received his doctorate from Paris in 1305. For the next two years he was *magister regens*, holding a solemn disputation called "*de Quodlibet*." He went to Cologne in 1307 as a professor and died there in 1308. The Vatican's complete edition of his works was begun in 1950 as *Ioannis Duns Scoti Opera Omnia*. The principal work is the *Ordinatio*. It has had more than thirty editions since 1472. His philosophy embraces the primacy of the will. The key to his philosophy is transcendent being, which is also important to his proofs of God's existence. The theology of Duns is that God elects people predestined to accomplish things and then gives them the means to do it. This idea put him in direct conflict with the other great thinker of the day, St. Thomas Aquinas. His most important work elevated Mary in status, and it was Duns Scotus who attributed the Immaculate Conception to her. Once considered to be merely a Scotist idea, the Immaculate Conception is now one of the principal dogmas of the Roman Catholic Church.[7]

As Duns was a Franciscan, and St. Thomas Aquinas was a Dominican, it was natural for them and for their supporters to be rivals. The Thomists thought the Dunses to be stupid, and thus the word dunce comes into the language.[8] Duns Scotus and St. Thomas Aquinas, are probably the two greatest medieval theologians. Duns Scotus perhaps received more interest in the centuries after his death.[9] The works of Duns Scotus were commended by Pope John XXIII, and he was beatified by Pope John Paul II in 1993.[10]

In the Conventual Franciscan Church in Cologne, there is an elaborate catafalque containing the remains of John Duns Scotus. It has this inscription:

Scotia me genuit,	(Scotland begot me)
Anglia me suscepit,	(England reared me)
Gallia me docuit,	(France taught me)
Colonia me tenet.	(Cologne holds me)

John Knox

(c. 1514–1572)

DURING THE REFORMATION when various countries of Europe broke away from the Roman Catholic Church, different systems were chosen so that in the end there were many types of Protestantism. It has been said that of all of the nations which left the Old Religion to become Protestant, England made the least change and Scotland made the most. Of course all of the countries remained Christian but the philosophical and practical fallout of the Scottish Protestant Reformation helped make Scotland the best educated and most democratic country, as well as the

John Knox,
Picture Collection, The Branch Libraries,
THE NEW YORK PUBLIC LIBRARY.

country most inclined toward participation in the Industrial Revolution which was to come. Partly as a result of its unique Reformation tiny, remote Scotland became intellectually and scientifically one of the leading countries of the world.

The principal figure in the Scottish Reformation was John Knox. Few details of his early life are known, but he is believed to have been born somewhere near the town of Haddington. His father's name was William and his mother was a Sinclair. He studied, but exactly when and where are not known. He was married twice, late in life, each time to scandalously young women who bore him five children. Records show that he had become a priest by 1540 and that after 1543 he became involved with Protestantism, perhaps because he was tutor to the sons of Hugh Douglas and Alexander Cockburn, who were involved in Protestant politics. In late 1545 Knox was in the company of George Wishart, a leading Protestant radical.

Wishart had been accused of heresy in 1538 and fled to England. Accused again in England, he fled to the Continent. Around 1543 he was back in Scotland where he began to influence Knox. In 1546 Wishart was arrested again and this time was taken to St. Andrews. Here he was tried in a court set up by Cardinal David Beaton, who was a de facto governor of the country due to his power in the Catholic Church and the infancy of Mary Queen of Scots. Wishart was found guilty and burned at the stake. A few months later Beaton was murdered by a band of Protestants. After the martyrdom of Wishart, John Knox ever after spoke reverently of his colleague.

Knox at this point was running for his life with his pupils when hearing that St. Andrews was in Protestant hands, he took his entourage there. Although he was still almost unknown several people at St. Andrews noticed that he possessed great talent and asked him to preach. Knox sincerely wanted to remain a tutor and refused. But finally after several requests and against his better judgment he accepted. From the moment he began to preach Knox captivated his audiences, and there was never any doubt that he would remain a preacher. He had passed the turning point in his life and since he hadn't wanted to preach on his own, he took his success as a divine intervention.[1]

In 1547 France intervened on the side of the Scottish government, and St. Andrews Castle was forced to surrender. Knox was arrested and spent the next year and a half as a slave on a French galley. After he was released he went to England where he became a licensed preacher in the Protestant reign of Edward VI. He was still strong in spirit, but his health had been weakened. In England he prospered for several years but when Edward died he had to flee again from the Catholic tyranny of Queen Mary I, also known as Bloody Mary.

This time Knox went to Geneva where he met and studied under John Calvin, accepting his doctrine of predestination. Here Knox spent the happiest days of his life in what he considered to be an ideal place ministering to English refugees. But it was in this peaceful setting that Knox formulated his fateful theory: that a Roman Catholic government which denies the right to practice the "true religion" (of Protestantism) may be overcome by violence.

In 1559 Knox returned to Scotland to find the Catholic Queen regent, Mary of Guise, trying to halt the spread of Protestantism. On May 11, 1559 Knox preached a sermon against "idolatry" in Perth, which started a rebellion. By June the Protestants had taken Edinburgh, Knox was preaching in St. Giles Cathedral, and Parliament had abolished papal authority. But the powerful Guise family of France still had to be dealt with. Their plan was to create a Catholic empire uniting France, Scotland, and England under King François II and his young Queen, the daughter of Mary of Guise—Mary Stuart, Queen of Scots. France was preparing to invade Scotland.[2]

It is at this time that John Knox became for a while perhaps the most important of all of the figures of the Reformation. Knox realized that his only possible aid against French designs was intervention from England. He reasoned that a French invasion and victory for the Guise family's strategy would not only be a possible end to the Reformation in Scotland; it would be a threat to Elizabethan England and perhaps to the Reformation in all Europe. He asked Elizabeth for help, pointing out that it was in England's best interest as well but help was not sent. The Protestants in Scotland were dejected with the news that the French were coming. There seemed to be no hope for Protestantism. But Knox remained a rock of belief in defense of his cause. Only his determination prevented the dissolution of the Scottish church. At last Elizabeth sent 10,000 soldiers to Scotland and the French decided not to fight. This was of course the beginning of the merger between Scotland and England, who had been enemies for centuries. The three countries signed the Treaty of Edinburgh in 1560, in which the forces of France and England were to leave Scotland. It was an official end to the *Alliance Ancienne* between Scotland and France, although there were pretensions of its existence for some time to come; and the dual nationality of Scots and Frenchmen was re-confirmed even after the union of the crowns of Scotland and England in 1603. The Auld Alliance had served both countries well, but had foundered on a difference of religion.

John Knox was now in control of his sober Calvinistic church, and proceeded to endow it with its most distinguishing characteristic—election of ministers by the people. He also gave it the beginnings of its tiered structure of democratic government. In 1561 Mary Queen of Scots—no longer Queen of France—returned to Scotland to govern, and to her hate-filled debates with Knox (see p. 306). Yet Knox had won his cause and set the course for Protestantism in Scotland, that would last up to the present. One of his greatest achievements was in the educational program begun during his leadership. The Kirk envisioned a grammar school in every parish, a high school or college in every town, and a university in each principal city of Scotland. Knox further proposed that education be compulsory, liberal, and free to the poor who qualified. Although this plan was never completely carried out, it is clear that Knox and his people realized the value of education, and in this were centuries ahead of the rest of the countries of the world. John Knox died in 1572, in his distinctive house on the Royal Mile in Edinburgh, which is visited by throngs of tourists every day.

The death of the dictatorial Knox created a great void in the leadership of the Scottish Kirk, and one man, Andrew Melville (1545–1622) soon filled it. Melville was a well-educated man who had studied at St. Andrews, Paris, and Geneva. In 1574 he returned to Scotland and reformed and invigorated her universities at Glasgow, Aberdeen, and St. Andrews, packing them with Scottish and foreign students. Also, it was Melville who completed the Presbyterian system of the Kirk in which the congregation elected the Kirk Session, and through a series of democracies extended power upward to the local presbyteries to the regional synods and finally to the national General Assembly at the summit. He was to defend this system against King James VI and I who wanted to exercise control by the institution of appointed bishops. At one point Melville told the king, "Sirrah! Ye are God's silly vassal; there are twa kings and twa kingdoms in Scotland; there is Christ Jesus who is King of the Kirk, whose subject James VI is, and of whose kingdom he is not a king, nor a lord, nor a head, but a member."[3] His defiance cost Melville several years in the Tower of London. When he was released, he left for France where he was given a professorship in biblical theology at the university at Sedan. He spent his last eleven years there in peace, never to return to his native land.[4]

But it was John Knox who had had the great influence on the world. He was the founder of the Kirk, and saw it through from its near demise, to its victory; and it was he who set its course. We will not discuss or defend here, the theological differences between the Scottish

Reformation and other religions. Nor will we recommend Presbyterianism, nor denigrate any other church. But it must be said, that what came out of the dour, grim Kirk created by Knox, has had an enormous impact on the world.

First, it pushed Scotland to become the best-educated country in the world.[5] By the seventeenth century the Church of Scotland had established parish schools all over the country. The ignorant yokel, so popular in the literature of various countries had no place in Scotland.[6] The English historian Trevelyan believed that at time of the union with England in 1707, the Scots were the best-educated people in Europe.[7] Even Dr. Johnson, a loud critic of the Scots, had to admit that on his tour of the remote Hebrides he "never encountered a house in which he did not find books in more languages than one."[8] By the beginning of the eighteenth century and indeed, well into the nineteenth, Scotland, with a population of only half a million people, had four universities, while huge England had only two. Moreover, while Oxford and Cambridge educated mainly the upper classes, Scotland's universities taught all who qualified. Esmond Wright says, ". . . in Scotland, where the son of the laird mixed with the son of the tenant, and it was indeed more important to come in 'at the heid o' the tenants than at the tail o' the gentry,' " blacksmith's son and minister's son sat side by side.[9]

In addition the Scots added the teaching of science to the classics earlier than any other country. Glasgow had the first university engineering faculty and the first college of applied science and technology in the world. By the end of the eighteenth century the great majority of the ordinary people of Scotland had at least a rudimentary education. From England, the Spectator wrote that the Scots were the best-educated and best-behaved people in the world.[10] Between 1750 and 1800, 87 percent of British physicians were Scottish-trained.[11] In the nineteenth century, St. Andrews gave Britain's first degrees to women, and Edinburgh was the first in the world to accept women as medical students. By the 1860s, 1 in 140 of the Scottish population were receiving a secondary education. In England it was 1 in 1,300. In 1865 Scotland had 1 in 1,000 of its population in a university, and led the world in that regard.[12]

When the Industrial Revolution came, Scotland was ready to produce entrepreneurs and engineers in quantities more appropriate to a major nation. And all over the world, emigrant Scots have been in the forefront of education. In what is now the United States, the minority Scots founded four of the first six major colleges (which became Princeton, the University of Pennsylvania, Columbia, and William and Mary) and all three of the first medical schools (at Penn, Columbia, and William and Mary).[13] In addition between 1780 and 1829, of the twenty-nine permanent colleges founded by religious organizations in all sections of the country thirteen were founded by Presbyterians and sixteen by all other religions.[14] In the United States, four centuries after the death of Knox, the census tells us that those claiming to be of Scottish or Scotch-Irish descent, have the most years of education of any national group in the country.[15]

There is not a single country in the British Commonwealth and many countries outside the commonwealth, where Scots have not been the most active people in promoting education and in creating schools and colleges. In Canada, Scots founded five of the first six colleges (which became the University of New Brunswick, Kings College in Nova Scotia, Dalhousie University, McGill University, and the University of Toronto). There were many other Scottish educational pioneers in Australia, New Zealand, South Africa, China, India, and many other lands.[16]

Second, the Presbyterian church of Scotland served as a model for the government of the United States. There are many people who have tried to disprove this, and some have even credited American Indian confederations. But after 1707, when the Scottish and English Parliaments were joined, the General Assembly of the Church of Scotland became the de facto government of Scotland. Here was an example of a modern nation operating a scaled democracy running from the precinct, to the local, to the regional to the national level. There was no other such model. And when it came time to choose the delegates to write the Constitution of the United States, Presbyterians and in particular Scottish and Scotch-Irish Americans, and others who had received their basic education from Scottish tutors and professors, were utterly over-represented.[17]

Third, the church created by John Knox united Scotland and gave it a purpose as never before. It is no coincidence that few Scottish geniuses were heard from before the Reformation. The overwhelming majority of the people of Scotland joined the new church with a zeal. Formerly, as Catholics, they had belonged to a world church where they had no special place. Knox gave Scotland a unique church of its very own. The church preached study, thriftiness, and achievement, and that is what it got, and what Scotland gave to the world. Scots felt that they were on a mission to prosper and succeed, that in fact, they were predestined to do so. The Scots believed that they were like the Jews, a covenanted people, the new Israel. In fact, they *were* a covenanted people. The National Covenant was written in 1638. It was both a religious and political declaration of Scotland's independence from England. And as Prebble observes it "challenged the King's prerogative, and by implication affirmed that the right to make and change the law rested in Parliament only." The National Covenant was copied and carried "to every burgh, parish, and university" where it was signed by the "whole people, landed and landless, rich and poor" of Scotland.[18]

The National Covenant had an important effect on America at the time it was becoming independent. As we have said, at the proceedings there were abundant Scots, Scotch-Irishmen, Presbyterians, and people who had Scottish educations. Many of these men must have been familiar with the National Covenant. The American Declaration of Independence ends with the signatories promising that in support of the document "we mutually pledge to each other our lives, our fortunes, and our sacred honor." The National Covenant says: "we promise and swear That we shall, to the uttermost of our power, with our means and lives" defend the religion, liberties, and laws of the kingdom. The preamble to the United States Constitution, a masterpiece of concise English, is only fifty-two words long and is printed below left in full. On the right are phrases excerpted from the National Covenant and the Act ordaining it, which can be read almost as if they *were* the preamble.[19] Many of the words and phrases are identical or nearly so in both documents. Italics are added for emphasis.

PREAMBLE TO THE CONSTITUTION OF THE UNITED STATES Philadelphia 1787	THE NATIONAL COVENANT AND ACT ORDAINING IT Edinburgh 1638 and 1639
We the people of the United States	we noblemen, barons, Gentlemen, burgesses, ministers and commons
in order to form a more *perfect union*	considering the great happiness which may flow from a full and *perfect union*

establish justice	judicatories be *established* and ministration of *justice* amongst us
insure domestic tranquillity	procure true and perfect peace
provide for the common *defense*	stand to the mutual *defence*
promote the general welfare	for the common happiness to conduce for so good ends and *promote* the same
and *secure* the blessings of liberty *to ourselves and our posterity*	security of said *liberties to ourselves and our posterity*
do ordain and establish this *Constitution* for the United States of America.	*do ordain* the Covenant and *Constitution* of this kingdom

These are just some of the legacies of the church founded by John Knox. Today some would call him a bigot. Certainly Mary Queen of Scots would have at least thought such a word to describe him. But without making excuses his life must be judged in the context of a harsh time when "heretics" of many persuasions were being burned at the stake. Also the Roman Church in Scotland was probably in the time of Knox, the most corrupt in Europe, and therefore, in need of the most reform. Knox was a harsh man, a violent man. But his life had an enormous influence on the progress of the world. He was the man who started Scotland on the road from backwater to influence. Thomas Carlyle says: "This Knox did for his nation, I say, we may really call a resurrection as from death. The people began to *live* . . . Scotch Literature and Thought, Scotch Industry; James Watt, David Hume, Walter Scott, Robert Burns: I find Knox and the Reformation acting in the hearts's core of every one of these persons and phenomena; I find that without the Reformation they would not have been."[20]

Mary Stuart

(1542–1587)

Mary Queen of Scots. Artist unknown. THE SCOTTISH NATIONAL PORTRAIT GALLERY.

T HE LIFE OF Mary Queen of Scots is Scotland's grand tragedy. From the day of her birth, to the day of her death, her life was dramatic. Her place on the stage of Scottish history was brief but crucial to the continuation of the Stewart dynasty, which was saved by her courage and intelligence. Even though she was a devout Catholic, her diplomacy during the Scottish Reformation ensured its success. And since the Scottish Reformation had so much to do with bringing Scotland into the modern world, and in making it a land of industry, learning, and science, her tolerance must be credited. The *Dictionary of National Biography* says, "The religious issues involved in the fate of Mary Stuart are in themselves sufficient to assign her a place in the first rank of historic personages. In her were concentrated the last hopes of catholicism in Britain."[1] To many she is still Scotland's biggest heroine, a fallen goddess brought forth from the myths of such as Mary Magdelene.

As Mary was born in Linlithgow Palace, her father King James V was dying in another room. When he heard the news that his heir was female he made the melancholy prediction, "It cam' wi' a lass and it will gang wi' a lass."[2] He was referring to the fact that the Stewart dynasty was founded by a woman, Marjorie Bruce, daughter of King Robert I, the Bruce, when she married Walter, sixth High Steward of Scotland. Their son became Robert II, the first Stewart king. But Mary's father was wrong. It was in fact this newborn daughter who would protect the dynasty, allowing it to continue and flourish.

The mother of this new princess was Mary of Lorraine, a member of the ultra-powerful Guise family of France. Her marriage to James V had been intended to help solidify the Auld Alliance, *l'Alliance Ancienne*, between Scotland and France against their mutual enemy, England. The perilous times would have tried the most experienced monarch. But at her father's death, the little princess became Queen of Scots on December 14, 1542 at the age of six days.

Immediately there was trouble. King Henry VIII of England wanted the infant Queen to be betrothed to his son and heir, Edward. But this proposal was rejected by Marie de Guise and her allies. Enraged, Henry sent an army north to invade Scotland, slashing, burning, killing, and destroying as it went. This was known as the "Rough Wooing." It was too much for the Queen Mother and her supporters. Queen Mary was in danger and her mother sent her to France in 1548, betrothed to the Dauphin, François. Here Mary Stewart became Marie Stuart as the French alphabet has no "w." She was educated with the French royal children, learning Latin, Greek, and Italian, but neither Scots nor English. In 1558 the fifteen-year-old Queen of Scots was married to the Dauphin in the Cathedral of Notre Dame in Paris in an elegant, elaborate ceremony. Within a year the Dauphin, the son of King Henri II and Catherine de Médicis, would become King François II upon the death of his father.

And so it came to be that Mary Queen of Scots was now Queen of France as well. But two countries were not enough for Mary. Her whole life was ruled by her desire for sovereignty, and Mary believed that she was the rightful queen of England. Catholics denied the validity of the marriage of Henry VIII to Anne Boleyn and since Queen Elizabeth was descended from this marriage, she was illegitimate in their opinion. Mary

Stuart was descended from the marriage of Margaret, the daughter of Henry VIII, to King James IV of Scots. Therefore, upon the death of Mary I, many people believed that Mary Stuart should have succeeded to the English throne rather than Elizabeth. In fact when the news of the death of Mary I reached Paris, heralds cried "Make way for the Queen of England."[3] Mary and François took the titles King and Queen of England, France, Scotland, and Ireland. At this point Marie Stuart had reached a pinnacle in her life: Queen of Scots, Queen of France, and claimant to the throne of England.

It was not to last. In July 1560, the Treaty of Edinburgh ended the centuries-old alliance between Scotland and France. It included a provision for Mary to abandon her claims to the throne of England, but she and François never ratified it. Instead the year marked the death of her husband and Mary was no longer Queen of France. Her mother, Marie de Guise, also died in 1560. Mary left France discouraged, arriving at the Scottish port of Leith on a French ship in August 1561.

The young Queen could not have arrived at a more dangerous time. The Protestant Reformation had blasted into Scotland. Parliament had passed laws abolishing the authority of the Pope and the Latin Mass. The great majority of her subjects were now Protestants. Immediately on her arrival she was confronted by the firebrand John Knox, the founder of Protestantism in Scotland, who hated anything to do with the Roman church. It is in her several conversations with Knox that Mary distinguished herself as a natural leader. Despite Knox's attacks on the Queen and her church, Mary held her ground. She made it clear to Knox that he could not intimidate her, and from the beginning she maintained that she felt no compulsion to force her Protestant subjects to return to the Church of Rome. But she made sure that he understood that she would practice and defend her religion to her death. Soon Knox realized that he was dealing with someone who had a mind and a will, and that she was not going away. Mary decided to try to be a great Catholic queen ruling over largely Protestant subjects. She even allocated money to the Protestant church. In fact, she was so broad-minded that her subjects began to love their beautiful young queen.[4]

Of course the presence of Mary on the island of Britain was a threat to Queen Elizabeth, since Mary after all had been claiming the right to sit on the throne of England. But Mary appeared ready to compromise and tried to put together a meeting with the English queen. Many letters were exchanged and delegations sent back and forth. Perhaps the simplest trade would have been for Mary to agree to do nothing to put forth her claim, in exchange for Elizabeth and her government recognizing her as heir to the English kingdom upon Elizabeth's death. But an arrangement was never reached and tragedy would come.

In 1565 Mary decided to marry her cousin Henry Stewart, Lord Darnley. Like Mary, Darnley was a Catholic and had claims to the thrones of both England and Scotland. Mary seems to have been infatuated with this ne'er-do-well, and quickly became pregnant with the future King James. But Darnley treated her badly, carousing and hunting with his friends, and Mary began to get close to her Italian secretary, David Riccio or Rizzio. Darnley became jealous and planned to get him out of the way. The conspiracy if successful, could have left Riccio dead, Mary and her unborn son dead or in prison, and Darnley as King.[5]

On a night in 1566 the plotters came up the back stairs to Mary's apartment in Holyrood Palace, interrupting a supper party. Riccio was dragged out and stabbed to death. If they intended to kill Mary as she always believed, they were foiled by their own commotion, which aroused Mary's loyal house guard, and she was saved.

The Queen must have suspected Darnley's complicity in the affair and her disgust with him must have been intense at this point. But she was much too clever to let it get the best of her. Instead, what she did next preserved the Stuart dynasty by lying to her husband, telling him that she was sure he was innocent of the plot and realizing that his lack of character might be the conspiracy's weakness, suggested to him that the only way for them to survive was as allies.[6]

With a few loyal soldiers, and Mary's courage, the King and Queen of Scots escaped to Dunbar Castle by night. From there the queen was able to muster a small army. One of her most helpful nobles in this regard was James Hepburn, the Earl of Bothwell. Within days several thousand men were gathered and Mary was back in Edinburgh, in complete control. The remaining conspirators fled. On June 19, 1566, Mary's heir, James, one of the most important monarchs in history was born. The Stuart dynasty had been saved.

Mary was now in a state of intense hatred of her husband Darnley, and in a state of love with her deliverer, Bothwell. At this point a plot developed to get rid of Darnley. It appears that the principal plotters were Mary and Bothwell. In January of 1567 Darnley, who was ill, was lured by Mary to a house in the city wall called Kirk O' Field, where Edinburgh University stands today. Suddenly on the night of February 9, she left the house to attend a wedding, and several hours later the house blew up in a tremendous explosion that woke the town. Darnley was found dead, but not of the explosion. Rather, he had been strangled.[7]

There was an immediate outcry and Bothwell, the prime suspect, was forced to stand trial. But the trial was rigged and in the farce Bothwell was acquitted. He and Mary were married a few months later. But the people's reaction to this anarchy was telling. For the first time the queen faced an outraged public. Scotland would not accept Bothwell and demonstrations against the Queen began. She was taken to the island stronghold of Loch Leven, and there the infamous Casket Letters were discovered. If genuine, they implicated Mary in the plot to kill Darnley. Mary was offered two choices—abdication or a trial for murder. She signed the abdication papers, and her year-old son was proclaimed as King James VI.[8]

In 1568 Mary escaped to England, still trying to negotiate with Elizabeth. Bothwell fled to Norway where he was arrested on a breach of promise suit. He was imprisoned in Denmark and died there it is said, babbling, chained to a wall.[9] Mary was moved by the English from one place to the next for almost two decades. At last in October of 1586, she was charged in a plot to assassinate Queen Elizabeth and brought to Fotheringay castle for trial. She defended herself with skill and self-assurance but in the end there was too much evidence against her and she was found guilty.

In her last hours Mary behaved with great courage. She made bequests to her servants, and told them to tell her friends that she had died for her religion. She wrote a long letter to her brother-in-law, King Henry III of France, explaining that she had been condemned and was to be executed as a criminal. But that the reality, she told him, was different. She was to die because of her right to the English throne and because of her religion. She begged the King to pay her servants, as their welfare was her greatest concern.

The next morning when they came for her she was calmly praying and asked for a few minutes to finish. She was offered a Protestant chaplain but refused, and requested a Catholic one, which was denied. With great deportment Mary, elegantly dressed and accompanied by a few of her servants, walked with regal dignity into the great hall of Fotheringay. Several hundred people were in attendance. There on a stage was the block, about two feet high and covered in black cloth. Next to the block was the axe. Mary mounted the stage and prayed in Latin. The executioner asked for her forgiveness, and the beautiful queen responded graciously. One of her servants blindfolded her, and Mary knelt before the block, fixing her head upon it. She died saying another prayer, at the age of forty-four.[10]

In France, the loss of their dowager queen was recognized as a national tragedy. A requiem mass was held at Notre Dame, with King Henry III, the former queen Catherine de Médicis, and the entire court in attendance. In Scotland the people felt a sense of outrage, and a vengeful war with England was promoted immediately. King James made the gestures of ordering a formal mourning for his mother and of breaking diplomatic relations with England, but did little else. Years later, he had his mother re-interred in Westminster Abbey.[11]

James Stewart

(1566–1625)

WHO ARE THE monarchs who founded Spanish America and the Spanish Empire? Almost anyone who has been to elementary school knows the answer—King Ferdinand and Queen Isabella who are universally recognized. Why is it then that King James, who performed the same function for England as Ferdinand and Isabella did for Spain, is not credited with being the founder of British America and the British Empire? The most likely reason is that people did not like him personally in his own

King James VI of Scots. Artist unknown.
THE SCOTTISH NATIONAL PORTRAIT GALLERY.

lifetime and this antipathy has carried forward to the present. A quick review of several well-known reference works, even Scottish ones, shows that King James is credited with very little. His many faults are made much of, but not a lot is said of his achievements. In other words people were and are prejudiced against James who was untidy, insensitive, and, from the English point of view, semi-barbarous—an enemy Scot speaking in what they perceived to be the uncouth Scottish tongue—an egalitarian of sorts, out of place in class-conscious England. Yet King James should have a place in the first rank of the world's leaders.

James Stewart, destined to become King James VI of Scots and King James I of England, was born in Edinburgh Castle, the son of Mary Queen of Scots and her cousin Henry Stewart, Lord Darnley. The parents were descended from both English and Scottish royalties. But soon after James's birth his father was murdered, and his mother was suspected of complicity in the plot. Queen Mary was forced to abdicate and flee Scotland for England. In 1567 her son was crowned James VI of Scots at Stirling when he was barely one year old.

While the country was governed by regents, the youthful King James was given a first-class education by tutors, among them the famous Scottish intellectual George Buchanan who also taught Michel de Montaigne in France. James was drilled in the Greek and Latin classics as well as theology, and became one of the best educated of Europe's monarchs. This allowed his critics to call him "the wisest fool in Christendom." James had a gift for languages and early in his life became a poet.

At age twelve, James began to be involved in affairs of state. But just at this time Esmé Stuart, a relative from France, arrived at James's court and the young king, having been deprived of parental affection, fell in love with this visitor and his elegant French manners. Esmé, the favorite, was promoted quickly to Duke of Lennox. Some feared that Lennox, a Catholic, was scheming to regain the throne for Mary and in 1582 James was kidnapped by the Protestant party and Lennox was exiled to France. The next year James escaped and asserted his control over the country while still a teenager.

In Scotland, Jamie the Saxt, as he was called in Scots, was a successful king, extending his authority to the farthest reaches of the kingdom including the wild highlands, something his predecessors had not been able to do. Also, Scotland under James was at peace and its finances usually in order. This relative tranquillity in the stormy history of the country was marred by constant battles with the Presbyterian church that commanded the loyalty of the overwhelming majority of the population. The trouble with Presbyterianism from the viewpoint of the king was that it was democratic and did not recognize the authority of the monarch over it. In 1584 James re-established the authoritarian Episcopal system with its bishops, giving him some control while allowing the democratic Presbyterian church to function underneath. This pragmatic compromise was typical of James' reign in Scotland.

But James wanted more than Scotland. He wanted to be King of England as well and he had a very solid claim. It was the same claim—descent from a sister of Henry VIII—that had been his mother's undoing. Mary Queen of Scots had always believed in her right to be Queen of England and this made her very existence a threat to the English monarchy. As a result she had been held as a prisoner by Queen Elizabeth for two decades and in 1587 she was tried and executed for treason. This left James as one of two main candidates for the throne of England.

In 1589 James was betrothed to the blonde Princess Anne of Denmark, who sailed for Scotland, but was able to get only as far as Norway due to bad weather. With great gallantry James went to collect his youthful princess in Norway and there he fell in love with her. The royal couple spent the winter in Denmark, returning in 1590 to Scotland where Anne was crowned queen with a great celebration. Anne and James were to have seven children, assuring the continuity of the Stewart dynasty.

In 1603, with Queen Elizabeth on her deathbed, the senior ministers of England chose James VI, King of Scots, to become her heir as James I of England. Since his person had united the two ancient kingdoms, James styled himself King of Great Britain without apparently asking anyone for consent.[1] Although both England and Scotland still maintained separate governments, it was James's idea that they were in effect, one country. But this idea never caught hold in either kingdom. The old animosities were still there.

James fulfilled an ancient prophecy when he was crowned in Westminster Abbey upon the ancient Scottish coronation stone. This was the sacred Stone of Destiny, the *Lia Fail*, that myth suggested had been Jacob's pillow, carried by the prehistoric Gaels in their wanderings from Egypt through Spain and Ireland, and finally brought to Scone in Perthshire, where all of the Scottish kings were crowned upon it until it was stolen in 1296 by King Edward I (The Hammer of the Scots). In his rage against the independent Scots Edward is said to have removed from the stone a prophecy which in Latin read:

> Ni fallat vatum,
> Scoti hunc quocunque locatum,
> Invenient lapidum,
> Regnare tenentur ibidem.

This is from an earlier oracular verse in Gaelic:

> Cinnidh Scuit saor am fine,
> Mur breug am faistine,
> Far am faighear an Lia-Fail,
> Dlighe flaitheas do ghabhail.

Or as it was rhymed in English by Sir Walter Scott:

> Unless the prophets faithless be,
> And Seer's words be vain,
> Where're is found this sacred stone,
> The Scottish race shall reign.

As the prophecy predicted, the royalty of the Scottish race followed the stone, and continues, through James and his descendants, to rule over Great Britain and the British Commonwealth to this day. The Stone of Destiny was finally returned to Scotland in 1997.[2]

James was not as successful as a sovereign in England as he had been in Scotland. He was set in his ways and didn't seem to be able to accommodate himself to English customs. He found it hard to use the English Parliament to rule his new realm. And he didn't understand English law, which is very different from that of Scotland. The English didn't like James's Scottish accent and informal manner. And they very much resented the retinue of Scottish courtiers that he brought with him, and whom he favored at every turn. In 1605 he came close to losing his life to the Gunpowder Plot of Guy Fawkes who intended to blow up the House of Lords on November 5 when King James would be in attendance. But the plot was foiled just in time by a security check. English children still chant:

> Remember, remember the fifth of November,
> The Gunpowder treason and plot!

Having founded Great Britain, James next moved toward founding what was to become the British Empire. In the Mercantile era colonies were deemed to be essential and in this regard Spain and Portugal were far ahead. When he became King of England there was not a single English (or Scottish) colony anywhere. Raleigh had tried but failed in what is now North Carolina. The East India Company had been formed but hadn't accomplished anything. So in 1606, James chartered the London and Plymouth companies giving them rights to colonize, respectively, the southeastern and northeastern coasts of what is now the United States of America. In the next year the London Company established the first permanent settlement in British America, naming their village Jamestown and the river on which it stood the James, in honor of their Scottish sponsor. Soon after, additional colonies were established by the English in Ireland, New England, Guiana, the East Indies, Bermuda, Newfoundland, and India; and by the Scots in Nova Scotia (New Scotland). King James took a great interest in these colonies, giving advice, defending their existence to Spain, and exercising considerable control over them. His Plantation in Ulster was fraught with turmoil from the start and the Scots (and some English) he "planted" there have never been reconciled to the native Irish population whom he greatly underestimated. Another result of the Plantation was the massive emigration of the Scotch-Irish to North America in the eighteenth century. But for the most part, his colonies were successful. By the end of his reign in 1625, British America and what was to become the British Empire, the largest and grandest in history, had been established.[3]

King James was a skilled author and poet. Among his many writings is his *Counterblaste to Tobacco*, perhaps the first warning of tobacco's danger to the lungs. His interest in literature brought fruit in his authorization of the King James Version of the Bible, a masterpiece of the English language. It was James's idea that ordinary people ought to be able to read the Bible in their own language, and instead of ordering his committee of scholars to produce a work with flowery Latinate translations, the overwhelming bulk of the work is in Anglo-Saxon-derived English words. "And God said, Let there be light: and there was light. And God saw the light, that it was good." The king is the first person mentioned in these Bibles, still in use all over the world today. They are dedicated:

TO THE MOST HIGH AN MIGHTY PRINCE
JAMES
BY THE GRACE OF GOD
KING OF GREAT BRITAIN, FRANCE, AND IRELAND
DEFENDER OF THE FAITH, ETC.

It continues: "Great and manifold were the blessings, most dread sover-eign, which Almighty God, the Father of all mercies bestowed upon us the people of England, when first he sent your Majesty's Royal Person to rule and reign over us."

Among the king's accomplishments is his charter authorizing the founding of Edinburgh University, one of the world's most distinguished, in 1582. He also gave money to support Ireland's most respected educa-tional institution, Trinity College in Dublin. He supported the great English writer John Donne, becoming his patron and making him Chaplain in Ordinary.[4] James was also instrumental in bringing golf and horse racing, both well established in Scotland, to England. During his reign Scottish noblemen opened a golf course at Blackheath, and races began at Croyden, Enfield, Newmarket, and Epsom.[5] He appears to have been one of the first initiates of the Freemasons while King of Scots, and so he can be said to have had a hand in the beginnings of the world's old-est and largest fraternity as well. It seems almost certain that he and his Scottish retinue brought the fraternity to England after 1603.[6]

But the greatest legacy of King James is as the founder of Great Britain, British America and the British Empire. What a show this is, measured in part by the growing use of the English language throughout the world. Spoken by only a few million people on a small island when he unified it, English is now spoken by a billion people with one hundred million more studying it in China. A few years ago, when an Indian Parliamentarian made a speech condemning the use of English in the Indian Parliament, he made the speech in English. When Italian pilots flying Italian planes between Italian cities converse with Italian air traffic controllers, they speak English. So do pilots in most of the world's major airports. Half of the world's telephone calls, 75 percent of the world's telegrams and letters and 80 percent of the world's computer data are in English. This is the legacy of the empire begun in the reign of King James.[7]

Patrick Gordon

(1635–1699)

I T IS POSSIBLE to argue that a Scottish soldier of fortune, Patrick Gordon, was the most important person in the creation of the Russian Empire after Peter the Great. Gordon was, in fact the emperor's trusted right-hand man. He was born at Auchleuchries in Aberdeenshire, the son of John Gordon, a small laird and his wife Mary Ogilvie. Scotland's poor economy forced young Gordon to seek his future elsewhere and in 1651, while still a teenager, he arrived at the port of Danzig (Gdansk in Polish) which was then teeming with Scottish traders.

It is not well known today, but then there were perhaps thirty thousand Scots throughout Poland, building Presbyterian churches, rising from peddlers to bankers-to-the-king, sometimes even being ennobled. Alexander Czamer (Chalmers) was four times elected mayor of Warsaw.[1]

Young Patrick Gordon was from Scotland's Roman Catholic minority, and he gained admission to the Jesuit College at Braniewo (Braunsberg). He left after two years to fight as a mercenary soldier in the Polish-Swedish War, changing sides for better pay several times. In 1661 Gordon saw service in Russia with the rank of major. The next year he was promoted to colonel for his role in putting down rioters in Moscow who were protesting the recently debased copper coinage.[2] In 1663 he married Catherine von Bockhoven, the daughter of a German in the tsar's service.[3]

In 1666 Gordon was sent to England as the tsar's ambassador to King Charles II. This mission was not consequential. But in 1678 Gordon successfully defeated the Turks at Chigirin and established his reputation. He was made a major general and received the right to be addressed in the third person and the name Patrick Ivanovitch.[4] The next year he was in command of Kiev and was promoted to lieutenant general. In 1687 he was made a full general and in 1694 a rear admiral as well. Gordon repeatedly asked for permission to leave Russia permanently, but this was never granted. Nevertheless in 1686–1687 Gordon was sent to England again to meet his fellow Catholic, King James II. On this voyage Gordon visited his boyhood home in Aberdeenshire. He returned to Russia as James's envoy extraordinary. Gordon was made the tsar's chief military advisor and was rewarded with many estates. Peter made a personal visit to Gordon's house. It was the first ever visit of a tsar to the house of a foreigner. Gordon wrote in his diary, "His Majesty came to supper with me, and we were very happy."[5]

Peter the Great was fascinated by the culture of Western Europe. His mother, Natalia Naryshkina, had influenced him to learn about the West in order to bring Russia into the modern world. She in turn had been educated by a relative, Madame Artamon Matveeva, who had been born a Hamilton. Additionally, Peter had been tutored as a boy by Paul Menezius, who had been born in Scotland as Paul Menzies.[6] In 1697–1698 Peter made his Grand Embassy to observe the West, leaving the country under the trusted care of Patrick Gordon. Not surprisingly, during the absence of the tsar in 1698, the *streltsy*, the military nobility attached to the crown, revolted in an attempt to put Sophia Alekseevna on the throne. Gordon met them with 12,000 men. He tried not to use violence but when they jeered at him, he simply crushed them. Many were executed, hung "by fives and threes," and all the rest were held until Peter could return. Gordon had saved Russia for Peter, then he rested. His wife and son John had come over from Scotland and the whole family went to the countryside to one of Gordon's estates. There Gordon received his serfs, listened to their grievances, then threw a gigantic party for all of the peasants. But the livid Peter had returned to Moscow and summoned Gordon to join him immediately. There, Gordon had to watch as the tsar set new standards for barbarity in torture and executions. Sophia was sent to a convent.[7]

Along the way Peter had given Gordon permission to build the first Roman Catholic church in Moscow. Gordon's first wife, Catherine, died before 1682, and he married a second woman of Dutch extraction. By his first marriage he had two sons and two daughters. By the second marriage, he had one son.[8] Gordon sent one of his sons, Theodore, to study at his old school at Braunsberg. He wrote to him not to forget Russian in his curious mix of Dutch and German, "Vergesse Nicht Din Russ Sprache."[9]

Gordon began to suffer from a stomach malady. In 1698 he wrote his last diary entry, "This year I have felt a sensible decrease in health and strength." Peter the Great visited Gordon constantly during his illness. The tsar was with Gordon and his priest when he died. Peter asked him, "Patrick Ivanovitch, do you know me?" Then Peter, his face washed with tears, closed his soldier's eyes. "He is indeed dead father," the tsar said to the priest. Peter arranged for a splendid funeral at the Roman Catholic cathedral. All of the generals and nobles of mighty Russia walked in the procession, with the tsar at the head.[10]

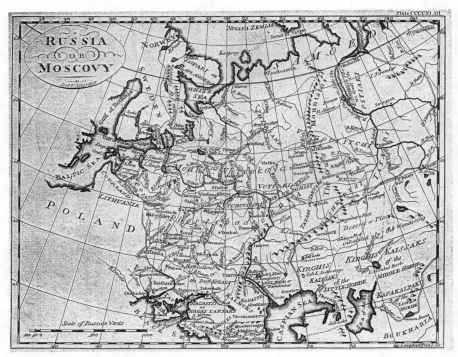

Russia, about 1700.
MAP DIVISION, THE NEW YORK PUBLIC LIBRARY, ASTOR, LENOX AND TILDEN FOUNDATIONS.

Robert Dinwiddie

(1693–1770)

NOT MANY CIVIL servants get to start a war, especially a war that would determine which language would be spoken on a third of a continent; a war which would spread to involve many nations on several continents. Not many get the opportunity to employ a young soldier, George Washington, barely out of his teens, and start him on a career in which he would become a nation's greatest hero. But Robert Dinwiddie did these things.

Robert Dinwiddie,
PICTURE COLLECTION, THE BRANCH LIBRARIES, THE NEW YORK PUBLIC LIBRARY.

Robert Dinwiddie was born at Germiston, near Glasgow, the son of Robert Dinwiddie, a merchant, and Elizabeth (or Sarah) Cumming. He attended Glasgow University and worked in his father's countinghouse. Later he and his brother Lawrence founded the Delftfield pottery company, which was successful enough to operate, from father to son, in Lawrence's line, into the nineteenth century.[1] At some point, Dinwiddie married Rebecca Affleck or Auchinleck,[2] the daughter of a minister. In 1721 he was appointed as a British representative in Bermuda. There, as a merchant ship owner, he made a substantial amount of money. In 1738 he was named surveyor general of the southern district of America, comprising everything on the mainland south of Pennsylvania, plus the Bahamas and Jamaica. He visited all of his territory and proceeded to act against crooked officials. Dinwiddie settled in Norfolk, Virginia in 1741. He became a member of the Virginia Council and presented the borough of Norfolk with a silver seal. In 1754 he donated a silver mace. Both still exist.[3]

Dinwiddie became a member of the Ohio Company that was formed to exploit a large tract of land in and around what is now the city of Pittsburgh. In 1751 he was appointed Lieutenant Governor of Virginia. Actually, he acted as governor for the second Earl of Albemarle who had a sinecure as Governor. Dinwiddie moved his wife and their two daughters to Williamsburg.[4] Although it might seem unusual to appoint a Scot as governor of a colony which was overwhelmingly English, in fact it was quite common. Over one hundred terms as American colonial governors were served by Scots, and it is remarkable to discover that Scottish governors presided most of the time in the colonies south of New England.[5]

Dinwiddie imposed a one pistole fee (a Spanish coin worth about sixteen shillings) for every land patent he signed. The House of Burgesses was angered, claiming that only they had the power to impose taxes. The Board of Trade in London upheld Dinwiddie but the Pistole Affair was one of the earlier sources of friction between the colonials and British rule.[6]

Dinwiddie's major work however was in confronting the encroachment of the French and their Indian allies on the western frontier, which he, the members of the Ohio Company, and all other Britons believed was British. The French had a good claim on the territory. In 1699 René Cavelier, sieur de La Salle, became the first non-Indian to see the land. In 1749 Pierre Joseph de Céloron de Blainville entered the area burying lead plates which claimed it for France. But the British had a better claim, the one that usually wins in the end. The British had settlers. In 1753, Dinwiddie gave twenty-one-year-old George Washington his first commission, as a major in the Virginia Militia. Dinwiddie dispatched Washington to the west to warn the French to get out of the lands south of Lake Erie, or be taken out. But Washington's trip through the wilderness accompanied by the trader Christopher Gist and a translator was futile, as the French told him they had no intention of leaving. Washington and Gist came near to freezing while crossing the Allegheny River on a flimsy raft. The place is marked by the Fortieth Street Bridge in what is now Pittsburgh.[7] When the young man returned to Virginia he made a full written report which Dinwiddie immediately sent to London in the hope of convincing the British government of the seriousness of the threat.[8]

In January of 1754 Dinwiddie sent letters to the seven most important governors between Massachusetts and South Carolina, warning them of the French menace and asking for support. He made an impassioned speech in the Virginia House of Burgesses in February in which he pleaded: "The dignity of the crown of Great Britain, the welfare of all the colonies on this continent and more especially of this dominion, engage me to have your advice and assistance . . . ."[9] Next, Dinwiddie ordered construction of a fort at the confluence of the Allegheny, Monongehela, and Ohio Rivers, where Pittsburgh now stands. William Trent[10] started to build the fort but before he could finish the French seized it and named it Fort Duquesne. Meanwhile Dinwiddie sent Washington back to the frontier with 160 men. Hearing that the fort was in French hands Washington proceeded carefully. Then on May 28, 1754, Washington attacked a detachment of French at a place he called Fort Necessity. The French were overwhelmed and their commander, Coulon de Jumonville, and nine soldiers were killed. The Seven Years' War, referred to as the French and Indian War by Americans, had begun.[11] The war soon spread to New England, Quebec, and Europe, and involved not only France and England but many German states, Spain, and Portugal.[12]

However Washington, now promoted to colonel, had to surrender Fort Necessity when it was stormed by 700 Frenchmen in July. Gallantly, the French allowed him and his men to return to Virginia upon their promising not to build a fort on the Ohio for a year. He was acclaimed at the House of Burgesses, and had gained fame in London. He was twenty-two years old.[13]

In 1755, Britain responded to the pleas of Dinwiddie and to Washington's defeat, sending General Edward Braddock to Virginia. In the summer of 1755 he and his 2,200 men marched towards Fort Duquesne and on July 9 were ambushed in a narrow ravine by about 250 Frenchmen and 600 Indians at the place now called Braddock, Pennsylvania, a few miles upstream from Pittsburgh. It is now the site of the Edgar Thomson steel works, the first major facility built by Andrew Carnegie. The French and Indians, shooting from behind trees, overwhelmed the British. Braddock was killed in the battle but Washington survived to return to Virginia where Dinwiddie promoted him to commander of all Virginia troops. He was now twenty-three years old.[14]

After Braddock's defeat, Dinwiddie's frontier communities were stung by marauding Indians. He formed ranger companies and gave Washington a regiment. In 1757 he was able to temporarily pacify his western realms, making a treaty with the Indians at Winchester.[15] He participated in conferences at Alexandria and Annapolis in 1755 and at Philadelphia in 1757. At these he tried to get more support, but was frustrated in these attempts, most likely due in part to the fallout of the Pistole Controversy. Dinwiddie, old and frustrated, retired and left Virginia in January of 1758, never to return. He was given a pension of £400 per annum, and made at least one trip back to Scotland. He died in Bristol, England.[16]

In his final twelve years, Robert Dinwiddie must have viewed with interest the constant stream of news which he himself had put in motion. In the same summer that he returned to Britain, a fellow Scot, General John Forbes, hacked his way through the dark forests between Philadelphia and Fort Duquesne. His force of 6,000, including many kilted Highlanders, was sufficient to convince the French and their Indian allies to leave the fort uncontested. It must have been a stirring sight, Forbes and his army marching toward the abandoned fort, with its three rivers, pipes skirling, tartans flapping in the wind. Forbes founded and named Pittsburgh at the site of Fort Duquesne.

The war which Robert Dinwiddie started became in some opinions the first world war. It raged on for several years across Europe and North America and as far away as India and Africa, until the treaty of Paris in 1763 ended it. A recent book by Fred Anderson finds a causality from the Seven Years' War to the American and French Revolutions, the Napoleonic wars, and the Latin American liberation movements.[17] Certainly, the Paris treaty meant that French-speaking Quebec would be part of the British Empire, and that the American Middle West would forevermore speak English. It was also the beginning of the end for the almost undisputed supremacy of France, which had lasted almost a thousand years, from the time of Charlemagne to the defeat of Napoleon. From 1754, when Robert Dinwiddie sent the young Washington to begin hostilities, to the Battle of Waterloo in 1815, there elapsed only sixty-one years.

Patrick henry

(1736–1799)

M OST AMERICANS KNOW of Patrick Henry's speech with its famous phrase, "Give me liberty or give me death." But few people know that he was perhaps the most influential radical in the colonies in the years leading up to the American Revolution. A decade before the rebellion when most Americans simply wanted better treatment by Britain, Henry was demanding full equality for the colonials as British subjects, and home rule or else. Henry was a truly great orator, probably not equaled in American history until Martin Luther King Jr. But of course, whereas King was pursuing peaceful change, Henry was inciting war. His speeches were inflammatory,

Patrick Henry,
PICTURE COLLECTION, THE BRANCH LIBRARIES, THE NEW YORK PUBLIC LIBRARY.

and inflame they did. Henry was the firebrand of the American Revolution.

Patrick Henry was born at Studley in Hanover County, Virginia. His father, John Henry, was a prosperous planter and a well-educated man. John Henry (or Hendrie) was an immigrant from Aberdeenshire. His brother Patrick (for whom our subject was named) won a scholarship to

Kings College, Aberdeen and graduated in 1718. John Henry also received a classical education at Aberdeen, but left without a degree. He was quite successful in Virginia, first as a surveyor and later as Justice of the Hanover County court. He married a widow, Sarah Winston Syme, of probable English descent, who had been married to another Scot named Syme.[1]

Young Patrick Henry received some formal education at the local school but was principally taught by his father. During the first two decades of his life, Henry was singularly unsuccessful. At age fifteen he clerked in a store. The next year he and his brother William opened a store of their own which failed. By age eighteen he had married Sarah Shelton with whom he would have six children. She brought a 300-acre plantation to the marriage, but a fire that destroyed their home ruined the couple. Henry then opened another store and after its failure went to work in a tavern owned by his father-in-law. Finally in 1760, nearing his twenty-fourth birthday, Henry found something he was good at. He decided to become a lawyer. Although his qualifications were meager, he was permitted to practice because the officials were so impressed by his great intelligence. At the law he prospered immediately and in the next few years built up a lucrative practice.[2]

Patrick Henry came into national prominence after May 29, 1765. On that day in Williamsburg he walked into the Virginia House of Burgesses, of which he was a member, and, demanding the floor, began to offer seven resolutions that he proposed should be passed. The immediate reason for these resolutions was his opposition to the recently passed Stamp Act, by which Britain had just levied what was perceived as an onerous tax on the colonies. But Henry's resolutions went much farther than just resisting the tax. His first resolution proposed that the colonists had come to America possessing all of the rights enjoyed by all British subjects. His second resolution said that these rights had already been confirmed. At his next resolutions some of the members began to squirm in their seats. Henry said that "taxation of the people by themselves" was "the distinguishing characteristic of British freedom . . . " and that Virginians had always enjoyed the right of self government. So far, Henry's resolutions were merely audacious. Then he presented his sixth resolution: "*Resolved*, That . . . the inhabitants of this colony are not bound to yield obedience to any law or ordinance whatever, designed to impose any taxation whatsoever upon them . . ." other than those made by their own House of

Burgesses. His last resolution set off a raucous debate. It *resolved*, in effect, that anyone who disagreed with the first six resolutions ". . . shall be deemed an enemy to his Majesty's colony."[3]

In the wild scene that ensued, Henry again took the floor to defend his resolutions. The words which he spoke made him America's first national hero. "Caesar had his Brutus, Charles the First his Cromwell, and George the Third . . ." Here he was interrupted by shouts of "Treason! Treason!" But he continued ". . . may profit from their example! If this be treason, make the most of it!"[4] Thomas Jefferson, who was present that day, said Henry spoke "as Homer wrote . . . with torrents of sublime elegance." Years later he recalled, "Henry spoke wonderfully. Call it oratory or what you please, but I never heard anything like it." Henry's resolutions were at once printed and distributed throughout the colonies with immediate effect. As far away as Massachusetts people became incited to think and speak differently about their relationship with Great Britain, sparked by the Virginian who had dared to say in public what many were afraid to say even in private.[5]

For the next decade Patrick Henry was a leader of the radical opposition in the colonies. He was a delegate to the Continental Congress in 1774 and 1775. An on March 23, 1775, at St. John's Church in Richmond, he delivered the speech which, says the *Encyclopaedia Britannica*, "assured his position as one of the world's great orators and advocates of human liberty."[6] The magic of Henry's speech held his audience entranced. Suddenly he stopped speaking, lowered his head and crossed his wrists, appearing to be a shackled slave. Quietly he then asked, "Is life so dear or peace so sweet as to be purchased at the price of chains and slavery?" Then he ended with his famous peroration, tossing his head towards the sky, his arms free of the imaginary bonds, wide open. In this posture he shouted, "Forbid it Almighty God! I know not what course others may take, but as for me, give me liberty or give me death!" The American War of Independence began twenty-seven days later at Lexington, Massachusetts.[7]

Patrick Henry served on the committee that drafted the constitution for the State of Virginia. He was elected governor of Virginia three successive times in 1776, 1777, and 1778, thus serving as long as the new constitution allowed. He authorized the expedition of General George Rogers Clark into the northwest, which proved to be very important. General Clark, who had Scottish ancestry on both sides of his family history, fought his part of the Revolution all alone in the wilderness. With a handful of unpaid soldiers, he captured the British forts of Kaskaskia and Cahokia and established such control over the area that it was awarded to the Americans at the peace treaty of 1783.[8] The lands Clark (and Henry) won for the United States, are now the states of Ohio, Illinois, Wisconsin, Michigan, and Indiana.[9]

Henry's first wife died and he married Dorothea Dandridge hoping to return to plantation life. But he was elected to the Virginia legislature, serving from 1780 to 1784. He was governor again from 1784 to 1786, and was back in the legislature from 1787 to 1790. Henry was initially skeptical of the federal idea and did not attend the Constitutional Convention. He finally approved of the Constitution after the Bill of Rights, with which he had a lot to do, had been passed. As his health declined, he began to turn down various government posts but was prevailed upon to run for the Virginia legislature in 1799. During his successful campaign, he made his last speech—a plea for American unity. But before he could take his seat he died at his plantation near Brookneal, Virginia.[10]

Thomas Jefferson testifies again, about Patrick Henry, the man who stoked the fires of revolution. "He left all of us far behind . . . He gave the first impulse to the ball of revolution . . . He was the idol of the country beyond anyone that ever lived."[11]

Alexander Hamilton

(1755–1804)

I T IS OBVIOUS to anyone who has studied the early history of the United States that Alexander Hamilton was one of the principal founding fathers. And few would argue with the view that he was the most important person of all in setting up the world's oldest and most stable constitutional government and in getting it running. Yet Hamilton is an unsung founding father, nowhere near to Washington, Jefferson, Madison, Franklin, and Adams in the perception of people today.

Alexander Hamilton, PICTURE COLLECTION, THE BRANCH LIBRARIES, THE NEW YORK PUBLIC LIBRARY.

Alexander Hamilton was born on the island of Nevis in the West Indies. His father, James Hamilton, was the fourth son of Alexander Hamilton, Laird of Cambuskenneth in Ayrshire. His mother, the former Rachel Faucett, was the daughter of a French Huguenot physician. Although married to a trader named Lavien, Rachel began living with James Hamilton around 1752 and did not divorce Lavien until 1758. This meant that her famous son was illegitimate, and it always pained him to acknowledge this. James Hamilton was a small trader and appears to have been a ne'er-do-well. In 1765 he brought his family to St. Croix and then abandoned them. Thus, although the parents of Alexander Hamilton were of excellent backgrounds, his birth and early years were not spent in the best of circumstances.

Rachel Faucett Lavien Hamilton ran a store in Christiansted to support her family and by all accounts was good enough at business to keep her family out of poverty. By the time she died in 1768 young Alexander Hamilton was clerking in the merchant house of New Yorkers Nicholas Cruger and David Beekman. In 1771 a Scotch-Irish Presbyterian minister, Hugh Knox, appeared in Christiansted and noticed the young clerk who was soon to be promoted to manager. With the help of Knox and Cruger, Alexander Hamilton was able to go to New York for his education. He wanted to study at Princeton but when he presented his request for a rapid promotion schedule the famous John Witherspoon turned him down. He was accepted at King's College (now Columbia University) in New York.[1]

Hamilton was a good student but he became distracted by the revolutionary politics of the day. Before he was twenty he had written pamphlets and publicly defended the Boston Tea Party. He was commissioned in the patriot army with the rank of captain in 1776, and displayed great bravery at the Second Battle of Trenton as his company shielded Washington's main army from attack. When the colonials took Princeton from the British in January 1777, Hamilton got to fire on Nassau Hall, which had spurned him as a student. Washington personally promoted Hamilton to be his aide-de-camp with the rank of lieutenant colonel. Since living with his mother had made him fluent in French, Hamilton became the liaison between Washington's staff and the French generals and admirals who supported the colonial army.

Hamilton stayed on the general staff, and in slow times continued his studies. In 1780 he married Elizabeth Schuyler who was from one of New York's most illustrious families.

At the siege of Yorktown in 1781, Hamilton led an assault against the British. With the war over, Hamilton moved to Albany, New York to study law. He was admitted to the bar in 1782 and was given a position as a tax collector. Shortly, he was elected to the Continental Congress. At this time he took the view that the new country could not survive and prosper without a strong central government. Under the *nom de plume* of "The Continentalist" he wrote articles for the *New York Packet* advocating these views. He also defended loyalists and was instrumental in getting a law repealed which had disbarred loyalist lawyers and which had taken the vote away from loyalist voters.[2]

In 1786 the new American states held a convention at Annapolis to discuss economic problems. Using this meeting as a platform, Hamilton urged that the states consider another convention to consider forming a new government that would be much stronger, "To render the Constitution of the federal government adequate to the exigencies of the union." He used these words in the document he drafted, which ordained the Constitutional Convention of 1787.[3] Having been the principal voice in creating the Convention, Hamilton was relatively quiet when it actually met. He made one speech in which he advocated that the United States use the British government "the best in the world," as he put it, as a model. This idea went nowhere, but since there was support for a strong central government along other lines, he remained relatively silent and the Constitution was written and approved by the Convention. Hamilton was the only delegate from New York to sign the Constitution.

But there was still much work to be done. Many citizens were wary of a strong central government. Accordingly, Hamilton, John Jay, and James Madison began to publish *The Federalist* papers advocating ratification of the Constitution by the various states. Hamilton wrote more than two-thirds of the eighty-five essays, which explained how the new government would work. These essays, published in New York newspapers (perhaps the beginning of New York as the media capital) were read throughout the new states and were very influential not only in getting the Constitution ratified but in presenting ideas about American political philosophy, still useful today. At the New York convention in 1788, Hamilton was "the chief champion" in persuading New York to ratify.[4]

Hamilton was appointed secretary of the treasury in the first cabinet. In 1790 he convinced the new federal government to assume all of the various states' debts and to implement taxes to pay them off. Within a few years the debt securities of the United States sold at a premium in Europe.[5] But some Southerners were so upset at this program that Hamilton had to bargain for votes with Jefferson to get it started. This trade resulted in establishing the permanent capital in the South, on the Potomac River. Hamilton founded the central bank of the country and established the Treasury. Even though the central bank was not envisioned in the Constitution, Hamilton argued that it could be established anyway. Thus his winning arguments established forever the "implied powers" inherent in the Constitution. Hamilton was close to Washington and behaved at times as if he were a sort of prime minister. This annoyed Jefferson, the Secretary of State, and they became enemies. Gradually, the two formed America's first political parties. Jefferson and Madison led the Republicans, who favored close ties with France. Hamilton was head of the Federalists, who wanted to be allied with Britain. Washington, so close to Hamilton for so long, usually backed him and was in effect, a Federalist.

Hamilton was also a great lawyer and it was he who came up with the concept of judicial review. The greatest chief justice, John Marshall (see p. 153) said that beside Hamilton he felt like a candle "before the sun at noonday."[6]

In 1794 the federal government faced its first major test as farmers in Western Pennsylvania rebelled against the excise tax which Hamilton had placed on whiskey, their most profitable product. Hamilton realized immediately that this Whiskey Rebellion was a threat to his concept of a strong central government. After a few tar-and-featherings and the burning of a tax collector's home, Hamilton was able to convince Washington to send 13,000 troops to the frontier, and went with them himself. The farmers, mostly Scottish and Scotch-Irish Presbyterians, were led by a Princeton-educated Scottish-American Judge, Hugh Henry Brackenridge, who became a principal founder of the University of Pittsburgh. But when the troops arrived the farmers' resistance ebbed. Hamilton had won this first test of federal authority.

In 1796 Washington gave his *Farewell Address* to the nation. It is one of the most important documents in American history and Hamilton was its principal author. Hamilton expected to be nominated for President but John Adams was elected as the second president. But much to the dismay of Adams, members of his cabinet still talked things over with Hamilton. In 1797, Hamilton became the subject of America's first political sex scandal, admitting his affair with Mrs. Maria Reynolds. In 1798 France threatened war and Hamilton demanded an army with himself as the head. Despite the vehement objections of President Adams, George Washington approved and made Hamilton second in command and a major general. The army of course never fought France, and Hamilton resigned in 1800.

In 1801 Alexander Hamilton built a country house in northern Manhattan, still called Hamilton Grange. He also opened the New York *Post*, now the city's oldest daily newspaper. In 1784 he founded the Bank of New York, the city's oldest bank today. Of the bank's first eight directors, at least four, Hamilton, William Maxwell, William Seton, and

General Alexander MacDougall were Scots. And in 1799, Hamilton, who has been called America's first big businessman, co-founded the Manhattan Company to bring fresh water to New York City. This company later merged with the Chase bank and is now America's largest bank, Chase Manhattan.

Aaron Burr, Hamilton's co-founder of the Manhattan Company, became a political enemy and this led to Hamilton's tragic end. After Hamilton had offended him by denouncing him in public, Burr, then Vice President of the United States demanded a duel. Hamilton thought this ridiculous, but his sense of honor compelled him to accept the challenge. The two combatants met on the morning of July 11, 1804 on a hill in Weehawken, New Jersey, across the Hudson, overlooking Manhattan Island. It was a sitting Vice President against a former Secretary of the Treasury. Imagine Al Gore dueling against Robert Rubin! Hamilton must have looked vulnerable. He was slender and only a little over five and one half feet tall. Below his wavy hair were the mournful, deep-set eyes which we see today on every ten-dollar bill. Two shots were fired. Alexander Hamilton was mortally wounded and died the next day. He had been an active member of Saint Andrew's Society of the State of New York.

Lachlan Macquarie

(1761-1824)

EW MEN, IF any, have ever done as much to influence the founding of a nation as Lachlan Macquarie did in Australia. When he arrived in 1809, as the fifth Governor of New South Wales (the first four had been notably inept) he found a distressed penal colony in a state of law-less chaos. When he left twelve years later Australia had been perma-nently established as a civilized place.

Macquarie was well chosen for his task. He was born on the isle of Ulva, just off the coast of the island of Mull, a kinsman to the chief of this small but very old clan. Among the clan's holdings was the island of Staffa, with its unusual rock cavern called "Fingal's cave." Mendelssohn was to make music of this rock. Johnson and Boswell visited Ulva in 1773 and Johnson found the island to be "a most dolorous country." But Boswell wrote that they found the chief to be poor, but "polite and worldly."[1]

Lachlan Macquarie joined the army in 1777. His years and places of service illustrate brilliantly the extent of the British Empire and the mobile life of a soldier in its service. Macquarie first served at Halifax. He became a lieutenant in 1781 and was stationed at New York at the close of the American Revolution. From there he was sent to Jamaica. On Christmas day, 1787, he was commissioned as a lieutenant in the Seventy-seventh regiment and served in India. He was in action at the sieges of Cananore in 1790 and Seringapatam in 1791. He saw duty at Cochin in China in 1795 and at Ceylon in 1796 where he became a major. He par-ticipated at the second siege of Seringapatam in 1799, and 1800 found him at the siege of Alexandria in Egypt. In the same year he became lieutenant colonel in the Eighty-sixth regiment, and in 1803 he was in London as assistant adjutant-general. In 1805 he went to India with the Eighty-sixth but was gazetted to the Seventy-third with which he served through 1806. In 1807 he took command of the Seventy-third in London.[2]

In 1809 Macquarie was appointed Governor of New South Wales and embarked with his Seventy-third regiment of Highlanders for Australia. What he found there must have shocked even the seasoned veteran he was. Almost the entire meager population of 6,000 were convicts, employed by the few free people in conditions approximating slave labor. Poverty was widespread. Alcohol abuse and prostitution were rampant. There was no proper infrastructure of sanitation, schools, churches, and roads. Crime was uncontrolled.[3]

Yet in this dismal scene there were prosperous people who had started an economy. These people were called the Exclusives, and were running the colony for their own benefit. At the head of the Exclusives was another Scot, John Macarthur, who had helped Macquarie to get his appointment. The two were to become enemies. Macarthur (1767–1834) had been born in Plymouth, Devonshire, England, the son of Alexander Macarthur, a fugitive from the battlefield of Culloden Moor who had fled to the Caribbean and then returned to England. John Macarthur had arrived in Sydney in 1790 as a member of the 102nd Foot, the New South Wales Corps. From the beginning, the Corps did more as businessmen than as policemen. Macarthur himself was the founder of the Australian wool industry that meant so much to the economy of the country. He improved the breed by crossing Irish and Bengal sheep, then in 1796, improved it further by importing merino sheep from the Cape, which had been a gift of the King of Spain to the Dutch Government. These new hybrids thrived in Australia. Macarthur planted, in addition, the first olive tree in Australia.[4]

In this lawless land Macarthur fought a duel against one of his own officers. Rum, illegal to distill, became the money of the colony. In 1806 William Bligh became the fourth Governor of New South Wales. He was the notorious Captain Bligh who in 1789, had incited the crew of the *Bounty* to mutiny. He would do worse in Australia. Bligh decided to enforce the letter of the law, particularly the law against distilling. He had Macarthur arrested for high misdemeanors. But Macarthur's friend, Major George Johnston, another Scot, arrested Bligh and deported him to England. Macarthur was acquitted and he and Johnston assumed control of a provisional government. In 1811, Macarthur returned to England to give testimony in favor of Johnston. He was not allowed back to Australia, and instead, went to France to study the wine industry. In 1817 he was honorably allowed to return to Australia and founded the Australian wine industry. He had created the two most important industries in the country's history. In 1825 he was elected a member of the first legislative council of New South Wales. Several of his descendants were knighted.[5]

When Macquarie took over from Bligh in 1809, he began, immediately, to bring the domain under his control. He ratified most of the acts of the provisional government, but otherwise, changed most things radically. He has been called a despot and he certainly was to those who wanted to keep the inequality between the free and the near slaves; the rich and the poor. His policy was, as Ritchie says, "that a convict, on the expiry or remission of his sentence, provided that he were well-behaved, ought to be treated as if he had never transgressed the law and should posses the same rights as a free man."[6] This policy was radically different from those of his predecessors and was successful, helping convicts and ex-convicts to become productive citizens. On the arrival of a new boatload of "transported" people, Macquarie would meet with them and tell them that rehabilitation was up to them. He told them that he had faith in them and that if they behaved, their past errors would be overlooked. He settled "emancipated" convicts on farmland, granting thirty acres to people whose sentence had been served.[7] During his term, 500,000 acres were distributed to free immigrants and former convicts. Whereas Bligh had given two pardons during his term, Macquarie gave 366 absolute pardons, 1,365 conditional pardons, and 2,319 tickets-of-leave.[8]

But Macquarie was a stern ruler. He condemned unmarried cohabitation, closed the pubs during Sunday services, and marched government employees to church. He sent his Seventy-third regiment into the bush, where hardened criminals were robbing and murdering. These men were hunted out and hanged.[9] When word came from London that the government had no plan to appoint a council to assist him, he said, "I entertain a fond hope that such an institution will never be extended to this colony."[10]

Macquarie widened the streets of Sydney and laid out their grid plan.[11] He gave the streets names and insisted that each building had a number. He introduced silver coinage, established a bank, opened a marketplace, controlled weights and measures, and opened foreign trade with China, Bengal, and the United States. He had a liberal attitude towards the Aborigines. He controlled alcoholism and prostitution. He built a hospital

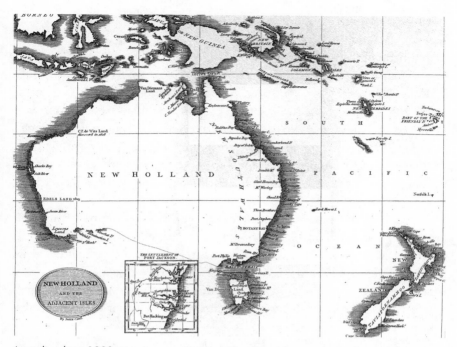

Australia about 1800. MAP DIVISION, THE NEW YORK PUBLIC LIBRARY, ASTOR, LENOX AND TILDEN FOUNDATIONS

costing £18,000. He built churches, schools, orphan institutions, bridges, and wharves. A botanical garden and a racecourse were started. He maintained fixed hours for interviews. He promoted flood control projects. He encouraged exploration, and built a road from Sydney over the Blue Mountains opening up a vast plain for agriculture. During Macquarie's term, the population tripled. For a while, the government noticed, promoting him to full colonel in 1810, brigadier general in 1811, and major general in 1813.[12]

But the British Colonial Office gave him little help for all of his projects in his increasingly large domain. They sent little money, but many more convicts. Accordingly, Macquarie taxed the colonists to pay for it all. This was his downfall. The powerful Exclusives resented the taxes and appealed to London for relief. They charged Macquarie with extravagance and leniency towards the convicts. These charges as well as declining health got him recalled in 1821. The grateful colonists gave him a piece of plate as he left the continent. He spent the rest of his years on a pension defending what was surely one of the best administrations in the history of colonization. In a switch that would have been fancied by Inspector Clouseau, Macquarie was denied a title, while the incompetent Captain Bligh was promoted to vice-admiral!

Lachlan Macquarie died in his house in Duke Street, London on July 1, 1824. His body was taken back to Ulva to be buried in the ancestral home that he had bought back from his father's creditors. His first wife had died in China in 1796. Therefore, it was his second wife Elizabeth (1778–1835), a distant cousin from the Campbells of Airds, who was left to defend his memory. They had one son who died without issue. Elizabeth spent the rest of her life righting the wrongs done to her husband's reputation.

It wouldn't be necessary now. Everyone knows who the Father of Austrailia was. Lachlan Macquarie has dozens of places named after him. There is Macquarie Road, Macquarie Street, and Macquarie Place in Sydney. There is a Lachlan River and a Macquarie River. There is Port Macquarie, Macquarie County, Macquarie Marsh, and Macquarie Plains. There is Macquarie Harbour in Tasmania, and Macquarie Island to the south.

There are some (including the *Encyclopaedia Britannica*) who propose two Scots, John Macarthur *and* Lachlan Macquarie, as joint Fathers of Australia[13] There is no doubt that Macarthur started the country's two great industries, wool and wine. These are significant achievements, but they do not take into account the forlorn state of the colony before the arrival of Macquarie, when Macarthur was exercising almost unlimited power. It was Macquarie who restored order and built the essential public facilities, which made the colony function. When he left in 1821, Australia was a civilized place on a firm foundation to become the great country it is today.

Andrew Jackson

(1767–1845)

ANDREW JACKSON WAS one of the most influential people in American history. As a soldier his actions caused Florida and large parts of Alabama and Mississippi to become part of the United States. As the seventh President, and the first born across the Appalachian Mountains, he gave the west its first strong voice in the national government, and ended the presidential dominance previously enjoyed by Massachusetts

Andrew Jackson, Washington, D.C.
COLLECTION OF THE AUTHOR.

and Virginia. He made the country truly democratic, and reinstated the strong two party system, which is still in place.

Andrew Jackson's parents were Andrew and Elizabeth Hutchinson Jackson, Scotch-Irish Presbyterian immigrants who left from Carrickfergus, County Down in 1765. Andrew Jackson was born on the frontier at the Waxhaw Settlement, an area then disputed by North and South Carolina. He arrived in the world less than two weeks after his father died, and was named in his honor. His penniless mother, Elizabeth, moved into the home of her sister, Jane Crawford. Her hope was that her third son, Andrew, would become a Presbyterian minister and she sent him to study at an academy run by William Humphries. Later he was tutored by James White Stephenson, a Presbyterian minister.[1]

But the American Revolution intervened, and, at age thirteen, Andrew Jackson joined the army. He was at the Battle of Hanging Rock and was captured in 1781. When he refused to shine the boots of a British officer he received a saber blow that left permanent scars on his head and hand. He also survived smallpox. Through some contacts, his mother secured his release but she in turn, died of cholera. His brothers, Hugh and Robert died also. The poverty his family had endured in Ireland, the scars on his face, and the deaths of his family were all in young Jackson's mind the fault of Great Britain. The fourteen-year-old orphan was filled with hatred for anything British thereafter.[2]

For the next few years, Jackson stayed with relatives and then settled in Salisbury, North Carolina where he studied law and became one of the wildest young men on the wild frontier. He gambled, drank, and wenched, all to excess, and fought at least one duel. Somehow, he was admitted to the bar in 1787 and became prosecutor for western North Carolina (soon to become Tennessee) in 1788. There, in and around Nashville, he built up a very lucrative law practice.[3]

Jackson boarded at the home of Colonol John Donelson, another Scotch-Irishman who had co-founded Nashville in 1779 with yet another Ulsterman, James Robertson. Their frontier village has grown into a city of more than 500,000, and is a world center of the music industry. Jackson was immediately attracted to Donelson's daughter Rachel, but she was stuck in a very bad marriage, estranged from her husband. Eventually her vengeful husband sued for divorce in Virginia, but on purpose he did not complete the action. Thinking that there had been a divorce, Jackson and Rachel were married in 1791. The former husband then pursued the divorce, charging Rachel with adultery and deliberately causing a scandal that never left the lives of Rachel and Andrew Jackson. The couple quietly remarried.[4] The Jacksons had no children, but they adopted one of Rachel's nephews, calling him Andrew Jackson Jr. They also adopted an Indian boy, Lyncoya, who died at age sixteen.[5]

In 1796 Andrew Jackson was on the committee which drafted the constitution for the new state of Tennessee, and was elected its first member of the House of Representatives. He was elected to the Senate in 1797 but resigned in 1798 to become judge of the Tennessee Superior Court.

He held that position through 1804. In 1812, as war with Britain became imminent, Jackson as a major general raised the Tennessee militia. In 1813 and 1814 he fought against the Creek Indians who were allied with the British, finally crushing them in Alabama. The victory was so complete that the Creeks were compelled to surrender 23 million acres, which are today almost half of the states of Alabama and Mississippi. People were beginning to call Jackson "Old Hickory." In August, 1814, Jackson, without orders, moved his army to the south towards Mobile with the idea of attacking the Spanish at Pensacola, using the excuse that they were allies of the British. But when he heard that the British were moving on New Orleans he hurried to that port city.[6]

Jackson was eager for the fight against the British he hated and just before the Battle of New Orleans he is quoted as saying, "I'll smash 'em, so help me God! I'll smash 'em."[7] But the odds were against him. He was commanding irregular troops made up of free blacks, frontiersmen, Creoles—even the pirate Jean Lafitte. And he was opposed by 8,000 British troops, fresh from their victory over Napoleon at Waterloo.[8] But on June 8, 1815, marching his men to "Yankee Doodle" and "La Marseillaise", Jackson completely defeated the British, causing them to leave Louisiana. No one on either side knew that the Treaty of Ghent, ending the war, had been signed in Belgium two weeks before! But news of Jackson's victory at New Orleans reached Washington and the Eastern United States before the news of the treaty. It was America's first major military victory, and Jackson was an immediate hero. This great triumph was an important tonic for the United States, which was fearful of Great Britain, and had already suffered the humiliation of having had its capital city sacked. Jackson was a national hero and when the news from Belgium finally arrived, a wave of euphoria swept through the land.

Jackson retired to his home, The Hermitage, near Nashville but was called to active duty again in 1818. He was given vague orders to oust some Indians in the south who were ignoring a previous treaty. But most people suspected that he would attack the Spanish in Florida: he did, capturing two Spanish ports. There was an immediate outcry from Spain, and some in the American government wanted to censure Jackson, but his friend, Secretary of State John Quincy Adams, stood by him and censure was avoided. His action hastened the acquisition of Florida by the United States. By 1822, Jackson was being touted for the presidency. He lost a close election in 1824, but won in 1828, besting his former ally John

Quincy Adams. But at every opportunity, his opponents had slandered Jackson and his wife about their "illegitimate" marriage. There is no question that it took its toll on both of them. Rachel was weakened, and in this, the hour of Jackson's greatest triumph, came his greatest tragedy. His wife of thirty-seven years died at The Hermitage.[9]

It is generally conceded that the election of 1828 was a turning point in American history. The country had its first "log cabin" President, the first "man of the people," born on the frontier. It was more democratic than previous elections, with the common people voting largely for their hero, the first self-made president.[10] More than a million votes were cast, triple the number cast in the previous election.

Jackson was re-elected easily in 1832. His presidency dealt largely with domestic issues, particularly involving banking. However, his own Vice President, fellow Scotch-Irishman John Caldwell Calhoun, made an issue out of state's rights when his state of South Carolina refused to impose a high federal protective tariff. Jackson asked for and received an authorization from Congress to send troops to South Carolina. Eventually, a compromise was negotiated, but Jackson had preserved the union and federal authority. He left the presidency in 1837, more popular than when he was first elected.

He retired to The Hermitage, an old man, semi-invalid. He received many visitors who came to render homage or just to curry favor. He officially joined the Presbyterian Church. On his last day, he was surrounded by his family and friends. He is quoted as saying, "What is the matter with my dear children? Have I alarmed you? Oh, do not cry. Be good children and we will all meet in Heaven."[11] He is buried next to Rachel at The Hermitage.

Old Hickory is honored with his picture on the $20 bill. He joins two other Scottish-Americans: Alexander Hamilton on the $10 bill, and U.S. Grant on the $50 bill. This is quite an honor for an ethnic group which now numbers fewer than five percent of the population of the United States of America.

Jackson's presidency reinstituted the two party system which is still in use today and he bequeathed to us a vigorous Democratic party. But his greatest contribution was in making the country a broad-based democracy. When he was first elected in 1828, there were many serious people who questioned the wisdom of such a government. It was never again in question after Jackson.[12]

Sam houston

(1793–1863)

AM HOUSTON WAS one
of the most important as
well as one of the most colorful
Americans in the nineteenth
century. His leadership in the
War for Texan Independence
established Texas as American
rather than Mexican, and
opened up the entire land to
the west to become American
as well.

Samuel Houston was born
near Lexington, Virginia, descended, it was said, from
Scottish archers who had
helped Joan of Arc win independence for France.[1] As far as
we can tell, Sam Houston was

General Sam Houston at the Battle of San Jacinto.
PICTURECOLLECTION, THE BRANCH LIBRARIES, THE
NEW YORK PUBLIC LIBRARY.

of entirely Scotch-Irish ancestry. His Presbyterian great-grandparents,
John and Margaret Houston, left Belfast for America in 1730. His mother and grandmother Elizabeth Paxton and Mary Davidson, and most of
the neighbors mentioned in his biographies were Scotch-Irish
Presbyterians as well.[2]

Sam Houston's father, also named Samuel, died in 1807 and his widow,
Elizabeth, moved her family to the frontier in Blount County, Tennessee.

Young Sam Houston was almost entirely self-educated. Somehow he got hold of a copy of Pope's translation of the *Iliad* and read it so often that he says in his memoirs, "I could repeat it almost entire from beginning to end."[3] His brothers tormented him and when they got him a job as a clerk in a store the free-spirited Sam ran away to live with the Cherokee Indians, who treated him like a prince. He made periodic visits to see his family to get new clothes, and when he reckoned that he owed his mother, he opened a country school, and was so good at it that he had to turn away students, even though he charged the high price of $8 a year. He says, "I thought that one who had graduated at an Indian university ought to hold his lore at a dearer rate . . . ."[4]

In the War of 1812 he fought with fellow Scotch-Irish frontiersman Andrew Jackson, who would later become president of the United States. It was the whites and the Cherokees against the Creek Indians, who had gone over to the British side. While storming a redoubt Houston received an arrow in a thigh, and later two balls in a shoulder. The attending physician was sure he would die, but somehow he survived, carried on a litter through the forest.[5]

In 1817 Houston became an agent in moving the Cherokees from Tennessee to a reservation in what is now Arkansas. He appeared before the noted Scotch-Irish politician John Caldwell Calhoun in Indian dress and was rebuked for it. He resigned this position in 1818. He then worked at a law office in Nashville for a while and was admitted to the bar. At age thirty he was elected as a congressman and at age thirty-four, running as a Jacksonian Democrat, Governor of Tennessee. Two years later Houston, who had many amorous affairs and fathered numerous half-breed children, married Eliza Allen. It was a disastrous union. After only three months the couple separated. The incident caused Houston to resign as governor and retreat to his haven with the Cherokees. This time, he was officially adopted into the tribe.[6]

In 1830 and 1832 Houston went to Washington "to expose frauds practiced upon the Cherokees by government agents." Then he was sent by President Jackson to go to Texas to make treaties with Indians, protecting American traders. He stayed in Texas and was a delegate at the constitutional convention at San Felipe in 1833, which tried for a peaceful solution with Mexico. But this was not to be. Relations worsened and in 1835 Sam Houston was chosen commander-in-chief of the Texan army. Only a few months later a group of 189 American volunteers occupied the Alamo, a former chapel in San Antonio. More than fifty of these were of Scottish ancestry, including the famous frontiersmen Jim Bowie and Davy Crockett, and bagpiper John McGregor.[7] Houston warned that the city could not be defended by such a small force but the volunteers refused to leave. On March 6, 1836 a Mexican army of about 4,000, commanded by General Antonio López de Santa Anna, overwhelmed the Americans. Santa Anna lost more than a quarter of his men and took no prisoners. All of the Americans were killed. "Remember the Alamo!" became the rallying cry of the Texans.[8]

On April 21, 1836, the Americans got their revenge. On the banks of the San Jacinto River, General Houston led an army of 743 irregulars against 1,600 Mexican veterans, again under Santa Anna. Houston's men completely won the day, and established the independence of Texas.[9] Houston was wounded in the battle and, lying on a pallet, ordered that the defeated Mexican general be brought to see him.

"General Santa Anna!" said Houston. "Ah indeed. Take a seat, general."

The Mexican replied, "That man may consider himself born to no common destiny who has conquered the Napoleon of the West, and now it remains for him to be generous to the vanquished."

Houston answered, "You should have thought of that at the Alamo." But Houston was generous, probably only because he knew that world opinion of him and of America in general would depend on his treatment of his prisoners.[10]

Houston was elected President of the Republic of Texas on September 1, 1836, and was elected again in 1841, serving through 1844. In 1840 he married Margaret Lea, a woman from Alabama. When Texas became a state in 1845, he was elected as one of its first two senators. From this position he tried to get justice for the Indians, but this was not popular and he was not re-elected. In 1859 he was elected governor of Texas, making him the only person to be governor of two American states. In this office he fought hard to keep his state in the union. When the Civil War began in 1861, he refused to swear allegiance to the Confederacy and was declared deposed as governor. He died two years later.[11]

The South's largest city, Houston, Texas, is named for Sam Houston and because "mission control" of the American Space Center was there in 1969, the first family name ever spoken on the moon was his.

James Knox Polk

(1795–1849)

JAMES KNOX POLK, as far as we can tell from his genealogists, was of entirely Scotch-Irish extraction, descended from Pollocks (the original form of the name), Taskers, Wilsons, and Knoxes.[1] He was born in Mecklenburg County, North Carolina, the son of Samuel Polk and Jane Knox. When he was eleven, the family moved to Maury County, Tennessee, where his father prospered as a surveyor and farmer. He was a frail boy, too often ill to get much formal schooling. Instead his mother taught him and brought him up in the Calvinist philosophy of hard work and individualism.[2]

When Polk was sixteen he and his father rode over 200 miles to Danville, Kentucky to see the famous Scotch-Irish-American surgeon, Ephraim McDowell. Only two years before McDowell had performed a medical marvel, the world's first elective abdominal surgery, and he had done it, not in London or Paris or Edinburgh. He had done it on the frontier. His patient, Jane (Jenny) Todd Crawford, also Scottish, had ridden on horseback some sixty miles to Danville. Without anesthesia, the Edinburgh-trained McDowell removed a twenty-pound tumor from Mrs. Crawford, who lived another thirty years to age seventy-nine. McDowell published his work but the medical world considered it to be a fraud. Confronted with the sickly James Knox Polk, McDowell removed gallstones, again without anesthesia. The boy's health improved dramatically.[3]

In 1815, despite his lack of schooling, Polk scored so well on the entrance examination at the University of North Carolina that he was admitted as a sophomore. He graduated first in his class and was as the *Encyclopaedia Britannica* says: "the preeminent scholar in both the classics and mathematics."[4] He was practically exhausted from the effort. Back in Nashville, he studied law and was elected to be clerk of the state senate. Here he developed a passion for politics, and in 1823 was elected to the state house of representatives. The next year he married Sarah Childress who was from a leading family in Murfreesboro. The couple had no children, but it proved to be a good marriage as his wife drew Polk out to socialize and meet people who were important to him. She was the perfect hostess.[5]

It was not well known then and is not now that the Polks owned a farm in the backwoods. It was operated by a tenant farmer who managed the property's seventeen slaves. The Polks visited the farm twice a year and made an income of between $3,500 and $6,300 per year. Polk wanted to sell the farm, but his wife insisted that they might need it during their old age. This may account for Polk's somewhat neutral and pragmatic stance on slavery.[6]

Polk became a friend of another Scotch-Irish-American politician, Andrew Jackson, who was known popularly as "Old Hickory." The powerful Jackson, soon to be President, backed Polk, helping to get him elected to the U.S. House of Representatives in 1825. Here the new congessman followed Jackson's expansionist policies to the point that he was called "Young Hickory." Polk was always in favor of the limited power of the federal government, and was devoted to "states rights." On the question of slavery, he maintained that the slaves were indeed human beings, implying that they should not be slaves. But, he said, the institution had to be borne. In 1828 Polk supported Jackson for President, and opposed the efforts of some to increase tarriffs.[7]

In 1835 Polk ousted John Bell, the incumbent Speaker of the House, and became a national figure. He maintained his loyalty to President Jackson, and became a skilled parliamentarian. People noticed his determination. It was obvious that he was brilliant. In 1839 he left the house and was elected governor of Tennessee. He tried and failed to get the Democratic party nomination for vice president in 1840. He ran again for governor and lost in 1841 and 1843.

The 1844 election was to be the biggest of Polk's life, and one of the most important in the country's history. There was a huge issue as to whether or not the United States should annex Texas and the Oregon country, both places claimed respectively by Mexico and Britain, but both populated mainly by immigrants from the United States. Most politicians were hedging on the issue but Polk was not. He demanded annexation of both Texas and Oregon. Polk went to the Democratic party convention hoping again to be nominated as vice president. But the overwhelming favorite for the Presidential nomination, Martin Van Buren had written an ill-advised public letter to the Washington *Daily Globe*, that predicted the annexing of Texas would start a war with Mexico. This greatly diminished his stature as a candidate and the first ballot produced no nominee. A compromise candidate was sought, and James Knox Polk was nominated for President of the United States on the eighth ballot. Polk campaigned on his annexation program with the slogan "54° 40' or fight!" This referred to his proposed latitude for the border with Canada in the Oregon Country. Polk won the election over Henry Clay by a bare 38,000 votes. The electoral votes, however, gave him a solid victory, 170–35. As someone seen as not likely to win, he became the first "dark horse" president, and was up to that time the youngest, at age forty-nine.[8]

Polk's inauguration was held in a rainstorm. Undaunted, he told the people exactly what he intended to do: support "states rights," annex Texas, solve the Oregon problem, lower the tariffs to increase trade, acquire California, and re-establish the independent treasury. Unlike so many presidents, he accomplished them all.[9] Polk announced that he would not seek a second term, undoubtedly with the idea that he could do and say as he thought best without giving any thought to re-election. He appointed a cabinet which had a broad geographical representation. It met twice a week, and Polk warned the members that if any had designs on the presidency, they may as well resign immediately, saying to them, "I intend to be, myself, President of the United States."[10]

Polk told Congress that the American people alone had the right to decide their destiny. He was modernizing the old idea of an American "Manifest Destiny." In his opinion, that destiny was to acquire all the lands within the latitudes north and south of the then United States, all the way to the Pacific Ocean. He made it clear that the United States should have no further claims, north or south, on the lands of Mexico and Britain.

Polk worked long hours. In his four years as president only six weeks were spent away from the capital. He didn't like to delegate, and was involved in all of the major decisions. "No President," he said, "who performs his duty faithfully and conscientiously can have any leisure."[11] Sarah, his faithful wife, arranged his social schedule—important to any leader—sometimes practically dragging her husband out of his office. Her spouse was all work, and had few real friends.[12]

Polk vetoed spending bills and got a bill passed to lower tariffs. He engaged Britain on the Oregon question, hoping to avoid a war. The British in Oregon were mostly fur traders. The Americans were settlers and far outnumbered them. Polk let Britain know that he would accept the forty-ninth parallel as the border, but Britain refused. Then he told them that he would submit the forty-ninth parallel proposal to the Senate if Britain would offer it. This time they accepted. Since it was known that Polk had campaigned for a more northerly border, (54° 40' or fight!) he asked the Senate instead for their advise and consent on the matter. The Senate voted 38–12 in favor of the forty-ninth parallel, which remains the border between the United States and Canada to this day. The area that now includes the states of Oregon, Washington, and Idaho had officially become part of the United States.

It was well that the Oregon question was settled, as it avoided a two-front war. The Mexican war had started. President Polk had sent General Zachary Taylor to Texas and had told him to march to the Rio Grande if requested to do so by the Texans. Then he sent an envoy to Mexico with an offer of $40,000,000, which was rejected. There were skirmishes between Mexican and American troops. Americans had been killed, and the President asked for a declaration of war which was approved by the House of Representatives 174 to 14.

Polk thought that Taylor was not prosecuting the war with enough vigor, and could not take Mexico by an overland route so he dispatched the army's senior officer, General Winfield Scott (see p. 233) to land at the port of Veracruz. Scott, whose grandfather had fought at the battle of Culloden Moor in 1746, led a brilliant campaign and within a few months, after an unbroken series of victories, flew the American flag on the Mexican National Palace. At the treaty of Guadeloupe Hidalgo in 1848, Mexico recognized the border between Texas and Mexico to be the Rio Grande and ceded to the United States most of what are now the states of California, Utah, Nevada, and Arizona, as well as parts of New Mexico, Colorado, and Wyoming. The United States paid Mexico $15,000,000, and agreed to assume the claims of Americans against Mexico. The United States, during the Polk regime, had become a transcontinental power, and had acquired about one-third of its present territory at very small cost. In addition, war with Britain had been avoided and both the northern and southern borders had been made secure.[13]

James Knox Polk had many other accomplishments during his term. He re-established the independent treasury; founded the U.S. Naval Academy; authorized the creation of the Smithsonian Institution; created the Department of the Interior; admitted Texas, Iowa, and Wisconsin as states; and ratified the Treaty of New Granada, which gave American citizens the right to cross the isthmus of Panama. President Polk governed, as the *Encyclopaedia Britannica* says, "with an extraordinary sense of duty." He left office with an unblemished reputation of integrity and fair dealing.[14]

James Knox Polk's monument is the western third of the United States. When his term expired he went immediately to his home in Nashville and died two months later, apparently of exhaustion.

THE ACQUISITION OF THE TERRITORY OF THE UNITED STATES OF AMERICA

Acquisition of Oregon Country, 1848
James Knox Polk, President
James Buchanan, Secretary of State

Aquisition of the Northwest Territory, 1783
George Rogers Clark, Soldier

Louisiana Purchase, 1803
Robert R. Livingston, Diplomat
James Monroe, Diplomat
Thomas Jefferson, President

Mexican Cession, 1848
Winfield Scott, Soldier
James Knox Polk, President

The Original Territory Colonized by Britain 1607-1783
James Stewart, King James VI & I, Founder

Gadsden purchase, 1853
Jefferson Davis, Secretary of War

Annexation of Texas, 1845
Sam Houston, Soldier
Jim Bowie, Soldier
Davy Crockett, Soldier
James Knox Polk, President

Annexation of Hawaii, 1898
Daniel Webster, Senator
R.C. Wyllie, Diplomat
William McKinley, President

Alaska Purchase, 1867
Andrew Johnson, President

Acquisition of Florida, 1819
Andrew Jackson, Soldier
Robert R. Livingston, Diplomat
James Madison, President
James Monroe, President

The acquisition of the territory of the United States of America, showing the names of prominent people of Scottish ancestry who played crucial roles in the process.
MAP BY BERNARD ADNET.

William Ewart Gladstone

(1809–1898)

GLADSTONE WAS THE "Victorian Colossus," the most important British statesman during the height of the British Empire. He served in Parliament a record sixty-one years, except for two brief periods, from 1833 to 1895. He was four times Prime Minister, also a record, being elected the last time at the age of eighty-two. He was also five times Chancellor of the Exchequer. Gladstone was a liberal, giving the Empire, which had been brought about by military and naval power, a more humanistic tone.

William Ewart Gladstone,
PICTURE COLLECTION, THE BRANCH LIBRARIES,
THE NEW YORK PUBLIC LIBRARY.

William Ewart Gladstone was born in Liverpool of purely Scottish ancestry. His father, Sir John Gladstone, was born in Leith as John Gladstones. His mother, Anne Mackenzie Robertson, was born in the Highland town of Dingwall. William Gladstone was the fourth son in a family of six. His father owned a sugar plantation in Demerara, West Indies and an estate in Scotland.[1]

From this privileged background, William Ewart Gladstone was sent to Eton at age eleven. He was not a great student but was good at football and cricket, and was interested in boating. At Oxford he became political, and took a double first in classics and mathematics in 1831. In 1832 he spent a half-year in Italy, learning the language. Near the end of the year he was elected to Parliament.[2]

Gladstone took strong positions during his long career. He was in favor of free trade, supported equality for Catholics, and although a staunch unionist, he advocated "national equity" for Scotland and Wales and Home Rule for Ireland.[3] He favored gradual emancipation for the slaves, and opposed the Opium War, defending China's right to resist the importation of drugs by force. He supported Baron Rothschild for admission to Parliament without taking the oath "on the true faith of a Christian." Gladstone was a voracious reader, including Homer and Dante in their original languages. He gave breakfast parties and went to many musical gatherings where he sang. In 1839 he married Catherine, elder daughter of Sir Stephen Glynne.[4]

In the winter of 1850–1851, Gladstone discovered while in Naples that Ferdinand II, king of the Two Sicilies, had dissolved the government and had taken twenty 20,000 political prisoners. Gladstone wrote a letter detailing the situation, to Lord Aberdeen who was about to become Prime Minister. Aberdeen cautioned against publication but Gladstone published anyway. The letter was translated into Italian and French. He then wrote two more which went through fourteen editions. The *Dictionary of National Biography* says, "Gladstone's letters undoubtedly contributed to the ultimate independence and unification of Italy."[5]

In 1852, Benjamin Disraeli was Chancellor of the Exchequer, proposing a tax that Gladstone opposed. Thus was begun the famous war between these two which ended only with Disraeli's going to the House of Lords a quarter of a century later. It is interesting to note that the running of the British Empire at the time of its greatest power and influence was entrusted alternately to these two men from minority groups, a Scot and a Jew. When the government reorganized in 1853, Gladstone became Chancellor of the Exchequer and proposed a budget that would reduce the income tax while paying the debt. He spoke for five hours conveying such a complete argument, there was no opposition. The speech was a political triumph which, says the *Dictionary of National Biography*, "has never been surpassed."[6]

In July 1868, Disraeli resigned and Gladstone was asked to form a government. From this new platform of Prime Minister, Gladstone advocated an Irish Land bill. This legislation guaranteed tenants' rights, with eviction allowed only for non-payment of rent and compensation permitted for improvements made by tenants. These reforms became law. He spoke for three hours about the Irish University bill explaining among other things, that Catholics wouldn't attend the Episcopal Trinity College. He proposed a network of schools. In 1885 he said that Ireland was entitled to Home Rule to the "utmost measure of local self-government consistent with the integrity of the United Kingdom." In 1886 he detailed his Home Rule bill for Ireland. How different the history of Britain and Ireland might have been had the bill been passed.[7]

As a young man Gladstone had been good looking with dark, piercing eyes. But in his last months he was stricken with cancer, and spent the winter of 1897–1898 at Cannes, on the French Riviera. He died in 1898 and lay in Westminster Hall on the 26 and 27 of May. He was buried in Westminster Abbey on May 28.[8] Roy Jenkins says that the "only comparable non-royal funerals" of the past 150 years were those of Wellington and Churchill. The pallbearers included the Prince of Wales, the Duke of York, (later King George V) and former Scottish Prime Ministers Balfour and Roseberry.[9] Lord Acton said, "in the three elements of greatness combined—the man, the power, and the result—character, genius, and success—none reached his level."[10]

James Bruce

(1811–1863)

JAMES BRUCE, THE eighth Earl of Elgin, was one of the two most prominent people in the history of Canada, the other being also a Scot, John A. Macdonald (see p. 360). Macdonald was Canada's Washington, the man who was the father of the present country. Lord Elgin who preceded him was Canada's Lincoln, the man who kept British North America together with strong commitments to civil rights and democracy. Lord Elgin, who served also in difficult assignments in Jamaica, China, India, and Japan, was one of the greatest colonial administrators of the British Empire.

James Bruce, who was to become the eighth Earl of Elgin and twelfth Earl of Kincardine, was born in London. His father the seventh Earl was Thomas Bruce, also a colonial administrator who became famous for his acquisition of the Greek statuary known as the Elgin Marbles. The controversy over taking the Marbles from Greece raged then and continues today. Bringing the Marbles to Britain did nothing but ill for the Elgins, since Parliament reimbursed the seventh Earl only a fraction of their cost. Today, they are thought of as the priceless jewels of the British Museum. The mother of James Bruce, the eighth Earl, was Elizabeth Oswald of Dunnikier, whose estate was near to Broomhall, the seat of the Elgins. Both estates are situated in Fifeshire.

James Bruce was educated at Eton and Christ Church, Oxford. There he would become close with fellow students William Ewart Gladstone, who was to become one of the greatest Prime Ministers (see p. 349), and James Andrew Broun Ramsay who was to become first Marquis of Dalhousie and the most influential governor of India (see p. 357). Bruce graduated in classics in 1841 and upon the death of his father returned to Broomhall as eighth Earl of Elgin. He found the estate to be heavily indebted. The principal activity at Broomhall, on the northern shore of the Firth of Forth, was the mining of some 60,000 tons of coal a year. Lime was produced and there was also a railway. Fifteen hundred people were dependent on the estate.[1]

In the same year of 1841, Elgin married Elizabeth Mary Cumming Bruce. It was the second auspicious marriage between noble Cummings and Bruces who had been rivals for the crown of Scotland half a millennium previously (see p. 211). Also in 1841, Elgin was elected to Parliament.[2] The next year he was appointed Governor of Jamaica and this would serve as a rough apprenticeship for his career as a colonial administrator. The Jamaican slaves had been freed for several years when Elgin arrived. The planters, having to pay more for labor than in neighboring Cuba and farming depleted soil, were in trouble. Elgin was only thirty-one years old and ruling over 377,500 people. To make matters harder for Elgin his wife died in 1843, at only twenty-two years old, leaving him with a daughter to raise. Elgin's rule in Jamaica was not a great triumph, but he did improve conditions both for the planters and the ordinary people.[3]

In 1846 Elgin married Mary Louisa Lambton, with whom he would have five children. In the same year he was appointed Governor General of Canada. He sailed from Liverpool, and on arriving at Halifax, it was found that it was too wintry to go directly to Montréal. Accordingly, the party proceeded to Boston where he was given a hearty welcome. From there he took a train partway and finished his journey riding in a sleigh in subzero weather. Lady Elgin joined him in May.[4]

Lord Elgin found Canada to be in a perilous position. There was great animosity between the British-Canadians, many of whom were Scots and the French-Canadians. The economy was poor and there were unfavorable relations with the United States. And even though Elgin was made a Knight of the Thistle, Scotland's highest honor, and danced Scottish reels with his wife, the British-Canadians were suspicious of this fluent French speaker. They were even more upset when he announced at the opening of Parliament that Westminster had put the French and English languages "on a parity" as the official languages of Canada. Elgin read this speech in both languages.[5]

The climax of Lord Elgin's career came in April of 1849. The country had been run by two mainly Scottish cliques—The Family Compact, in

Toronto and The Château Clique, in Montréal.[6] Before the arrival of Elgin they had had their way. But Elgin was steadily increasing democracy and most British-Canadians didn't like it. On April 25 they erupted. A mob pelted Elgin's coach with stones and rotten eggs. When he escaped, the crowd became uglier and destroyed the Parliament House and most of the country's records. On April 30, Lord Elgin ventured out of his home on what author Sydney Checkland calls "the only occasion on which the Sovereign's representative has ever been put in physical danger." This time it was paving stones which hit the carriage and Elgin was forced to retreat to his mansion. His opponents grew bolder. The St. Andrew's Society of Montréal struck his name from its roll of members. It complained "that the Earl of Elgin having so conducted himself as to insult and outrage the feelings of every British subject in Canada and to disgrace the Scottish name . . . should be expelled from membership . . ." The Thistle Curling Club followed suit. But all was not lost. The St. Andrew's Society of Toronto drank to his lordship's health.[7]

After five months in seclusion, Lord Elgin made a tour of Upper Canada (now Ontario) collecting 164,000 signatures in support of a democratic Canadian government. He regained his power and established a responsible government, saving Canada for the British Empire. For this he was made a baron in the British peerage. In the same year Mary Louisa had a son; Queen Victoria agreed to be his godmother and asked that he be given her names as Victor Alexander.[8] In 1854 Elgin traveled to Washington where he was well received. He was able to get a new treaty and improve Canada's relations with the United States. Later in the year, he went home.

In 1857, Lord Elgin, still struggling with the finances at Broomhall, was appointed as special envoy to China, as the Chinese were ignoring the 1842 Treaty of Nanking. By the time he got to Calcutta, he had heard of the Indian mutiny then underway and decided to leave most of his troops in India where he reasoned, they would be most needed. It turned out to be a very good decision as they were important at Lucknow and Kanpur.

Moving on to China, Elgin tried to reason with the Chinese, but they only stalled. With the French envoy, Baron Gros, he put together a strong force and bombarded Canton on December 28 1857. Then the united troops of France, Britain, Russia, and the United States moved to within fifty miles of Peking. Elgin went ashore carried in a sedan chair with 150 marines and the band of the HMS *Calcutta*. He got the Treaty of Tientsin in June of 1858 that opened more treaty ports and gave traders access to the Chinese interior.[9]

The very next month Lord Elgin journeyed to Edo (now Tokyo) with a small force, as a diplomat rather than the aggressor he had been in China. Two Americans of Scottish ancestry, Matthew Calbraith Perry and Franklin Buchanan had already secured a treaty with Japan several years previously. Commodore Perry—his fleet at anchor in a Japanese harbor in 1853—was told by isolationist Japan to leave. Instead Perry demanded "as a right . . . those acts of courtesy which are due from one civilized country to another." He had sent his documents ashore with Admiral Franklin Buchanan, who jumped into the surf ahead of his crew, becoming the first American to set foot on Japanese soil.[10]

In the wake of the American treaty, Lord Elgin sailed the *Furious* into Edo Bay, the first western ship to enter since the seventeenth century. He landed August 17, 1858, "resplendent in full dress and the ribbon and star of a Knight of the Thistle." Crowds of Japanese watched from the shore as "Rule Britannia" was played triumphantly by the ship's band. The Treaty of Edo took effect July 1, 1859, giving Britain five treaty ports, three naval bases, and the right of Britons to trade in Japan. The *Daily Telegraph* wrote: "The Earldom of Elgin is just now a new and mighty wonder to the Eastern world. It passes like the Comet over islands, continents, and seas and emperors and nations bow down . . . ." As ordinary British subjects saw it, Lord Elgin had saved India, and humbled China and Japan.[11]

In 1860, Lord Elgin, after a brief stint as postmaster general, had to return to China to enforce his treaty. In charge of forces led by the Scottish generals Hope Grant and Sir Robert Napier, the Summer Palace was sacked and torched after a diligent search for important records. The Chinese had to capitulate again.[12] Lord Elgin returned to Britain but in 1862 was appointed Viceroy and Governor General of India. He was the first governor of India to report directly to the crown, the East India Company having been deposed in 1858. This was a very difficult task and his health had become frail. But he was well on his way to establishing a new system when he died in Dharmsala, Punjab in 1863.

The *Encyclopaedia Britannica* calls the eighth Earl of Elgin "a classic example of the great British proconsuls of the nineteenth century," and describes him as "self-reliant and decisive, adaptable and indefatigable."[13]

His son, Victor Alexander Bruce, ninth Earl of Elgin, followed him as Viceroy of India and was made a Knight of the Garter. Today Andrew Bruce, the eleventh Earl of Elgin and fifteenth Earl of Kincardine, is Chief of the Name of Bruce, ruling still from Broomhall with his charming wife Victoria, Countess of Elgin. After performing many services for his country, the present Earl has been made a Knight of the Thistle, following his great-grandfather in Scotland's most-esteemed order.

Lord Elgin in Peking, 1860. THE ILLUSTRATED LONDON NEWS PICTURE LIBRARY.

James Andrew Broun Ramsay

(1812–1860)

J AMES ANDREW BROUN Ramsay, first Marquess and tenth Earl of Dalhousie, had more to do with the creation of modern India than any other single person. His military ventures resulted in huge additions of land and created a nation-state out of numerous principalities. His importation of Western technology to India revolutionized transport and communications there. Yet despite the brilliant results of his eight-year term as governor general, he is one of the most controversial figures in Indian history.

Lord Dalhousie was born at Dalhousie Castle, Midlothian, where his ancestors had lived for centuries.

James Andrew Broun Ramsay, 10th Earl and 1st Marquess of Dalhousie. By Sir John Watson Gordon. THE SCOTTISH NATIONAL PORTRAIT GALLERY.

His father George, the ninth Earl was a general in Wellington's army in the Peninsular War and became Governor General of Canada in 1819. The ninth Earl married Christina Broun of Coulston and the couple had three sons, two of whom died young leaving James as the only child. The family moved to Canada in 1816 but in 1825 young James was sent back to Britain to study at Harrow. In 1829 he went up to Christ Church, Oxford, where he met the future Prime Minister W. E. Gladstone and the future Lord Elgin. In 1836 he married a Scottish noblewoman, Lady

Susan Hay, eldest daughter of the Marquess of Tweeddale. The following year he was elected to Parliament. In 1838 his father died and he became the tenth Earl, taking his seat in the House of Lords. He was also a member of the General Assembly of the Church of Scotland, maintaining an active role. In 1845 he succeeded Gladstone as President of the Board of Trade, showing a strong interest in the burgeoning new railroad industry.[1]

In 1848, Dalhousie became at age thirty-five the youngest-ever Governor General of India. In his first year he put down a Sikh rebellion and annexed the Punjab. For this he was made a marquess. Before his term ended in 1856 he had added Oudh, part of Burma, and much of central India to British control. Effectively, Dalhousie drew the map of modern India. He also built the first few thousand miles of Indian railway, which has become the largest in the world, carrying 10 million passengers and close to a million tons of freight each day.[2] He reorganized the post office which when he arrived was so disorganized and overpriced, it was not generally used. He made postage cheap and the system flourished. He constructed 4,000 miles of telegraph. Dalhousie called the railway, the post office and the telegraph "the three great engines of social improvement."[3] He saw to the building of 2,000 miles of roads, constructed canals, and began irrigation systems and tea plantations. During his administration the civil service was opened to both Indians and Europeans. Exports and imports doubled. He stressed primary education and gave grants to high schools and colleges, and established engineering colleges. He ended female infanticide, and permitted the remarriage of Hindu widows.[4]

Even Dalhousie's enemies agree that the accomplishments of his regime were brilliant. But controversy surrounded him. Some people called him ruthless. The Queen, to whom he sent the Koh-i-noor diamond, elevated him to a Knighthood of the Thistle, Scotland's highest honor. The Collins Encyclopaedia of Scotland says that he "despised Indians." But Andrew Dewar Gibb recounts Dalhousie saying, "My lady. . . gave a ball . . . and to this I caused the native officers to be invited. Some of the old school and some of the young gentlemen did not like this I believe. I intend to make it the rule."[5]

The controversy became worse when Dalhousie, his health weakened, returned to Britain in 1856. The grateful East India Company voted him £5,000 a year. But then in 1857 came the Indian Mutiny and Dalhousie's reputation plummeted. There can be little doubt that his iron rule, which provoked traditional Indians, was a cause of this revolt. But it is obvious that the people who succeeded him should have thrown blame his way to save themselves. The newspapers had a fine time blasting him every day. Dalhousie refused to utter a word in his own defense. The *Dictionary of National Biography* says that the negatives heaped on him were "in no way shared by those acquainted with the actual facts."[6]

Dalhousie's wife had died at sea in 1853, leaving him with two daughters. He died alone in 1860 on the family estate in Scotland and without a son, the marquessate died with him.

John A. Macdonald

(1815–1891)

NEXT TO SCOTLAND itself, Canada is the most Scottish country. The French and the English of course were there ahead of the Scots, but after France ceded Quebec to Britain in 1763 a constant flow of immigrants from Scotland to what is now Canada began and continues still. Perhaps one in six Canadians claims ancestors from Scotland, but the influence of the Scots on the country is far greater than what would be expected of such a minority. The Scottish prominence in the fur trade, that in Canada's early days was the country's principal economic activity, is illustrative. The great fur-trading Hudson's Bay Company was founded in England, and as of the year 1700, there were no Scots in the company. But by 1800 four out of every five of the company's employees were Scots,[1] and by 1900, the principal shareholders were Scots as well. Also the chief rival of the Bay, the Northwest Company, was founded by a Scottish immigrant, Simon McTavish. At his death in 1804, forty of its forty-six partners were Scots.[2] In addition, five of Canada's first six colleges were founded by Scots;[3] and two political groups, the Family Compact in Upper Canada (now Ontario) and the Château Clique in Lower Canada (now Québec) were controlled by Scots and dominated the politics of the country. As the Canadian historian, Pierre Berton says: "The Irish outnumbered them, as did the English, but the Scots ran the country. Though they formed only one-fifteenth of the population, they controlled the fur trade, the great banking and financial houses, the major educational institutions and to a considerable degree, the government."[4]

Of the many boatloads of Scottish immigrants in 1820, one contained a five-year-old boy who was to become by far the most important politician in Canadian history. John Alexander Macdonald was born in 1815 in George Street, Glasgow. His father, Hugh Macdonald had come from the far north, Dornoch in Sutherlandshire, to seek his fortune in the industrial south. He had married Helen Shaw who was the granddaughter of John Grant, a nephew of the Laird of Rothiemurchas. This famous family has produced among others the actor Hugh Grant and the painter Duncan Grant. Hugh Macdonald did not prosper sufficiently in Glasgow and he and his family joined the great stream of Scottish immigrants to cross the Atlantic. The Macdonalds settled in Kingston, in what is now Ontario where Hugh Macdonald operated a mill. This business failed in 1836, at which time Hugh Macdonald admitted that he was not sufficiently motivated to own a business.[5]

Despite their poverty Hugh and Helen Macdonald found the means to educate their children. At age ten, young John A. Macdonald was sent to the Royal Grammar School in Kingston where he excelled in mathematics, but not in the classics. The young Macdonald was a voracious reader, and exhibited early an excellent speaking ability and a good memory for faces and names, all of which would serve him well in his political career. At age fifteen, he was apprenticed to a lawyer, George Mackenzie, an arrangement that lasted six years. He was admitted to the bar in 1836, only twenty-one years old.[6] Young John A. Macdonald had a flair for the law, that he demonstrated in 1837 while defending a rapist. Although the defendant was found guilty and was hanged, Macdonald's stylish defense gained him an excellent reputation and won him many clients. Macdonald hired two Scottish law students for the law office who would became prominent. Oliver Mowat became premier of Ontario, and Alexander Campbell became Lieutenant Governor of Ontario.[7]

In 1843 Macdonald married Isabella Clark. The couple had two sons, who died in infancy, and Isabella herself died at age forty-five. In 1844 Macdonald's career changed from the law to politics as he was elected at age twenty-nine as Conservative member for Kingston to the House of Assembly, the home-rule government of Upper and Lower Canada. In 1847 he joined the cabinet as receiver-general.[8] He was then only thirty-two years old. But his party lost in 1848, and Macdonald went into the opposition. For the next six years Allan Mac Nab was the titular head of the party, but Macdonald was the real power. These were difficult times, as some Tories were in favor of seceding from the British Empire. Opposed to this, Macdonald sought closer ties to Britain and advocated a confederation of the British lands in North America. His principal foe throughout his career was George Brown, who had come from Edinburgh and owned what became Canada's national newspaper, the Toronto *Globe*, also known as the Scotchman's Bible. Not only were Macdonald and Brown political opponents, they personally disliked each other. Macdonald's principal ally was Georges Étienne Cartier of Lower Canada.

In 1854 Macdonald formed a coalition of Conservatives and French-Canadians that became the Liberal-Conservative Party. From this point on, until his death almost four decades later, it was Macdonald's party and he was the most powerful man in Canada. In 1857 he became Premier of Upper Canada and Cartier became the leader in Lower Canada. In 1858 Cartier was premier and Macdonald, the real power behind the scenes, was Attorney-General. This government lasted until 1862 when another member of Scotland's largest clan, John Sandfield Macdonald, with the backing of George Brown, led the government.

By 1864 John A. Macdonald was back in power. In the United States the outcome of the Civil War seemed certain to result in a Union victory. There was a real threat that the Union Army with its momentum might invade Canada. Macdonald preached unity but instead there was division in the country. Macdonald and Cartier began to work with their enemy, George Brown, for confederation. Late in the year Nova Scotia, New Brunswick, and Prince Edward Island, called a conference at Charlottetown on Prince Edward Island to decide whether to have some sort of unified government for the Maritime Provinces. Macdonald seized the opportunity. Without any authority or invitations he, Cartier, and Brown went to the conference, taking a boat from Quebec City stocked with ample champagne. With the exception of a nasty row between Brown and Macdonald, that was patched up, the whole affair took on the aspects of a great traveling party. Macdonald, who had often been criticized for his heavy drinking, now found himself to be "the life of the party."[9]

When Macdonald, Cartier, and Brown arrived at the conference in Charlottetown as uninvited guests they were welcomed anyway and the party continued. Almost immediately Macdonald convinced the Maritime delegates that they should be discussing a union of all of the provinces, not just the Maritime Provinces in the east. There was virtually no opposition. The uninvited and unauthorized Macdonald's stature was so great that he became the de-facto head of the conference. He was in his best form, dancing with the ladies and drinking with the men.[10] At a dinner in Halifax he said, "For twenty long years, I have been dragging myself through the dreary waste of colonial politics. I thought there was no end, nothing worthy of ambition, but now I see something which is well worthy of my little country . . . a great British-American nation, under the government of her majesty . . . "[11]

In 1866 Macdonald went to London as the chairman of the conference to draft the British North America Act. In 1867 it was enacted into law and Ontario, Quebec, Nova Scotia, and New Brunswick became the Dominion of Canada. Tiny Prince Edward Island had in the end become concerned that it would be overwhelmed, and didn't join. Macdonald became the new country's first Prime Minister and was made a Knight Commander of the Order of the Bath. Oxford University awarded him the degree of D.C.L. His old ally Cartier was knighted also. Canadian school children learn of the ten principal "fathers of Confederation" of their country. Of the ten, D'Arcy McGee and Georges E. Cartier were, respectively of Irish and French heritage. The other eight, including Macdonald and George Brown, were Scots.[12] At the time, and still today, however, Macdonald is recognized as the principal "father."

Macdonald strove for unity in his first cabinet, that had five men from Ontario, four from Quebec, and two each from New Brunswick and Nova Scotia. The members included Presbyterians, Catholics, Anglicans, Methodists, French, English, Scots, and Irish.[13] Almost immediately Nova Scotia talked of leaving the confederation. Macdonald used all of his political skill and tact to keep the province in. By 1873 Rupert's Land, Manitoba, the Northwest Territories, British Columbia, and Prince Edward Island had joined the Dominion. Macdonald's domain then con-tained close to 4 million people spread out through approximately 4 mil-lion square miles. In 1873 his government created the Northwest Mounted Police. Colonel James F. Macleod was given three hundred men to patrol a territory as wide as Europe.[14]

Up until the Canadian confederation, relations between the United States and the British provinces had usually been hostile. In 1870 Macdonald went to Washington to try to change this. His personality and stature were so great that he was able to present a convincing case for bet-ter relations. Macdonald made the government of the United States realize that they had a new, united, powerful neighbor on their northern border, and were dealing directly with the world-class statesman who had been its principal creator. This expedition resulted in the Treaty of Washington of 1871, that amicably settled some old disputes, including duty-free shipping of goods destined for Canada from ports in the United States and vice versa. But the most important effect of the treaty was in ending the hostility between the two countries forever. Since that time, not a shot has been fired and relations between the two countries have been competitive but cordial.

One of Macdonald's most important achievements was his consistent promotion of the Canadian Pacific Railway. It was obvious to him that Canada, thinly populated and strung out over several thousand miles, could not exist as a nation without a railroad connecting Nova Scotia with British Columbia and all of the points in between. But a scandal broke out. Sir Hugh Allan had been awarded the contract to build the railway, but it was discovered that there had been substantial campaign contributions to Macdonald's party and there were rumors that American railway barons were part of the deal. Just then Cartier died. Macdonald had lost his most trusted ally with whom he had cooperated for so many years. He was left to face the criticism alone. Macdonald defended himself eloquently and he was found to be personally not guilty but he and his cabinet were forced to resign. He offered to quit as head of his party but this was rejected. Another Scot, Alexander Mackenzie, was now running Canada.[15]

For the next five years, 1873–1878, Macdonald headed the opposition to the Mackenzie government. Finally, a severe recession in the economy led the people of Canada to return "the old corruptionist," as his opponents called Macdonald, back to power. Immediately he raised tariffs, protecting Canadian industries such as steel and textiles. In 1880 Macdonald sponsored a new group to complete the postponed Canadian Pacific Railway. The principal partners in the end, were George Stephen, President of the Bank of Montreal and his cousin, Donald Alexander Smith. Others involved were Duncan MacIntyre, Robert B. Angus, and John Rose. All were Scots. Smith and Stephen sold personal assets and borrowed heavily as funds to complete the project ran short. At one low point, Stephen cabled Smith from London, "Stand Fast, Cragellachie!" remembering the inspiring slogan of Clan Grant from whose territory they had both come. At last on November 7, 1885, Smith was given the honor of driving the last spike of the Railway at Craigellachie, British Columbia. Stephen was made Baron Mount Stephen and Smith was made Baron Strathcona and Mount Royal. Smith was also the principal

Sir John A. Macdonald and Lady Macdonald aboard a CPR transcontinental train, July 1886. CANADIAN PACIFIC ARCHIVES, IMAGE NO. NS.10217

shareholder of the Hudson's Bay Company and was its governor until his death in 1914.[16]

So John A. Macdonald had seen the railway built, unifying the country he had done so much to create. In the summer of 1886 he and his beautiful second wife, Susan, with whom he had a daughter, went west for the first time in a private car. He was elected again as Prime Minister in 1891 and died in office, at age seventy-six, of a stroke. He had been in public office almost half a century. He had brought the British and French Canadians together. He had improved relations with the United States from hostility to a cordiality, which continues to this day. He had been the architect of Canadian unity, the delegate who dominated the conferences, which created the confederation. As the *Dictionary of National Biography* puts it, Macdonald was "the organizer of the Dominion of Canada." He had appointed cabinets, which were religiously and ethnically inclusive. He had been the principal proponent of the Canadian Pacific Railway that unified the country and made it a reality. He had created the legendary Mounties to patrol the vast domain. He had been Prime Minister for more than twenty of the Dominion's first twenty-five years. At his death he was the foremost statesman in North America. Thousands of Canadians attended his wake in the Parliament building, and thousands more lined the tracks as his body was returned to Kingston for burial.

Allan Octavian hume

(1829–1912)

POPULATION PROJECTIONS SHOW that India will soon become the largest nation in the world. It is already the world's largest democracy. And the man who is called the "father" of that democracy was an unassuming Scot.

Allan Octavian Hume was born in London, the son of Joseph Hume, a radical member of Parliament who was a native of Montrose, Scotland. Allan Hume was educated at Haileybury College and London University. At age twenty he joined the Bengal Civil Service, and was posted to the district of Etawah. There he founded 181 free schools for Indians in his district and offered scholarships for higher studies.[1] During the Indian Mutiny (1857–1858) Hume displayed great courage and fought in the field with distinction. He was decorated in 1860.[2]

Hume was promoted to the central government of India in 1870 as secretary in the revenue and agriculture department. But his too liberal political views got him banished back to the provinces in 1879. He retired from the service in 1882. He became convinced that India needed a Parliament that he believed would help the masses and quell the discontent of the educated people of the country. On March 1, 1883 Hume addressed a circular letter to the graduates of Calcutta University. He asked them "to scorn personal ease and make a resolute struggle to secure greater freedom for themselves and their country."[3]

With Hume's guidance, important Hindus convened the first Indian National Congress in Bombay in December, 1885. The government adopted a stance of "passive goodwill," but the viceroy, the Earl of Dufferin, who approved the plans never had any thought that anything would actually change. Hume was able to get his Congress important British supporters but of course there were significant difficulties. Perhaps the main one was the Hindu-Moslem split, and the fact that some educated Hindus often thought all Moslems to be beneath them. Hume cried out, "The wretched plea about the Mahomedans so inferior to Hindus . . . is monstrous!"[4] Gradually the congress contained more radical elements and by the time Hume left the country in 1894 he had lost control of the movement.

Hume returned to Britain to live in Upper Norwood in England. There he continued to push his agenda, publishing Indian news in major British journals and forming a Congress organization in Britain.[5] He lived to see the Minto-Morely reforms which were passed in the early twentieth century during the regime of the Scottish viceroy, the Earl of Minto. At last the government had taken responsible steps towards Indian democracy.

Hume married Anne Grindall in 1853. She died in 1890. He was an ornithologist and the author of *The Game Birds of India, Burmah and Ceylon*, which was published in 1879. He formed and endowed the South London Botanical Institute.[6] But the main result of Allan Hume's toil is Indian democracy. The Congress Party, a direct consequence of his work brought the country to independence after World War II and has ruled the country for most of the time since. When Hume died in 1912, the Bankipore Session of the Congress unanimously passed a resolution recognizing Allan Octavian Hume as the father and founder of the Indian National Congress.[7]

India, about 1881.
MAP DIVISION,
THE NEW YORK PUBLIC LIBRARY,
ASTOR, LENOX AND TILDEN
FOUNDATIONS.

Arthur James Balfour

(1848–1930)

L ORD BALFOUR WAS a brilliant politician who served Great Britain for half a century in various positions, including Prime Minister. His record was distinguished, his contributions were many, and he was given a title, first Earl of Balfour, in recognition of all of his accomplishments. But it is unlikely that we would remember him now had it not been for something he did in the twilight of his career. Holding the office of foreign secretary Balfour decided in 1917 to sanction a homeland for the Jewish people in Palestine enabling the creation of Israel. Abba Eban the great Jewish intellectual calls the Balfour Declaration "the authentic turning-point in Jewish political history."[1] This is a very significant statement from a man who well knew the unparalleled record of the Jews over several millennia.

Arthur James Balfour was born an aristocrat in Whittingehame, East Lothian. His father was James Maitland Balfour, the son of James Balfour who had made a fortune in India as a contractor. The mother of Arthur James Balfour was Lady Blanche, daughter of the second Marquess of Salisbury. Young Arthur James Balfour was near-sighted and not at all robust. He was educated at Eton and Trinity College, Cambridge. He was not a great scholar but developed a love of literature. In addition he became a philosopher. In 1879 he published *Defence of Philosophic Doubt* which argued that science depends on an act of faith as does religion and for this reason it is rational to believe in religion.[2]

Balfour began his career by being elected to Parliament in 1874. His progress at first was very slow. In 1875 he became virtually engaged to May Lyttleton, the sister of a close friend. But she died soon after and the shock prevented him from ever considering marriage again. In 1886 Balfour was secretary for Scotland and in 1887 was given the Irish chief-secretaryship. In Ireland, Balfour managed to rule firmly but bring improved conditions for the Irish people. He became Prime Minister in 1902, a position he held until 1905, without any great distinction. By 1911, it seemed as if his political career was over. But World War I intervened. Balfour was appointed to succeed Winston Churchill as First Lord of the Admiralty. Gradually he moved toward the position of Foreign Secretary. In 1917, at the age of sixty-nine, he made a trip to the United States to see President Wilson, a Scottish-American, to promote the English-speaking alliance. By all accounts, Balfour charmed the Americans and helped increase America's participation in the war, that virtually guaranteed a British victory.

Balfour had expressed an early interest in Zionism. A feeling of brotherhood with the Jews was a common idea among Scots and Presbyterians throughout the English-speaking world. Balfour had met Chaim Weizmann, the Zionist leader in 1906. In a conference that was supposed to last only fifteen minutes, the two men had talked for more than an hour. They met again in 1914, and Weizmann was astonished to find that Balfour remembered everything said in their previous encounter. In this second meeting, Weizmann described the pogroms and expulsions of the Jews by the Russian armies, and later said of Balfour, "He listened for a long time and was, I assure you, most deeply moved—to the point of tears." Balfour called the Jews, "a great and suffering nation." He also said, "The Jews are the most gifted race that mankind has seen since the Greeks of the fifth century . . . " " They have been exiled, scattered and oppressed . . . " He added that civilization should "find them an asylum, a safe home, in their native land . . . "[3] In addition Balfour had met with Mr. Justice Louis Brandeis while in America that same year. Brandeis was shocked at Balfour's grasp of the Jewish situation and stunned when the Scot told him, "I am a Zionist."[4]

Balfour had a great deal of trouble in getting support for the Jewish national home in the cabinet. Some of the most heated opposition was from British Jews such as Edwin Montagu, who thought that such a place would encourage countries to exile Jews to the new state. But eventually Balfour won out and on November 2, 1917, wrote and signed his momentous letter to a Zionist leader:

Foreign Office,
November 2nd, 1917.

Dear Lord Rothschild,

I have much pleasure in conveying to you, on behalf of His Majesty's Government, the following declaration of sympathy with Jewish Zionist aspirations which has been submitted to, and approved by, the Cabinet

"His Majesty's Government view with favour the establishment in Palestine of a national home for the Jewish people, and will use their best endeavours to facilitate the achievement of this object, it being clearly understood that nothing shall be done which may prejudice the civil and religious rights of existing non-Jewish communities in Palestine, or the rights and political status enjoyed by Jews in any other country".

I should be grateful if you would bring this declaration to the knowledge of the Zionist Federation.

The Balfour Declaration, 1917.
BY PERMISSION OF THE BRITISH LIBRARY.

The Balfour Declaration was approved by the Paris Peace Conference of the League of Nations in 1922. Balfour received an earldom. When Hebrew University opened in Jerusalem in 1925, Lord Balfour was an honored guest. At his death "Jewry mourned him with honours perhaps never before accorded" to a non-Jew. Arthur James Balfour was buried at the Church of Scotland Cemetery in Whittingehame, Scotland.[5]

John Napier

(1550–1617)

J OHN NAPIER, EIGHTH Laird of
Merchiston, was born at
Merchiston Castle, the son of
Archibald Napier and Janet
Bothwell. He was one of the world's
greatest scientists, as well as one of
the earliest. Napier invented logarithms and decimal fractions, the
mathematical tools which were the
foundation of all scientific calculation and progress for the next 350
years, and beyond. He lived in the
same two centuries as the great
Italian, Galileo, who is considered
by many to be the father of modern
science. It would be fair to consider
Galileo and Napier as the co-
founders of modern science.

John Napier of Merchiston.
ARTIST UNKNOWN.
THE SCOTTISH NATIONAL PORTRAIT GALLERY.

John Napier entered the university of St. Andrews at the age of thirteen. Records show that he did not stay long enough to get a degree. It is
believed that he went to the Continent for further studies, but his where-
abouts in this period are hazy. At any rate he was back in Scotland in
1571 and married Elizabeth Stirling with whom he had two children. She
died in 1579, and his second wife, Agnes Chisholm, bore him five sons
and five daughters. Napier's father died in 1608 and he removed to

Merchiston Castle. There he led a contentious life as property holder, appearing in court often to settle disputes. Despite this he was considered to be fair in his dealings.[1]

Napier invented a machine, a hydraulic screw with a revolving axle that drained water from coal mines. It proved to be a great advantage for Scottish mines and the king gave him a monopoly. In 1594 Napier, a devout Protestant, wrote *A Plaine Discovery of the Whole Revelation of Saint John*, which was the first Scottish work on interpreting the scriptures. In 1596 his *Secret Inventions* were plans for military defense which included two varieties of burning mirrors, a piece of artillery, and a sort of primitive tank in the form of a metal chariot which could withstand musket shot. This vehicle was controlled from the inside and had holes in the sides for people to shoot out of. He was sometimes suspected of black magic.[2]

In 1594 Napier conceived the principles of logarithms and spent the next two decades perfecting their method of construction and writing the tables. At last in 1614 he published *Mirifici Logarithmorum Canonis Descriptio*, presenting the world with a tool that greatly aided the explosive growth of science for the next three and a half centuries. By the use of logarithmic tables, it became possible to multiply and divide complex numbers by simple addition and subtraction. It also made it possible to obtain roots of numbers by division and the raising of roots to any power by multiplication. Thus the most complicated problems in science, even in such as astronomy, could be solved with relative ease. Logarithms "came on the world as a bolt from the blue. No previous work had led up to it, nothing had foreshadowed it or heralded its arrival."[3]

Napier's work began a new era in science. An Englishman, Henry Briggs, visited Napier in Scotland twice and the two men worked out common logarithms, an improvement over the original version. Briggs published tables in 1617.[4] By 1632 William Oughtred of England was able to produce the first slide rule using logarithms. These systems were the basis for all scientific calculation and engineering right up to the computer age.[5]

Napier also made calculations using logarithms and a series of rods made of bone or ivory. These are familiarly referred to as "Napier's bones" and were a basis for the slide rule. He also made a calculating device "the most expeditious of all" by means of metal plates arranged in a box. This is usually thought to have been the world's first attempt to create a calculating machine.[6]

Although clumsy use of decimal fractions had been made before him, Napier, through his development of logarithms, was the real inventor of modern decimals. Early in this century, celebrating the tercentenary of logarithms, it was said that "In the works of John Napier we find the theory and practice of decimal fractions as firmly established and as well understood as they are at the present day, throughout the whole civilised world." Napier was the first to explain and use decimals in ordinary calculation. In an appendix to his *Constructio* he says: "In numbers distinguished thus by a period in their midst, whatever is written after the period is a fraction, the denominator of which is unity with as many ciphers after it as there are figures after the period. Thus:[7]

10000000.04 is the same as 10000000 4/100; also 25.803 is the same as 25 803/1000; also 9999998.0005021 is the same as 9999998 5021/10000000."

It is estimated that John Napier, who said he should have had dozens of research assistants, but had in fact none, had to make something like seven million calculations to produce his tables of logarithms. He died, at his own admission, of overwork at the age of sixty-seven.[8]

Another Scottish genius, David Hume, proclaimed John Napier of Merchiston as "the person to whom the title of *great man* is more justly due than to any other whom his country ever produced."[9]

James Hutton

(1726–1797)

J AMES HUTTON WAS the founder of modern geology. Although others had made observations before him, it was Hutton who came up with a comprehensive theory of the earth that has proved to be essentially correct. His idea was "that geologic phenomena can be explained in terms of observable geologic processes."[1] In 1785 he presented his *Theory of the Earth, or an Investigation of the Laws Observable in the Composition, Dissolution, and Restoration of Land Upon the Globe* to the Royal Society of Edinburgh. At a time when most people thought that the world was a few thousand years old, Hutton, reasoning from a great

James Hutton,
PICTURE COLLECTION, THE BRANCH LIBRARIES, THE NEW YORK PUBLIC LIBRARY.

deal of evidence, concluded that the earth had existed from a remote past. He could see "no vestige of a beginning—no prospect of an end."[2] The Huttonian theory is that "natural agents now at work on and within the earth have operated with general uniformity through immensely long periods of time."[3] In other words, the processes that created the earth are the same as those now operating. These ideas, now universally accepted, were first put forward by Hutton and demolished several other theories then current. He thought of the earth as a great heat producer, with volcanoes as the safety valves. He discovered the igneous nature of granite.[4]

James Hutton was born in Edinburgh, his father a successful merchant and sometime City Treasurer. Unfortunately, he died very young, and James was brought up entirely by his mother, who sent him to Edinburgh High School. At seventeen, he was apprenticed to a lawyer, but was let go for using the office as a chemistry laboratory.[5] He attended Edinburgh University and studied as well at Paris and Leyden, qualifying as a physician, but he never practiced medicine. He went instead to Norfolk where he became involved in agriculture. He returned to Scotland in 1754 to farm in Berwickshire. Then it was on to Edinburgh, where he became a partner in a venture which used soot to produce sal ammoniac, also called ammonium chloride, a substance used in metallurgy and in dying. The profits from this venture made him independent and he retired in 1768. From then on he devoted himself to geology.

Hutton was slender and had "penetrating eyes." He never married and lived with his three sisters. His dress was very plain. So plain that Robert Louis Stevenson called his clothes "quakerish," and noted that Hutton "cared more about fossils than young ladies . . . " Hutton rose late and worked until dinner. He drank no wine and walked often. He was usually in the company of intellectuals. He was an original member of the Oyster Club in Edinburgh, which included Joseph Black, Adam Smith, Adam Ferguson, and Dugald Stewart.[6] But he spent most of his life in the field, studying rocks. James Hutton is buried in Greyfriars Kirkyard where the National Covenant was signed in 1638. He is there in the company of many famous Scots.

But Hutton was not a very good writer. His prose is difficult to read and the immediate effect of his work was not well known when he died. It was a noted mathematician and fellow member of the Oyster Club, John Playfair (1748–1819), who made Hutton universally known in his 1802 work, *Illustrations of the Huttonian Theory of the Earth*.

Geology has been called The Scottish Science with good reason. There was soon a flood of talent following the lead of Hutton and Playfair. Sir James Hall (1761–1832) born near Dunbar, is considered the founder of experimental geology. Sir Roderick Murchison (1792–1871) born in Ross-shire, identified the Silurian, Devonian, and Permian systems and made a geological survey of Russia (1840–1845) at the request of the tsar.[7] In 1838 Thomas Dick, a native of Angus, wrote *Celestial Scenery* that for the first time described the movements of the earth's surface that we now call continental drift and plate tectonics. Dick suggested that such things as that the bulge of Brazil had once fit into the west coast of Africa and proposed the revolutionary idea that the continents had once been joined.[8] Sir Archibald Geikie (1835–1924), born in Edinburgh, was known as The Prince of Geologists. He was director general of the Geological Survey of the U.K. and president of the Geological Society. Geikie was decorated by France, Italy, and the United States, and was elected president of the Royal Society in 1908.[9] William Maclure (1763–1840), born in Ayr, was the father of American Geology and completed the first American geological survey, perhaps the first in the world, in 1809.[10] Hugh Miller (1802–1856), a stone mason born in Cromarty, wrote extensively on geology and did more to popularize its study than anyone else. According to Forbes Macgregor, "practically the entire population of Edinburgh, besides many famous scholars," attended his funeral.[11] Sir Charles Lyell (1797–1875), born in Angus, wrote works on geology, generally supporting Hutton, which became standard textbooks on the subject. All of these great geologists were born in Scotland.

James Hutton conceived the theory that founded modern geology. Research in this century shows that he can be credited with, or at least given partial credit for, what is an even greater theory in science—natural selection. About a half century ago E.B. Bailey discovered an unpublished manuscript which Hutton had written, *The Elements of Agriculture*. Of course Hutton has been mentioned as an influence on Darwin and his ideas of natural selection since his geological theories maintain that very slow changes have happened over a very long time. But in *The Elements* Hutton goes much farther. He actually describes natural selection without using the term. He says that in an environment where dogs must hunt by being fleet of foot and sharp of sight, then those who adapt best will prosper while those "that are less adapted to this manner of chase will be the first to perish . . . " Further, he says, that in a situation where a keen sense of smell is more valuable than fleet feet or sharp eyes, a race of animal will develop appropriately, with a keen sense of smell. This of course is the theory of natural selection, written by a man who died a dozen years before Darwin was born.[12]

There is no doubt that Darwin was influenced by the work of James Hutton. Sir Charles Lyell, while a member of the Royal Society, promoted Hutton's ideas to Darwin and encouraged him in his work.[13] In addition, the grandfather of Charles Darwin, Erasmus Darwin, became a friend of Hutton's while studying medicine at Edinburgh.[14]

Joseph Black

(1728–1799)

I T IS DOUBTFUL if any doctoral thesis ever written by any student anywhere in the world had an impact even close to that made by the thesis which Joseph Black presented to the medical faculty at Edinburgh University in 1754. Young Black called his work, *De humore acido à cibis orto et Magnesia alba* (on acid humors arising from food and magnesia alba). In the paper he describes an experiment he had made that demonstrated that chalk (calcium carbonate) could be created by the absorption of carbon dioxide by quicklime (calcium oxide); and that the process could be reversed when the chalk was heat-

Joseph Black,

ed.[1] He showed that by heating magnesium carbonate, carbon dioxide was distinct from air, and that it could be produced by fermentation, respiration, and by burning charcoal. These revolutionary experiments in effect provided the first chemical formula in history for making and taking apart a substance; proved that a gas could be present in a solid, and that air was made up of more than one gas. These proven facts, unknown before Black, completely overthrew all of the existing useless theories then current and in effect began modern chemistry. Scientists throughout Europe enthusiastically followed up Black's work. Within twenty years Joseph Priestly of England had discovered oxygen and Antoine Lavoisier in France had begun his experiments which established the science of chemistry.

Joseph Black was born in Bordeaux, the son of a wine dealer from Belfast. His father, John Black, was of Scottish ancestry and moved up high enough in France to become a friend of Montesquieu. Joseph Black's mother was also Scottish, being the daughter of another wine merchant, Robert Gordon of the Gordons of Hillhead in Aberdeenshire. In addition to Joseph Black, the couple had seven sons and five daughters.[2] At age twelve, Joseph Black was sent to a grammar school in Belfast and in 1746 to Glasgow University. There he studied under the revered William Cullen, author of the *Edinburgh Pharmacopaeia*. From 1751 to 1756 Black was at Edinburgh where he submitted his momentous thesis.

In 1756 Black returned to Glasgow where he succeeded Cullen as professor of chemistry. There he began investigations that led to his discoveries of latent and specific heat. Having founded modern chemistry, Black now advanced physics. He noticed that when melting ice takes up heat, the temperature of the ice remains the same. Thus the heat must have combined with the ice and become latent in it. Also he noted that the same amount of different substances needed different amounts of heat to raise them to the same temperature. This he called specific heat. Thus the specific heat of a substance was the ratio of the heat needed to raise it one degree versus the amount of heat needed to raise water one degree.

Most importantly Black discovered that the latent heat of steam was several times that of water. It is obvious that this must have affected James Watt, who arrived at Glasgow University one year later than had Black. Watt and Black became friends at Glasgow, and although Watt took no classes of Black's, the two men often worked together. Black even loaned the then great sum of £1,000 to Watt to help him get through his work.[3] Thus Black's efforts in physics produced not only the beginnings of modern thermal science, but also merit an assist in the practical steam engine, the key invention of the Industrial Revolution.

Black, a man distrustful of fame, never published his work on latent and specific heat, but the world knows that he did it. He lectured on the subject as soon as he made his discoveries and for many years thereafter. In 1766 he returned to Edinburgh where he succeeded Cullen again as professor of medicine and chemistry. From there on his life was spent as a teacher and occasional physician. He did no more research, probably because he had a delicate constitution, and the profession of teaching took all of his strength. He was an excellent teacher, so good that even the poorer students understood him. He popularized chemistry, and non-students attended his lectures in increasing numbers throughout his thirty-odd years as a professor. He was tall and good-looking, and had a good voice capable of excellent articulation. He never married, but had many friends, including David Hume, James Hutton, Dugald Stewart, John Robison, and Adam Smith.

Joseph Black was honored by gaining membership in the Royal Society of Edinburgh, the Royal College of Physicians, the Paris Academy of Science, and the St. Petersburg Academy of Science. He was First Physician to His Majesty in Scotland. Perhaps the best compliment paid to him was from Lavoisier who acknowledged himself to be Black's "disciple."[4]

Joseph henry

(1797–1878)

O N JUNE 16, 1776, a shipload
of immigrants from Britain
arrived in New York Harbor. The
newcomers could not have guessed
what an auspicious date it was, nor
that they would not always be
British subjects. They had landed
on the day before the Battle of
Bunker Hill, the first full combat of
the American Revolution. The
Americans would fight well against
Gen. Howe's troops the very next
day, and inspire the colonists, who
would declare their independence
only two weeks hence. The passengers must have felt an uneasiness as
the situation developed. Not only
had they left their friends, families
and familiar surroundings; they
might have left their king as well.

There were two families of
Scottish Presbyterians aboard the
ship as it sailed through The
Narrows. The Hendries were an
Argyllshire clan of farmers distantly

Statue of Joseph Henry outside the
Smithsonian Museum, Washington, D.C.
COLLECTION OF THE AUTHOR.

related to the Earl of Stirling. Hugh Alexander was a miller. The two families made their way up the magnificent Hudson River to Albany and there separated. But they would meet again. William Hendrie took his family to a farm in Delaware County and prospered there. He was well read in Presbyterian theology and Scottish history. He was also loyal to the deposed Stuart dynasty, and always told the story of how he had seen Bonnie Prince Charlie in Edinburgh in 1745. Hugh Alexander had built a mill, but fortune had not been kind to him. First he and his family had been driven off their land by Indians. Later their mill was destroyed in the Revolution. Hugh Alexander became a salt manufacturer.[1]

The two immigrant families were reunited after the Revolution for a wedding. Their children, William Henry (the name had been Americanized) and Ann Alexander, had fallen in love on their voyage to New York and were married. The new couple resided on South Pearl Street in Albany, the capital city of New York. Their son, Joseph Henry was baptized, according to the register, at the First Presbyterian Church in Albany December 9, 1797, although a cousin claimed years later that it was really in 1799.[2]

As a boy, Joseph Henry showed very little interest in school and received almost no formal education. The family was poor and by the age of ten he was working. Things got worse when his father, William Henry died when Joseph was merely thirteen. Joseph had entertained ideas of being an actor but was apprenticed to a watchmaker and silversmith, and failed in these trades. One day the young Henry discovered a hole in the floor underneath the church library and entered surreptitiously. There he was entranced reading George Gregory's *Popular Lectures on Experimental Philosophy, Astronomy, and Chemistry*. Many years later, when Joseph Henry gave a copy of this work to his only son, he wrote on the flyleaf that the book had " . . . opened to me a new world of thought and enjoyment; fixed my attention upon the study of nature, and caused me to resolve at the time of reading it that I would immediately devote myself to the acquisition of knowledge."[3]

There were many more excursions through the hole in the library floor after that as Henry began to read extensively. At the age of twenty-two, finally ready for school, and much older than his classmates, he entered Albany Academy where he studied chemistry, anatomy, and physiology to prepare as a physician. But a post to survey a road for the State of New York changed his studies in the direction of engineering. He supported himself mainly as a tutor, his most distinguished pupil being the elder Henry James, father of the psychologist William James and the author Henry James.[4]

In 1826 he became professor of mathematics and natural philosophy (as physics was called then) at Albany. Here Henry began his outstanding career in science. He was the first to insulate wire for magnetic coils, and devised the spool winding.[5] His magnets were more powerful than any that had been made before, and the scientific community began to notice Joseph Henry. He found the laws governing electromagnetic force and coil resistance. His short coil magnet invented in 1829 is basically the same as that used in present day electric motors and generators. In the same year he made what was essentially the world's first electric motor. The *Encyclopaedia Britannica* says, "The principles of efficient long distance transmission of current with his long-coil intensity magnet serve as the basis of every electromagnetic telegraph since invented."[6] Henry built a working telegraph before anyone else. But the inventor of the electric motor and the telegraph did not patent his inventions, leaving the field open to others. Joseph Henry said, "The only reward I ever expected was the consciousness of advancing science, the pleasure of discovering new truths, and the scientific reputation to which these labors would entitle me."[7]

In 1830 Henry discovered electromagnetic induction, the generation of an electric current by magnetism, beating the Englishman Faraday—who made the same discovery independently—by a year. Faraday published first, but in 1893 The International Congress of Electricians recognized Henry's priority of this discovery by giving his name to the standard unit of inductive resistance, the Henry. In the same period he first used the earth as a return conductor.[8] Also in 1830, he married his cousin, Harriet Alexander, with whom he had four children.

In 1832, despite the fact that he had no college degree of any kind, Joseph Henry became Professor of Natural History at the College of New Jersey, which was to become Princeton University. He taught an astonishing number of subjects, including chemistry, physics, mathematics, mineralogy, geology, astronomy, and architecture.[9] He was very popular with the students who were in awe of his knowledge. While at Princeton, he improved his relays and invented the transformer, discovering that a low current could become stronger by an arrangement of coils. He then wrote the laws by which transformers could be built. Henry was the first to record the action of radio waves when he magnetized a needle from a lightning flash some miles away. This proved that currents could be induced at great distances. He discovered the oscillatory nature of the discharge of a capacitor.[10] He did work on auroras and ultra-violet light, and also proved that sunspots radiate less heat than the surface of the sun in general.

Henry supported the efforts of a young American of Scottish descent, Samuel Finley Breese Morse, to build a practical telegraph system. Morse was one of the country's most popular artists in his time. His pictures occasionally trade today for millions of dollars. One day Morse visited the great Joseph Henry at Princeton. It is said that Henry telegraphed lunch orders to his wife to be delivered later to show his students how his invention worked.[11] Morse may have seen this, but Henry discovered in conversation that his visitor was not a scientist and knew nothing about physics. Still, he tried to encourage Morse. But Morse was to become a problem.

In 1844 Morse constructed the world's first practical telegraph line between Washington and Baltimore, sending the first message, "What hath God wrought!" Immediately he became enmeshed in lawsuits over his patent. He called Joseph Henry as a witness and Henry proceeded to tell the truth—that he himself had invented the telegraph and that when he first met Morse he knew nothing of physics. This enraged Morse who feared that this testimony might hurt his case. Morse then attacked Henry, practically calling him a liar. Henry, in turn, sought not money but rather vindication of his reputation. He called a witness, Professor James Hall, who testified that he had seen and heard Henry's telegraph ring a bell in 1832. A specially appointed tribunal completely vindicated Henry saying, "Mr. Morse's charges not only remain unproved but they are positively disproved."[12] Morse won his patent suits and is recognized as the inventor of the practical telegraph. His reputation however suffered for his attack on Henry.

In 1846 Joseph Henry was named as the first secretary (chief operating officer) of the newly formed Smithsonian Institution in Washington. The Board of Regents also chose a Scottish-American architect, James Renwick Jr., better known for his St. Patrick's Cathedral in New York, to design its buildings. Henry was responsible for the excellence of the Smithsonian in its early years. He got rid of the library and gave the books to the Library of Congress. He got government support for the Institution as a museum and a research organization in anthropology, archaeology, botany, zoology, meteorology, geophysics, and astronomy. At one point he had five hundred volunteer observers of meteorology reporting from around the country.[13] This department became the National Weather Service. Henry stayed at his post at the Smithsonian until his death.

From 1868 to 1878 he was President of the fragile National Academy of Sciences, keeping it alive. In 1849–1850 he was President of the American Association for the Advancement of Science. He was a life-long Presbyterian, although he formally became a member of the church only in 1844. He had no problem finding harmony between religion and science. He tried to reconcile the Bible with geology and publicly supported Darwin. He ridiculed Evangelicals as suffering from hysteria, but was sympathetic towards Catholics. He took up the cause of J. J. Sylvester, a British scientist who wasn't hired at Columbia University because he was Jewish.[14]

The influence of Joseph Henry on science, and particularly on American science, continues to this day. Yet the man who did the pioneering work on the electric motor, electromagnetic induction, the telegraph, and the transformer and so many other things is not nearly as well known as Faraday and Morse. They filed patents. Henry didn't.

But in the main reading room of the Library of Congress he is one of the sixteen immortals depicted. He is there, along with Newton, Herodotus, Michaelangelo, Shakespeare, Plato, and the others.[15]

William Thomson

(1824–1907)

ORD KELVIN WAS one of the most important scientists of the nineteenth century. His work on the first successful transatlantic cable, which reduced the time of communications between Europe and America from days or weeks to seconds, would be enough to prove this. But his influence on the development of physics during his century may have had a greater impact over the long term.

William Thomson, who was to become better known as Lord Kelvin, was born in Belfast of what appears to be entirely Scottish ancestry. We can call him Scotch-Irish. His great-grandfather, John Thomson, left Scotland for County Down in 1641 during the Plantation of Ulster. His grandfather James Thomson married a woman with the Scottish name of Agnes Nesbitt. Lord Kelvin's father, also named James Thomson, was a Presbyterian born at

Lord Kelvin with his compass. PICTURE COLLECTION, THE BRANCH LIBRARIES, THE NEW YORK PUBLIC LIBRARY.

Annaghmore in 1786 who married Margaret Gardner, the daughter of a Glaswegian merchant.[1] William Thomson was the second son and fourth child of this marriage. His father was a professor of mathematics at the Royal Academical Institution of Belfast, and moved the family to Glasgow in 1832. There he became professor of mathematics at Glasgow University.[2]

Young William Thomson never attended primary school, being entirely educated by his father until 1834 when at age ten, he entered Glasgow University. Until very recently, when someone pulled a stunt at a diploma factory, *The Guinness Book of World Records* called him the youngest undergraduate in the entire history of education.[3] In 1841, Thomson left Glasgow for Cambridge. He was then seventeen years old and produced his mathematical analogy between heat and electricity. He rowed for Cambridge in 1844, winning the Colquhoun silver sculls, and was a founder of the Cambridge University Musical Society. Then it was on to Paris for more study. By age twenty-one he had studied at three universities in three countries. In 1846, at age twenty-two, he became professor of natural philosophy at Glasgow, a position he held for more than half a century. By age twenty-six he had published more than fifty scientific papers, some of them in French. In 1848 Thomson put forth his absolute scale of temperature. The world now honors him by calling it the Kelvin scale. In 1852 he married his second cousin, Margaret Crum, whose father Walter Crum was a fellow of the Royal Society.[4]

In the same year his paper, "On the Dynamical Theory of Heat," that stated what is now called the Second Law of Thermodynamics, was published. This paper resolved the work of several physicists and is basic to the design of all engines using heat and for all cooling and refrigeration appliances. This work led to air conditioning and the subsequent population boom in warm climates. Simply stated the law says, "It is impossible, by means of inanimate material agency, to derive mechanical effect from any portion of matter by cooling it below the temperature of the coldest of the surrounding objects."[5]

Thomson also worked on magnetism and electricity, influencing his fellow Scot James Clerk Maxwell, whose discoveries became the most important in physics in the nineteenth century (see p. 388). Thomson introduced the term "kinetic energy" to the world. But it is as a practical scientist or inventor that he became famous. He overcame the problems of long-distance telegraphy, that led to the first successful trans-atlantic cable in 1866. As a director of the Atlantic Telegraph Company, he invented the electric apparatus for the cable, supervised its construction, and sent the first signals between the continents. He was knighted for this work. In 1874 he was elected President of the Society of Telegraph Engineers. Thomson also invented and patented the mirror galvanometer, a tide gauge and a tide-predicting machine, and a sounding apparatus, that worked in shallow or deep water. He redesigned and improved the mariner's compass so completely that his version became virtually universal. Thomson became a partner in James White & Co., the firm that produced his inventions, and became prosperous enough to build a mansion on the water at Largs where he kept boats for his pleasure.[6] His first wife died in 1870. In 1874 he married Frances Blandy of Madeira.

Thomson was liberal in politics, except that he was an Ulster unionist. A sometime Episcopalian, he attended Presbyterian services at Largs. He was three times offered the professorship at the Cavendish Laboratory at Cambridge and declined each time. He was elected a Fellow of the Royal Society in 1851 and was President from 1890 to1904. In 1883 he was awarded the Copley Medal. He was made Lord Kelvin in 1892, the name being derived from the River Kelvin which runs through Glasgow University. He resigned his professorship there in 1899. In semi-retirement, Lord Kelvin lectured often, traveling as far away as Baltimore. In 1904 he was named Chancellor of Glasgow University and founded the Glasgow University Music Society. He won the Legion of Honor and many honorary degrees, and was nominated for a Nobel Prize after his death. It was not given, however, as the trustees decided that only the living should receive the award. Lord Kelvin is buried in Westminster Abbey.[7]

James Clerk Maxwell

(1831–1879)

ORE THAN TWO hundred years passed between the publication of Newton's *Principia* and Einstein's theory of relativity, generally agreed to be the most important points in the progress of physics. But there was another work, *Treatise on Electricity and Magnetism*, published by James Clerk Maxwell, in 1873, which bridged the gap between Newton and Einstein. Maxwell's *Treatise* was the most necessary part of the progression of knowledge and theory that Einstein needed before he could develop his ideas and draw his conclusions. The world likes things to be presented in threes and thus physics finds its trinity in the geniuses of Sir Isaac Newton, James Clerk Maxwell, and Albert Einstein.

James Clerk Maxwell,
PICTURE COLLECTION, THE BRANCH LIBRARIES, THE NEW YORK PUBLIC LIBRARY.

Unlike Newton and Einstein, born in the large countries of England and Germany, the *Treatise* was published by a man born in the small country of Scotland. A one-third share in this triumvirate is a fine score for Scotland, but it could be even higher if Newton's claim of Scottish ancestry could be proven. But even third place between Newton and Einstein is more than one would expect from such a small nation. It is even more remarkable to postulate that four more places in an impartial

ranking of the world's eight or ten greatest physicists might well be awarded to Ernest Rutherford, Joseph J. Thomson, Lord Kelvin, and Joseph
Black. All of these men, who are discussed in this book, were Scots, born
respectively in New Zealand, England, Ireland, and France. Perhaps we
should also mention that one of the most famous scientists since Einstein
is Stephen W. Hawking, who is the grandson of a Scottish physician.

The greatest scientist ever produced by Scotland was James Clerk
Maxwell, who was born in Edinburgh. His family also owned an estate of
1,500 acres, Glenlair, in Kircudbrightshire, in the southwestern province
of Galloway. Maxwell showed his scientific inclinations even as a small
boy, taking toys apart, fixing things, noticing how water flowed in a
stream, and building machines. He was sent to Edinburgh Academy
where his quiet personality earned him the nickname Dafty, a Scots term
for a dull person. Soon, however, this daft boy was far ahead of his classmates. At age fourteen Maxwell wrote a paper on a way to draw ovals that
was so good that it was read at the Royal Society of Edinburgh. In 1847,
at age sixteen, Maxwell entered Edinburgh University, later transferring
to Trinity College, Cambridge, where he graduated with high honors.[1]

In 1856 Maxwell was given the chair of natural philosophy at
Marischal College, Aberdeen, and two years later married Katherine
Mary Dewar. In 1859 he won one of his many prizes for describing the
composition of the rings of the planet Saturn. His theory was that the
rings were made of dusty clouds of individual particles, and this description was confirmed in the twentieth century by an unmanned spacecraft.[2]

In 1860 Maxwell was made professor of physics at King's College,
London. The Saturn research led him to study the properties of gasses and
he published his brilliant kinetic theory of gasses, the laws of which are
still in use. In 1861 he demonstrated the principles of color photography
by showing an audience a patriotic picture of a tartan ribbon. Thus,
Maxwell became the founder of color photography. He resigned from
King's College in 1865 to return to the solitude of Glenlair where he
spent several productive years.[3]

But his eminence caused Maxwell to be called away from peaceful
Galloway and in 1871 he was asked to become the first professor of experimental physics at Cambridge. It took the urging of many friends to get
him to accept. At Cambridge he designed and created what is perhaps the
most famous physics laboratory in the world, the Cavendish Laboratory.

The climax of Maxwell's career came in 1873 upon the publication of his *Treatise on Electricity and Magnetism*, which the Encyclopaedia Britannica calls "one of the most splendid monuments ever raised by the genius of a single individual."[4] Maxwell's greatest achievement is his discovery that electricity and magnetism are different aspects of the same thing, which he named "electromagnetism." He said, "The theory I propose . . . may be called a theory of the electromagnetic field." In order to prove this he reduced, as his biographer, Ivan Tolstoy has said, "a whole universe of electromagnetic phenomena, miraculously contained in a few lines of elegant mathematics."[5] Here, for those scientifically inclined, are the famous "Maxwell's equations":[6]

$$\Delta \times E + \partial B / \partial t = 0$$
$$\Delta \times H - \partial D / \partial t = J$$
$$\Delta \cdot B = 0$$
$$\Delta \cdot D = \Theta$$

E is the electric field; D is the electric displacement; H is the magnetic field; B is the magnetic induction; J is the current density; and Θ is the density of the electrical charge.

The German scientist Boltzmann asked, quoting Goethe, "Was it God who wrote these lines?" Maxwell's equations not only prove his theory, they bring out another since they require, implicitly, that electromagnetic waves travel at the speed of light. If the speed of electricity in a wire is the same, approximately, as the speed of light then Maxwell says, "We can scarcely avoid the inference that light consists in the transverse undulation of the same medium which is the cause of electric and magnetic phenomena."[7] In other words, light is an electromagnetic phenomenon. Maxwell's exquisite equations consolidated the theories of Gauss, Ampère and Faraday.

The influence of Maxwell's *Treatise* is immense. His electromagnetic field is the basis of much of modern science and made possible the development of radio, television, and radar. He is the "father" of electronics and the "New Economy." He predicted that radio waves would exist and could be produced. Around 1886, Heinrich Hertz proved this to be true.

Of almost equal importance to his discoveries were his constructions of the equations that have inspired later theoreticians to construct similar models. Albert Einstein described Maxwell's work as " a change in the conception of reality" which was the "most fruitful since the time of Newton."[8] Einstein kept a photograph of Maxwell on his office wall.[9]

Einstein's theory of relativity overturned much of physics but not the work of James Clerk Maxwell. In fact, the Collins *Encyclopaedia of Scotland* quotes Einstein as saying: "It was Maxwell who fully comprehended the significance of the field concept; he made the fundamental discovery that the laws of electrodynamics found their natural expression in the differential equations for the electric and magnetic fields."[10]

Most people today have never even heard of James Clerk Maxwell, but all physicists know him well. The Nobel Prize winner Richard Feynman says: "From the long view of the history of mankind—seen from, say, ten thousand years from now—there can be little doubt that the most significant event of the nineteenth century will be judged as Maxwell's discovery of the laws of electrodynamics."[11]

William Ramsay

(1852–1916)

SIR WILLIAM RAMSAY discovered the entire family of elements that are known as the noble gases: argon, helium, neon, krypton, xenon and radon. It is an achievement that will last forever.

William Ramsay was born in Glasgow, the only child of William Ramsay, a civil engineer, and his wife, Catharine Robertson, who belonged to a family of physicians. From 1866 to 1869, William Ramsay studied classics, logic, and mathematics at the University of Glasgow. In 1870 he went to Heidelberg where he studied under the famous Robert Wilhelm Bunsen. He ended his studies at Tübingen, where he earned a Ph.D. In 1872 he was an assistant professor of chemistry at Glasgow and in 1880 was made professor of chemistry at University College, Bristol. In 1887 he rose to the chair of general chemistry at University College, London where he stayed until his retirement in 1913. He built a career as one of the most distinguished chemists of his time and along the way he married Margaret Buchanan, with whom he had a son and a daughter.[1]

Then in 1892 the distinguished physicist Lord Rayleigh asked chemists to try to find the reason for the difference between the densities of chemical and atmospheric nitrogen. Ramsay became interested in the problem and theorized, contrary to Rayleigh's supposition, that a hidden gas was involved. He succeeded in removing oxygen and nitrogen from the air and found a new gas, previously unknown. He and Rayleigh made the announcement of the discovery of the gas in 1894. They called it argon after the Greek *argos*, meaning idle, because it was inert and would not combine with other elements.[2]

In 1895 Ramsay conducted an experiment, heating cleveite with acid. This produced a gas with a spectrum identical to helium, that had been detected on the sun but not previously on earth. Thus, Ramsay brought in his second element and after examining positions of helium and argon in the periodic table, he concluded that at least three more noble gases must exist. With M. W. Travers, Ramsay discovered them in 1898, using liquid air, from which oxygen and nitrogen had been removed. These new gases were called neon, krypton, and xenon.[3]

In 1903 Ramsay had found that helium was produced from radium emanation. In 1910, in an ingenious experiment he discovered a gas emanating from a three-millionth part of a cubic inch of radium. He was able to determine its atomic weight, which proved that this was the last of the noble gases. Initially it was called niton, but is commonly referred to today as radon.[4]

Sir William was a man of great personal charm and generosity. His students loved him. He was a linguist, a musician, and a humorous speaker. He received many honorary degrees, was elected a Fellow of the Royal Society in 1888, was knighted in 1902, and was awarded the Nobel Prize in Chemistry in 1904. The *Dictionary of National Biography* says that he was the greatest chemical discoverer of his time, and that he "will rank with the greatest scientific discoverers of any age."[5]

Group O
He 2
Ne 10
Ar 18
Kr 36
Xe 54
Rn 86

From the Short-Form Periodic Table
COLLECTION OF THE AUTHOR

Joseph J. Thomson

(1856–1940)

Joseph J. Thomson,

IR JOSEPH JOHN Thomson, born at Cheetham Hill near Manchester in England, is one of the founders of modern physics. His paternal grandparents, James Andrew Thomson and Margaret Cuthbertson Sword,[1] both with triply Scottish names, may have been born in Scotland. The *Dictionary of National Biography* says more simply, "So far as is known . . . ," his father's ancestors " . . . were entirely lowland Scottish."[2] Thomson's father, a bookseller, sent his son to Owens College in Manchester at age fourteen. Later, the college, distressed to find someone so young to have qualified, changed its admission policy. By 1876 Thomson was at Cambridge, where he stayed for the rest of his life.

Young "J. J.," as he was usually called, was of average height and strongly built, with large bones. He wasn't athletic however, but was a lifelong "fan" of rugby and cricket. He paid little attention to his clothes being, perhaps, the stereotypical rumpled academic. In 1881, while still quite young, Thomson made his mark with a paper proving that an electrical charge must possess inertia. The *Dictionary of National Biography* says, " . . . even had this achievement stood alone it would have established him as a scientist of the first rank."[3]

In 1893 he produced *Notes and Researches in Electricity and Magnetism*, that some have called "the third volume of Maxwell," referring to the brilliant 1873 work of James Clerk Maxwell, whose treatise we have discussed earlier. In 1896 Thomson lectured at Princeton and in 1904 at Yale in the United States. During these eight years he reached the summit of his career. On April 30, 1897, he lectured that he had discovered "a corpuscle" of electrically charged matter smaller than the hydrogen atom; the particle now called the electron. In 1903 he produced what is thought of as his best book, *Conduction of Electricity Through Gasses*. For this he was awarded the 1906 Nobel Prize in physics.

J. J. Thomson married one of his students, Rose Paget, and it is interesting to see his correspondence with her change as their relationship progressed from professor and student to lovers. He begins writing things to "Dear Miss Paget," discussing work assignments and signing off as J. J. Thomson. Some letters later he is on a much more familiar basis and signing off as J. J. T. It appears that she was the only woman in his life.

The only son of J. J. Thomson and Rose Paget was Sir George Paget Thomson (1892–1975) who became a noted scientist in his own right. Having graduated from Trinity College, Cambridge in 1914, he was in military service in France in World War I. Afterward he spent some time at the Cavendish Laboratory at Cambridge. From there he became a professor at Aberdeen and later at the University of London. He won a Nobel Prize in physics in 1937 for his work on the diffraction of electrons in crystals. How interesting and satisfying it must have been for the Thomsons that the son received science's ultimate recognition for having made a significant discovery in the properties of a particle discovered by his father!

During World War II Sir George headed the committee that reported that it was possible to build an atomic bomb. He was sent to the United States to inform the American government and scientists of the feasibility of the powerful destructive force which could aid the Allies.[4] His mission resulted in the Los Alamos project and eventually, on the bombings of Hiroshima and Nagasaki, which shortened the war, saving hundreds of thousands, perhaps even millions of American and Japanese lives, including civilians.

The influence of J. J. Thomson was vast. He wrote several of the most widely used textbooks. He held the Cavendish Professorship, the most important scientific professorship in the world, from 1884 to 1919. From this position he trained " . . . nine Nobel Prize winners, thirty-two Fellows of Britain's Royal Society, and eighty-three professors of physics."[5]

J. J. Thomson received many honors, including honorary degrees from twenty-three colleges and universities. In addition he was president of the Royal Society from 1915 through 1920. His ashes are buried in Westminster Abbey near such greats as Newton, Darwin, Kelvin, and Rutherford.[6]

Ernest Rutherford

(1871–1937)

L ORD RUTHERFORD WAS one of the greatest scientists in all history. His work in radiation and atomic structure, in the early part of the twentieth century was absolutely basic to all subsequent developments in nuclear physics. He was born at Brightwater near Nelson, New Zealand, and is often called "New Zealand's greatest son." Rutherford's father, James Rutherford, was born in Scotland and immigrated at age three in 1842 with his parents. The arduous sail from Dundee to New Zealand took six months. James' father,

Lord Rutherford,
PICTURE COLLECTION, THE BRANCH LIBRARIES,
THE NEW YORK PUBLIC LIBRARY.

George Rutherford, was a wheelwright from Perth who came to New Zealand to build a sawmill. James Rutherford grew up to marry Caroline Thompson Shuttleworth, a young woman from England.[1] Their son, Ernest Rutherford, would make history.

Young Ernest Rutherford had a happy childhood and good teachers. He won a scholarship to Nelson College, scoring 580 out of a possible 600 points in an examination. His excellent work there won him another scholarship to the University of New Zealand where he played football and graduated with first-class degrees in both mathematics and physics.

Then came a scholarship to Cambridge, that had been almost too much for the young man to hope for. He was digging potatoes when his mother brought the telegram notifying him of his acceptance. He knew that his life's destiny was fixed then, and is said to have flung aside his spade saying, "These are the last potatoes I shall ever dig."[2]

He arrived at Cambridge in 1895, fearing what he imagined would be a stern professor, the world-famous J. J. Thomson. How surprised he was when the affable Thomson invited the young student to his home for lunch. There Rutherford met Thomson's little son, George. Within a few years all three of these men would win Nobel Prizes.[3] Thomson was immediately and favorably impressed by young Rutherford and the two began to work together.

In 1898 Rutherford accepted a position at the Macdonald Laboratory at McGill University in Montreal. There he discovered that the radiation from radium was complex. There were relatively weak rays, which he named alpha rays. Stronger rays, from uranium, which could penetrate a sheet of aluminum, he called beta rays. These were found to be high-speed electrons.[4]

In 1907 Rutherford became a professor at Manchester University in England. A year later he was awarded a Nobel Prize in Chemistry for his work in radiation. But his most important work was still ahead. It was around 1910 when he theorized the structure of the atom as being a positively-charged nucleus, surrounded by negatively-charged electrons. The two electrical charges would be equal, and the atom therefore balanced. He deduced that this should make it possible to disintegrate atoms. This is known as the "atom-smashing theory." In 1919 Rutherford was able to prove this theory by bombarding an atom with alpha particles. In 1920 he deduced the nucleus and suggested calling it by the name "proton," Greek for "the first" because they are primary things. In the same year he speculated that there might be another part to the nucleus, a neutrally-charged particle—the neutron. Within a few years all of this was proved to be true by the experiments of others. Rutherford's work was the beginning of atomic science.

Thus it was that two Scots—Thomson, who discovered electrons, and Rutherford who found neutrons and protons—determined the basic structure of the atom. They had many followers who went on to discover how to use the enormous power of the atom for peace and war. One young man who studied with both of them was the Danish-Jewish Niels Bohr who set up his famous Institute for Theoretical Physics in Copenhagen in 1920. Bohr was forced to flee the Nazis during World War II, and ended up playing a crucial role in the American development of the atomic bomb. Rutherford was, until his death in 1937, like a second father to Bohr.[5]

Ernest Rutherford was a large man, "enthusiastic, absolutely direct" who "made great discoveries look ridiculously simple."[6] He married Mary Newton, a woman he had known in New Zealand. In 1919 he succeeded J. J. Thomson in the chair at the Cavendish Laboratory where he trained eleven future Nobel Prize winners. It is noted that of the first four heads of the world's greatest physics laboratory, Maxwell, Rayleigh, Thomson, and Rutherford, all but Rayleigh were Scots. If Lord Kelvin had wanted the job it might have been all four. From Kelvin through Maxwell, Thomson and Rutherford, Scots dominated physics for almost a century, with each man learning from the others.

Rutherford was knighted in 1914, and was made President of the Royal Society in 1925, the same year he was awarded the Order of Merit. In 1931 he became Lord Rutherford as first Baron of Nelson and Cambridge.

His former student, Niels Bohr made things simply clear. "Rutherford," he said, "is not a clever man, he is a great man."[7]

Mary Leakey

(1913–1996)

Mary Leakey,
LOS ANGELES TIMES. THE LEAKEY FOUNDATION.

T HE LEAKEY FAMILY of Kenya have lifted paleontology to its place among the sciences. Their name is "synonymous with the study of human origins." The Leakeys were the ones who proved beyond any doubt that the origin of mankind was in Africa rather than in Asia as was previously thought. They also found that our ancestors walked upright before they could make and use tools. And it was a discovery by the Leakeys in 1959 that gave momentum to modern paleoanthropology. After that more people became involved. The work became more scientific and discoveries came faster. "Geologists and anatomists, not just bone hunters, joined the quest, a multidisciplinary approach that the Leakeys did much to promote."[1] Louis and Mary Leakey often jointly shared in the honors accorded for their work but in fact—probably because she was a woman—Mary Leakey's English-born husband, Louis Leakey, was usually given most of the credit. This article is not intended to belittle the great work done by

Louis Leakey. But in fact the two most important discoveries made by this exceptional team were made by Mary Leakey.

She was born in London as Mary Douglas Nicol, the daughter of the painter Erskine Nicol, and his wife, Cecilia Frere, who was of English and Irish descent. Mary Leakey says in her autobiography, "My father's family was essentially Scottish."[2] Mary Douglas Nicol's schooling has been described as sporadic, but at an early age she did excavations at a neolithic site at Hembury in Devonshire, England.[3] It is not true, then, that she knew nothing of the subject, as is claimed in some works, before she met Louis Leakey in 1933. They were married in 1936 and worked together, side by side, for over thirty years. The couple had three children.

In 1948 Mary Leakey made the discovery of *Proconsul Africanus*, "an apelike ancestor of both apes and humans" which was about 25 million years old. The first of her two most important discoveries was made at Olduvai Gorge in 1959. It was the skull of an early hominid, which Louis Leakey named *Zinjanthropus*.[4] On that particular day, Mary Leakey was working alone as her husband was suffering from influenza back at their camp. "Mary saw two large teeth set in the curve of a jaw." Immediately she jumped in her Land Rover as fast as she could to tell her husband the news. "I've got him! I've got him! I've got him!" she yelled. "Got what?" answered Louis Leakey. "Him, the man! Our man . . ." She had discovered the world's earliest known hominid.[5] It is not known how the Leakeys celebrated this triumph, but in an earlier celebration they "cast aside care" with the result that their son Philip "came to join" the family.[6]

Mary Leakey believed that her most important discovery was made at Laetoli, south of Olduvai Gorge, in 1978. Here she found "several sets of footprints made in volcanic ash by early hominids who lived about 3.5 million years ago." The footprints meant that these ancient ancestors walked upright, moving the date for bipedalism back to a much earlier time than had been thought, to a time long before the advent of tool making.[7] Mary Leakey called a press conference at the headquarters of the National Geographic Society in Washington to announce her find.[8]

The Leakey's son, Richard Erskine Frere Leakey (1944–) has continued the work of his parents, and has made important discoveries on his own. He has proved that tool-making "ancestors of true man lived in East Africa as early as 3 million years ago." This is almost twice the previous estimate. In 1967 on the shores of Lake Rudolph (now Lake Turkana) he discovered a treasure trove of ancient human remains, the largest in the world. In a decade he found 400 hominid fossils representing about 230 individuals. Richard Leakey also proved that *homo habilis* was the ancestor of man, "the evolutionary link between australopithecines and *homo erectus*, the direct ancestor of man (*homo sapiens*).[9]

Mary Leakey died in 1996. During her life, she had been showered with honors. She received an Honorary DSc from Chicago in 1981, Cambridge in 1982, and a DSSc from Yale in 1976. In 1981 Oxford awarded her an Honorary DLitt. She received the Linneaus Gold Medal from the Royal Swedish Academy in 1978. In the same year she shared the Hubbard Medal of the National Geographic Society, with her husband.[10] The work of Mary Douglas Nicol Leakey will stand forever.

James D. Watson

(1928–)

NOT SO LONG AGO, a half century or so, no one knew exactly how hereditary traits were passed along from one generation of plants or animals to another. Genes were only a concept. Today scientists are able to splice genes to rearrange genetic material from different organisms. An immense biotechnology industry has developed throughout the world. All of this progress rests upon two essential discoveries.

The first was made at Rockefeller University in New York City during World War II. There, three scientists, Oswald Avery, Maclyn McCarty, and

Dr. James D. Watson,
COLD SPRING HARBOR LABORATORY ARCHIVES

Colin Munro MacLeod proved that DNA (deoxyribonucleic acid) was the substance of the genes. This was a great surprise to the scientific world because it had been assumed that it would be found that the genetic code was carried in proteins. All subsequent developments in genetics and biotechnology depend on this discovery.[1] It is another example of the capricious nature of recognition that these three scientists did not receive Nobel Prizes. Two of the three had Scottish backgrounds. Dr. McCarty is of Scotch-Irish descent. Dr. MacLeod was the son of a Presbyterian minister from Nova Scotia.

But a second discovery was essential towards the progress which has resulted in the biotechnology we have today. That would be to discover the structure of DNA. This work fell to a young American.

James Dewey Watson was born in Chicago in 1928, the son of James D. Watson, a businessman, and his wife Jean Mitchell, whose father was born in Scotland. Young Watson was an unusually good scholar. He spent eight years at Horace Mann Grammar School and two years at South Shore High School in Chicago. In 1943, while the scientists in New York were on the verge of proving that DNA was the substance of genetics, he received a tuition scholarship to the University of Chicago. He was only fifteen years old. Four years later, already an avid bird-watcher, James Watson received a bachelor's degree in zoology. By 1950 he had a Ph.D. from Indiana University. In the same year he went to Copenhagen as a National Research Council Fellow. In 1951 he went to Cambridge, England to join Francis H. C. Crick in the quest to discover the structure of DNA.[2]

In England at that time, Maurice Wilkins was the only scientist working on DNA, and in England, it was not considered polite to begin research on a project which had been begun by another. But Linus Pauling—an American who would later win two Nobel Prizes—was known to be working on the structure of DNA. Watson and Crick decided that, manners or no, they had to try to beat Pauling to the discovery.[3]

Watson and Crick were given a clue by the work of Erwin Chargaff, an Austrian scientist working at Columbia University in New York. Chargaff had noticed some regularities in DNA chemistry through painstaking analysis. As Watson relates in his famous book, *The Double Helix*, "In all their DNA preparations the number of adenine (A) molecules was very similar to the number of thymine (T) molecules, while the number of guanine (G) molecules was very close to the number of cytosine (C) molecules." Chargaff of course was also interested in solving the problem of the structure of DNA. At one point, he visited Watson and Crick, scorning them as if they were amateurs. Later Watson and Crick discovered that the A-T pairs and G-C pairs tended to stick to each other. They began to formulate the theory that DNA was shaped in the form of a helix; a spiral form. To discover and prove the shape, they would have to make a model of DNA.[4]

Another clue came from an X ray photograph of DNA which had been made by Rosalind Franklin, a colleague of Maurice Wilkins. Watson says, "The instant I saw the picture my mouth fell open and my pulse began to race." The evidence for a helix was now overwhelming.[5] Then one morning, Watson went to the office early and cleared off his desk to try to put the model pieces in some order that would work. He says, "Suddenly I became aware that an adenine-thymine pair held together by two hydrogen bonds was identical in shape to a guanine-cytosine pair held together by at least two hydrogen bonds . . . Chargoff's rules then suddenly stood out as a consequence of a double-helical structure for DNA."[6]

Watson had made the discovery of the double-helix structure of DNA. Watson says that Crick didn't even get halfway through the door on his arrival at the office when Watson told him that "the answer to everything is in our hands." Crick started pushing the model bases together in a number of different ways "which did not reveal any other way to satisfy Chargaff's rules."[7] But there was still work to do. They had not yet built a convincing model. Watson didn't want to "cry wolf" and suggested that they keep the discovery quiet until a model would give them absolute proof. Crick didn't agree, and Watson says, "Thus I was slightly queasy when . . . Francis winged into the Eagle (a favorite local pub) to tell everyone within hearing distance that we had found the secret of life."[8]

So it is now known that the structure of DNA is a double helix, that it looks like a spiral staircase or a twisted ladder, with each rung consisting of a pair of bases of which there are only four: adenine, thymine, guanine and cytosine. Further, the chains come apart like a zipper and reproduce their missing halves. All of subsequent biotechnology and genetics springs from this discovery.

Linus Pauling came to see for himself. Watson and Crick stood in breathless anticipation as the great American chemist examined their model. They showed him Rosalind Franklin's photograph. As Watson says of their former competitor, "All the right cards were in our hands and so, gracefully, he gave his opinion that we had the answer."[9] On April 25, 1953, Watson and Crick published their work in *Nature*. They began conservatively, "We wish to suggest a structure for the salt of deoxyribose nucleic acid (DNA)."[10]

James D. Watson married Elizabeth Lewis, with whom he has two sons, Rufus and Duncan. He has continued to have a very productive career. He was long a professor of biology at Harvard University. He was the first director of the Human Genome Project at the National Institute of Health. He has had a long association with the Cold Spring Harbor Laboratory on Long Island. When he began there it was in financial difficulty, and Watson made it financially sound. He is currently the director at Cold Spring where thousands of scientists have worked and studied. Watson has received many honors. He shared the Nobel Prize in 1962 with Crick and Wilkins. He was awarded the Presidential Medal of Freedom. He is a member of the American Academy of Arts and Sciences and the National Academy of Science. He was awarded the Wallace Award of the American-Scottish Foundation.

Linus Pauling said, years after the event, "I believe that this discovery of the double helix and the developments that resulted from the discovery constitute the greatest advance in biological science and our understanding of life that has taken place in the last hundred years."[11] Pauling is a good source, as he is the only person ever to win two unshared Nobel Prizes in different fields. As an American of Scottish ancestry he, too, received the Wallace Award.

James Naismith

(1861–1939)

J AMES NAISMITH WAS the inventor of basketball, the principal winter sport of the United States that is now played all over the world. He was born in Almonte, Ontario, near Ottawa, the son of Scottish immigrant parents. His father, John Naismith, was a lumberman and carpenter. His mother was Margaret Young. The parents of James Naismith died in a typhoid epidemic in 1870, leaving the boy to be raised by his sternly religious grandmother and later by a bachelor uncle. Young James Naismith worked five years in a lumber camp, and it was not until 1888 that he was able to enter McGill University in Montréal. During his last year at McGill he directed undergraduate gymnastic classes. He received his AB degree in 1887.[1]

After McGill, Naismith studied theology at a Presbyterian seminary for three years. Upon graduation he was still interested in physical education and went to Springfield, Massachusetts where the YMCA had a strong program. At Springfield, Naismith played football under the soon to be legendary coach Amos Alonzo Stagg. But interest in sport flagged in the rough New England winters and Naismith was asked to invent a game that could be played indoors. It wasn't easy for him to come up with the game but as he says, "All the stubbornness of my Scotch ancestry was aroused."[2] Finally he conceived the sport. He nailed two peach baskets to the gymnasium balcony and found that a soccer ball would go through the baskets perfectly. He made some rules, including nine men on a side, and the first basketball game was played in December of 1891.[3]

As basketball developed over the years, Naismith was on the committees that changed the rules. In 1894 he married Maude Evelyn Sherman, with whom he had five children. In 1898 he was appointed the first instructor of physical education at the University of Kansas, where he coached basketball and track until 1905. In 1916 he was ordained as a Presbyterian minister and became a chaplain in World War I. On the side he pitted French- and Italian-soldier basketball teams against Americans. Naismith, who became a United States citizen in 1925, derived no immediate fame and absolutely no fortune from his invention of basketball. The 1936 Olympic games, staged in Nazi Berlin, were what made basketball a world game. A fund was raised by coaches to send Naismith there. Fittingly, Canada and the United States were the finalists, with the latter winning 19–8.[4]

There is a compelling parallel story here. Naismith's closest friend back in Almonte, had been another child of Scottish immigrants, Robert Tait McKenzie. McKenzie's father, William, was a minister of the Free Church of Scotland. McKenzie's mother was Catherine Shiels. "Rob," as he was called then was their third child. But tragedy struck the McKenzies as it had the Naismiths. For health reasons, William and Catherine returned to Scotland leaving their son to live with the same people as the orphaned Naismith. When James Naismith was in Springfield in 1891, Tait McKenzie visited him and helped him to perfect the game of basketball. McKenzie got his M.D. from McGill in 1892, and was best man at Naismith's wedding in 1894. McKenzie was in charge of a large part of the therapy program for soldiers in England in World War I.[5] As R. Tait McKenzie, he became the greatest sculptor ever produced by Canada. He is the creator of the Scottish-American War Memorial in Edinburgh, as well as the statue of the young Benjamin Franklin arriving in Philadelphia, that graces the campus of the University of Pennsylvania, where Dr. McKenzie was long involved in physical education.

Many great athletes have been of Scottish birth or descent. Jim Clark and Jackie Stewart were two of the best auto racers of all time. Don Budge was the first tennis player to win the "Grand Slam." Billie Jean (Moffat) King was the first woman tennis player to make $100,000. Otto Graham was arguably, the best American football player ever. Arnold Palmer, of Scotch-Irish descent, was the golfer who made the sport a big money game. Bobby Orr (Robert Gordon Orr) was hockey's best defenseman. Kenny Dalglish and many others have been great footballers. Scotland has also been involved in the formation and development of several important games such as football (British), golf, hockey, horse racing, boxing, and curling.[6]

But only one Scot created an important international game. In 1959 at the founding of the Basketball Hall of Fame in Springfield, Massachusetts, James Naismith was made a charter member.[7]

The Scottish-American War Memorial, Edinburgh, by R. Tait Mckenzie.
COLLECTION OF THE AUTHOR.

Notes

ROBERT ADAM
1. *EB*, vol. 1, pp. 118–119.
2. *DNB*, vol. 1, pp. 88–89.
3. Macgregor, F., p. 285.
4. *DNB*, vol. 1, pp. 88–89.
5. C. Edmiston Douglas, *Scottish Field*, August 1972, p. 71.
6. *EB*, vol. 5, p. 661; *EB*, vol. 11, p. 384.
7. Musgrave, p. 75.
8. *DNB*, vol. 18, p.69.
9. *EB*, vol. 1, p. 119.
10. *Ibid.*, vol. 17, p. 1011.
11. Bruce, pp. 235–237.
12. Bryant, p. 5.
13. *DNB*, vol. 1, p. 89

CHARLES RENNIE MACKINTOSH
1. Crawford, pp. 9, 10.
2. *DNB* 1922–1930, pp. 546, 547.
3. *Scottish World*, pp. 290, 291.
4. *DNB*, 1922–1930, pp. 546, 547.
5. *Scottish World*, pp. 290, 291.
6. *DNB*, 1922–1930, pp. 546, 547.
7. Crawford, pp. 187, 193.
8. R. W. Apple Jr., *New York Times*, 15 April 1982, C 12.
9. *DNB*, 1922–1930, pp. 546, 547.

ALLAN RAMSAY AND HENRY RAEBURN
1. *CES*, p. 803.
2. Macgregor, F., pp. 223, 224.
3. *Ibid.*, pp. 271, 272.

4. *CES*, p. 804.
5. *Dictionary of Art*, vol. 25, p. 881.
6. *DNB*, vol. 16, pp. 598, 599.
7. *Ibid.*, pp. 599–602.

MARY CASSATT
1. *EB*, vol. 5, p. 18.
2. Matthews, pp. 324, 325.
3. Hale, pp. 3–5.
4. *ANB*, vol 4, pp. 551–553.
5. Davis, pp. 3, 4.
6. *ANB*, vol. 4, pp. 551–553.
7. *Ibid.*
8. *Ibid.*
9. Matthews, p. 320.
10. *ANB*, vol. 4, pp. 551–553.

ALEXANDER CALDER
1. *Dictionary of Art*, vol. 5, p. 422.
2. *Philadelphia Journal*, 22 March 1978, p. 6.
3. *Dictionary of Art*, vol. 5 p. 422.
4. Ted Morgan, *New York Times Magazine*, 8 July 1973, p. 29.
5. John Russell, *New York Times*, 12 November 1976, A1, D14.
6. *Ibid.*
7. *Ibid.*

JACKSON POLLOCK
1. Bruce, p. 233.

2. Michael Brenson, *New York Times*, 1 May 1982, p. 17.
3. *Dictionary of Art*, vol. 25, p. 165.
4. *ANB*, vol. 17, p. 639.
5. Cernuschi, p. 12.
6. *Dictionary of Art*, vol. 25, p. 165.
7. *Ibid.*, p. 166.
8. *ANB*, vol. 17, p. 641.
9. *Ibid.*, p. 642.
10. Cernuschi, p. 310.
11. Rita Reif, *New York Times*, 3 May 1988, C16.

WILLIAM PATERSON

1. *DNB*, vol. 15, p. 469.
2. *EB*, vol. 17, p. 456.
3. *DNB*, vol. 15, p. 469.
4. Bruce, pp. 19–21.
5. Hart, pp. 91–93.
6. *EB*, vol. 17, p. 456.
7. *DNB*, vol. 15, p. 470.
8. *Ibid.*, p. 471.

JOHN LAW

1. *DNB*, vol. 11, pp. 671–675.
2. *EB*, vol. 13, p. 820.
3. *DNB*, vol. 11, pp. 671–675.
4. *Ibid.*
5. *Ibid.*
6. *Ibid.*
7. Hyde, *John Law* p. 150.
8. Train.
9. *DNB*, vol. 11, pp. 671–675.
10. *Ibid.*

WILLIAM JARDINE AND JAMES MATHESON

1. Bruce, passim.
2. *DNB*, Missing Persons, p. 347.
3. *Ibid.*, p. 452.
4. *Ibid.*, p. 348.
5. *Ibid.*, pp 347, 348.
6. *Ibid.*
7. *Ibid.*
8. *Ibid.*, p. 453.
9. Jardine, pp. 15–45.
10. Nicholas D. Kristof, *New York Times*, 1 December 1986, D1.

ANDREW CARNEGIE

1. *ANB*, vol. 4, pp. 408–414.
2. *Ibid.*
3. Wilson, p. 5.
4. *ANB*, vol. 4, pp. 408–414.
5. *Ibid.*
6. *Ibid.*
7. *New York Times*, 20 Dec 1999, C 27.
8. Ron Chernow, *New York Times*, 27 September 1999, A 23.
9. Lynch, p. 12.
10. *ANB*, vol. 4, pp. 408–414.
11. Wall, p. 1041.

THOMAS BLAKE GLOVER

1. Vivienne Forrest, *The Highlander*, May/June 1992, pp. 48, 49.
2. *Ibid.*
3. Nicholas D. Kristof, the *New York Times*, 16 February 1997, XX9.
4. Forrest, op. cit., p. 50.
5. *CES*, pp. 276, 277, 355.
6. *Historical Catalogue of the St. Andrew's Society of Philadelphia*, vol. 3, pp. xiv, 61, 127.
7. Fox Butterfield, the *New York Times*, 2 October 1988, p. 13.
8. Dinita Smith, the *New York Times*, 1 December 1999, C31.
9. Kristof, op. cit. XX9.
10. Forrest, op. cit., pp. 50, 51.

ELIZABETH ARDEN

1. Shuker, p. 8.
2. *ANB*, vol. 1, pp. 579–580.
3. *Ibid.*
4. *Ibid.*
5. *Ibid.*
6. Telephone conversation with Lorna Gui at Elizabeth Arden, 8 December 1999.
7. Lewis and Woodworth, pp. 20–23.
8. *Ibid.*, p. 22.

DONALD DOUGLAS

1. *ANB*, vol. 6, p. 793.
2. *EB 15th*, vol. 4, p. 196.
3. Richard Witkin, *New York Times*, 3 February 1981, B14.
4. *ANB*, vol. 6. p. 793.

5. Ralph Blumenthal, *New York Times*, 1 December 1985, p. 30.
6. *Ibid.*
7. Morrison, p. ix.
8. Witkin, op. cit., B14.
9. Morrison, p. ix.
10. *ANB*, vol. 6, p. 794.

THOMAS J. WATSON AND THOMAS J. WATSON JR.

1. Rodgers, p. 16.
2. Watson, Thomas J. Jr., p. 12.
3. Rodgers, p. 54.
4. Watson, Thomas J. Jr., p. 14.
5. *Ibid.*, pp. 15, 16.
6. *Ibid.*, p. 33.
7. *Ibid.*, p. ix.
8. Bruce, p. 106.
9. Watson, Thomas J. Jr., p. viii.
10. Steve Lohr, *New York Times*, 1 January 1994.
11. Watson, Thomas J. Jr., p. viii.
12. Steve Lohr, *New York Times*, 1 January 1994.
13. *Ibid.*

SEAN CONNERY

1. Yule, p. 3, 4.
2. Callan, pp. 29–31.
3. Yule, pp. 16–29.
4. Freedland, p. 225.
5. For more Scots in film, see Bruce, pp. 248–252.

JOHN MUIR

1. *CES*, p. 713.
2. James Wilson, *Highlander*, March/April 1988, pp. 6, 10.
3. *ANB*, vol. 16, p. 63.
4. Wilkins, p. 10.
5. Bruce, p. 227.
6. *ANB*, vol. 16, p. 63.
7. *CSBD*, p. 325.
8. *ANB*, vol. 16, p. 63.
9. Muir, pp. 313, 314.
10. *EB*, vol. 19, pp. 607–608; *ANB*, vol. 16, p. 63.
11. Muir, p. 378.

RACHEL CARSON

1. Lear, pp. 9–10.
2. *ANB*, vol. 4, p. 474.
3. *Ibid.*, p. 475.
4. *Ibid.*, p. 476.
5. Gartner, p. 107.
6. *U.S. News and World Report*, 27 December 1999, p. 65.

ROBERT R. LIVINGSTON

1. Francis, p. 19.
2. Francis, pp. 19–21.
3. Bruce, pp. 115, 125, 236, 266.
4. *ANB*, vol. 13, p. 774.
5. Francis, p. 41.
6. Dangerfield, p. 78.
7. St. Andrew's Society, p. 158.
8. Burrows and Wallace, pp. 296–298.
9. *Ibid.*
10. *Ibid.*
11. *EB*, vol. 14, p. 358.
12. *Ibid.*
13. Francis, p. 37.
14. *EB*, vol. 14, p. 358.
15. St. Andrew's Society, p. 158.
16. *ANB*, vol. 13, p. 775.
17. *EB*, vol. 14, p. 154.

JAMES WATT

1. Carnegie, pp. 13–14.
2. *CSBD*, p. 449.
3. Carnegie, pp. 41–42.
4. *CES*, p. 967, 968.
5. Maclean and Dunnett, p. 168.
6. *EB*, vol. 23, p. 310.
7. *DNB*, vol. 20, p. 963.
8. *EB*, op. cit.
9. Carnegie, preface.
10. *CES*, op. cit.

WILLIAM MURDOCH

1. *DNB*, vol. 13, pp. 1221–1225.
2. *Light*, pp. 12–14.
3. *DNB*, vol. 13, pp. 1221–1225.
4. *Light*, p. 17.
5. *DNB*, vol. 13, pp. 1221–1225.
6. *Light*, p. 21.
7. *DNB*, vol. 13, pp. 1221–1225.
8. *Ibid.*
9. *Light*, p. 26.
10. *DNB*, vol. 13, pp. 1221–1225.

11. *Ibid.*
12. *Ibid.*
13. *Ibid.*
14. *Light*, pp. 33, 48.
15. *DNB*, vol. 13, pp. 1221-1225
16. *Light*, p. 20.
17. Black, p. 620.

WILLIAM SYMINGTON
1. Harvey, pp. 2, 3.
2. *DNB*, vol. 19, p. 269.
3. Harvey, p. 50.
4. *DNB*, vol. 19, p. 269.
5. *Ibid.*
6. Harvey, p. 139.
7. *Ibid.*, p. 8.
8. *DNB*, p. 270.

KIRKPATRICK MACMILLAN
1. *DNB*, Missing Persons, 1999, p. 435.
2. Norrie McLeish, *The Highlander*, May/June 1999, p.10.
3. *EB*, vol. 3, p. 594.
4. Irving, *Brush Up Your Scotland*, pp. 33–36.
5. McLeish, op. cit., p. 12; Irving, *The Devil on Wheels*, p. 16.
6. *DNB*, Missing Persons, 1999, p. 435.
7. Irving, *Devil*, overleaf.

SANFORD FLEMING
1. *DNB*, 1912–1921, pp. 190, 191.
2. *EB*, vol. 9, p. 437.
3. *DNB*, 1912–1921, pp. 190, 191.
4. *Ibid.*
5. Burpee, p. 140–151.
6. *Ibid.*
7. *Ibid.*, pp. 220–223.
8. *Ibid.*, p. 158, 159.
9. *DNB*, 1912–1922, pp. 190, 191; Burpee, p. 163.
10. *DNB*, 1912–1922, pp. 190, 191.

ALEXANDER GRAHAM BELL
1. Stevenson, O., p. 22.
2. *DNB*, 1922–1930, pp. 73–74; CES, p. 71, 72.
3. Macgregor, F., p. 154.
4. Stevenson, O., pp. 130–135.

5. *ANB*, vol. 2, p. 498.
6. Stevenson, O., pp. 140, 141.
7. *CFS*, pp. 18–19.
8. Bruce, p. 125.
9. Watson, T.A., pp. 171–173.
10. Macgregor, F., p. 154.
11. *CFS*, pp. 18–19.
12. Conaway, pp. 172–188.
13. Cunningham, pp. 24–25.
14. Bruce, p. 112.
15. *Ibid.*
16. *CFS*, p. 19.

THOMAS A. EDISON
1. Dyer, pp. 18–19.
2. *Ibid.*, pp. 25–26.
3. *Ibid.*, pp. 27–29.
4. *Ibid.*, pp. 30–31.
5. *Ibid.*, pp. 35–36.
6. *Ibid.*, pp. 37–40.
7. *ANB*, vol. 7, pp. 310–314.
8. Dyer, pp. 54, 55.
9. *Ibid.*, pp. 65, 66.
10. *ANB*, vol. 7, pp. 310–314.
11. *DAB*, Supp. I and II, p. 278.
12. *Ibid.*
13. *EB*, vol. 7, p. 978.
14. *ANB*, vol. 7, p. 310–314.
15. *EB*, vol. 7, pp. 978.
16. *DAB*, Supp. I and II p. 279; *EB*, vol. 7, p. 978.
17. *DAB*, Supp. I and II, p. 279.
18. Dickson, p. i.
19. Josephson, p.337; Dickson, p. i.
20. Bruce, p. 107.
21. *DAB*, Supp. I and II p. 279.
22. Josephson, p. 485.

GUGLIELMO MARCONI
1. Marconi, pp. 4, 5.
2. Dunlap, p. 6.
3. Marconi, p.14.
4. *EB*, vol. 14, p. 856, 857.
5. Marconi, pp. 19–20.
6. Ibid, pp. 32–38.
7. *EB*, vol. 14, pp. 856, 857.
8. *Ibid.*
9. Lessing, p. 11.
10. Ibid pp. 300–304.
11. *EB*, vol. 14, pp. 856, 857.

12. Richard Severo, *New York Times*, 19 December 1982.
13. Dunlap, p. 21.

JOHN LOGIE BAIRD
1. *DNB*, 1941–1950, p. 39.
2. *Ibid.*
3. Tiltman, p. 75.
4. *DNB*, 1941–1950, p. 39.
5. Tiltman, p. 97.
6. Macgregor, F., p. 155.
7. *DNB*, 1941–1950, p. 39.; *EB*, vol. 2, p. 1042.; Tiltman, p. 14.
8. Letter to the Editor, *New York Times*, 9 June 1989, A30.
9. *DNB*, 1941–1950, p. 39.
10. *CFS*, p. 13.
11. *DNB*, 1941–1950, p. 39.
12. Tiltman, pp. 29, 30.
13. Bruce, p. 109.
14. Tiltman, p. 40.
15. *Ibid.*, pp. 41–43.
16. *DNB*, 1941–1950, p.39.

ROBERT WATSON-WATT
1. *DNB*, 1901–1980, pp. 887, 889.
2. MacGregor, F., p. 156.
3. *DNB*, 1901–1980, pp. 887, 889.
4. *Ibid.*
5. Macgregor, F., p. 156.
6. *DNB*, 1901–1980, pp. 887 889.
7. *DNB*, 1951–1960, p. 998.
8. Macgregor, F., p. 156.
9. *DNB*, 1951–1960, p. 998.
10. Cave Brown, p. 814.
11. *DNB*, 1951–1960, p. 998.

HENRY SINCLAIR
1. Sinclair, p. 12.
2. *DNB*, vol. 18, p. 296.
3. Pohl, p. 103.
4. Bruce, p. 10.
5. Brown, Ian.
6. This included tree trunks and other jetsam.
7. *EB*, vol. 6, p. 111.
8. Brown, Ian.

JAMES COOK (CAPTAIN COOK)
1. *EB*, vol. 6, pp. 442, 443.
2. Alan Villiers, *National Geographic*, September 1971, p. 300.
3. Beaglehole, pp.2, 3.
4. *EB*, vol. 6, pp. 442, 443.
5. *Ibid.*
6. Villiers, op. cit. p. 325.
7. *EB*, vol. 6, pp. 442, 443.; Bruce, pp. 87, 91, 92.
8. Villiers, op. cit., pp. 328, 329; Rand McNally, p. 213.
9. Villiers, op. cit. p. 339.
10. *EB*, vol. 6, pp. 442, 443.; Rand McNally, p. 214.
11. Beaglehole, p. 697.

ALEXANDER MACKENZIE
1. The spelling Mackenzie is used here, as that is the most usual Scottish spelling, and the way his name appears on maps and in the *Encyclopaedia Britannica*. The explorer sometimes spelled it McKenzie, and abbreviated his first name as Alex or other variations. This was common in the eighteenth century.
2. Mackenzie, pp. 2, 3.
3. William N. McDonald III, the *Highlander*, November/December 1980, p. 44.
4. *DNB*, vol. 12, p. 578.
5. Gough, p. 76.
6. McDonald, op. cit, p. 44.
7. *EB*, vol. 14, p. 532.
8. McDonald, opp. cit., 44.
9. Mackenzie, p. 381.
10. *DNB*, vol. 12, pp. 578, 579.

DAVID LIVINGSTONE
1. Bruce, p. 12.
2. Moncreiffe, p. 117.
3. Campbell, R.J., pp. 25, 26.
4. *DNB* vol. 11, p. 1264; Jeal, p. 8.
5. *EB*, vol. 14, pp. 154, 156.
6. *Ibid.*
7. Ransford, p. 275.
8. Jeal, p. 1.
9. *Ibid.*, pp. 1–3.
10. Ransford, p. 2.

11. Jeal, pp. 1, 2, 345, 346.
12. CES, p. 628.
13. Holmes, pp. xiii, xiv.
14. Bruce, p.13.

WILLIAM STEPHENSON
1. *DNB*, vol. 1986–1990, p. 429.
2. Albin Krebs, *New York Times*, 3 Feb 1989, p. D17.
3. Stevenson, William, p. xvii.
4. *Ibid.*, p. xix.
5. Hyde, *The Quiet Canadian*, p. xi.
6. *Ibid.*, p. xii.
7. Albin Krebs, *New York Times*, 3 February 1989, D17.
8. John le Carre, *New York Times Book Review*, 29 February 1976, p. 1.

JAMES GORDON BENNETT AND JAMES GORDON BENNETT
1. *EB*, vol. 3, p. 480.
2. *ANB*, vol. 2, pp. 584, 585.
3. Seitz, pp. 46, 47.
4. *ANB*, vol. 2, p. 585.
5. Seitz, p. 15.
6. Carlson, pp. 387–396.
7. *ANB*, vol. 2, p. 586.
8. *Ibid.*, op. cit., p. 587.
9. Carlson, p. 386.
10. Seitz, Foreword.
11. *New York Times*, 4 October 1987, p. 55.

LILA ACHESON WALLACE AND DEWITT WALLACE
1. *ANB*, vol. 22, p. 529.
2. Heidenry, p. 28.
3. *ANB*, op. cit., p. 529.
4. Letter dated April 20, 1983 from Dorothy Little, assistant to Lila Acheson Wallace.
5. Heidenry, p. 44.
6. *ANB*, vol. 22 p. 539.
7. *Ibid.*, p. 529.
8. *Ibid.*, pp. 530, 539.
9. Alden Whitman, *New York Times*, 1 April 1981, p. D23.

1. Bruce, p. 207.
2. *Ibid.*
3. Kiernan, p. 6.
4. *Ibid.*, pp. 8–10.
5. *Ibid.*, pp. 38–44.
6. *Who's Who in Australia*.
7. Tuceille, p. 265.

JAMES WILSON
1. Political stability seems to be a special talent of the English-speaking people. Canada, Australia, and New Zealand are also among the oldest countries, politically, in the world.
2. *DAB*, vol.10, part 2, pp. 326–330.
3. *Ibid.*
4. *Ibid.*
5. Seed, p. 182.
6. *EB*, vol. 22, p. 622.
7. Lorant, p. 14.
8. *Ibid.*, p. 16.
9. This was Governour Morris, a member of Saint Andrew's Society of the State of New York.
10. Lorant, pp. 18–20.
11. *DAB*, vol.10, part 2, pp. 329–330.
12. *Ibid.*
13. Pascal, pp. vii, xi; Seed, p. 182.

JOHN MARSHALL
1. *EB* vol. 14, p. 960.
2. Bruce, pp. 153, 156.
3. Beveridge, vol. 1 and 2, p. 17.
4. Ibid.
5. *EB*, vol. 14, p. 959.
6. *Ibid.*
7. *Ibid.*
8. *EB*, vol. 21, p. 435.
9. *EB*, vol. 14, p. 960.
10. *Ibid.*, p. 961.
11. *Ibid.*
12. Beveridge, vol. 3 and 4, p. 588.
13. *EB*, vol. 14, p. 961.
14. Mason, p. 343.
15. *Ibid.*, p. 345.

RUPERT MURDOCH

JAMES MACPHERSON

1. Smart, J. S. *James Macpherson, an Episode in Literature* (1905), p. 11, quoted by Adam Potkay, in Modern Language Association pamphlet (1992).
2. Clark, pp. 302–304.
3. *Scottish World*, pp. 254–255.
4. Hook, p. 167, note 9.
5. Macpherson, *Fingal*, Book I, p. 3.
6. *Ibid.*, Book III, p. 45.
7. *DNB*, vol. 12, pp. 707–709.
8. Ibid.
9. Gaskill, p. 5.
10. *DNB*. vol. 12, pp. 707–719.
11. *CSBD*, p. 297.
12. *EB*, vol. 14, p. 545.
13. Gaskill, p. 1.

ROBERT BURNS

1. *DNB*, vol. 3, p. 426.
2. EB, vol.4, p. 454.
3. Randall, p. 50
4. *Ibid.*, p. 39.
5. Guinness, p. 218.
6. *EB*, vol. 4, p. 456.

SIR WALTER SCOTT

1. *EB*, vol. 20, p. 80–83.
2. *Ibid.*
3. *CES*, p. 851.
4. *EB*, vol. 20, pp. 81–83.
5. *CES*, p. 851.

WASHINGTON IRVING

1. Adams, p. 17.
2. *ANB*, vol. 11, p. 686.
3. *Ibid.*
4. Adams, pp. 54–60.
5. *New York Times*, 19 December 1999, 2CY.
6. *ANB*, vol. 11, p. 687.
7. *Ibid.*, pp. 688, 689.
8. Johnston, pp. 361, 362.

GEORGE GORDON, LORD BYRON

1. *DNB*, vol. 3, p. 584.
2. Doherty, pp. 11–12.
3. *DNB*, vol. 3, pp. 587–590.

4. Doherty, pp. 17–19.
5. *Don Juan, Canto the Third*, quoted by Steven V. Roberts, *New York Times*, 19 Apr 1974.
6. Steven V. Roberts, op. cit.
7. From *She Walks in Beauty*, quoted in *The Family Book of Best Loved Poems*, David L. George, ed., New York 1952.
8. Quoted in Rutherford, Andrew, *The Works of Byron*, p. 213. Edinburgh, 1951, quoting *The Works of Byron: Poetry*, ed. E.H. Coleridge, London, 1950.

THOMAS CARLYLE

1. Neff, p. 14.
2. *DNB*, vol. 3, p. 1020.
3. Macgregor, F., p. 246.
4. *EB*, vol. 4, p. 923.
5. *CSBD*, p. 77.
6. *EB*, vol. 4, p. 923.
7. *DNB*, vol. 3, pp. 1032, 1033.
8. Raymond Lamont Brown, *The Scottish Banner*, May 1998, p. 24.
9. *EB*, vol. 4, p. 924.

EDGAR ALLAN POE

1. Phillips, vol. I, pp. 7–9; Quinn, p. 16; Black, p. 667.
2. *DAB*, vol. 8, p. 20.
3. *ANB*, vol. 17, pp. 608–611; *EB*, vol. 18, p. 87.
4. *ANB*, vol. 17, pp. 608–611.
5. *Ibid.*
6. Phillips, vol. II, pp. 1511, 1513.
7. Quinn, p. 695.

ROBERT LOUIS STEVENSON

1. *EB*, vol. 21, p. 240.
2. *DNB*, vol. 18, pp. 1132–1133.
3. *CFS*, pp. 210, 211.
4. *DNB*, vol. 21, pp. 1132–1134.
5. *Ibid.*, p. 1135.
6. Cooper, p. 77.
7. *CFS*, p. 212.
8. *DNB*, vol. 18, p. 1136.
9. *Ibid.*, pp. 1137, 1138, 1140.
10. *CFS*, p. 212.
11. Cooper, p. 169.
12. Ellison, pp. 280–282. Samoan poem

translated by Lloyd Osbourne.

WILLIAM HUNTER AND JOHN HUNTER
1. Wills, E., p. 24.
2. Bruce, pp. 221–227.
3. *DNB*, vol 10, pp. 302–304.
4. Fox, p. 11.
5. *DNB*, vol. 10, pp. 288–292.
6. *Ibid.*
7. Dobson, p. v.
8. Begley, p. 123.

RONALD ROSS
1. Ross, p. 3.
2. Megroz, p. 32.
3. *CES*, p. 679.
4. *DNB*, 1931–1940, pp. 752, 753.
5. *EB*, vol. 19, p. 634.
6. *DNB*, 1931–1940, p. 753.
7. Bruce, p. 221.
8. Letters dated 12 December 1996 and 28 January 1997, from F.W. Henderson, M.D.; *JAMA*, 12 December 1996, p. 189.
9. Lewis J. Amster, *Hospital Practice*, 15 May 1987, p. 244.
10. *Scottish World*, pp. 248, 249.

JOHN J.R. MACLEOD AND FREDERICK GRANT BANTING
1. Lawrence K. Altman, *New York Times*, 14 September 1982, C6.
2. *DNB*, 1931–1940, p. 585.
3. Stevenson, p. xiii.
4. *DNB*, 1941–1950, p. 53.
5. *DNB*, 1931–1945, p. 585.
6. Altman, op. cit., C6.
7. *Ibid.*
8. *DNB*, 1941–1950, pp. 54, 55.
9. *DNB*, 1931–1940, p. 585–586.

ALEXANDER FLEMING
1. *DNB*, 1951–1960, pp. 361–364.
2. Ibid; *EB*, vol. 9, p. 437.
3. *CES*, p. 377.
4. Ludovici, pp. 133–135.
5. *DNB*, 1951–1960, pp. 361–364.
6. *CES*, pp. 337, 338.

7. *DNB*, 1951–1960, pp. 361–364.
8. *Ibid.*
9. Howard Goldberg, *New York Times*, 12 November 1986.
10. *Scotia News*, Jan 1976.

IAN DONALD, ALLAN MACLEOD CORMACK, AND JAMES M.S. HUTCHISON
1. *CSBD*, p. 119.
2. *DNB*, 1986–1990, p. 108.
3. Wills, E., p. 32.
4. *DNB*, 1986–1990, p. 108.
5. *Ibid.*, pp. 108, 109.
6. Bruce, p. 226.
7. Lawrence K. Altman, *New York Times*, 12 October 1979, A1.
8. Letter dated May 11, 2000 from Dr. James M.S. Hutchison.
9. *Ibid.*
10. *Ibid.*
11. *Ibid.*

WILLIAM WALLACE
1. *EB*, vol. 23, p. 166.
2. *DNB*, vol. 25, p. 564.
3. *EB*, vol. 23, p. 166.
4. *DNB*, vol. 25, p. 565.
5. Bruce, p. 174.
6. Prebble, p. 87.
7. Grimble, *Scottish Clans and Tartans*, p. 76.
8. *DNB*, vol. 20, p. 571.
9. Macgregor, F., p. 15.
10. *CES*, p. 965.

ROBERT BRUCE (KING ROBERT I)
1. Scott, p. 74.
2. *Ibid.*, pp. 87, 88.
3. *Ibid.*, pp. 128, 129.
4. Barbour, *The Bruce*, Book X, 821–824.
5. Munro and Pottinger.
6. Scott, pp. 169–171; Barrow, p. 236.
7. Bruce, pp. 39–41.
8. *Ibid.*
9. Barrow, p. 256.

JOHN HEPBURN
1. John Keegan, *New York Times Book*

Review, 20 Oct 1991, reviewing
Weigley, Russell F. *The Age of Battles*,
Bloomington, Indiana, 1991.
2. Bruce, pp. 158–160.
3. *DNB*, vol. 9, pp. 609–610.
4. *Ibid.*
5. *EB*, vol. 10, p. 1049.
6. *DNB*, vol. 9, pp. 609–610.
7. Grant, pp. 104–106.
8. *Ibid.*, pp. 190–192.
9. *DNB*, vol. 9, pp. 609–610.
10. Fischer, pp. 87–89.

JOHN PAUL JONES
1. *ANB*, vol. 12, p. 220.
2. Morison, p. xi.
3. *ANB*, vol. 12, p. 219; *EB*, vol. 13, p. 72.
4. *DNB*, vol. 10, p. 1029.
5. *ANB*, vol. 12, p. 219.
6. *EB*, vol. 13, p. 72.
7. *Ibid.*
8. *ANB*, vol. 12, p. 219.
9. *EB*, vol. 13, p. 73.
10. *ANB*, vol. 12, p. 219.
11. *EB*, vol. 13, p. 73.
12. Morison, p. 148.
13. *EB*, vol. 13, p. 73.
14. *Ibid.*
15. *Ibid.*
16. *ANB*, vol. 12, p. 220.
17. Morison, pp. 403, 404.
18. *Ibid.*, p. 407–408.

MIKHAIL ANDREAS BOGDANOVICH BARCLAY DE TOLLY
1. Bruce, pp. 155, 156, 187.
2. Josselson, p. 7.
3. *Ibid.*, p. 1.
4. *Ibid.*, p. 219.
5. *EB*, vol. 21, p. 107.

WINFIELD SCOTT
1. Elliott, pp. 1–2.
2. *ANB*, vol. 19, pp. 513–516.
3. *Ibid.*
4. *Ibid.*
5. Eisenhower, p. 298.
6. Johnson, p. 7.

7. *Ibid.*
8. *ANB*, vol. 19, pp. 573–576.
9. *Ibid.*

THOMAS COCHRANE (LORD DUNDONALD)
1. Firsts, p. 67.
2. *DNB*, vol.4, pp. 621–629.
3. *Ibid.*
4. *Ibid.*
5. *Ibid.*
6. *Ibid.*
7. *EB*, vol. 4, p. 123.
8. *DNB*, vol. 4, pp. 621–629.
9. *CES*, p. 177.
10. Grimble, *The Sea Wolf*, p. 171.

ULYSSES SIMPSON GRANT
1. *EB*, vol.10, p. 684.
2. Hanna, R., p. 2.
3. *Ibid.*, p 7.
4. *ANB*, vol. 9, p. 415.
5. Hanna, R., p. 19, quoting Thayer, *From the Tannery to the White House*, p., 122.
6. *EB* vol. 14, p. 302.
7. *ANB* vol., 9, p. 417.
8. *Ibid.*, p. 419, quoting Grant's Personal Memoirs.
9. Burrows and Wallace, p. 1044.

DOUGLAS MACARTHUR
1. J. Thomson, *Highlander*, March/April 1986, pp. 41–43; Caradon, p. 4.
2. Caradon, p. 6.
3. *Ibid.*, p.7.
4. *Ibid.*, p. 8.
5. *Ibid.*, pp. 11–14.
6. J. Thomson, op. cit.
7. *ANB*, vol. 14, p. 196.
8. *EB*, vol. 13, pp. 469, 470.
9. Caradon, p. 33.
10. Manchester, p. 3.
11. *Ibid.*, p.4.
12. *Ibid.* p.17.

STEPHEN FOSTER
1. Bruce, p. 243. Carmichael's best songs include "Stardust" and "Georgia on My Mind"; Mercer's include "Moon

River," "Blues in the Night," and "Laura."
2. Mornweck, vol. I, pp. 1–5.
3. ANB, vol. 8, p. 304, 305.
4. Ibid.
5. Walters, p. 11.
6. Ibid., p. 23.
7. ANB, vol. 8, p. 305.
8. Walters, p. 11.
9. ANB, vol. 8, p. 305.
10. Walters, p. 53.
11. EB, vol. 15, p. 555.
12. ANB, vol. 8, pp. 305, 306.
13. Guinness, p. 218.
14. ANB, vol. 8, pp. 305, 306.
15. Ibid.
16. Ibid.
17. Ibid.
18. Mornweck, vol. II, pp. 558–562.

EDVARD GRIEG
1. Bernard Holland, New York Times, 9 Jan 1993, p. 13.
2. EB, vol. 10, p. 923.
3. Greig, pp. 6–8.
4. Benestad, p. 14.
5. Layton, p. 15.
6. Gibb, Scotland in Eclipse, p. 17; Mcfall, p. 34.
7. EB, vol. 10, p. 923.
8. NBC Nightly News, 21 Dec 1982.
9. Greig, p. 14.
10. Bernard Holland, op. cit., p, 13.

MARTHA GRAHAM
1. Jennifer Dunning, New York Times, 27 May 2000, B16.
2. Anna Kisselgoff, New York Times, 2 April 1991, A1.
3. De Mille, pp. 15–17.
4. ANB, vol. 9, pp. 384–388.
5. Ibid.
6. Jennifer Dunning, New York Times, 12 June 1990, C15.
7. Bruce, pp. 245, 246.
8. ANB, vol. 9, pp. 384–388; Kisselgoff, op. cit. A1.

JOAN SUTHERLAND
1. Major, p. 9, 10.
2. Madame Melba (1861–1931) was born Helen Mitchell to a Scottish father. Mary Garden (1874–1967) for whom the operas Der Rosenkavelier by Strauss and Pelléas et Mélisande by Debussy were written, was born in Aberdeen.
3. Major, p. 203.
4. Ibid.

FRANCIS HUTCHESON
1. CES, p. 530.
2. CDP, p. 351.
3. Wills, Inventing America, p. 150.
4. Scotia, p. 10.
5. Paine, p. 28.
6. Lehmann, p. 162.
7. Wills, op. cit., p. 229.
8. Lehmann, p. 163.
9. CES, p. 530.

DAVID HUME
1. Garry Wills, New York Times, Travel Section, 9 Jan 1983, p. 39.
2. EB, vol. 11, pp. 833, 834.
3. Clark, p. 259.
4. CDP, pp. 343, 344.
5. EB, vol. 11, pp. 833, 834.
6. Ibid.
7. Hume, Political Essays, Part 2, Essay 16, pp. 487, 488; quoted by Wills, Explaining America, p. 169.
8. CDP, p. 346.
9. Scottish World, p. 194.
10. Wills, Inventing America, p. 197.
11. EB, vol. 11, pp. 833, 834.
12. Scottish World, p. 194.
13. EB, vol. 833, 834.

THOMAS REID
1. EB, vol. 19, p. 90.
2. Ibid.
3. CDP, p. 684.
4. EB, vol. 6, p. 166.
5. Lehrer, p. 20.
6. EB, vol. 6, p. 166.
7. CDP, p. 719.
8. EB, vol. 6, pp. 166, 167.

9. *CDP*, p. 685.
10. *EB*, vol. 6, p. 167.
11. *Ibid.*, vol. 19, p. 91.
12. *CES*, p. 366; *CDP*, p. 264.
13. *CSBD*, p. 414; *CES*, p. 900.
14. *DNB*, vol. 21, pp. 742–744.
15. *Ibid.*
16. Wills, *Explaining America*, p. 18.
17. Esmond Wright, *Pennsylvania Gazette*, February/Mararch 1990, p. 46; Wills, op. cit., p. 7.
18. Lehmann, p. 156.
19. Hook, pp. 19, 20.
20. Haws, p. 57.
21. Wills, op. cit., pp. 14, 23.
22. Edwards, p. 10.
23. Lehmann, p. 174.
24. *EB*, vol. 6, p. 167.

ADAM SMITH

1. Macgregor, F., p. 51.
2. *CES*, p. 885.
3. *Ibid.*
4. Smith, pp. 581, 582.
5. *Ibid.*, p. 549.
6. *Ibid.*, p. 577.
7. *Ibid.*, p. 587.
8. *Ibid.*, p. 589.
9. *Ibid.*, p. 423.
10. *Ibid.*, p. 425.
11. *Ibid.*, p. 459.
12. *Ibid.*, p. 365.
13. *Ibid.*, p. 555.
14. *CFS*, p. 202.

IMMANUEL KANT

1. *EB*, vol. 13, p. 217.
2. Windelband, vol. II, p. 532.
3. *CCE*, p. 430.
4. *CDP*, p. 398.
5. *EB*, vol. 13, p. 217, 219.
6. Fischer, p. 231. Fischer says that Kant meant Memel, not Tilsit, and suggests that Kant was relying on his father's license to be a saddler, given at Tilsit, some fifty miles from Memel.
7. Black, p. 132. Black also says that Kant's grandfather was Scottish.
8. Bruce, p. 175.
9. Fischer, p. 312.

10. Black, p. 395.
11. Fischer, p. 312.
12. Windelband, vol. II, pp. 529, 530.

JOHN STUART MILL

1. Packe, p. 3, 4.
2. *EB*, vol. 15, pp. 459–460.
3. *DNB*, vol. 13, pp. 383, 390; *EB*, vol. 15, p. 460.
4. Cox, Catherine Morris, *Genetic Studies of Genius, Vol.II*, Stanford, California, 1926, p. 707.
5. *DNB*, vol. 13, pp. 391–397.
6. David Spitz, *New York Times Book Review*, 28 Jul 1974, p. 15.
7. *DNB*, vol. 13, pp. 396–397.
8. *CDP*, p. 496.

MICHAEL SCOT AND JOHN DUNS SCOTUS

1. Broadie, p. 2.
2. Macgregor, F., pp. 46, 47; *DNB*, vol. 17, p. 997.
3. *DNB*, vol. 17, p. 998; Macgregor, F., p. 47; *CES*, p. 849.
4. *DNB*, vol. 17, p. 998; Macgregor, F., p. 47.
5. *DNB*, vol. 17, p. 999.
6. Thorndike, pp. 1, 3, 12.
7. *EB*, vol. 7, pp. 765, 766.
8. Macgregor, F., p. 47.
9. Cross, p. 3.
10. *CES*, p. 274.

JOHN KNOX

1. *EB*, vol. 13, p. 433.
2. *Ibid.*, vol. 13, p. 434.
3. McCosh, p.79.
4. *EB*, vol. 15, p. 134.
5. See Bruce, pp. 307–309.
6. Donaldson, p. 20.
7. Scottish Tradition in Canada, p. 9.
8. Brown, *Scottish Historical Review* 10, p. 130.
9. Esmond Wright, *Pennsylvania Gazette*, Feb/Mar 1990, p. 44.
10. R.K. Webb, *Scottish Historical Review* vol. 33, p. 100.
11. Wills, E. p. 24.
12. Kellas, pp. 58, 59.
13. Bruce, p. 25.

14. Lehmann, p. 120.
15. Bruce, pp. 4, 5.
16. *Ibid.*, passim.
17. *Ibid.*, pp. 28, 37, 38.
18. Prebble, p. 242.
19. Bruce, pp. 41, 42.
20. Hanna C., vol. I, p. 103, quoting Thomas Carlyle, *On Heroes and Hero Worship*, IV.

MARY STUART

1. *DNB*, vol. 12, p.1273.
2. Macgregor, F. p. 159.
3. *EB*, vol. 14, p. 995.
4. Fraser *Mary Queen of Scots*, pp. 178–183.
5. *EB*, vol. 14, p. 995.
6. Fraser, pp. 293–294.
7. *EB*, vol. 14, p.995, 996.
8. Ibid.
9. Prebble, p. 207.
10. Fraser, pp. 614–624.
11. Fraser, pp. 628–630.

JAMES STEWART (KING JAMES VI & I)

1. Fraser, *King James*, p. 92.
2. Bruce, pp. 60, 61.
3. *Ibid.*
4. Fraser, pp. 140, 145.
5. *EB*, vol. 11, p. 714.
6. Bruce, p. 291.
7. *Ibid.*, pp. 100, 101.

PATRICK GORDON

1. For more on the Scots in Poland, see Bruce, pp. 184–186.
2. *EB*, vol. 10, p. 582.
3. *DNB*, vol. 8, p 223.
4. Steuart, p. 47–63.
5. *EB*, vol. 10, pp. 582, 583; *DNB*, vol. 8, p. 223; Buxhoeveden, pp. 285–287.
6. Steuart, pp. 38–43.
7. Buxhoeveden, pp. 305–307.
8. *DNB*, vol. 8, p. 223.
9. Buxhoeveden, p. 313.
10. *Ibid.*, p. 317; *DNB*, vol. 8, p. 223.

ROBERT DINWIDDIE

1. Koontz, p. 31; *ANB*, vol. 6, p. 620.
2. Black, p. 9, says these are variants of the same name.
3. *ANB*, vol. 6, p. 620.
4. *EB*, vol. 7, p. 458.
5. Bruce, pp. 265–268.
6. *ANB*, vol. 6, p. 620.
7. *EB*, vol. 16, p. 889.
8. *Ibid.*, vol. 23, p. 238.
9. Koontz, p. 256.
10. Trent's father, also William Trent, was born in Inverness. Trenton, New Jersey's capital, is named for him.
11. *EB*, vol. 23, p. 238.
12. *Ibid.*, vol. 9, p. 864.
13. *Ibid.*, vol. 23, p. 238.
14. Bruce, p. 45.
15. *EB*, vol. 7, p. 459.
16. *ANB*, vol. 6, p. 621.
17. Charles Royster, *New York Times Book Review*, 13 Feb 2000, p. 13, reviewing Anderson, Fred, *The Seven Years' War and the Fate of Empire in British North America*, New York, 2000.

PATRICK HENRY

1. Mayer, p. 15.
2. *ANB*, vol. 10, p. 615.
3. Willison, pp. 4–6.
4. *EB*, vol. 11, p. 380.
5. Willison, pp. 8, 9, 123.
6. *EB*, vol. 11, p. 380.
7. *Ibid.*, Bruce, p. 29.
8. *EB*, vol. 15, p. 890.
9. Bruce, p. 48.
10. *EB*, vol. 11, p. 380.
11. Willison, p. 9.

ALEXANDER HAMILTON

1. Brookhiser, pp. 16–28; *EB*, vol. 11, p. 28.
2. *EB*, vol. 11, p. 29.
3. *WA*, p. 538.
4. *EB*, vol. 11, p. 29.
5. Richard Brookhiser, *U.S. News and World Report*, 10 Nov 1997, p. 72.
6. *Ibid.*

LACHLAN MACQUARIE

1. Richie, pp. 11, 12.
2. *DNB*, vol. 12, pp. 715–717.
3. Macgregor, F., p. 171.
4. *DNB*, vol. 12, pp. 401–402.
5. *Ibid.*
6. Ritchie, p. 132.
7. *DNB*, vol 12, p. 716.
8. Ritchie, pp. 132, 133.
9. Macgregor, F., p. 171.
10. *DNB*, vol. 12 p. 716.
11. *CES*, p. 671.
12. Ritchie, pp. 123–128; Macgregor, F., pp. 171, 172; *DNB*, vol. 12, p.716; *CSBD*, p. 297.
13. *EB*, vol. 2, p. 788.

ANDREW JACKSON

1. *ANB*, vol. 11, p. 732.
2. *EB*, vol. 12, p. 827.
3. *ANB*, vol. 11, p. 732.
4. Davis, Burke, p. 17; *EB*, vol. 12, p. 827.
5. Kennedy, p. 64.
6. *EB*, vol. 12, p, 828.
7. Davis, B., p. 119.
8. Carlo D'Este, *New York Times Book Review*, 19 Dec 1999, p. 13, reviewing Remini, Robert V., *The Battle of New Orleans*, New York, 1999.
9. *EB*, vol. 12, p. 827.
10. *Ibid.*
11. Rimini, p. 188.
12. *EB*, vol. 11, p. 830.

SAM HOUSTON

1. For more on Scots with Joan of Arc, see Bruce, p. 152.
2. James, pp. 3–7; De Bruhl, pp. 8–16.
3. Houston, p. 5.
4. *Ibid.*, p. 8.
5. *EB*, vol 11, p. 790; De Bruhl, pp. 43, 44.
6. *EB*, vol. 11, p. 79.
7. *EB*, op. cit; *Highlander*, September 1979, p. 10.
8. *EB*, vol. 1, p. 492.
9. *Ibid.*, vol. 11, p. 790.
10. Houston, p. 121.
11. *EB*, vol.11, p. 790.

JAMES KNOX POLK

1. Hanna, Charles, vol. 2, p. 187.
2. *ANB*, vol. 17, pp. 622–626.
3. Williams, p. 40.
4. *EB*, vol. 18, p. 174, 175.
5. *ANB*, vol. 17, pp. 622–626.
6. Williams, p. 49.
7. *ANB*, vol. 17, pp. 622–626.
8. *EB*, vol. 18, pp. 174, 175.; *ANB*, vol. 17, p. 623.
9. Williams, p. 40.
10. *ANB*, vol. 17, p. 623.
11. *Ibid.*
12. Williams, p. 63.
13. *ANB*, vol. 17, p. 623.
14. *EB*, vol. 18, pp. 174, 175.

WILLIAM EWART GLADSTONE

1. Ramm, p. 1.
2. *DNB*, Supp., p. 706.
3. Ramm, p. viii.
4. *DNB*, Supp., pp. 706–710.
5. *Ibid.*, Supp., p. 710.
6. *Ibid.*, Supp., pp. 711, 712.
7. *Ibid.*, Supp., pp. 721, 724, 725, 740.
8. Ramm, p. 117.
9. Jenkins, p. 630.
10. *EB*, vol. 10, p. 446.

JAMES BRUCE (8TH EARL OF ELGIN)

1. Checkland, pp. 101–106.
2. *Ibid.*, pp. 105–106.
3. *EB*, vol. 8, p. 280, Checkland, pp. 108–110.
4. Checkland, p. 118.
5. *Ibid.*, pp. 120–124.
6. Bruce, pp. 71–75, 81.
7. Checkland, pp. 128–131.
8. *Ibid.*, p. 132.
9. *Ibid.*, pp. 150–155.
10. Bruce, p. 167.
11. Checkland, pp. 155–164.
12. *EB*, vol. 8, p. 280; Macgregor, p. 176.
13. *Ibid.*, vol. 8, p. 280.

JAMES ANDREW BROUN RAMSAY (LORD DALHOUSIE)

1. *DNB*, vol. 16, pp. 690–691; *EB*, vol. 7, p. 6.
2. Paul Theroux, *National Geographic,*

Jun 1984, p. 747.
3. Ghosh, p. 145.
4. Ghosh, p. 145.
5. Gibb, Scottish Empire, p. 225.
6. *DNB*, vol. 16, p. 697.

JOHN A. MACDONALD
1. *Scottish Tradition*, p. 30.
2. Campbell, p. 51.
3. Bruce, p. 83.
4. *Scottish Tradition*, p. 199.
5. Swainson, pp. 16–19.
6. *DNB*, vol. 12, pp. 487–490.
7. Swainson, p. 19, 20.
8. *EB*, vol. 14, pp. 504, 505.
9. Swainson, pp. 60–69; *DNB*, vol. 12, p. 488–490.
10. Swainson, pp. 60–69.
11. *DNB*, vol. 12, p. 489.
12. Scottish Tradition, pp. 289–291.
13. Swainson, p. 83.
14. Gibbon, pp. 143, 144.
15. Swainson, pp. 97, 98.
16. *EB*, vol. 21, p. 301.
17. *DNB*, vol. 12, p. 487.

ALLAN OCTAVIAN HUME
1. *CES*, p. 525.
2. *DNB*, 1912–1921, pp. 277, 278.
3. *Ibid.*
4. Wedderburn, p. 73.
5. *CES*, p. 525.
6. *DNB*, 1912–1921, pp. 277, 278.
7. *CES*, p. 525.

ARTHUR JAMES BALFOUR
1. Eban, p. 256.
2. *EB*, vol. 3, p. 1.
3. Zebel, pp. 239–241.
4. *Ibid.*, p. 244.
5. *DNB*, 1922–1930, pp. 54–55; Zebel, p. 247.

JOHN NAPIER
1. *DNB*, vol. 14., pp. 59–64.
2. *Ibid.*
3. Napier, p.3.
4. *EB*, vol. 4, p. 212; *EB*, vol. 14, p. 208.
5. *EB*, vol. 16, p. 1164.

6. *DNB*, vol. 14, p. 64.
7. Napier, pp. 2, 27.
8. *DNB*, vol. 14, p. 64.
9. Napier, p. 33.

JAMES HUTTON
1. *EB*, vol. 11, p. 915.
2. *EB*, vol. 10, p. 178B.
3. *Ibid.*, p. 178A.
4. Macgregor, p. 112.
5. *Ibid.*
6. Bailey, pp. 21–24.
7. *CES*, p. 717.
8. John McPhee, *The New Yorker*, 14 September 1992, p. 47.
9. Black, p. 294; Bruce, p. 219.
10. *EB*, vol. 14, p. 540.
11. Macgregor, pp. 116, 117.
12. Bailey, pp.16–17; Paul Pearson, *Paleontology Newsletter*, 37:17–18.
13. Wills, E. p. 21.
14. Bailey, pp. 16–17.

JOSEPH BLACK
1. *EB*, vol. 5, p. 391.; Simpson, p. 8.
2. *DNB*, vol. 2, p. 571.
3. *The Scottish World*, p. 187.
4. *DNB*, vol. 2, p. 573.

JOSEPH HENRY
1. Coulson, pp. 5–6.
2. *Ibid.*, p. 7.
3. Conaway, p. 44.
4. *Ibid.*, pp. 44, 45.
5. *EB*, vol. 11, p. 379.
6. *Ibid.*
7. Conaway, pp. 42, 44.
8. *EB*, op. cit; *WA*, p. 611.
9. *EB*, vol. 11, p. 379.
10. *Ibid.*
11. Riedman, p. 11, 12.
12. Coulson, p. 231, 232.
13. *ANB*, vol. 10, pp. 613–615.
14. *Ibid.*
15. *Ibid.*

WILLIAM THOMSON (LORD KELVIN)
1. Thompson, pp. 1–5.

2. *DNB*, suppliment 1901–1911, vol. 3, pp. 508–510.
3. Guinness, 1987, pp. 416–417.
4. *DNB*, 1901–1911, pp. 508–510; Sharlin, p. xi.
5. *DNB*, 1901–1911, pp, 508–510; Sharlin, p. 114.
6. Bruce, pp. 108, 111, 229; CES, p. 940.
7. *DNB*, 1901–1911, pp. 508–510.

JAMES CLERK MAXWELL
1. *EB*, vol.15, pp. 3, 4.
2. *CES*, p. 168.
3. *EB*, vol. 15, pp. 3, 4.
4. *Ibid.*
5. Tolstoy, pp. 125–126.
6. There are several ways to state Maxwell's equations.
7. Tolstoy, p. 124.
8. Bell, p. 75.
9. Timothy Ferris, *New York Times Magazine*, 26 September 1982, p. 44.
10. *CES*, p. 168.
11. Hans Christian von Baeyer, *New York Times Book Review*, 26 September 93, p. 34.

WILLIAM RAMSAY
1. *DNB*, 1912–1921, pp. 444, 445.
2. *EB*, vol. 18, p. 1150.
3. *Ibid.*
4. *Ibid.*
5. *DNB*, 1912–1921, pp.444, 445.

JOSEPH J. THOMSON
1. Rayleigh, p. 1.
2. *DNB*, 1931–1940, p. 857.
3. *Ibid.*, p.859.
4. *New York Times*, 11 Sept 1975.
5. Marcia Bartusiak, review of *Discovering* (1990), by Robert Scott Root-Bernstein, *New York Times Book Review*, 28 January 1990, p. 24.
6. *DNB*, 1931–1940, p. 861.

ERNEST RUTHERFORD (LORD RUTHERFORD)
1. Crowther, pp. 7–11.
2. *Ibid.*, pp. 11–19.

3. *Ibid.*, p.19, 20.
4. *EB*, vol.19, p. 834.
5. Shapiro, p. 73.
6. Crowther, p.5.
7. *Ibid.*, p.5.

MARY LEAKEY
1. John Noble Wolford, *New York Times*, 30 October 1984, C1.
2. Leakey, p. 14.
3. *EB 15th*, Macropaedia, vol. 7, pp. 222, 223.
4. *Ibid.*
5. Morell, p. 181.
6. Wolford, op. cit. C9.
7. *EB 15th*, Macropaedia, vol. 7, pp. 222, 223.
8. Morell, p. 482.
9. *EB 15th*, Macropaedia, vol. 7, pp. 222, 223.
10. *Who's Who*, 1991.

JAMES D. WATSON
1. Nadine Brozan, New York Times, 2 February 1994, B5.
2. Nobel Foundation, Biography of James D. Watson, 1999.
3. Watson, James D. pp. 19–37.
4. *Ibid.*, p. 83.
5. *Ibid.*, p. 107.
6. *Ibid.*, pp. 123–125.
7. *Ibid.*, p. 125.
8. *Ibid.*, p. 126.
9. *Ibid.*, p. 140.
10. Harold M. Schmeck, Jr., *New York Times*, 12 Apr 1983, C1.
11. *Ibid.*

JAMES NAISMITH
1. *ANB*, vol. 16, pp. 221, 222.
2. Naismith, p. 42.
3. *ANB*, vol. 16, pp. 221, 222.
4. *Ibid.*
5. Consentino, pp. 1–5, passim.
6. Bruce, pp. 253–264.
7. *ANB*, vol. 16, pp. 221, 222.

Bibliography

Adams, Charles. *Memoir of Washington Irving*. Freeport, New York, 1870.
American National Biography. New York, 1999.
Bailey, E. B. *James Hutton, The Founder of Modern Geology*. New York, 1967.
Barbour, John. *The Bruce*. 1375.
Barrow, Geoffrey W. S. *Robert Bruce & The Community of the Realm of Scotland*.
   Edinburgh, 1988.
Beaglehole, J. C. *The Life of Captain James Cook*. Stanford, California, 1974.
Begley, Eve. *Of Scottish Ways*. Minneapolis, 1977.
Bell, Brian, ed. *Insight Guides, Scotland*. 1990.
Benestad, Finn. *Edward Grieg*. Lincoln, Nebraska, 1988.
Beveridge, Albert J. *The Life of John Marshall*. Boston, 1929.
Black, George Fraser. *The Surnames of Scotland*. New York, 1946.
Bliss, Michael. *The Discovery of Insulin*. Toronto, 1982.
Broadie, Alexander. *The Shadow of Scotus*. Edinburgh, 1995.
Brookhiser, Richard. *Alexander Hamilton, American*. New York, 1999.
Brown, Anthony Cave. *Bodyguard of Lies*. New York, 1975.
Brown, Ian F. *The Sinclair/Columbus Connection*. In *The Sinclair Genealogist*. Worcester,
   Massachusetts, 1993.
Bruce, Duncan A. *The Mark of the Scots*. New York, 1996.
Bryant, Julius. *Robert Adam*. London, 1992.
Burpee, Lawrence J. *Sandford Fleming, Empire Builder*. London, 1915.
Burrows, Edwin G. and Mike Wallace. *Gotham, a History of New York City*. New York,
   1999.
Buxhoeveden, Baroness Sophie. *A Cavalier in Muscovy*. London, 1932.
Callan, Michael Feeney. *Sean Connery*. New York, 1983.
Cambridge Dictionary of Philosophy, The. Robert Audi, ed., Cambridge, England, 1995.
Campbell, R. J. *Livingstone*. London, 1929.
Campbell, Wilfred. *The Scotsman in Canada*, Vol. 1. Eastern Canada, Toronto, 1911.
Carlson, Oliver. *The Man Who Made News*. New York, 1942.
Carnegie, Andrew. *James Watt*. Edinburgh, 1905.
Cernuschi, Claude. *Jackson Pollock, Meaning and Significance*. New York, 1992.
Chambers Scottish Biographical Dictionary. Rosemary Goring, ed., Edinburgh, 1992.

Checkland, Sydney. *The Elgins, 1766–1917*. Aberdeen, 1988.

Clark, Kenneth. *Civilisation*. New York, 1969.

Collins Encyclopaedia of Scotland. John Keay and Julia Keay, eds., London, 1994.

Collins Gem, Famous Scots. Glasgow, 1995.

Consentino, Frank. *Almonte's Brothers of the Wind, R. Tait McKenzie and James Naismith*. Burnstown, Ontario, 1996.

Concise Columbia Encyclopaedia. New York, 1989.

Conaway, James. *The Smithsonian; 150 Years of Adventure, Discovery, and Wonder*. New York, 1995.

Cooper, Lettice. *Robert Louis Stevenson*. London, 1969.

Coulson, Thomas. *Joseph Henry, His Life and Work*. Princeton, 1950.

Crawford, Alan. *Charles Rennie Mackintosh*. London, 1995.

Cross, Richard. *Duns Scotus*. New York, 1999.

Crowther, J.G. *Ernest Rutherford*. London, 1922.

Cunningham, Frank. *Skymaster: The Story of Donald Douglas*. 1943.

Cyclopaedia of Canadian Biography. Toronto, 1919.

Dangerfield, George. *Chancellor Robert R. Livingston*. New York, 1960.

Davis, Burke. *Old Hickory: A Life of Andrew Jackson*. New York, 1977.

Davis, Patricia Talbot. *End of the Line: Alexander J. Cassatt and the Pennsylvania Railroad*. New York, 1978.

De Bruhl, Marshall. *Sword of San Jacinto: A Life of Sam Houston*. New York, 1993.

De Mille, Agnes. *Martha: the Life and Work of Martha Graham*. New York, 1956.

De Peyster, Frederic. *A Biographical Sketch of Robert R. Livingston*. New York, 1876.

Dickson, W.K–L. *The Biograph in Battle*. Introduction by Richard Brown, Trowbridge, England, 1995.

Dictionary of American Biography. New York, 1936.

Dictionary Of Art, The. Jane Turner, ed., New York, 1996.

Dictionary of National Biography. Oxford, 1917.

Dictionary of Scientific Biography. New York, 1974.

Dobson, Jessie. *John Hunter*. Edinburgh, 1969.

Doherty, Francis M. *Byron*. London, 1968.

Donaldson, Gordon. *The Scots Overseas*. London, 1966.

Dunlap, Orrin E., Jr. *Marconi, the Man and His Wireless*. New York, 1938.

Dyer, Frank Lewis and Thomas Commerford Martin. *Edison, His Life and Inventions*, vol. I New York, 1910.

Encyclopaedia Britannica. 14th ed., 1969.

Encyclopaedia Britannica. 15th ed., Chicago, 1998.

Eban, Abba. *Heritage*. New York , 1984.

Edwards, Samuel (Noel Gerson). *Rebel—A Biography of Thomas Paine*. New York, 1974.

Eisenhower, John S. D. *Agent of Destiny: The Life and Times of General Winfield Scott*. New York, 1999.

Elliott, Charles Winslow. *Winfield Scott, the Soldier and the Man*. New York, 1937.

Ellis, Malcolm Henry. *Lachlan Macquarie, His Life, Adventures and Times*. Sydney, 1958.

Ellison, Joseph W. *Tusitala of the South Seas*. New York, 1953.

Fischer, Th. A. *The Scots in Germany*. Edinburgh, 1902.

Fox, R. Hingston. *William Hunter*. London, 1901.

Francis, John W. *Address: Delivered on the Anniversary of the Philolexian Society*. New York, 1831.

Fraser, Antonia. *Mary Queen of Scots*. New York, 1971.

————. *King James*. New York, 1975.

Freedland, Michael. *Sean Connery*. London, 1994.

Gartner, Carol B. *Rachel Carson*. New York, 1983.

Gaskill, Howard. *Ossian Revisited*. Edinburgh, 1991.

Ghosh, Suresh Chandra. *Dalhousie in India, 1848–56*. New Delhi, 1975.

Gibb, Andrew Dewar. *Scotland in Eclipse*. London, 1930.

————. *Scottish Empire*. London, 1937.

Gibbon, John Murray. *Scots in Canada*. Toronto, 1911.

Gilmour, Weir. *Famous Scots*. Glasgow, 1979.

Gough, Barry M. *First Across the Continent: Sir Alexander Mackenzie*. Norman Oklahoma, 1997.

Grant, James. *Memoirs and Adventures of Sir John Hepburn*. Edinburgh, 1851.

Greig, J. Russell. *Grieg and His Scottish Ancestry*. London, 1952.

Grimble, Ian. *Scottish Clans and Tartans*. New York, 1973.

————. *The Sea Wolf: the Life of Admiral Cochrane*. London, 1978.

Guinness Book of World Records. New York, 1987.

Hale, Nancy. *Mary Cassatt*. New York, 1975.

Hanna, Charles A. *The Scotch-Irish*. New York, 1902.

Hanna, Ronnie. *Never Call Retreat: The Life and Times of Ulyssees S. Grant, Ulster-American Hero*. Armagh, 1991.

Hart, Francis Russell. *The Disaster of Darien*. Boston, 1929.

Harvey, W. S., and G. Downs-Rose. *William Symington, Inventor and Engine Builder*. London, 1980.

Haws, Charles H. *Scots in the Old Dominion*. Edinburgh, 1980.

Heidenry, John. *Theirs was the Kingdom—Lila and DeWitt Wallace and the Story of the Reader's Digest*. New York, 1993.

Highlander, The. Vandalia, Ohio, 1963.

Holmes, Timothy. *Journey to Livingstone*. Edinburgh, 1993.

Hook, Andrew. *Scotland and America*. Glasgow, 1975.

Houston, Sam. *The Autobiography of Sam Houston, edited by Donald Day and Harry Herbert Ullom*. Norman, Oklahoma, 1954.

Hyde, H. Montgomery. *The Quiet Canadian: The Secret Story of Sir William Stephenson*. London, 1962.

Hyde, H. Montgomery. *John Law, the History of an Honest Adventurer*. London, 1969.

Irving, Gordon. *Brush Up Your Scotland*. 1972.

Irving, Gordon. *The Devil on Wheels: the Story of Kirkpatrick Macmillan, Inventor of the Bicycle*. Ayr, 1986.

James, Marquis. *The Raven: A Biography of Sam Houston*. Indianapolis, 1929.

Jardine, Matheson & Company, Ltd. *Jardines and the EWO Interests*. New York, 1947.

Jeal, Tim. *Livingstone*. London, 1973.

Jenkins, Roy. *Gladstone, a Biography*. London, 1995.

Johnson, Timothy D. *Winfield Scott, the Quest for Military Glory*. Lawrence, Kansas, 1998.

Johnston, Johanna. *The Heart That Would Not Hold, A Biography of Washington Irving*. New York, 1971.

Jolly, W.P. *Marconi*. 1972.

Josephson, Matthew. *Edison, a Biography*. New York, 1959.

Josselson, Michael and Diana Josselson. *The Commander, a Life of Barclay de Tolly*. Oxford, 1980.

Kellas, James G. *Modern Scotland*. Winchester, Massachusetts, 1980.

Kennedy, Billy. *The Scots-Irish in Tennessee*. Londonderry, 1995.

Kiernan, Thomas. *Citizen Murdoch*. New York, 1986.

Koontz, Louis Knott. *Robert Dinwiddie, His Career in Colonial Government and Westward Expansion*. Glendale, California, 1941.

Layton, Robert. *Grieg*. London, 1998.

Leakey, Mary. *Disclosing the Past*. Garden City, New York, 1984.

Lear, Linda. *Rachel Carson, Witness for Nature*. New York, 1997.

Lees-Milne, James. *The Age of Adam*. London, 1947.

Lehmann, William C. *Scottish and Scotch-Irish Contributions to Early American Life and Culture*. Port Washington, N.Y., 1978.

Lehrer, Keith. *Thomas Reid*. London, 1989.

Lessing, Lawrence. *Man of High Fidelity: Edwin Howard Armstrong*. Philadelphia, 1956.

Lewis, Alfred Allan and Constance Woodworth. *Miss Elizabeth Arden*. New York, 1972.

Light without a Wick, a Century of Gas Lighting. North British Association of Gas Managers, Glasgow, 1892.

Lorant, Stefan. *The Glorious Burden*. New York, 1968.

Ludovici, L. J. *Fleming, Discoverer of Penicillin*. London, 1952.

Lynch, Frederick Henry. *Personal Recollections of Andrew Carnegie*. New York, 1920.

McArthurs of Milwaukee, The. Milwaukee, 1979.

McCosh, James. *The Scottish Philosophy*. New York, 1875.

McFall, Haldene. *Ibsen*. New York, 1907.

Macgregor, Forbes. *Famous Scots*. Edinburgh, 1984.

MacGregor, Geddes. *Scotland Forever Home*. 1980.

Mackenzie, Sir Alexander. *The Journals and Letters of Sir Alexander Mackenzie*. W. Kaye Lamb, ed., Cambridge, England, 1970.

Maclean, Alistair and Alastair M. Dunnett. *Alistair Maclean Introduces Scotland*. New York, 1972.

Maclean, Fitzroy. *A Concise History of Scotland*. London, 1970.

Macpherson, James. *Morison's Edition of the Poems of Osssian the Son of Fingal, Translated by James Macpherson, Esq.* Perth, 1795.

Major, Norma. *Joan Sutherland*. London, 1987.

Manchester, William. *American Caesar*. Boston, 1978.

Marconi, Degna. *My Father, Marconi*. Toronto, 1996.

Mason, Frances Norton. *My Dearest Polly, Letters of Chief Justice John Marshall to His Wife, with Their Background, Political and Domestic, 1779–1831*. Richmond, Virginia, 1961.

Matthews, Nancy Mowll. *Mary Cassatt, a Life*. New York, 1994.

Mayer, Henry. *A Son of Thunder: Patrick Henry and the American Republic*. New York, 1986.

Megroz, R.L. *Ronald Ross, Discoverer and Creator*. London, 1931.

Moncreiffe, Sir Iain and David Hicks. *The Highland Clans*. London, 1967.

Morell, Virginia. *Ancestral Passions: The Leakey Family and the Quest for Humankind's Beginnings*. New York, 1995.

Morison, Samuel Eliot. *John Paul Jones, A Sailor's Biography*. First Edition. Boston, 1959.

Mornweck, Evelyn Foster. *Chronicles of Stephen Foster's Family* (Two Vols.). Pittsburgh, 1944.

Morrison, Wilbur H. *Donald W. Douglas, a Heart with Wings*. Ames, Iowa, 1991.

Muir, John. *His Life and Letters and Other Writings*. London, 1996.

Munro, Jean and Don Pottinger. *Robert, the Bruce; Maps of the War of Scottish Independence and the Battle of Bannockburn*. Edinburgh, 1974.

Musgrave, Clifford. *Adam and Hepplewhite*. London, 1966.

Naismith, James. *Basketball, Its Origin and Development*. Lincoln, Nebraska, 1996.

Napier Tercentenary Volume, The. Edinburgh, 1915.

National Geographic. Washington, D.C.

Neff, Emery. *Carlyle*. New York, 1932.

Nobel Foundation, The. *Biography of James Dewey Watson*. 1999.

Norton, David Fate. *David Hume; Common-Sense Moralist, Skeptical Metaphysician*. Princeton, 1982.

Orr, James. *David Hume and His Influence on Philosophy and Theology*. Edinburgh, 1903.

Packe, Michael St. John. *The Life of John Stuart Mill*. London, 1954.

Paine, Thomas. *Common Sense*. Philadelphia, 1776.

Pascal, Jean-Marc. *The Political Ideas of James Wilson*. New York, 1991.

Petrie, A. Roy. *Alexander Graham Bell*. Don Mills, Ontario, 1975.

Phillips, Mary E. *Edgar Allan Poe*. Chicago, 1926.

Pohl, Frederick J. *Prince Henry Sinclair*. New York, 1974.

Pope, Joseph. *Memoirs of the Rt. Hon. Sir John Alexander Macdonald*. London, 1894.

Prebble, John. *The Lion in the North*. New York, 1971.

Quinn, Arthur Hobson. *Edgar Allan Poe*. New York, 1969.

Ramm, Agatha. *William Ewart Gladstone*. Cardiff, 1989.

Rand McNally. *New Cosmopolitan World Atlas*. Chicago, 1968.

Randall, Eric Lemuel, ed. *The Merry Muses*. London, 1966.

Ransford, Oliver. *David Livingstone: The Dark Interior*. London, 1978.

Rayleigh, Lord. *The Life of Sir J.J. Thomson*, Cambridge, England, 1943.

Riedman, Sarah Regal. *Trailblazer of American Science; the Life of Joseph Henry*. Chicago, 1961.

Rimini, Robert V. *Andrew Jackson*. New York, 1966.

Ritchie, John. *Lachlan Macquarie: A Biography*. Melbourne, 1986.

Rodgers, William. *Think; a Biography of the Watsons and IBM*. New York, 1969.

Ross, Sir Ronald. *Memoirs, with a Full Account of the Great Malaria Problem*. London, 1923.

Rutherford, Andrew. *Byron, a Critical Study*. Edinburgh, 1961.

Saint Andrew's Society of the State of New York. *200th Anniversary*. New York, 1956.

Scotia; American-Canadian Journal of Scottish Studies. Norfolk, Virginia, 1977.

Scott, Ronald McNair. *Robert the Bruce, King of Scots*. New York, 1982.

Scottish Tradition in Canada, The, W. Stanford Reid, ed., Toronto, 1976.

Scottish World, The. Joanne Greenspun, ed., New York, 1981.

Seed, Geoffrey. *James Wilson*. Millwood, New York, 1978.

Seitz, Don Carlos. *The James Gordon Bennetts*. Indianapolis, 1928.

Shapiro, Michael. *The Jewish 100*. New York, 1994.

Sharlin, Harold Isadore. *Lord Kelvin, the Dynamic Victorian*. University Park, Pennsylvania, 1979.

Shuker, Nancy. *Elizabeth Arden*. Englewood Cliffs, New Jersey, 1989.

Simpson, A.D.C., ed. *Joseph Black, 1728–1799: A Commemorative Symposium*. Edinburgh, 1982.

Sinclair, Andrew. *The Sword and the Grail*. New York, 1992.

Smith, Adam. *The Wealth of Nations*. 1776.

Smout, T. C. *A History of the Scottish People, 1560–1830*. New York, 1969.

Steuart, Archibald Francis. *Scottish Influences on Russian History*. Glasgow, 1913.

Stevenson, Lloyd. *Sir Frederick Banting*. Toronto, 1946.

Stevenson, Orlando J. *The Talking Wire; the Story of Alexander Graham Bell*. New York, 1947.

Stevenson, William. *A Man Called Intrepid*. London, 1976.

Stohlman, Martha Lou Lemmon. *John Witherspoon*. Philadelphia, 1976.

Swainson, Donald. *John A. Macdonald: The Man and the Politician*. Toronto, 1971.

Taylor, W. L. *Francis Hutcheson and David Hume as Predecessors of Adam Smith*. Durham, North Carolina, 1965.

Thompson, Silvanus Phillips. *The Life of Lord Kelvin*. New York, 1976.

Thorndike, Lynn. *Michael Scot*. London, 1965.

Tiltman, Ronald Frank. *Baird of Television*. 1933.

Tolstoy, Ivan. *James Clerk Maxwell*. Edinburgh, 1981.

Train, John. *Famous Financial Fiascos*. New York, 1984.

Tuccille, Jerome. *Rupert Murdoch*. New york, 1989.

Wall, Joseph Frazier. *Andrew Carnegie*. Pittsburgh, 1989.

Walters, Raymond. *Stephen Foster*. Princeton, 1936.

Watson, James D. *The Double Helix*. New York, 1968.

Watson, Thomas A. *Exploring Life*. New York, 1926.

Watson, Thomas J. Jr. *Father Son & Co*. New York, 1990.

Wedderburn, Sir William. *Allan Octavian Hume, C. B. "Father of the Indian National Congress."* London, 1913.

Wilkins, Thurman. *John Muir, Apostle of Nature*. Norman, Oklahoma, 1995.

Williams, Frank B. Jr. *Tennessee's Presidents*. Knoxville, Tennessee, 1981.

Willison, George F. *Patrick Henry and his World*. Garden City, New York, 1969.

Wills, Elspeth. *Scottish Firsts*. Glasgow, 1985.

Wills, Garry. *Inventing America*. New York, 1978.

———. *Explaining America*. New York, 1981.

Wilson, William Bender, *Robert Pitcairn*, Holmsburg, Pensylvania, 1913, p.5.

Windelband, Wilhelm. *A History of Philosophy*, vol. 2. New York, 1958.

World Almanac and Book of Facts 2000, The. Mahwah, New Jersey, 2000.

Yule, Andrew. *Sean Connery*. New York, 1992.

Zebel, Sidney Henry. *Balfour: A Political Biography*. Cambridge, England, 1973.

Index

bold indicates main selection; 'i' indicates illustration